PRICE: $25.00 (3798/anfarp)

UNPRECEDENTED

FOREWORD BY Michele Romanow

UNPRECEDENTED

CANADA'S TOP CEOs ON LEADERSHIP DURING COVID-19

COMPILED AND EDITED BY
Steve Mayer and Andrew Willis

Library and Archives Canada Cataloguing in Publication

Title: Unprecedented : Canada's Top CEOs on leadership during
COVID-19 / edited by Steve Mayer and Andrew Willis.
Other titles: Unprecedented (Toronto, Ont.)
Names: Mayer, Steve (Editor), editor. | Willis, Andrew, 1962- editor.
Identifiers: Canadiana (print) 20210391022 | Canadiana (ebook) 20210391138 |
ISBN 9780771002137 (hardcover) | ISBN 9780771002144 (EPUB)
Subjects: LCSH: Leadership—Canada. | LCSH: Chief executive officers—Canada. |
LCSH: COVID-19 Pandemic, 2020-—Economic aspects—Canada.
Classification: LCC HD57.7 .U57 2022 | 658.4/092—dc23

Jacket design by Matthew Flute
Jacket art: senicphoto / stock.adobe.com
Typeset by M&S, Toronto

Printed in Canada

Published by Signal,
an imprint of McClelland & Stewart,
a division of Penguin Random House Canada Limited,
a Penguin Random House Company
www.penguinrandomhouse.ca

1 2 3 4 5   26 25 24 23 22

Penguin
Random House
Canada

SIGNAL
McCLELLAND
& STEWART

We dedicate this book to the front line workers across Canada
who carried us through unprecedented times, and continue to do so.

—SM & AW

To my beautiful wife Alina. You are the foundation of our family
and make every day fun and meaningful.

To our wonderful children who bring tremendous joy
to our lives every single day:

Leora, Ian, and Emmie
Josh and Daphna
Jonah
Arielle
Abby

—SM

To Jen, Hannah, and Rachel,
who make everything worthwhile.

—AW

CONTENTS

FOREWORD

For the past seven years, I have been proud to be part of the *Dragons'*
Den television series, showcasing entrepreneurs pitching for the money
they need to achieve their dreams, from often-skeptical backers.

There is a tension on the show that makes for great TV. Contestants vie
for life-changing investments in their businesses, while facing the fear of
failure before their families, their friends, and a national audience.

Being an entrepreneur on the *Dragons' Den* stage is an intense, stripped-
down, pressure-packed version of the quest for capital that every founder
faces when starting a company. If you're an entrepreneur who faces the
spotlight on *Dragons' Den*, you emerge from the experience a better business owner. Even if Dragons like me refuse to back your plans.

The pandemic, in my opinion, made us all contestants on *Dragons' Den*.
We all knew fear in the early days. We are all now coming out of COVID
far stronger for the experience. The title of this book sums it up—it was
an *unprecedented* experience.

If you were a working Canadian during the first lockdowns in March
2020, you experienced something terrifying. In the space of a few days,
COVID challenged the way we have done business for centuries. You
couldn't meet a customer face-to-face, brainstorm with colleagues over
coffee, or shake hands to close a deal. We all needed to adapt to survive—
and fast.

Business leaders, including the CEOs who contributed their stories to this book, faced making critical decisions with little or no data. In a crisis, all eyes turn to the leader. Everyone expects the CEO to have the answers. Yet when COVID hit, no CEO had a game plan.

In my business—as Co-founder and President of artificial intelligence-based ecommerce investor Clearco—data is the heart of everything we do. Information informs all our actions. We crunch reams of statistics, every hour of every day, to invest more than $3 billion into 6,500 companies. In essence, this is true of what every good business leader does—you gather all the available facts, and only then do you act.

That proven, logical approach went out the window when COVID came along. There just was no data on how to run a company during a global pandemic. Nothing we've experienced in the past served as a guide. We needed to figure out a new way to work. Leaders had to find different ways to inspire their shell-shocked teams.

The pandemic forced leaders of all stripes—in business, government, health care, and education—to make decisions based on values. For CEOs, that meant considering the needs of customers, of employees, of all stakeholders, rather than simply focusing on the bottom line, on maximized profits.

The pandemic was (and continues to be) a brutal experience. We lost loved ones, friends, and colleagues. Everyone suffered to some extent. The most vulnerable members of our society, the aged and young people, shouldered the greatest hardships and made the greatest sacrifices. Businesses struggled, some failed.

Yet the pandemic also brought out the best in us.

I see Canada emerging from COVID as a stronger nation, with a clearer sense of where we need to raise our game if we want to hand over a better country to the next generation. I see our business leaders changed for the better, along with an economy that is more inclusive. In addition, I see enormous opportunities for entrepreneurs, the community that drives innovation and economic growth.

My own experience in the pandemic speaks to the journey that many of the leaders in this book experienced.

When the pandemic hit, we had an entirely office-based culture at Clearco. We had no work-from-home policies. Candidly, prior to March 2020, I would have said that if you were working from home, you weren't really working. That most businesses, certainly ours, could not survive away from the office. That all changed in the months to follow, after we had to send everyone home. In contrast to what I expected, once we got everyone set up, our business thrived.

Entrepreneurs are our main client base. They needed our support more than ever, and we were there for them. From our home offices, we kept investing and during the pandemic, our team exploded from 150 to 500 employees. I have never met the majority of those 350 new colleagues face-to-face.

In my opinion, business leaders universally underestimated people's ability to work remotely. The improvements in productivity we have seen during the pandemic show that going forward, companies can and should be flexible around how to structure their workplace. This is and can continue to be an incredibly important shift for women in the workforce, one that removes huge barriers to advancement.

During the pandemic, many women shouldered the burden of being both care-giver and wage-earner. It was a near impossible balancing act, one that brought stress and sacrifices, at home and in careers. Going forward, our goal should be a more equitable work force. The consulting firm McKinsey did a study that showed women's jobs were almost twice as vulnerable to the pandemic as men's jobs. Their research also found that if we strive for true gender parity, through digital inclusion, education, and childcare, we could add $13 trillion to global GPD by the year 2030. That opportunity should inspire all of us.

We also had a corporate culture at Clearco that was heavy on travel. Our vision is to build a global company; we have customers and backers in Asia, Australia, and Europe, along with our base in North America. We hit the road to build relationships. Personally, I took about 125 business flights in the year before the pandemic. I used to think nothing of flying to Boston for a meeting and coming back to Toronto the same day.

Yet during the pandemic, especially at the time when no one was flying, we raised capital from investors around the world without leaving our homes. We did over one hundred virtual investor pitches in less than four weeks, cutting months from our typical fundraising campaigns. We ended up with new financial backers, including institutional investors from Asia and Silicon Valley. The SoftBank deal made Clearco a unicorn—a startup that is now valued at over $1 billion. And we hit this milestone during a global health crisis.

This is not to say that face-to-face meetings have lost their value—I am writing this from a finance conference in Portugal, where I'll network at dozens of sessions before heading home—but for companies that want to expand globally, the shift to virtual conferences and online commerce offers huge growth opportunities, not to mention cost savings and a reduced environmental impact.

The pandemic sped up the fourth industrial revolution: the shift to businesses powered by interconnectivity, artificial intelligence, and automation. That's a digital economy where success is largely based on skills. It's a workplace environment that's far more open to women and visible minorities than one dominated by a traditional mentality that promotes within itself, heavily favouring those that look and talk just like them.

Many leaders—in business, in health care, in government—made mistakes during the pandemic, and those included in this book were no exception. It was to be expected. Running a company during a pandemic was new territory for everyone. The important thing for all of us, as a society, is to learn from those errors. We need to share these lessons, like the leaders in this book, to ensure we do better when the next crisis arises, as it inevitably will.

My first venture, a caviar fishery business based in New Brunswick, failed in 2008 during the financial crisis. Guess what? It is next to impossible to sell caviar during a global recession! Yet I learned more from that failure than most of my more successful ventures.

It is now easier to be an entrepreneur than it has ever been. The shift to a digital economy, decades in the making, gained major ground during the pandemic. A generation back, it took at least $2 million to get a website up and running. Now you can launch an Internet-based business for a few hundred bucks, creating a platform that reaches customers and brings in financial backers.

The pandemic gave us a reason to step back and consider our priorities. A great many people—including folks with secure, well-paying jobs— nurture entrepreneurial dreams. Many want to build businesses that tie their passions to their careers. I see those people every day on the *Dragons' Den* set, and among Clearco clients. COVID is the spark lighting a fire in many potential entrepreneurs. Having been liberated from their offices and business as usual, they see what is now possible by breaking out on their own terms.

But what has been always true about making it as an entrepreneur is that you have to get back up after you've been knocked down—and you will get knocked down. The same is true for the CEOs in this book: In the face of adversity, these inspiring men and women had to find the way forward. That is what is at the core of the stories you will find in this impressive and instructional book—what it takes to move your company forward during unprecedented times.

The pandemic, while incredibly difficult, has reinforced my belief that a great deal of success in business can be traced to resilience and perseverance. You need to have a dream, and the discipline to make that vision a reality. This book is full of lessons from leaders across all sorts of industries, stories from executives and business owners who faced the full fury of COVID and came out the other side.

Michele Romanow
"Dragon", CBC's *Dragons' Den* and Co-Founder and President, Clearco
November 2021

A Note from Dan Clement, President and CEO, United Way Centraide Canada

The COVID-19 pandemic has been a global crisis at a local scale in all regions of Canada and around the world. It is a singular global health crisis not experienced in generations that has affected everyone—individuals, families, local businesses, community service organizations, corporations, and government. It has shown us the best of our communities as people and organizations have rallied in response, and it has revealed the fault lines of inequity, poverty, privilege, precarious work, and racism present in our society.

Each year, over 1 million donors, volunteers, and staff come together as part of the United Way Centraide Movement to ensure every Canadian in every community can reach their full potential.

From the outset of this crisis and as we work to build a better future, United Way Centraide Canada has been guided by four principles.

First, the pandemic has been an "all-in moment for communities," requiring a singular focus on collaboration and coordination among all levels of government, corporate, labour, and foundation partners. It has placed local decision making at the centre of the response to address the unique circumstances of communities across Canada.

Second, equity and anti-racism must be at the centre of our recovery efforts. This means building new relationships with the communities and organizations serving those most affected, challenging our current funding practices, and committing our organizations and our leadership to building a more diverse and inclusive community and philanthropic sector.

Third, building trust and transparency has been paramount. This includes openly sharing our experience and learning, advocating on behalf of the community services sector and needs of each community, and transparently and clearly demonstrating how and where our investments are being made in communities.

Fourth, we are committed to having a long memory of the disproportionate impacts of the pandemic on Indigenous Peoples, people living in poverty, and people of colour. We do not seek a return to normalcy but a new, more inclusive and prosperous future. This means having uncomfortable discussions about the history of philanthropy in Canada, which has not adequately addressed the underlying inequities in our communities, and being willing to change.

This focus has allowed United Ways and Centraides to leverage our local relationships to coordinate action and to work in deep partnership with government, donors, corporations, and labour organizations to mobilize over $200 million in emergency response funding to support over six thousand community service organizations since March 2020. This is on top of our flexible and sustained annual funding of Canada's essential community services, at a time of growing demand and declining revenues.

This book shares the stories and experiences of corporate leaders and their organizations as they navigated this crisis. Similarly, throughout the pandemic, United Way Centraide Canada witnessed thousands of community service organizations respond, adapt, and innovate in the face of rising demand. These are stories of resilience and response, and they serve as a guide as we look to recover to a more prosperous and inclusive future.

We deeply appreciate the support from Steve Mayer and Andy Willis and the CEOs participating in this book. The pandemic has had a deep impact on the communities where United Ways and Centraides work, and we are grateful for their philanthropic contributions and proceeds from the book's sales.

Proceeds from *Unprecedented* will be invested in local programs and supports to address ongoing challenges and barriers facing Canadians in vulnerable situations such as housing, employment, child and youth development, and mental health.

Across Canada, there is a yearning for a return to normal, but this cannot be our goal or purpose. Let us have a long memory of this pandemic and its disproportionate impact, and let's harness the energy and desire of Canadians to reconnect with family, friends, and communities to achieve a more just and equal future.

For more information about the work of United Ways and Centraides in your community and our response to the COVID-19 pandemic, visit unitedway.ca.

INTRODUCTION

A sense of awe inspired this book.

In the early, darkest days of the COVID-19 pandemic, investment banker Steve Mayer reached out to his CEO clients to ask how they were faring, from a personal and from a corporate perspective, and to find out if there was anything his firm, Greenhill, could do to help. That started lengthy conversations in which the CEOs discussed how they were doing their best for their employees, customers, and communities. The leaders of Canada's largest companies described how they were flying blind through a storm. From a business standpoint, the stories were fascinating. From a personal standpoint, they were inspiring.

Chief executives talked with raw emotion. They opened up about their initial reactions to the pandemic, their fears and frustrations. Then the conversation turned to leadership, to how their businesses retrenched and retooled. For leaders at grocery stores, retirement homes, and toilet paper makers, shutting down the business was never an option.

Their CEOs talked about innovation, dedication, and sacrifice. They described gut-wrenching decisions on layoffs and plant closures, and the sorrow and grief that came with losing employees to COVID. Their CEOs spoke of the Canadian values that guided decisions and carried their teams forward—traits such as resilience, creativity, and compassion.

There was no playbook for COVID. When they went to business school, no future CEO worked through a case study on how to handle a global health crisis. The pandemic was unprecedented. While much was being written about the coronavirus, the story of how corporate Canada stepped up during the pandemic was largely untold. Steve believed that this was a story that needed to be told and he conceived of a book in which the leading Canadian CEOs would tell their personal stories, in their own words, of how they confronted COVID-19. The proceeds from the book would go to COVID recovery charities. However, it was only in March 2021, after Steve had a Zoom meeting with Scott Thomson, the CEO of Finning, that the book started to progress. During the meeting, Scott mentioned that over 750 of his employees around the world had COVID-19. Steve was inspired by Scott's leadership and his story and suggested the idea of the book. Scott enthusiastically encouraged Steve to move forward, and that was the catalyst Steve needed to turn an idea into reality.

When the pandemic took hold in Canada in March 2020, business reporter Andrew Willis began writing stories for the *Globe and Mail* that detailed how companies were adapting to the crisis. The articles, told through the eyes of CEOs, took readers to Toronto's Pearson Airport, Enbridge's pipelines, and Stelco's steel mills.

Stories from the front lines of the pandemic showed how CEOs embraced the adage "Keep calm and carry on," balancing leadership responsibilities with the challenge of family life and community commitments. Those stories proved hugely popular with *Globe* readers. When Steve broached the idea of partnering on a COVID leadership book, with the proceeds going to charity, Andrew signed on instantly.

By the end of 2020, COVID vaccines had been developed. CEOs began turning their attention to building back better. However, the experience of leading through the storm was fresh. Canadians realized that the pandemic and the social justice issues playing out simultaneously were permanently changing the way we work, and the way we live.

Business leaders shared the sense that Canada was going through a period of extreme challenges and profound changes. When approached about sharing first-person accounts of leadership during this era, CEOs at a diverse group of twenty-nine companies—unified by the fact that they faced the worst of the COVID storm—enthusiastically agreed to contribute their stories.

Each chapter takes the reader into the CEO's office and behind the scenes at their company. Air Canada's Calin Rovinescu reveals that in the midst of a company party his team decided to shut down flights to China. Sobey's Michael Medline deals with a grocery store cashier being punched in the face during a dispute with a customer over wearing masks. Canada Goose's Dani Reiss discusses how he changed his production lines to produce personal protective equipment. Dino Bianco at toilet paper producer Kruger takes readers on a drive to Costco, where he confirms shoppers are hoarding toilet paper. Brian Hannasch at Alimentation Couche-Tard (Circle K) discusses how the company flew a private plane to China to acquire masks for their employees. Greg Hicks from Canadian Tire describes how he heard about the NBA season being cancelled while he was having dinner to celebrate his first day as CEO.

This isn't a book about COVID or business. It's a book about leadership. The companies that contributed chapters touch the lives of every Canadian. They play critical roles across Canada in health care, restaurants, seniors homes, factories, fitness centres, hotels, shopping malls, office towers, retailers, airlines, and banks. Most are public, several are family controlled, and others are the domestic arms of leading foreign companies. Collectively, these businesses employ approximately a million people around the world and have a combined valuation of $510 billion on the Toronto Stock Exchange.

This is a book about businesses that are thriving coming out of the pandemic, along with companies that continue to struggle with COVID. CEOs reveal what they got right as leaders and own their mistakes. Several CEOs point out that many of the challenges they faced were compounded by inaction, vacillation, or lack of clarity from political leaders and government institutions. It is our hope that this book helps lay the groundwork for a more harmonious, productive relationship between government and business, ahead of the inevitable next crisis.

While every CEO has a different story to tell, there are common lessons learned from COVID. Business leaders recognize that getting through a crisis requires shared corporate values. Several leaders highlight their company's "North Star," a shared set of principles that guided every employee during the pandemic. With that North Star as a guide, it became far easier to delegate responsibility and empower employees during the crisis. CEOs stressed the importance of going the extra mile on communication, especially when they themselves didn't know all the answers and were feeling vulnerable. Leaders highlighted the need to act quickly and to embrace mistakes as part of the learning process.

All net proceeds from this book are going to COVID recovery charities. We are honoured to be partners with United Way Centraide in supporting pandemic-related causes across the country. In addition to sharing their experiences, the twenty-nine companies in this project contributed $3.4 million to United Way.

The book is meant for anyone in Canada who wants to know how the brands they touch each day, the companies they rely on, kept moving forward through COVID. We hope those in business, now and in the future, learn something from these shared experiences. Going forward, we hope this book serves as a reminder of an unprecedented challenge to Canada. A crisis we overcame together, and one we emerged from stronger than ever.

AIR CANADA

As 2020 dawned, Air Canada was flying high.

In the first few weeks of the year, the country's largest airline launched its first flights from Vancouver to New Zealand, signed a marketing deal with Quebec's famed Cirque du Soleil, and took delivery of its first ultra-efficient Airbus A-220 regional jets.

It was a heady time. Air Canada was coming off a year when its stock delivered the best performance of any airline in the world. In 2019, the Montreal-based carrier was voted Best Airline in North America for the third year in a row and the eighth time in ten years. The global economy was strong, and the 33,000-employee airline expected to soar past records set the previous year—its busiest ever—with its 250-strong fleet expected to carry more than 50 million passengers to 217 destinations on six continents.

President and Chief Executive Officer Calin Rovinescu was looking forward to joining the exclusive ranks of the Canadian Business Hall of Fame in the spring. And as 2020 began, the CEO had a secret.

After spending his career as an Air Canada advisor and then executive—he was a successful lawyer and investment banker earlier in his career—Rovinescu was on the verge of announcing his retirement. The airline already had a successor in place. Air Canada had named Chief Financial Officer Michael Rousseau its deputy CEO the previous January. Rousseau had proven his mettle in recent months by stickhandling the ongoing grounding of Air Canada's two dozen Boeing 737 Max aircraft.

On January 29, Air Canada first signalled turbulence ahead. The airline suspended flights to Beijing and Shanghai, two of its most profitable routes.

Calin Rovinescu

AUGUST 2021

Whether it is *The Poseidon Adventure* or *The Towering Inferno*, every fan of director Irwin Allen's classic disaster films knows this: A good calamity always begins with a party. Ours was on January 29, 2020, at the Montreal Airport Marriott Hotel. Three hundred senior leaders, from all Air Canada branches and subsidiaries, had flown in from dozens of countries around the world to attend our annual senior management conference.

While primarily a planning and strategy session, in recent years the conference had become just as much a celebration of our company's turnaround and an opportunity to recognize many of the airline's talented women and men from around the globe. In just over ten years, we had doubled our revenue to nearly $20 billion, expanded our network to all six inhabited continents, created more than 11,000 new jobs, and turned a crippling $4.2 billion pension solvency deficit into a $2.5 billion surplus. We were carrying more than 51 million people a year and winning numerous customer and employee awards. And our shares, which had traded under a dollar for most of 2009, had hit an all-time high above $52 earlier in the month of January 2020, a return exceeding 6,500%.

For me, that year's event also had special piquancy. Although no one knew it then, I had already decided that that year's management conference would be my last as Air Canada's leader. After an incredibly stimulating and highly satisfying eleven-year run as Air Canada's CEO, I was planning to retire later that summer. It was an extremely difficult decision as almost my entire career had gravitated, in one fashion or another, toward Air Canada, starting with my role as a young partner at Stikeman Elliott leading the legal work on its privatization some thirty-two years earlier. For me, Air Canada was never just a job or a career; it was in many respects my life's work, even my second family.

The excitement in the room that morning was palpable. As in prior years, the opening slot was my opportunity to tout our 2019 results and outline future ambitions. It had been a remarkable year, with record performance across the board—especially in the face of the unexpected regulatory grounding of the Boeing 737 Max, the backbone of Air Canada's narrow-body fleet. We had, in effect, achieved what I desperately wanted for Air Canada—sustainability and adaptability. Little did I know then how essential those traits would be in light of what was to come.

Among the many large numbers in our year-end results was our eye-popping unrestricted liquidity of nearly $7.4 billion, amassed over several years of strong performance, cost discipline, and opportunistic financings led by Mike Rousseau, our outstanding CFO and Deputy CEO whom we had identified as my successor. Such a sum prompted many questions from analysts and others, including why we would ever need such a war chest.

Convivial as the atmosphere was, an undercurrent of unease coursed through the room and certainly was front of mind for me. For weeks there had been news items about a new coronavirus identified in Wuhan, China, that had already infected 7,711 people, 170 of them fatally. Sam Elfassy, our VP of safety, together with Dr. Jim Chung, our chief medical officer, and our external epidemiological experts from BlueDot, had been carefully monitoring the virus's development, warning that initial signs were that it was likely more contagious and more lethal than was SARS in 2003. Sam reported on the virus risk to me frequently, sometimes daily, as circumstances changed.

That very morning, World Health Organization (WHO) officials finally sounded an alarm about increased person-to-person contact, after suggesting for weeks that there was "no evidence of human-to-human transmission." Overnight, we learned that British Airways planned to suspend flights to China. More importantly, we received detailed information from our people in Beijing about the worsening situation on the ground—expansion of emergency mass quarantine and lockdown plans; beginnings of makeshift hospitals; closures of hotels, restaurants, and public transportation; and a general sense of unease from both customers and crews. At this point, Canada had taken no steps whatsoever to suspend travel to China, nor were any sanitary requirements or tracking and tracing measures proposed by the government. Indeed, both the WHO and the Public Health Agency of Canada (PHAC) categorically recommended against the imposition of international travel restrictions to China or elsewhere in Asia. Dr. Theresa Tam, Canada's chief public health officer, and Patty Hajdu, minister of health, both assured the public that the risk to Canada was "low."

Despite this, given what we had learned overnight, after my remarks I convened an emergency meeting of the executive committee (ExCom), which included Mike Rousseau; Arielle Meloul-Wechsler, EVP and head of human resources and public affairs; Lucie Guillemette, EVP and chief commercial officer; Craig Landry, EVP of operations; and David Shapiro, chief legal officer. We added our executives responsible for maintenance and engineering, flight operations, system operations control, in-flight service, safety, cargo, and government affairs. There were very few executives left to attend the management conference by this point!

We met in a small room beside the management conference ballroom, where the somber mood contrasted starkly with the boisterous enthusiasm of the management conference next door. But a frank and courageous discussion about the increasing risk to our crews and customers left no doubt about next steps, despite the difficulty of the decision. And we had to act very quickly—as we had five flights that day heading to China, some of which were literally boarding passengers in Vancouver and Toronto as we were deliberating. We decided to immediately suspend all flights to Beijing and Shanghai and to dispatch aircraft only to repatriate our crews and passengers back to Canada. In a matter of minutes, China, key to our international expansion plans—a long-nurtured, very profitable market where we had acquired valuable landing slots and invested billions in aircraft and facilities over decades—was suddenly a no-go zone. We were unanimous that the safety of our staff, crew, and customers trumped commercial considerations, despite the assurances of the Canadian government that the risk was low. The date was January 29, some forty-two days before a global pandemic was declared—and I still wonder what the impact would have been had governments and health organizations taken action starting then.

In relaying our decision to peremptorily suspend our China services, we advised the Canadian government that morning that if it wanted to truly contain the spread of the virus it should suspend *all* flights between Canada and China for some period of time, as there continued to be five Chinese airlines with daily service to Canada, transporting thousands of travellers. To my disappointment, the federal government demurred—a troubling signal that our knowledge, experience, and boots on the ground internationally would not be factors in Canada's response to the growing risk.

Back at our headquarters, over the coming week we began a series of meetings to grapple with the unfurling global pandemic. In attempting to sketch the best- and worst-case scenarios given the scant information available, we drew upon our experience with SARS, studied epidemics elsewhere, and even set up a new commercial team specialized with AI algorithms and big data on the problem, mapping performance and potential recovery of other industries such as tourism, hotels, cruise lines, business conferences, etc. On the optimistic side, based on SARS, we thought the worst might be over by April or May and that we could salvage the summer.

Lucie Guillemette, who had seen it all in her thirty years at the airline, came to ExCom in February with our senior in-house economist and best revenue forecaster, Lian Qiu. Their initial prognosis, given the suspensions of flights to mainland China and Hong Kong, and an emerging travel malaise, was a $500 million revenue decline, which was reluctantly increased a week later to a number Lucie could barely bring herself to utter—a potential $1 billion decline. Of course, knowing now what we did not know then, this underestimated the enormity, depth, and duration of the pandemic and the impact of government-imposed travel restrictions and quarantines. Our 2020 year ended with a $13.3 billion revenue decline over 2019, a 70% reduction in total revenues.

COVID-19's shadow crept over what should have been a glorious year end for our company. During the analyst conference call in early February, discussing our 2019 results, we candidly admitted we did not know what the impact would be. Based on our understanding at the time, we thought mainland China and Hong Kong services might recover by the third quarter. By March, we began to think in terms of years, and we were the first major airline that predicted a minimum three-year recovery period to get back to 2019 levels.

While cancelling our China flights in January had seemed drastic, it rapidly became evident that this would in no way propitiate the gods of COVID-19. Hong Kong, Italy, Iran, France, and several other COVID hot spots emerged quickly in February. In fact, at one point, at a meeting of the International Air Transport Association (IATA) board of governors, consideration was seriously given to shutting down all air travel globally for some period of time, as unbelievable as that concept would have been since the start of commercial aviation a hundred years earlier.

So we began working feverishly behind the scenes, metaphorically nailing plywood over the windows and filling sandbags in dread of the financial storm we sensed coming. By March, we were no longer talking about a $500 million to $1 billion revenue loss but about the potential loss of our entire second and third quarter, the most important quarters for Air Canada. This was much worse and much deeper than what we faced after 9/11. Air Canada would become, far and away, the Canadian company most affected by COVID, given our size and scale, our global network, and the fixed-cost nature of a large international airline.

Our ability to act quickly and in a "battlefield" dynamic throughout the pandemic was due to our nimble corporate culture honed over the years. We were now, yet again, in survival mode. Our regular weekly ExCom meetings had morphed into full-time, hours-long crisis management meetings, with attention firmly on devising a viable COVID-19 Mitigation and Recovery Plan as soon as possible. Everything would be on the table—fleet, workforce, operations, capital commitments, finances. And we were learning that we could count only on ourselves.

Our foremost concern was, however, the safety and well-being of our employees and customers. Arielle Meloul-Wechsler skillfully built and led a robust employee communications network that was both sensitive and highly responsive to the overwhelming questions and concerns about COVID-19 safety and international travel. Through our daily *Horizons* newsletter, our Yammer chat group, town halls, special bulletins, and other vehicles we did our best to provide information, squelch rumours, and rally the troops as the crisis deepened.

With Arielle's help, I recorded a number of videos to reach out directly to employees and respond frankly to all questions of concern given the gravity of the situation. In preparation, I did extensive research on COVID-19, becoming quite conversant regarding its Re or effective reproductive number, antigen versus PCR testing, theories of its zoonotic origins, status of development of therapeutics and vaccines, and the virtues of N95 masks versus cloth ones. I spent much more time researching and discussing health care during those weeks than aviation. My late father, a surgeon who tried to lure me into medicine as a career numerous times, would have been pleased.

As a fillip to these employee videos, I took to adding an inspirational quote—ranging from Winston Churchill on war and traversing hell, to Maya Angelou on courage as a virtue, to Barack Obama on hard things being "hard." Looking back on these videos and my sleep-deprived, somewhat harried appearance, the wartime analogy may not have been too much of a stretch.

Beyond just words, we also took concrete action to protect people, without waiting for governments or regulators to require us to do so—often leading the way for the international aviation community. We joined the global scavenger hunt for medical masks, gowns, and gloves to outfit our people amid a worldwide shortage of personal protective equipment (PPE). We were among the first to require masks for crew and customers, and to mandate temperature checks and other monitoring tools despite initial protestations from privacy experts. We instituted procedures for customers testing positive for COVID-19, revised aircraft grooming protocols, made provisions for protective self-isolation, and procured drum-loads of disinfectant and PPE. We eventually packaged these measures together as the Air Canada Clean Care+ program, with a view to making it clear to customers we were taking concrete steps to protect them and thereby preserve customer confidence in flying.

On the operational side, we urgently needed to shrink our footprint, reduce services, and ground aircraft at an unprecedented rate, while continuing to run a safe operation where we could. Craig, our EVP of operations, worked with our SVP of operations and VPs of flight operations, maintenance and engineering, in-flight service, airports, and Operations Centre (OC) to plan for the exponential reduction in both workforce and aircraft while defending our key business facilities, such as our OC. Housed in a high-tech building, where on a vast open floor dozens of employees crouch within rings of computers, the OC looks like a NASA control centre for an interplanetary mission. It choreographs the airline's day-of operations, ensuring crews, aircraft, meals, fuel, passengers, and everything else all come together to make routine the daily miracle of launching 1,500 flights.

As part of earlier business continuity planning, we had built a second Disaster Recovery OC to give the system complete redundancy. While normally it sat dormant, we dusted off and activated the Doomsday site to divide our operations in case the primary site went into lockdown. It was just one of many extraordinary steps we took to ensure system redundancy, promote social distancing, and infuse COVID precautions into workaday habits.

While necessary, the results of these precautions were sometimes depressing—such as when I would pull up to our Montreal base each morning to find an expansive empty lot where normally hundreds of vehicles would be parked, but now there were essentially only mine, Mike's, and the one belonging to Amos Kazzaz, our SVP of finance and planning, who dutifully came in every day to help plan the cost and capital expenditure transformation we urgently needed to survive and who would later deservedly succeed Mike as CFO.

Keeping the flights going was imperative because people continued to travel—although, with only 73,100 customers on March 21, our loads were now less than half of what we would typically carry. But those booked to fly were incredibly anxious to get home as countries around the world closed their borders, with some, beginning with Italy, going to an extreme state of total national lockdown. These slamming doors played havoc with our schedule, such as in Peru, where the government barred all flights with less than twenty-four hours' notice, stranding hundreds of Canadians for weeks.

Despite these impediments and the changeable patchwork of international and domestic regulations, we were, of course, fully committed to help meaningfully with the repatriation efforts, as we had in the past with humanitarian crises in places such as Lebanon, Haiti, or Syria. Between March 15 and April 20, we repatriated hundreds of thousands of Canadians, including some forty-eight special repatriation missions on behalf of the Canadian government. I often found myself speaking with Francois-Philippe Champagne, Canada's very dedicated minister of foreign affairs, very late at night to deal with complex logistics or seek help when a country pulled the rug out from under us and changed the rules, often with a flight in progress. We repatriated Canadians from far and wide—China, India, Morocco, Spain, Ecuador, Peru, Algeria, Argentina, and Colombia. In some of these places, our crews heroically operated into military airports, under extreme conditions, with no facilities, reassuring travellers we were there to bring them home and out of harm's way.

Along with this, Air Canada Cargo moved nearly 250 tonnes of PPE from around the world and across Canada, contributing to the global effort to make this crucial resource available where it was most needed.

In fact, one glimmer in the pandemic's darkness and, for me, a gratifying example of the company's adaptability, was Air Canada Cargo. It is little appreciated that most of the world's air freight travels in the bellies of passenger planes, and with the mass grounding of aircraft as carriers cut schedules, IATA was estimating that up to 82% of world air cargo capacity was suddenly no longer available. Our people quickly spotted this opportunity and we were among the first airlines to reconfigure several of our wide-body aircraft by removing seats from the cabins, effectively doubling the volume of space available to carry cargo.

In a year in which our total revenues fell 70%, our cargo revenue grew 28% to $920 million. The success of the operation catalyzed other, more permanent changes to Air Canada's cargo business, including permanently converting some of our Boeing 767s into dedicated freighters. We also hatched Rivo, an e-commerce delivery service with a "first and last mile" capability that gives us a foothold in the lucrative online shopping world.

Commercially and outwardly, we needed to soldier on and continue to run our business where we could do so safely, to so-called green zones. We celebrated any small accomplishments—such things as customer awards, alternative payment options, our growing cargo business, and a new celebrity chef. Despite consuming significant resources, we also carried on development of our much-anticipated new Aeroplan loyalty program. After years of work, and a lot of corporate drama, the project was nearing completion and I was determined for it to be completed even though that required expending some capital. Once relaunched that fall, it would serve an important role in our future recovery and, more immediately, would signal our determination that there would be life after COVID-19.

Behind closed doors, however, executive meetings grew ever more grim, with one participant likening them to group therapy. By the end of March, daily passenger loads were down to 27,000—a number that fell to 11,650 by April 2 and halved again to 5,500 by April 16. Breathtakingly fast, we were now at less than 5% of the number of passengers carried the prior year. Asia was non-existent. Europe was non-existent. Latin America and the Caribbean were shut down. The U.S. border was closed. Our finances were similarly deflating, and our shares were tumbling along with the broader stock market to bottom out at $9.26 in March. The cash burn raged like a wildfire, consuming as much as $25 million a day in the second quarter. We noted sardonically that a three-hour ExCom meeting would now represent a $3 million session.

Such dark humour was the only levity at these gatherings, where all options were thrown on the table, including an outright shutdown of the entire company, as other airlines in Canada and around the world had done. This was a move we considered but ultimately rejected because of our essential role in moving PPE, perishables, manufacturing inputs, medicines, and ventilators—not to mention returning Canadians home and transporting others whose travel continued to be required.

Another plan jettisoned after what was really a perfunctory consultation with Arielle was my retirement, slated for the end of the summer. There was no way I was leaving while all hands were on deck valiantly straining to prevent the ship from capsizing. Moreover, my continued presence would allow Mike to fully devote his energies to bolstering our finances. With second quarter net cash burn hitting $1.7 billion and no let-up to the pandemic in sight, that $7.4 billion cash hoard no longer seemed so inexhaustible. I knew that our finance team were extremely adept at pulling rabbits from hats. I had every confidence that we would be able to access capital markets to their fullest potential, and if push came to shove, we would find ways to "go it alone"—to boldly restructure our costs, operations, and finances, without counting on sector support from the Government of Canada, which never came prior to year end.

Having seen the Canadian banks yank Air Canada's credit lines during the 2008 global financial crisis, we immediately drew down our $1 billion in revolving credit facilities. To augment this, we sold stock and issued notes that raised $1.6 billion, and secured additional liquidity of $840 million using aircraft and spare parts, real estate, and even airport slots as collateral. We topped this up with a $426 million EETC, a specialized type of aircraft securitization pioneered in North America with leadership from David Shapiro, our chief legal officer.

With these efforts, we ended the second quarter with unrestricted liquidity of $9.1 billion, more than we had at the start of the year. Still, with the indeterminate length and depth of the pandemic, even this amount was no guarantee. Due to their high-fixed-cost structure, international airlines consume massive amounts of liquidity when revenues dry up in a crisis, and covenants with lenders, lessors, and credit card companies require certain minimum cash levels running into the billions. We needed to stay well clear of these triggers—both to avoid complications and also to maintain confidence in the broader financial community and among our remaining customers in anticipation of the post-COVID recovery.

There were other, more painful steps. After having refused to implement travel restrictions on China in January, the Government of Canada imposed what were among the most stringent travel restrictions in the world starting in mid-March, including an absolute closure of the U.S. border virtually overnight. We thus began wholesale cancellations and took a scythe to our network, which was largely interdependent on connecting flights that no longer had any relevancy. In mid-March we had anticipated cutting our second quarter schedule by a shocking 50% from the prior year; however, by the end of June we had chopped it by 92%. The number of daily flights fell from 1,500 in mid-March to as few as 72 on April 30. For our network planning group, which had spent the last decade growing Air Canada's reach to nearly 100 international destinations, it was soul-destroying as no one knew where the bottom would be found. By May, we saw days with 5,000 customers booked, of whom fewer than 3,000 might actually show up. It was an inverted game of musical chairs where we could not remove seats fast enough as customers disappeared.

The collapse in loads left us with an infrastructure that was far too big for the amount of business we were doing and that we were likely to do for the foreseeable future. To right-size, we retired 79 older aircraft from our fleet, including the entire Boeing 767 Rouge fleet. We packed 114 more off for storage at airports scattered around the continent, including in the southwest U.S. desert. This was another massive, unprecedented logistical undertaking, involving careful preparation of aircraft for storage by our maintenance and engineering experts. Whereas pre-pandemic we had 253 aircraft in the fleet, on May 1, 2020, we had about 60. There were management pay cuts across the board and a company-wide cost reduction and capital deferral initiative that ultimately delivered $1.3 billion in savings.

And then there were our people . . .

Over the past decade, in expanding our network, our workforce had grown to 37,000 from 26,000. Of all we had accomplished together, the thing of which I was proudest was that Air Canada created 11,000 good jobs with good benefits and pensions, and stimulating work for people to do in a company going places. It was largely unprecedented in Canada or pretty much anywhere in this age of part-time, contract, and precarious employment. While inevitable, it was thus the most painful decision of my career when on March 30 we announced that we would furlough 15,200 unionized employees and 1,300 managers, or approximately 50% of the workforce. We still kept 50% of our employees even though we were only operating at less than 10%, so as to allow for an eventual recovery.

Adding to my frustration was the apparent indifference of the Government of Canada respecting our industry's plight relative to what was going on elsewhere in the world—as regards both sector support and travel restrictions. We watched as governments worldwide, grasping the importance of airlines to national economies, committed by early May to US$123 billion in sector-specific support to our global competitors, with promises of more too, if needed.

Canada did adopt the Canada Emergency Wage Subsidy (CEWS) program, a form of wage subsidy for employees still on the payroll, available to all Canadian employers. And we did access this program for the benefit of our employees, but, while welcome, it was nowhere near enough given the gravity of the impact of the pandemic and travel restrictions on our company. All in, the subsidy compensated for about 42 days of cash burn. For the year's other 323 days, we were completely on our own.

From mid-March through the rest of the year, Canada adopted and kept in place some of the world's most draconian travel restrictions, often at odds with what other G7 countries such as the U.S., the U.K., and European countries were doing with travel bubbles, green zones, or other techniques designed to help their aviation and tourism businesses salvage some portion of their businesses. Often uninformed by science, these restrictions permitted virtually no one other than a Canadian to enter the country while an array of ever-tightening regulations and quarantines discouraged anyone thinking of leaving. In addition, several Canadian provinces, including all of the Atlantic provinces, prohibited any visitors from entering their provinces, including Canadians, which greatly affected interprovincial trade and commerce.

By mid-June, there was great frustration among Canadian businesses in response to the restrictions and the virtual decimation of Canada's travel and tourism industry, with no end in sight. This prompted twenty-seven CEOs of leading companies, including banks, telecoms, transportation, asset management, energy, manufacturing, and airlines (including me) to write to the prime minister to urge the Government of Canada to "thoughtfully open aviation and lift restrictions to safely resume travel throughout all provinces of Canada as well as from select countries." Again, we were disappointed to see Canada demur and keep all restrictions in place.

Adding to these challenges were Health Canada's daily bulletins on every flight after which a passenger was *later* found to have COVID, whether or not it had anything to do with that flight. These were eagerly picked up by the media, producing a steady drip-drip of "COVID Flight" stories that reinforced in the public mind that airlines were the fount of all COVID. Some took to describing aircraft as "flying petri-dishes."

The reality, however, was quite different. The government's own statistical reporting revealed that travel accounted for less than 2% of COVID-19 cases. Moreover, due to the use of medical grade HEPA air filters and our own extensive precautions, instances of people contracting COVID-19 on aircraft were extremely, extremely rare. So much so that Canada's chief public health officer and minister of transport both admitted they knew of no such occurrences and Harvard concluded in a scientific study undertaken by its School of Public Health that "flying can be safer than grocery shopping."

Our leadership team knew that we would need to coexist with the virus for a while even after effective vaccines were developed and that this was the only path to some recovery for Air Canada. I therefore concluded that we needed to actively participate in the scientific dialogue and analysis, and to work with private sector and research partners to develop our own studies—both to prove that travel was safe and to help source affordable rapid tests so that we would have a shot at reopening both travel and the economy. Rather than wait, we pressed ahead on our own, benchmarking what other countries were doing and collecting data on the disease. To leave no stone unturned, we joined with companies in our sector, groups in the broader hospitality industry, and local and national business organizations. We formed partnerships with specialists such as Cleveland Clinic to seek advice and explored the possibilities of applying new preventative technologies, some not fully approved for use yet. We also reached out to academia.

We were a founding member of the Rapid Screening Consortium led by the highly energetic and creative Ajay Agarwal of Creative Destruction Labs to establish rapid screening systems. In addition, we separately funded McMaster HealthLabs to establish a comprehensive study of arriving international travellers at Toronto Pearson Airport. The CDL Rapid Screening Consortium is a private-led, not-for-profit initiative formed in August 2020 with the goal of establishing a robust rapid screening system and implementation strategy as a public good. It is an unprecedented collaboration among businesses and researchers for a public interest objective.

The McMaster HealthLabs study, announced in September 2020, was the largest of its kind in the world. It involved more than sixteen thousand participants completing more than forty thousand tests. It found that 99% of people landing in Canada did not have COVID and were being subject to a blanket fourteen-day quarantine to no purpose. Second, it showed that proper testing, combined with shortened quarantine, was highly accurate in detecting COVID cases. Finally, the results strongly suggested that since testing can achieve 100% compliance, it was more effective than full quarantine. The Government of Canada eventually implemented arrival testing in Canada in February 2021. As for quarantine, despite the study's findings, the policy unfortunately not only remained in place but was stiffened to require arriving passengers to check into quarantine hotels, which continued to exist well into the summer of 2021.

While our studies produced highly optimistic results, by the fall of 2020, caseloads began ramping up as a second, more threatening wave rolled over the world. In Canada, travel restrictions bit down even harder, airlines extended their groundings, and regional communities lost air service. At the same time, thousands more travel and hospitality workers saw their jobs disappear.

In early November, we reported an 86% year-over-year third quarter revenue decline of $4.8 billion. Given the mounting losses, we advised the minister of transport that unfortunately we planned ninety-five more route suspensions, including many domestic routes that had virtually no demand. Following this, Minister Garneau announced that the government would establish a process with major airlines regarding financial assistance, subject to certain conditions, including providing refunds to customers holding non-refundable tickets for flights that had been cancelled. The industry's decision not to provide such refunds sooner had been a hot button item since the start of the pandemic, when, uncertain of its depth and duration, airlines took every step to conserve cash in light of the unprecedented circumstances. In our case, this amounted to approximately $2 billion in advance ticket sales, so we viewed it as an extremely critical component of our cash reserves. Moreover, the Canadian Transportation Agency had expressly confirmed that a one-year voucher in lieu of a refund was appropriate given the unprecedented situation. And Air Canada went further and offered credits with no expiry at all.

Still, while it was perfectly legal and provided for in our tariffs, the decision to suspend our regular refund policy was ulcer-inducing for senior management. Beyond worries around brand damage, there was deep unease about the impact on individuals who might need the money. In the event, once refunds were made available in April 2021, including to those who cancelled the flights themselves, little more than half requested refunds.

The other half held on to their credits, intending to fly with Air Canada again soon. To this day I am grateful to our customers for their forbearance and understanding.

Parallel to all this, I needed to make a decision on the timing of my delayed retirement announcement. So, in October, after much reflection, I set and announced February 15, 2021, as the retirement date. I wanted to be there for the delivery of Air Canada's year-end results and I calculated that, by that date, the pieces of our Mitigation and Recovery Plan would have adequately come together. I agonized as the date approached and the pandemic continued to rage on, but its second wave had by then crested. Moreover, our Mitigation and Recovery Plan was indeed fully in place. Our available liquidity at $8 billion was higher than when COVID had struck. Our fleet, including future aircraft orders, had been significantly rationalized, leaving it leaner and greener to compete. The painful work-force reductions were behind us, and in fact we would begin rehiring a few months later. The government sector support negotiations had progressed to such a level that, with the release our 2020 results, I felt comfortable enough to express qualified optimism for the first time. For customers, we had instituted industry-leading safety measures, unveiled an appealing new loyalty program, and, in what proved a very complex IT project, developed a user-friendly online refund tool. With all this done, it was an appropriate moment for a transition and for Mike to take his place as CEO.

Those who know the Air Canada story and our ten-plus-year trans-formation from near-bankruptcy to global champion know how much I value the culture that we created in re-engineering the airline: A nimble "Just Do It" mindset. Sustainability, both financial and otherwise. Clarity in planning. Courage in execution. COVID-19 may have incinerated a decade's worth of financial results; an intricately crafted, world-spanning network; and billions of dollars, together with nearly twenty thousand jobs. But it did not incinerate Air Canada's culture.

Instead, I look back to 2009 when we set out to reimagine Air Canada. Our goal was to create a nimble, resilient airline that would be sustainable over the long term in an industry notoriously susceptible to Black Swan events. COVID-19 proved we accomplished this. Our team delivered against long odds, standing alone. We not only overcame the worst of the pandemic but made significant societal contributions, such as repatriating Canadians from abroad, advancing science-based safety, preserving fifteen thousand jobs, and delivering essential cargo. I have every confidence that the airline will thrive once more, its network rebuilt and many of the twenty thousand hired back. We are already seeing the exciting possibilities of this next phase.

A&W FOOD SERVICES

Susan Senecal was just a kid when her parents took her and her sisters to an A&W restaurant in the Montreal suburbs. Her strongest memory of that meal is trying her first onion rings. She loved them, and still does. Now she offers those onion rings, Mama and Papa burgers, and A&W Root Beer to 130 million guests each year as chief executive at A&W Food Services of Canada, one of the country's largest restaurant chains.

A&W Canada is all-Canadian owned and led, with over a thousand outlets run by franchisees who, as business owners, employ over twenty thousand employees. When you run drive-thru restaurants or can deliver through Uber Eats and other services, you don't stop serving burgers just because there's a global pandemic.

Senecal and her team at A&W ensured front-line staff could keep serving meals as COVID-19 swept across the country, while supporting employees whose outlets in shopping malls and urban streets were shut down during lockdowns.

A graduate of McGill University, where she studied biology and computer science, Senecal joined A&W in 1992 as an area manager after working for two smaller chains in Montreal, Cultures and Croissant Plus. She fed on the dynamic pace of what are known in the industry as QSRs, or quick-service restaurants. Within four years, she was running all of A&W's operations in Quebec. Senecal moved to A&W's Vancouver head office in 2002, in operations, then stepped up as chief marketing officer in

2012. After Senecal took charge of the brand, one reporter wrote that A&W had become the burger joint with a conscience.

A&W staged a series of product launches all based on what Senecal describes as the concept of "good food makes good food." That meant that burgers made from beef raised without the use of artificial hormones (and now also grass-fed), chicken raised without antibiotics, fair trade coffee, and Beyond Meat plant-based proteins became staples on the menu.

In 2015, A&W promoted Senecal to chief operating officer, and she was named CEO three years later. In Senecal's first year as CEO, A&W's sales rose 15% to a record $1.4 billion.

In early March 2020, Senecal jetted off to A&W's national convention in the Bahamas, part of a thousand-person gathering that featured awards dinners, high-fives, and goodbye hugs as the CEO prepared to head back to Vancouver. She came home to a pandemic.

Susan Senecal

JUNE 2021

A hush descended on the office as the light faded that February evening in Vancouver. This was in sharp contrast to the crescendo of activity that had built up over the previous few days. A worry, triggered by our awareness of an infectious new illness spreading in some parts of the world, had generated a flurry of fact-finding, consulting with experts, and conversations with our teams at the office and across the country. Adding to that spike of activity was the already intense bustle and energy of the final preparations for a national convention, over a year in the making and about to kick off. The day's energy surrounding this new emergency had been intense, but by evening I felt very ready.

From what was believed about the virus in those very early days, it appeared to spread through surface contact. If "fomites" were the enemy—and "clean" to be our salvation—then the plan seemed actionable and familiar. After all, at restaurants, "clean and safe" is an integral part of what we do. We doubled down, adding substantially to our inventory of sanitation supplies and enhanced our protocols. Given the advice that was beginning to emerge, my feeling was that "we had this."

While we remained alert and vigilant, this mingled with a sense of excitement, anticipating the celebratory, family reunion feel that highlights our conventions. In fact, the very reason for their existence is the opportunity they provide for us all—hundreds of franchised operators, suppliers, and the members of the corporate team who support them—to see one another, renew friendships, and rejoice in the togetherness of the growing A&W family.

I took a final look around before leaving, desk tidied, ready for the flight the next day. It was late, and the hush had tapered to silence. But, perhaps if I had been listening closely, I would have heard the click of a seat bar, locking us into place at the front of the roller coaster, gearing up for what would become a ride like no other.

For us at A&W, those first few days of March 2020 began as a celebration. We enjoyed a fabulously sunny, noisy, exciting National Convention in the Bahamas. It was a real hit, with unprecedented attendance, gorgeous weather, and beautifully planned social and business events. The more than one thousand attendees enjoyed every moment; there was a feeling of great optimism for the future. The finale was our traditional Awards Dinner, where the sense of pride burst forth—the heartfelt speeches, fancy dress, and phone flashes, the hugs and high-fives and the robust applause.

On an emotional high as we gathered one last time in the lobby after checkout the following morning, it was hard to say goodbye—and easy to miss the significance of the increasingly worrisome news of more and more outbreaks of the "novel coronavirus." While we continued to feel a vague sense of unease, the virus was still lurking in the shadows.

The virus felt distant. China had locked down, with what people at the time considered "draconian health measures." Overseas travel appeared to be the key risk factor. Airport signage warned us to report any out-of-country trips. As we made our way home, the few international travellers wearing masks were an anomaly.

Two flights later, as I touched down in Vancouver, reality began setting in. COVID-19 cases in Canada were climbing, including dozens related to large Canadian conferences that had just ended in Toronto and Vancouver. Suddenly it all felt very close to home. Fear struck. Could we have encountered and maybe been a source of spread for this virus at our convention? On high alert to hear of any symptoms or illnesses, we took action to create our own version of tracking and self-isolation. Health guidelines began to emerge, and we rushed to implement the recommendations, while nervously counting down the days since we had been all together and at risk. Thankfully, none of our convention attendees fell ill, but that sense of relief was short-lived as we immediately began to confront the challenges of operating over one thousand restaurants and an office with over one hundred people.

There was so much to do. Where to start? We needed a plan. I began to reach out for information and help. At that point, the guidance was scant.

We would need to provide our own clarity and direction, and to do so right away. Every one of our operators and their restaurant teams needed to take immediate action to keep themselves and our patrons safe. The rush of deciding, acting, and communicating was all-consuming, and that busyness muted whatever personal fears may have been cropping up for me. We rallied. I set up daily calls and conversations with our department heads—which they did in turn with their teams—and initiated a crisis response to COVID.

For our first crisis team meeting, I had convened a group with leaders from every area of the business. We sat together (at our boardroom table, for the first and last time!). I opened the meeting by saying, "We probably won't need all of us here at every meeting. This is just to start off." As it turned out, this was the first of what would be over two hundred meetings. And we needed every one. We had a huge responsibility. The actions and decisions we made would impact the well-being of everyone connected to A&W. As we exited that first meeting, we learned that Italy had announced they were locking down the whole country. Not long after, "*le confinement*" had spread to France and across Europe, and we now expected that it would find its way here. I could not at all picture what this would be like. Would restaurants be needed? Could and should we stay open? And if yes, how? Time and information were both scarce. We did our best to ask questions and listen to experts.

Our operators told us that things were quickly changing at their restaurants. More guests were asking for their food to go. Our restaurants in shopping centres were seeing sales plunge. Our suppliers were reaching out to ask what we needed, and when. Restaurant staff were asking operators what would be done to keep them safe. And we began to wonder, could they even come to work? Many Canadian schools were on spring break, and we started hearing that students might not return. Who would take care of the children? What impact would all these closures and "pauses" have?

At the same time, many A&W restaurants were reporting that they were hearing more and more "thank you's" from their guests. With so much shut down, they were seeing truck drivers parked at the side of the road, jumping down from their cabs, hoping for a place to get a quick bite. Our washrooms were in high demand. Healthcare workers appeared at our drive-thrus, at the end of a long day, to pick up food for their families. We began to understand the importance of our restaurants and were determined to remain open if we could. Government directives had just identified restaurant employees as "essential workers." Seeing the line-ups, and sensing the urgency at our drive-thrus and outside many of our restaurants, we certainly felt that was true. Our restaurants were open seven days a week, and they needed the support of our home office now more than ever.

We were clearly in the midst of a global pandemic, and yet our teams' experiences were vastly different—province to province, restaurant to restaurant, person to person. Smaller restaurants struggled to find ways to maintain physical distancing, while bigger restaurants had a hard time finding enough staff able to work. Shopping centre restaurants closed. Our downtown restaurants faced shuttered office towers and traffic that was down to a trickle. Our drive-thru restaurants needed to adapt to a whole new pattern of business.

Operators were contending with multiple, frequent changes to accepted protocols. It often felt like one step forward, two steps back. Travel restrictions were a huge obstacle for restaurants about to open, as new franchisees typically rely on experienced trainers from across the country. And the challenges our people faced spanned everything from fears of contracting COVID, to concerns for vulnerable family members and friends, to the practical effects of shrinking availability of groceries and household items and reductions in public transit.

Events were moving swiftly and we needed to act as such. I made a list of everyone I could think of who might be able to provide some insight and advice. We started reaching out to connections at home and in the world. Who had experience with the Asian and European outbreaks? Who was connected to the medical community? What plans did our suppliers have in place? Our landlords? What information could our operators provide? Experiences differed by region, by type of restaurant, by community.

To find the answers we went all in to listen and learn, divided up the work, and then regularly reconnected briefly, to share information. At the same time, every day brought new questions. For a high-touch organization like A&W, the impact of losing the ability to travel, visit, and see things with our own eyes sent us for a loop. Apart from one another, we faced change at every turn.

There was so much we needed to know and say! We needed a way to get all of A&W together, fast. We signed up for Zoom teleconferencing in the morning. By 2 p.m. that day we were on our first call with operators and A&W staff from across the country, to provide information and answer questions. We had hundreds of people show up to begin what became a daily opportunity to share knowledge, connect with one another, and face our fears together. A global crisis was unfolding at breakneck speed, and our job was to see around the corner and set a path forward. There was an otherworldly feel as we tuned in to the first of what would become many updates from the provincial authorities, the prime minister, and other world leaders. We sensed that there would be big directives and actions to come. But we couldn't wait.

Most of what we learned we were hearing, not seeing. The one place change was visible was at the office. Person by person, department by department, ideas and actions streamed in. Our IT team was first off the mark, deciding to dramatically accelerate the implementation of some new online collaboration tools. The planned weeks of rollout were compressed into a short number of hours instead. None of us imagined just how essential these tools would become! The team then rallied to figure out how every single A&W office employee could get what they needed to work from home. This was all happening very fast, but so was everything about the pandemic. What felt like possible overkill at 8 a.m. felt insufficient just a few hours later.

That afternoon, the office emptied out. I vividly remember the scene playing out below my window. A parade of employees, laptops in their backpacks, monitors tucked under their arms, heading for the SeaBus. Heading for an uncertain future. Heading for home.

I don't remember what I was thinking as I left the office that day, but I do recall waking up the next morning with a question: "Now what?" While the twists and turns of the past few days had been dizzying and scary, they were also filled with people and action and important work that needed to be done right away. Today felt open and empty, waiting for me to fill it in. I knew that in a time of crisis you should play to your strengths. What was I good at? One answer was immediate—I was good at working! So I decided to head to the office.

Only the sounds of nature greeted me as I stepped out the door. The world was still. No one and nothing was moving. Every clunk and click seemed to echo as I opened my car door and switched on the engine. I caught my breath as the solemn notes of the song "If the World Was Ending" sounded on the radio. Hopefully not a prophecy, but it certainly felt relevant. The streets were deserted. I had green lights all the way. It was my fastest drive to work ever, and by far the eeriest. The parking lot was empty; I unlocked the building myself. I entered, turned on the lights, and sat down. And then jumped up, thinking of all the things I had touched. I rushed to wash my hands.

Anyone who has spent more than a few minutes with someone from A&W has no doubt heard us say that Strategy and Climate are at the core of our success. What we mean by that is an unwavering commitment to continuous, bold renewal of A&W's strategies and the hard work and discipline of successful implementation, accompanied by a deep belief in the need to create a Climate that defines the behaviours that we will need to demonstrate with one another in order to succeed.

In the quiet of the office that day, I started by reading through all of our Strategy documents. I was looking for inspiration and direction, but what I felt instead was a sense of nostalgia, already convinced that we would need a new Mission and new objectives to deal with the dramatic changes we were seeing in the world and in our business. That work would have to wait, but many of the Climate goals felt exactly right. One of them—"We earn the trust of our guests by always doing what's right"—was particularly apt. Another stated "We work together as partners, pursuing common goals and shared success." These two Climate goals would guide the work ahead.

My reading and thinking that day was punctuated by the occasional ting of the elevator, announcing a few new arrivals. It felt good to have company. We sought one another out several times a day—to check in, to bounce around ideas, to hear what each other had learned. We wanted to be present for our restaurants and for one another. "How are you?" had taken on a whole new meaning.

Everywhere in the business, our teams mobilized to prepare for what might lie ahead. This would be a massive undertaking, and it started with realizations and personal initiatives. "We will need lots of takeout packaging." "I've started to track down sources for personal protective equipment." "Our media is set to launch for a new promotion. Wait, that doesn't feel right—we have to change." "What do our suppliers need to know?"

The World Health Organization had just declared COVID-19 a pandemic. Conversations intensified. Given our strategic focus, we were used to thinking about and aiming for beacons that were years away. Now, we also needed to look ahead in terms of hours and days. To focus our thinking, we put our restaurants first. Everything we were doing started with a focus on what would be needed to operate safely and what would be right for our restaurants, their teams, our operators, and our guests. We pictured ourselves building a bridge from where we were to a post-COVID future. We now knew the impact on our restaurants would be sudden and severe.

At first, the theme was survival. Could we keep on track? The swerves and sense of danger were unsettling. We needed and invited creativity. With our restaurants so firmly at the centre of our thinking, our teams were rising to the challenge to invent novel responses to the crises each was facing. Those working in real estate flipped their work from finding new leases to managing the ones we had. In operations, attention zeroed in on the financial health of our operators and helped ensure they had the ability to take care of their business and the people it touched. Our purchasing teams had to change course constantly to ensure our restaurants had what they needed.

Lots of energy and effort went to avoiding waste and diverting what we couldn't use to feed those in need. Government assistance was not yet in place. We hosted calls, every single day, so that we could be there for any questions and issues that arose. We did not always have answers. Some people needed help right away. We launched an emergency fund to help our operators respond to immediate needs for some of their team members. It felt good to be doing something, even though we knew that this was only the beginning of what was likely to be a very long and emotional ride.

Information and science regarding the spread of COVID began to accumulate. We learned that a choir practice in Washington State had turned deadly, even though distancing and hand hygiene had been in place. Experts were confused. This was different and dangerous news. Not knowing what it meant, it was difficult to know what to do—but we wanted to take whatever action we could. We made the heart-wrenching decision to close our restaurants' doors to all guests until we could figure out what was going on. No eating in. No takeout. No pickup. For our restaurants without drive-thru, this meant shutting down completely.

For our operators, this meant seeing revenues dry up, for themselves and, in many cases, their family members, who were often employed in the business. The bright future they had worked hard to create now seemed bleak. They were crushed by the prospect of needing to scale down their operations or even close, conscious of the devastating impact this would have on their staff. Despite their worry and sadness, the idea of working together as partners kicked in. For restaurant operators facing temporary closure, their first thought was how to transfer food and supplies to restaurants that were able to safely operate. Avoid waste. Help one another. Some opened their kitchens to supply free meals to healthcare and other essential workers. Our entire operator community came together as one. For some, this was the first time they had closed their doors since going into business. From twenty-four hours to none.

To strengthen our ability to deal with decisions and situations in the moment, our operations team articulated some simple, deeply held principles and obligations:

1. To act as responsible citizens to help reduce the risk of spreading the COVID-19 virus and the subsequent stress on the healthcare system.
2. To make business decisions that support the personal health and economic well-being of ourselves and our employees.
3. To continue providing our services to our guests in a manner that is consistent with #1 and #2 above.

These principles gave us the ability to respond quickly, consistently, and with confidence, even when faced with a myriad of different and unique situations. It didn't take long for us to have the principles memorized and for our actions to begin to make a positive difference.

Science was closing in on what really mattered in terms of human behaviour and the spread of COVID. Our response team sought out the experience of experts: knowledge about and supply of personal protective equipment (PPE), medical and scientific expertise, and insights from industry associations doing their best to ensure the right guidance for safe food service operations. Our own health and safety leaders worked closely with the operations team, our operators, and especially our Standards Board, to create the policies, procedures, and practices that defined the "best-known ways" to operate safely. These changed again and again.

Creating, communicating, and implementing our first COVID safety manual was a monumental task. But it allowed many of our restaurants to resume partial operation with confidence. From now on, while outside information would still be important and acted upon, an even quicker source of data would come from our restaurants. Tracking the health of our operators and their teams meant being available all day, every day, to hear, guide, and learn. We wished our goal could be to never have a single case among any of our A&W family. But the explosion of cases in every community, right across the country, meant we would not achieve that ideal. Our operators and their teams lived in and were subject to the same day-to-day risks as their neighbours. Our realistic objectives: To never have spread of COVID in or through any of our restaurants. To protect one another and our guests. To earn their trust. We received our first shipments of masks. The battle for safety at A&W was in full swing.

The A&W office became the nerve centre for everything COVID—measuring, learning, deciding, communicating. For members of the COVID response team, our mornings began with situation updates. The information dashboard was updated constantly. If we couldn't be in restaurants ourselves, we could immerse ourselves in their status and assess and continuously improve our protocols. Health checks felt odd at first but soon became a normal part of our daily routines.

Our updates included reports from operators and our own experience in our corporate restaurant market in Ottawa. Our operators found creative ways to manage tricky restaurant issues like physical distancing, and we were able to share those ideas. Our Standards Board, composed of franchisees and members of the corporate team, worked late into the night to create the right operating systems for the business, exemplifying "working together as partners." The decisions were not easy. There was lots of learning. Who knew that spraying sanitizer on the PIN pads would make them short circuit?

Thankfully, the majority of our restaurants never experienced even a single case. For those that did, our safety team created a concierge-like level of support. Operators could call anytime to ask questions and walk through the steps they needed to follow. Our COVID manual was updated almost weekly. In addition to direct support for operators we looked at the big picture. Were we experiencing any unusual trends? What was happening in different parts of the country? What regulations and directives did we need to follow?

We analyzed the data, looked for hot spots, took preventative action where we could, and kept health and safety at the absolute centre of our decision making as we helped operators navigate their particular challenges. We worried along with them when a staff member was ill and waited anxiously for positive news about their recovery. Each case was taken with the utmost seriousness. The success of our protocols in preventing any in-restaurant transmission gave us and our operators confidence, and this helped us build trust. Some of the hills and swerves were starting to feel more manageable.

What we did day-to-day had changed overnight. Everything in-person had virtually disappeared: restaurant visits, franchisee meetings, site visits, and workshops were replaced by endless video conferences and phone calls. At home, our teams were managing child care, virtual school, lineups for groceries, and disrupted routines of all kinds.

The social isolation, the stress of the pandemic, and the anxiety amplified by the uncertainty of a life unmoored created a pressured cauldron that began to impact the mental health of many members of our A&W community. Almost everyone suffered from a kind of strain and worry that sapped much of the joy from our lives. As a leadership team we wanted to help, but this was challenging. Our best response: to create and deliver whatever certainty we could. Change was happening to us—what change could we bring about and manage ourselves?

First, we decided that since many of our franchisees' businesses were still operating, our Home Office would stay in business too. There would be no layoffs at the office or among the field team; we would keep our talent. We would share tasks differently and find work for everyone. This provided security and hope, especially to those who had family members who had lost their jobs. That choice led to a raft of "secondments"— moving people from areas of the business that had been paused or slowed down to areas where we needed more help.

We created centres of expertise—health and safety, sourcing of PPE, restaurant closures and reopenings, supply chain, government programs. Our people dove in to learn everything and become go-to sources of information for our operators and our staff. With 90% of our team working from home, we defined a hybrid future for the workplace and announced it right away, so that our team knew that our office would remain open, with more flexibility, as we evolved post-pandemic. We created new rhythms for the business—things we did daily, things we did weekly. Same times, same agenda, but always new information and new insight.

We began work on our new Strategy and aimed to size up, develop, and launch it more quickly than ever before—targeting getting underway with the new direction in just a few months. We made the summer a time for vacations for everyone, so that we would be ready, all together, in the fall. We shared staycation ideas. The flexibility and dedication of our teams made us proud. None of it was easy, but all of it delivered valuable clarity and a degree of peace of mind as we moved from a feeling of helplessness to a sense of more action and control. For a while, we even felt better about our ability to see ahead. That proved to be an illusion.

May 25, 2020. George Floyd's arrest and murder at the hands of a police officer, in broad daylight, was witnessed by members of the public from all walks of life, filmed in its entirety by a concerned seventeen-year-old. The video ignited an international firestorm of fury and jolted the Black Lives Matter movement into public consciousness with force and emotion. Our work on what we were calling "JEDI," for Justice, Equity, Diversity and Inclusion, suddenly took on new urgency. I used our weekly staff update to share my thoughts and invite feedback and ideas about what this meant for A&W.

Some of my words were awkward, maybe even wrong for the situation, but they began a conversation and a journey that has already made the kind of difference I was hoping for. One of the most powerful impacts has been the creation of a new climate goal: "I build a safe environment by welcoming, accepting, and respecting everyone in our community." Commitment to the Climate goals extends to every part of the A&W organization—from the cook or cashier who started work in a restaurant yesterday to the forty-year Home Office veteran. The addition of this goal has allowed conversation, education, and action to touch all of us in our day-to-day interactions, building on our efforts to make A&W, and our communities, more inclusive and fair. We are learning and changing, focused on making a difference. I'm very proud of the work we are doing, but I know we have a long way to go.

In contrast to the global health crisis and the upheaval in world events were the little milestones and everyday matters that continued to chug along, though changed. Retirements, which were celebrated in unfamiliar ways. New employees joining teams they would not meet in person for months. Restaurant openings, using new and untried ways to assemble training teams who could find their way to the restaurants and lead safely amid travel restrictions, quarantine requirements, and ever-changing protocols.

Horror at the mounting case counts, serious illnesses, and deaths was a backdrop to the daily sadness and personal fears for people we knew who were impacted by COVID in so many different ways—illness, worry, loneliness, grief. We learned to experience many emotions at the same time, and we especially needed to find ways to let happiness in.

These included: A karaoke-like "screaming singalong" at the end of the fiftieth consecutive day of COVID crisis team meetings. A socially distant kefir tasting (good for immunity?) for the smattering of people at the office. Competing for excellence at the ritual of perfect handwashing. Handwritten notes of appreciation and encouragement. A digital place to share good news. Everything helped, a little. I found myself buying anything that sounded soothing—building an eclectic collection of products with names that contained words like "nourishing" and "calm." Anything "sweet" worked well too!

We all needed to find ways to maintain our own positive energy. Many of my soul-sustaining activities, like yoga and family visits, had been cancelled or were unsafe. I needed to find alternatives. I started a regular routine of taking walks outside at lunch. It was nice to get outdoors, a welcomed break, some time to think and breathe the outdoor air. Soon I was meeting more and more A&W people out for their own walks, and that was a boost too! I already had bottles of sanitizer, along with lip balm and hand cream on my desk. I expanded that collection to include sunscreen! I found myself outside, a lot.

I also discovered just how many ways music can alter your mood—adding calmness or energy, or helping me connect with and manage my emotions. Finding the right song or the right lyrics to match a moment felt like a little victory, and I turned the music up loud. Finally, I started to pay much more attention to sleep. After decades of hotel nights almost every week I was now in my own bed every single night. That helped! The restorative trio of walking, music, and sleep turned into a daily regime and the core of my self-care.

Every morning, new information, new questions, new choices and decisions awaited. There was a hunger—from our team, and especially from our restaurant operators—for the certainty and vision we could provide, and the information and guidance we could share. But we were never overwhelmed. Our restaurants were the horizon our eyes could focus on to steady ourselves.

Our operators, far from giving in to the weariness, the uncertainty, and the financial challenges, remained committed, bringing their best to their work and their teams. Many reached out with kindness to their colleagues and to us, and that caring meant the world. The strong ties, the compassion, the practical help, and the sense of togetherness were the daily tonic that invigorated us and gave purpose to our efforts. Restaurant staff, at the front lines to serve our guests, anchored us. The generous acts of our operators in their communities across the country inspired us. And their belief and optimism gave us the collective strength and resilience we needed to get through.

The COVID-19 pandemic has forged change that has marked people from every part of the world, and from every generation. Fighting COVID has been unique. It has required everyone's participation and made us realize that for some things, we really are all in it together. Embracing change, we adapted to dramatic disruption in societal norms and saw first hand the impact we could create.

I believe we will emerge with more openness, more empathy, and a greater appreciation for our interconnectedness. Our experiences and our willingness to work together to protect and support one another will give each of us more confidence in our own ability to tackle other big problems—at home, at work, and in the world. We are more prepared than ever to face the future with creativity and courage. There are doubtless other roller coasters to confront and tame. I feel ready.

BANK OF NOVA SCOTIA

Bank of Nova Scotia takes pride in being a leading bank in the Americas. Scotiabank's founders in Halifax followed their clients to the Caribbean in the 1880s, opening a branch in Jamaica to finance trade in sugar, rum, and fish. By the time Brian Porter became president and chief executive officer in 2013, Scotiabank was operating in fifty-four countries across seventeen time zones.

Porter effectively doubled down on Scotiabank's international strategy. As CEO, he expanded the bank's presence in countries that stand to benefit from the growth of Pacific economies—Chile, Peru, Colombia, and Mexico—while exiting smaller nations. Porter runs the show from an antique desk in Toronto that previously served as the bank's boardroom table in Halifax during the 1800s.

On Porter's watch, Scotiabank came to have more Spanish-speaking employees in its workforce of ninety-two thousand than those who claim English as their first language. For years, the outward-looking strategy translated into a premium stock market valuation compared to other Canadian banks, reflecting Scotiabank's unique mix of geographies and business lines.

A global health crisis, however, posed unique challenges to Canada's most international bank. Scotiabank's share price fell more than 30% in mid-March 2020, on concerns over COVID-19's impact, particularly on export-based economies such as Mexico, Chile, and Peru. Porter, a hands-on leader who spends considerable time with teams in South America, suddenly had to set strategy from a home office with a wonky printer.

It was the challenge of a lifetime for a banker who has spent his career at Scotiabank. A Calgary native, Porter earned a business degree at Dalhousie University, then joined employee-owned investment dealer McLeod Young Weir in 1981. Scotiabank acquired the firm seven years later. Over the next four decades, Porter worked closely with corporate clients as an investment banker, then took senior roles in risk management and treasury before being named president in 2012 and chief executive the following year.

Brian Porter

AUGUST 2021

Two days before the first coronavirus case was identified in Canada, I was in Santiago, Chile, with the senior management team for Scotiabank's Investor Day. This regular event, being held outside Canada for just the third time in the bank's 188-year history, was an opportunity to speak directly with some of our largest investors, to update them on our strategy, successes, and plans for growth.

We had accomplished a lot since I'd become president in 2013. We'd undertaken a highly complex international repositioning that involved reducing our footprint from fifty-four to thirty countries, focusing on high-quality business and decreasing numerous types of risk. After years of targeted investment and heavy lifting, the bank's repositioning program was largely complete, and we were looking forward to showcasing our progress and our leadership team in Santiago.

At the very same time, the World Health Organization was holding a meeting of its emergency committee to assess whether the outbreak of a mysterious respiratory virus constituted a health emergency of international concern. Cases had been identified only in China (where it had originated), South Korea, Thailand, and Singapore and numbered in the hundreds. Members of the committee could not reach a consensus based on the available evidence. As the world waited, the number of coronavirus cases grew.

Though our focus was on our shareholders and the investment community over those two days in Santiago, the gathering storm clouds were very much on our radar. We had no idea that COVID-19, as it would later be known, would become the defining story of the year, if not the early twenty-first century. Nor did we realize the toll it would take on lives and economies around the world, but we were paying attention.

On our first day in Chile, I walked with Jake Lawrence and James Neate, co-group heads of our global banking and markets division, along

Apoquindo Avenue, a beautiful thoroughfare lined with glass buildings, to a meeting with investors. Jake and James, who had responsibility for our operations in Asia and were getting regular updates from leaders there, briefed me as we walked. Detailed information was scarce, but case counts were rising quickly in China, which had all but sealed off the city of Wuhan, where the virus originated. Cases had also begun to emerge elsewhere in Asia. Further spread of the virus seemed inevitable. We discussed restricting company travel to and from China.

Some of the decisions we made were difficult at the time, but with the benefit of hindsight they were clearly right for our team and our customers. A good example was the call to restrict company travel to and from China well before any government travel advisories. In fact, by the time we returned to Toronto from Santiago, not only were the restrictions in place but our senior response team was fully set up to monitor and manage the issue. The travel restriction raised some eyebrows among authorities external to the bank. I received one rather pointed phone call from a senior Canadian government official, in which it was suggested that I was over-reacting, even undermining public confidence.

It was a choice that had, at its core, one principle that would guide us in all of the critical decisions the leadership team had to make during the difficult months ahead: that the well-being of our employees, customers, and communities must always be our first priority. It was clear, particularly in the early days of the pandemic, that our employees were going to be feeling fearful about the virus, its impact on them and their families, and the financial impacts it could have on them and the bank. As the senior leadership team, we needed to be role models and project a sense of calm and confidence across the organization and publicly.

There were two other principles that I adhered to throughout the crisis: that communicating transparently and frequently with our employees was crucial, and supporting our customers in their time of need was key.

Every crisis is unique in its particulars, but that doesn't mean you respond to each one differently. Experience matters. It helps you see beyond the headline of the day, or in the case of a spreading pandemic, the minute. It enables you to avoid panic because you know every problem can be solved with the right people and the right approach. It also informs how you behave *before* the crisis, so that you have the right systems and processes in place to deal with whatever arises.

During my forty-year career in banking, I have experienced and led through many crises of various kinds: debt crises in Asia and Latin America; the dot-com bubble; natural disasters such as hurricanes and earthquakes in some of our most important markets; and, of course, the global financial crisis of 2007–2008. I was Scotiabank's chief risk officer during that time and saw first-hand the rate and pace at which financial contagion spread from financial markets to Main Street. That experience was formative for me, both personally and professionally. I distinctly remember the sleepless nights and thousands of hours of calls and meetings with my colleagues, counterparts, government leaders, the Bank of Canada, regulatory bodies, and, of course, our clients.

The COVID-19 pandemic was different. It was a health crisis with financial consequences, not a financial problem at its root. As different as it was, experience, as well as new information, would inform how our team would deal with it. And my experience told me this: when you operate from a set of strong principles, when you have trust in your team, when you have patience and a willingness to communicate, you are already well equipped to deal with whatever fate may hand you. We had all those things heading into the pandemic. That didn't mean we had all the answers. Quite the contrary: we were staring into an abyss with no idea of its depth. Nevertheless, I was confident that we—the bank and its employees, our customers, and our communities across many countries— would emerge stronger on the other side. As I said often to our team, every crisis has an ending.

As January 2020 rolled over into February, the senior response team, led by Barb Mason, the chief human resources officer and a member of the bank's operating committee, and Tracy Bryan, executive vice-president in

charge of global operations, were meeting daily to oversee complex preparations and safety measures across the bank.

The efficient execution of the bank's business continuity plans (BCPs)
would be critical. BCPs are detailed blueprints for how the bank can continue to operate—to serve retail customers, finance corporate transactions,
manage clients' savings, conduct trades, and so on—during a service disruption caused by a natural disaster, for example. Or a pandemic.

On February 25, BCPs were invoked for our teams in the United
Kingdom, with key employees being split up over two sites; over the coming days, other countries followed suit. Travel restrictions and self-isolation
guidelines were put in place for employees returning from the most seriously affected countries and jurisdictions, including Iran, northern Italy,
and South Korea. An incident in which an employee went to work at a
Canadian branch displaying flu-like symptoms triggered a full review of
health and safety measures and communications. The employee did not
have COVID-19, but the incident helped strengthen our awareness of and
adherence to established health and safety protocols.

I can remember the week our BCP for Canada was implemented. On
Monday, March 9, my team and I were planning for a trip to Montreal.
I was going there to meet with clients and to deliver remarks at a 250-per-
son luncheon. By Thursday, the trip was off, the luncheon was cancelled,
and we were making sure we had the necessary equipment in place to lead
the bank and connect with team members and customers while we worked
to invoke BCPs in every geography Scotiabank operates in, more than
thirty countries globally.

Our employees were incredibly adaptable. Within a short period of
time, 60% of our employees moved to a largely virtual work environment
with hardly any interruptions. Over the coming weeks, that number
would grow to 80% of non-branch employees who were enabled to work
from home.

The preparations we had made, both long-term and short-term,
ensured the transition to a work-from-home scenario was seamless. The
long-term ones consisted primarily of the significant investments we

had made in technology over the previous five years—some $15 billion across our geographic footprint. The purpose of those investments, in talent as well as the technology itself, was to put us at the leading edge of digital banking. We have since been recognized with many awards for our best-in-class digital platforms and services, including from J.D. Power and *The Banker* magazine. The teams, processes, and management practices we developed along the way also allowed us to handle technology-related risks much more effectively. Nobody knew the pandemic would come, but having those teams in place, having those playbooks ready, and having developed the connectivity across different geographies created an organization that was probably more prepared than others to respond quickly.

The work our technology teams—led by Michael Zerbs, group head of technology and operations—did as the COVID situation became more fraught deserves special mention. In the leadup to the first of the lockdowns, these teams made sure we would be ready. One of the priorities was ensuring we had enough virtual private networks (VPNs), which allow a computer to connect to the bank's systems over the Internet securely. This was an absolute necessity so we could continue to manage clients' private financial information without risk. Until the pandemic, the most concurrent users on the bank VPNs at one time was around nine thousand, during a major snowstorm in Ontario. Suddenly we needed to accommodate five or six times that number. By late January we were placing orders for additional equipment and network bandwidth globally to prepare for the tsunami of demands that would soon come. Because of the foresight and hard work of our technology teams, we went into the pandemic at the end of March 2020 with eighty thousand connections globally. Unlike some of our banking peers, we were never forced to ration VPNs or make people work at odd hours so the licences could be shared around. A peak concurrent user count of over forty-six thousand was achieved in May 2021. We have since further improved our resiliency and security in support of a remote workforce by enabling capabilities such as Always On VPN and cross-regional access between major hub countries (e.g., Mexico employees can connect to a VPN hub in Canada or the inverse in the event of a widespread technical issue).

I decided to use our family's property just northwest of Toronto as my home base, and for the first time in my career, I started working from home. While the bank's technology systems were running smoothly thanks to steps we had taken over the previous years to boost our platforms and capabilities, I experienced some growing pains—paper jams being chief among them!

Those first six weeks of BCP were simultaneously a blur and incredibly vivid. I would wake up at 5 a.m., have breakfast, and catch up on emails. I would go for a walk to clear my head and prepare myself for the day to come: calls, emails, and decisions that would impact millions of people. It was during those days that I was grateful for my experience with handling emergencies a decade before. It didn't take long for my "crisis muscle memory" to be activated.

One of the core principles our team adhered to was to communicate, communicate, and then over-communicate. I'm a private person and it's not in my nature to talk about myself, but it was clear that our employees needed to know that the leadership team was listening. More than that, we understood what they were going through, and we were in this battle together. Our transparency and consistent communication enabled us to build trust with our people and to ensure resilience as a team.

I started sending weekly emails to all our employees, telling them what we knew, and what we didn't know, without wrapping it all up in corporate-speak. We decided it was okay to say we don't have all the answers yet, particularly when it came to our return-to-work plans. We weren't going to set arbitrary deadlines and commitments without knowing we could follow through. We launched a Scotiabank Heroes series, highlighting examples of our employees going over and above for one another. These incredibly moving stories were profiled in emails, videos, and infographics, and shared with our 90,000+ employees. As an example, one of our employees in Mexico moved to a different town in order to keep one of our branches open to serve our customers there. By recognizing exceptional service and celebrating our wins, we fostered an attitude of gratitude and deep respect for one another.

I recorded videos with members of our team in which I answered questions submitted by employees. In each one, my tone was calm and measured. Often, I would end with my go-to phrase of reassurance: "Every crisis has an ending." Each member of the leadership team increased the frequency of employee communications, keeping our people up to speed on the latest developments and how new measures might affect them. Employees greatly appreciated the transparency, and employee engagement, as measured by regular surveys, stayed very high throughout the pandemic. More importantly, we matched words with actions, implementing new programs and benefits to help employees deal with the financial and health impacts brought about by the crisis.

Within the leadership team, the communication was non-stop. I would have short calls throughout the day with some of my team members, in between calls with customers, government officials, regulators, and our competitors. It was sometimes chaotic—more like playing improvisational jazz than conducting a symphony orchestra, as Dan Rees, our head of Canadian banking, described it—but the calls were effective in keeping a constant flow of information moving. That was an approach I favoured even before the pandemic, picking up the phone and speaking directly to people rather than having a three-hour management meeting. The nimbleness that we had already built into our management processes and communications served us well during those chaotic early COVID days. We were also in regular contact with our board of directors, who supported our decisions and provided thoughtful and strategic guidance throughout.

We also needed to talk to our investors, who were naturally concerned about the impact of the crisis on the banks and markets. Very early in the pandemic, I convened a call with shareholders and was shocked by how many people were on the line. They were worried about things like our energy portfolio, or credit cards, or mortgage deferrals. And my message was "Don't panic, it isn't Armageddon." This was something that we were ready for. We had ample liquidity and ample capital, and we could take this shock. It was weeks before the other banks had similar calls. I didn't like the situation any more than anyone else, but you have to talk about it. You can't hide.

Some of my favourite moments from 2020 were my visits to our branches—delivering hot coffee and Sobeys gift cards to thank our teams on the front lines for their courage and dedication to our customers. I recently received an email from a satisfied customer. The customer wrote, "All Canadian dreams run through a branch." I couldn't agree more, which is why deciding what to do with our branches was something Dan and I discussed during the first weekend after the BCPs had been invoked.

The safety of employees and customers was of course the highest priority, but we were also certain that our customers would need us to be there for them during the difficult times ahead. Some of our competitors were closing hundreds of branches, but Dan refused to overreact. We knew many customers, including elderly patrons and small businesses, preferred or needed to go to branches to do their banking. Our view was that the pandemic would only increase the need for financial advice.

As volume increased dramatically at our call centres (at the peak they received ninety thousand calls a day in Canada, an increase of 50% over pre-pandemic), we made sure our digital platforms were as accessible and easy to use as possible, but the need for the in-person human touch would not disappear. From our call centres, we proactively reached out to our customers to offer help before they asked for it. We know our customers, and this outreach certainly helped to save many thousands from unnecessary interest payments, or even insolvency.

Dan made the decision: we would keep as many of our more than nine hundred Canadian branches open as possible—98% in total—with shorter hours and with the most comprehensive health measures we could implement. It was the right call. It showed our customers that we were serious about serving them and that we would be there for them, come what may. That was one of the moves that contributed to Scotiabank being the only major bank to see its customer satisfaction rating go up during the pandemic, and that drew positive comments from several levels of government.

Keeping our branches sanitized and ensuring physical distancing could happen was no small task. In the early days, branch employees would improvise, placing lunchroom tables in front of wickets to create some distance between customers and staff. Soon our operation shifted into high gear and supplies rolled out. Over the course of the next few months we would purchase twelve thousand pieces of plexiglass for our Canadian branches; five million disposable masks for use in branches and offices; two hundred thousand bottles of hand sanitizer; and seventy-five thousand containers of wipes. From my visits, I can tell you that the pride our branch teams felt in being able to continue to help their customers was palpable. Those visits and the feedback frontline employees were getting from customers confirmed for me that keeping the branches open was the right call.

Banking is all about relationships, and the strongest relationships are forged during challenging times. Keeping our branches open during the pandemic was one of the ways we directly served our customers, but there were other ways too.

Liquidity—the ability to access cash quickly—is the lifeblood of a business. If you can't meet payroll or you miss a payment to a supplier because of a sudden downturn, it can kill your business. That was the great concern of many Canadian business owners and executives by the end of March as large segments of the economy—especially travel, hospitality, and entertainment, as well as in-person retail—began to shut down. There was tremendous apprehension about the coming weeks and how bad the economic situation would become. It's at times like these that the importance of the relationships we have forged with our clients is most acutely felt, and our stability and ability to withstand hard times are most appreciated.

One of the services banks offer their corporate and commercial clients is a revolving credit facility, or revolver. It's essentially a line of credit for business, money that can be drawn on at any time, usually to meet short-term needs, and then repaid. Rather than wait for our clients to call us, we set out to make sure they knew we had their backs and would be there when they needed to access their revolvers. During that stretch from mid-March through late April, large parts of my days were filled with calls to the CEOs of some of our biggest clients, reassuring them that we were there for them.

In a matter of weeks, we loaned out tens of billions of dollars to corporate and commercial clients. We were able to handle that avalanche of funding requests comfortably because the bank's financial resiliency and capital liquidity were excellent, and we were set up to be nimble. Jake Lawrence and James Neate and their global banking and markets teams skillfully managed the client needs as well as the market volatility that was causing such concern. They turned a crisis into an opportunity to strengthen ties with our customers and even grow our business.

I have often described the role of Scotiabank, and of other financial institutions, as being that of shock absorber for the economy by providing liquidity when it is needed most. That social and economic responsibility, especially during down times, is part of the reason that I consider banking to be more of a calling than a career. We are responsible for most of the capital allocation in this society. During difficult times like the ones we just went through, that capital provides a backstop for the businesses, large and small, upon which the economy depends.

For capital to be allocated efficiently and properly, the engines of allocation—the banks—need to be healthy. Our strong, stable banking system helped us recover quickly from the 2007–2008 financial crisis and helped us get through the worst of the pandemic. It's a system of which I'm proud to be a part. I think our employees share that view, which is part of why we were so successful and productive. They were helping customers, families, and companies get through a really difficult time, and that sense of mission pulls people together.

That personal touch matters and isn't forgotten. We recently led an equity financing for a significant Canadian company, a company to whose CEO I had reached out in the early pandemic days to offer whatever support I could. We put a credit facility in place to make sure he had the liquidity to get through those challenging times. He chose us to lead the company's next transaction because we had provided them with liquidity when it was needed. People always remember who stood by them during challenging times.

One of Scotiabank's key differentiators from our peers is our international footprint, with a particular focus on Latin America and the Caribbean. Ninety-five per cent of our revenue comes from six countries—Canada, the U.S., Mexico, Chile, Colombia, and Peru—but we have a presence in twenty-four other countries. We're proud of this diversity, and some of the best experiences of my career at Scotiabank have been the many international trips I've made, meeting the people and learning about the cultures of those countries.

During the pandemic, our presence across such a vast geographic area presented some unique challenges as well as some tremendous opportunities. The challenges included the simple fact that the course of the virus and the ability of governments to react varied from country to country. We would have to be nimble to stay on top of the evolving situation in so many places.

The opportunities arose from a couple of sources. One was, again, our experience. We had often dealt with crisis situations in Latin America and the Caribbean, including natural disasters such as hurricanes and earthquakes, and had quickly implemented the kinds of deferral programs that the pandemic now called for. In our international banking division, since the beginning of the pandemic and following regulatory guidelines, the bank has launched customer assistance programs to provide financial relief to approximately three million customers ($25 billion or 37% of total retail lending balances). The programs have mostly expired, with small balances remaining.

Indeed, our experience in setting up such programs prepared us well when we needed to quickly do the same in Canada. We also knew from experience that deferral programs—allowing customers to postpone payments on mortgages, car loans, and other kinds of credit—not only were hugely helpful to our customers but also did not lead to the kinds of massive defaults down the road that external commentators feared. We were able to provide 370,000 Canadian customers with over $54 billion of payment relief, ensuring they could get through those difficult early months with peace of mind.

The other opportunity that arose was that we could call on the digital capabilities that we had carefully developed across our footprint and that I mentioned earlier. We had built what we called digital factories in our key countries and sought out the top technology talent to help us fully digitize our operations. Our Peruvian team was the first to develop a digital tool that allowed customers to access deferral programs online. Similar tools were rolled out across the footprint, and in the end some 70% of customers accessed their assistance programs digitally. The crisis ultimately drove digital adoption to record levels and showed that we had built the capability to reimagine the way we operate as a bank.

We also had in Ignacio ("Nacho") Deschamps—who oversaw both our international operations and our digital transformation company-wide— a seasoned leader who had managed through challenging times before. Again, experience matters. As Nacho said to me about his response to the crisis, "I just had to reach into my internal shelf and grab the playbook." Nacho also recognized early on the need to access outside sources of information to inform our decision making and began weekly calls with leading thinkers, political figures, and business people from across the region. Those calls really helped me prepare to answer questions from investors and the board and helped inform how we were thinking about the evolution of this awful virus. I was reaching out to finance ministers and health ministers in our Latin American countries, to the heads of central banks, and of course to our country heads, to push beyond the headlines to get an informed view from experts in the field and triangulate the different facts and figures and opinions.

Seeing the way our employees reacted to the crisis right across our vast footprint was among the proudest moments for me. We did everything we could to support them, and they in turn gave their all to ensure we were there for our customers. We were truly a family working together toward a common goal.

I have long believed that ours is an office culture. We produce better results working together from the office. Of course, forcing people to come back before we had reached established vaccination thresholds and could put the necessary safety precautions in place would be foolhardy, and flexibility would be required. We have always focused on returning to work the right way.

I returned to the office in late April 2020 to prepare to report the bank's second quarter results. We had strict safety protocols in place, as well as weekly COVID-19 tests, and you could count the number of people on the two executive floors on both hands. Following Q2, some of us continued to come into the office. We were happy to be there, a nimble team that could keep us connected at the leadership level as well as with all the people working remotely. Later in the spring, as some of the restrictions were loosened, to keep spirits up my team and I would host lunches with a few members of the management team. We would order in food from local restaurants and sit together, at a distance, in a room that could easily fit twenty-five. These lunches were not only a welcome escape from the ever-changing news of the day; they were an opportunity to socialize and have fun. We laughed a lot during those lunches. I think we were all grateful for them.

One day in late April 2020, with the pandemic just over a month old, I was at Scotiabank Arena helping to put together meals that would be distributed to frontline workers at hospitals, charities, and shelters. The initiative—a partnership between Maple Leaf Sports & Entertainment (MLSE), Scotiabank, and other donors—was supplying ten thousand healthy meals a day to people putting themselves at risk to help others during the pandemic. As we worked in the kitchen and, later, on the playing surface at the arena, I was moved by the efforts of the people there giving of themselves for their community, both the people helping making the meals and those they were intended for. Moved, but not surprised. Canada is a generous, open place where people look out for one another, especially in hard times. I knew then that however difficult this challenge proved to be, we would pull together and come out stronger on the other side.

We were getting close to that other side in late June 2021 when another event took place at Scotiabank Arena. This time, we had helped organize a mass vaccination clinic with our partners at MLSE, the University Health Network, and the City of Toronto. Over the course of the day, more than twenty-six thousand people would get their first or second vaccines, a global record for the number of vaccines administered in one day at a single clinic. It was another shining example of a community coming together to help one another in a time of need. The event had a joyous, celebratory feel, one of those moments when we all felt like life might soon start getting back to some kind of normal.

Getting back to normal was what we all hoped for, but I couldn't help thinking that maybe we could do even better than getting back to where we had been before the pandemic. Those difficult eighteen months revealed this great country's many strengths, but they also exposed shortcomings that need to be addressed, both to prepare for the next crisis—and there will be a next one—and to ensure our prosperity in the decades ahead.

On the first count, we simply must make our healthcare system better, and that means investing in it. As chair of the University Health Network, a research and teaching hospital network in Toronto, I saw first-hand the impacts of the pandemic on health professionals and the health system more broadly. Yet the issues existed before the pandemic. Although the population density in the Greater Toronto Area has grown substantially, the number of hospital beds has not. In fact, it has fallen. The answer isn't just more beds; many services can be delivered in the home or the community if the necessary funding is there. As well, this country used to have vaccine manufacturing capability, but it no longer did by the time COVID struck. We were reliant on others for the life-saving shots that have gradually returned us to near normal. That is an issue of sovereignty, of being self-reliant in the most basic sense. We also saw some unfortunate dynamics between levels of government during the crisis, with finger-pointing and friction over responsibilities. Canadians don't want to hear any of that—they just want their leaders to get it done. And they want them to have a plan for the next pandemic.

On the broader economic questions, the pandemic highlighted several issues that need serious attention. One is a housing shortage that has seen real estate prices skyrocket even amid an economic downturn. While Canada has significantly increased the number of new Canadians it welcomes every year—a move I fully support—our housing stock hasn't kept pace with the population growth. It is getting to the point where first-time buyers and young families are having trouble entering the market. Governments at all levels must work together to remove the obstacles to the construction of all types of housing.

A second issue is child care. While there was already a shortage of high-quality, affordable child care pre-pandemic, the extent of the problem became even more clear during the crisis. Women's participation rate in the workforce, already lower than that of men, declined even further during COVID. For Canada to prosper, women must be able to fully participate and reach their full potential in the workforce. Ensuring families have access to affordable child care is one of the ways to help reach that gender parity. The federal government has promised steps in that direction. We must make sure it follows through.

We also have to look at our economy and determine where the strengths are and how we sustain them. Where do we have a strategic competitive advantage? How can the government enhance investment? We've had issues with productivity—a key measure of economic growth—in this country for a long time. As an example, many retailers realized during the pandemic that they needed a digital strategy to survive. That has been the case for almost a decade, yet many hadn't made the necessary investments.

A certain amount of complacency seems to have set in. For years we have been satisfied living in what some call the 2% trap, with modest economic growth of that order being the norm. How do we break out of that trap to create the robust growth that will add to the prosperity of all Canadians? Part of the answer may be to fashion what one might call a modern industrial policy. Our approach has often been to spread our attention and resources around evenly, according to political rather than economic priorities and leading to suboptimal outcomes. Instead, we must identify the sectors where we can lead and win and make sure those sectors get the support they need to compete globally. It could be agriculture, various forms of energy, technology, or something else. We must aggressively pursue our economic interests and encourage entrepreneurship, innovation, and creativity in all their forms.

We've learned a lot about ourselves and our communities over the past eighteen months—about our many strengths and the challenges that remain. We've lived through the pain of losing loved ones, and we've seen what we can accomplish when we work together. Let's not allow the lessons of this difficult time slip past us. Rather, let's seize the opportunity to make Canada an even better country for all.

BLACKNORTH INITIATIVE

Hollywood would be hard pressed to script a success story that matches Wes Hall's journey.

Raised by his grandmother in a tin shack in Kingston, Jamaica, Hall arrived in Canada as a teenager with no cash and no connections. He held a series of menial jobs—chicken processing, cleaner, security guard, mailroom clerk—while getting a college degree. At that point, a Global Television Network executive decided to take a chance and hired him for a corporate role.

Hall thrived on detail-oriented tasks and had a passion for people that lit up every encounter. He gravitated to deal making, launching shareholder advisory firm Kingsdale in 2003. Hall became the guy Bay Street called to help close friendly acquisitions or fend off hostile takeovers. Blue chip clients—Air Canada, Barrick, CN Rail, Suncor, CP Rail—entrusted their biggest deals to Kingsdale. Hall's success translated into a home in an exclusive neighbourhood and support for philanthropic causes such as Toronto's SickKids Hospital.

Yet for all his achievements, Hall could never overcome the slights—the micro-aggressions—that come with being a Black executive in a white business world. Renovators who ask if Mr. Hall is home when they come to work on his century-old home. Partygoers who hand Hall the keys to park their car when the entrepreneur is standing in front of a hotel at a charity event. While Hall was in the top echelon of corporate leaders, it was always disconcerting to look around and see so few people who looked like him.

Long before George Floyd was murdered, Hall created BlackNorth as a networking platform for Black executives. It was a passion project: Hall would gather a few dozen BlackNorth members at his home and invite then-Finance Minister Bill Morneau over for a fireside chat.

However, when the pandemic hit, the Kingsdale CEO found himself working flat out for his clients, who were all struggling to turn deals that traditionally got done face to face into online sessions. Social justice was not his priority in the early stages of COVID. Until a cop put his knee on a Black man's neck, with cellphone cameras rolling, and kept it there for more than nine minutes.

Wes Hall

AUGUST 2021

I first heard about George Floyd's murder when a friend asked me, "Have you seen the video?" I thought he was referring to the news story about Ahmaud Arbery, the Black man who was shot while out jogging through an affluent neighbourhood in Georgia, or the incident with Christian Cooper, the Black man who was out birdwatching in Central Park and had a woman call the police on him because he rightfully asked her to leash her dog. So, naturally, I responded by saying that I'd seen these videos. But he said, no—not those ones. There is another that is even more egregious, and it involved the murder of another Black man by the police in plain sight. See, all these videos, though painful to watch, have become all too commonplace in our lives—even among Black folks—and the response they generate had become equally predictable, though unacceptable. A shocking video emerges, there is outrage for forty-eight hours, people talk about change, yet nothing happens. Despite this I had no choice but to watch this latest release, perhaps hoping something would be different.

I was in my home office when I clicked on that video, which at the time had already been viewed by millions. I watched this police officer kneel on George Floyd's neck for eight minutes and fifty-seven seconds, while his fellow officers, who were there to "serve and protect," were directing traffic. Bystanders were yelling to render aid to George Floyd, but the officers ignored them as well as Mr. Floyd's own plea, "I can't breathe." The officer kneeling on George Floyd's neck had one hand in his pocket and he was as cool as if he was just taking a smoke break. As a Black man, it was completely devastating to watch George Floyd die, slowly, with no dignity, almost as if watching a medieval execution of someone just like me and my sons. At least in medieval times the executioner's face was covered. In the case of the execution of George Floyd, his executioner's expression was so chilling that it appears as if it was just another day at the office.

How many other incidents were there like this that we do not know about? I shut down, emotionally and physically. I literally dropped into a chair. I saw myself in George Floyd. What happened to him could easily happen to me, not just in Minnesota but where I live. In my hometown of Toronto, 70% of civilians killed in police shootings are Black.

George Floyd was killed on May 25, 2020. At that point, we were only two months into the pandemic. We were crisis footing at all my companies as well as the not-for-profit organizations in which I volunteer a substantial amount of my time. At Kingsdale Advisors, my shareholder advisory firm, for example, spring is always the busiest time of our year. Some years, we book 80% of our revenues in those three months of the year.

We help our clients stage their annual meetings, so we are running management's most important session with the shareholders who own the company. We were also working on proxy votes and shareholder activism, advising investors and boards on high-profile campaigns over governance and contested issues. Every one of these proxy battles typically consists of dozens of one-on-one meetings with investors. These are enormously important moments in the life of a company. We built our reputation on executing at the highest possible level for corporate Canada.

Suddenly annual meetings were moved online, for the very first time. Proxy campaigns became fully digital, no face-to-face meetings. We needed to make this huge shift while our team at Kingsdale, who are used to being side by side at our office in the financial districts in Toronto and New York, were suddenly working on their laptops, from their kitchen tables, while simultaneously home-schooling their children, caring for elderly family members, among other things. It was incredibly intense. We were coordinating remotely with boards, with CEOs, with lawyers, with regulators, and with technology suppliers. At this point, no one had ever heard of Zoom meetings, so we were all learning on the fly. We were flat out. However, we were prepared for this. Just a year prior we had rolled out the teams platform company wide. We recognized that as a 24/7 firm we needed to ensure our employees could provide service to our clients from wherever they were, and we wanted to ensure our employees had balance in their work and personal lives. So our employees pivoted and had grown accustomed to working from outside the office when the pandemic hit, and I have to say . . . they thoroughly impressed me.

Other businesses I own faced similar challenges, all reeling because of COVID. For example, my four-star hotel in St. Lucia, the Harbor Club, had opened just two years prior and had finally found its footing, projecting a record year for 2020. There were also three new restaurants on the grounds. The resort went from fully booked to completely shut down in the blink of an eye as the world was forced into mandatory lockdowns for months on end. I also own a business that supplies rigging and wear products to oil and gas companies. We had to rework the operations to ensure the employees were safe and healthy while the doors stayed open. Nothing was the same. I recognized early that the pandemic would have a significant economic impact on my businesses, but how much remained to be seen. I quickly initiated a weekly leadership meeting with all my holding company's management teams to scenario plan. We needed to stay one step ahead of often unpredictable events, something that ended up lessening the financial impact on all my businesses.

On top of my business interests, I was working on several philanthropic initiatives at the time COVID hit, including as a board member of the SickKids Foundation in Toronto. The pandemic only served to highlight the inequalities faced by our society and the way we deal with underserved communities and our elderly, especially when it comes to health care.

Almost immediately after watching the video of George Floyd's murder, I dropped everything I was engaged in at the time—my work, my charities, all my business interests. I just sat in my backyard. I needed a mental break to process it all. Nothing else mattered at the time, even COVID, believe it or not.

Despite the endless challenges and roadblocks put in place due to COVID—I knew I still had all these pressing obligations. I decided to write a note to the board members of the charities I was serving on as well as to the leadership teams of my companies. The SickKids Foundation was having its Annual General Meeting as well as our end-of-year board meeting that week. These were very big events in the Foundation's calendar. I explained in my note how I was feeling—my sadness, my anger, my grief, and this sense of being paralyzed.

The SickKids Foundation board is one of the best group of people I have had the privilege of serving with. They immediately grasped what I was struggling with as a Black man, and in solidarity the board voted to postpone the Foundation's board meeting and Annual General Meeting as well as the planned reception after the meetings, out of respect for me and my community following the murder of George Floyd. That meant a great deal. It demonstrated that business leaders were willing to set aside what they were doing, even things they felt were important, to engage in a conversation around anti-Black systemic racism.

I knew it was essential to continue this uncomfortable conversation surrounding race, inclusion, and diversity. It was very upsetting to me to see statements made by our corporate and political leaders that I felt were disingenuous and inauthentic, lacking action or substance. There was just nothing concrete that these leaders were committing to that I felt helped our BIPOC (Black, Indigenous, and people of colour) communities or that would permanently change the narrative for Black Canadians. In addition, it was clear by their statements that in their minds this was exclusively a U.S. issue and that Canada was much better when it came to systemic anti-Black racism. The fact is that Canadians needed to recognize that we have our own dark history and that anti-Black systemic racism exists in all aspects of our society. As a country, we needed to make real change rather than just sending out a Tweet or a press release expressing solidarity and then moving on to the next corporate or political challenge. Canadians needed to know what Black Canadians experience in our own backyard.

While on my mental break, I felt the need to express my feelings more broadly. I decided to write about my personal experiences of being a Black man in Canada and took my story directly to major press outlets. I wanted to make it clear that anti-Black systemic racism is just as much a problem in this country as it is in downtown Minneapolis. I opened that story by saying, "When I look into the mirror, I see George Floyd." After writing my thoughts, I contemplated the next step.

I wrote about being out for a jog in my affluent Toronto neighbourhood and seeing an elderly white woman take a tumble. I hesitated to help her, worried that she might be startled by having a Black man standing over her as she was sprawled on the sidewalk. I feared my neighbours would call the police if they saw a Black man standing over an elderly white woman while she was seemingly fighting him off. It was clear to me that even though I live in an affluent neighbourhood and am "successful" on Bay Street, Canada's financial capital, I still unfortunately face systemic racism daily and my skin colour is still the first thing people use to determine how to treat me. My wealth will never provide me with a shield against anti-Black racism in a moment like that. I told my story to make a point: the psyche and the system that led to George Floyd's death transcend national borders. I made it clear that each of us needs to take meaningful action to dismantle the system we inherited and make an unparalleled effort to build a better one.

During the pandemic, healthcare workers and pharmaceutical companies showed that they could achieve incredible results by focusing on specific goals—treating those infected with COVID-19 and developing vaccines. In corporate Canada, we made significant strides on gender diversity in recent years, in part by tracking the number of women on boards and in executive jobs. Why couldn't we make the same sort of commitment to eliminating systemic racism? At least this was my thinking. My article urged the Canadian business community to change attitudes that date back four hundred years, to the introduction of slavery in North America. I challenged our leaders to make a meaningful, permanent commitment to ending systemic racism.

In early June, about a week after George Floyd's murder, the article I wrote ran on the front page of the *Globe and Mail*. First thing that morning, my phone started ringing. Victor Dodig, the chief executive at CIBC, was one of the first to call. His message: "I get it. How can I help?" Then Prem Watsa, the chief executive officer of Fairfax Financial, called and asked to meet with me in person. Prem is an immigrant to Canada like me. We met, socially distanced, and had a great conversation. Prem opened by saying, "Wes, I am from India and came here with nothing. I know Black people are treated differently, but until you put it the way you did, I didn't get it. How can I help?"

My solution was very simple. Why don't we as business leaders take a business approach to solving the problem of anti-Black systemic racism? I thought we could treat this social problem like any other business problem we encounter. But first, let us start within our own organizations. Let's first look around the boardroom table and see if there are Black members on the board, and if not, ask yourself, *Is there a systemic reason for that?* Then apply the same scrutiny and pressure to the executive suite and, after that, the pipeline of the company.

As we addressed the problems within our own companies, it allowed us to recognize the fact that as CEOs we have power, especially if applied collectively. So, we said, let us investigate society to see whether our Black employees are treated differently. When a Black individual interacts with the police or the healthcare system, when their kids go to school, when Black entrepreneurs try to access capital—we are simply treated differently. Then let us use our collective power to ensure we have a fair system. By the end of the day, we had a group of CEOs committed to taking a business approach to fixing a social problem. Shortly after, during the worst days of the first COVID lockdown, Victor, Prem, Rola Dagher, the then CEO of Cisco Systems Canada, and I designed a strategy to get the resources needed to address the problem of systemic racism head on. Having this level of support was hugely important to me because it told me I wouldn't be on my own, I wouldn't be an outcast, if I took on this mission. I recognized that this is a lonely and sometimes dangerous task for any one individual, and that there is strength in numbers. I had seen what happened to other leaders who spoke out against systemic racism—take Colin Kaepernick, for example. Kaepernick was a Super Bowl quarterback with a bright future—that is, until he took a knee to protest police brutality against minorities and ultimately lost his job in the NFL.

In writing the BlackNorth pledge, I ensured it clearly stated our stance on taking a business-centric approach to end anti-Black racism in Canada's business world. As a devout Jehovah's Witness, my faith dictates that I steer clear of involvement in political movements, so I had to be extremely cautious when putting together our pledge message as I did not want our mission to read as a political move in any way. Because of this, my faith has always prevented me from taking a role in social justice campaigns such as Black Lives Matter—I wanted the BlackNorth Initiative to be something different entirely.

However, though politicians may view the subject of systemic racism as a political one and therefore stay clear of making statements one way or another, this is in fact a human rights issue, and it should not be a taboo subject. By approaching the subject from a non-partisan perspective, I was able to cast a wider net and get large-scale support from corporate leaders.

The BlackNorth Initiative is meant to help people and companies realize their full potential with a more diverse approach—one that ultimately makes their businesses stronger. Studies have proven the benefits of having a more inclusive workspace—that it strengthens their employees' morale and boosts the economy overall. I felt a personal responsibility to share this information with Canada's largest employers by using my platform to bring awareness and inclusion directly to the source of the problem.

Victor Dodig, Prem Watsa, and Rola Dagher joined me as co-chairs of the BlackNorth Initiative. We agreed to set up an organization to work through barriers to fight anti-Black systemic racism and formed the Canadian Counsel of Business Leaders Against Anti-Black Systemic Racism.

All the CEOs who joined the cause—over two hundred business leaders—agreed to personally sign a BlackNorth Initiative pledge to meet specific goals, including a commitment that by 2025, a minimum of 3.5% of their executive and board roles would be held by Black leaders. The target reflects the percentage of Black Canadians in the population. CEOs also promised to recruit at least 5% of their student workforce from the Black community, and to channel 3% of donations and sponsorships to causes geared toward the Black community.

The interesting thing about the BlackNorth pledge is that it is not a nameless, faceless corporate pledge. It is the company CEO who signs the pledge who is making a personal commitment to lend their voice to the conversation and to ensure the conversation does not die out. It is also evident that this important mandate is being championed by the CEO and does not reside on the desk of the HR department. However, if that CEO leaves the company, the new CEO is not obligated to follow through. This makes the pledge easy for anyone to sign because they are binding not their company but themselves. If as a CEO you make statements against systemic racism and then fail to sign the BlackNorth pledge, then one could make the reasonable argument that your statements are meaningless. There were CEOs who thought they could not sign the pledge without their lawyers first vetting it. Others felt it must be approved by their boards, while some wanted it watered down drastically. Still others just wanted to sign a simple statement that they "would do better." None of these options were acceptable to us. Going through the motions without meaningful actionable commitment was unacceptable. History will judge those who refused to make changes within their companies or those who refused to make a written commitment to change by signing the BlackNorth pledge. Accountability will bring about positive changes in the way businesses operate. I also noticed that many companies don't currently track diversity in their workforce, for various historic reasons. Think about that. CEOs at some of Canada's largest companies don't even know how many BIPOC employees are in their workforce. There is an old saying in business—what gets measured gets managed. The BlackNorth Initiative ensures we measure progress.

By signing the pledge, CEOs also have an incentive to review their employee development plans. If there are no Black leaders climbing through the management ranks, they need to ask why that is the case. CEOs need to look at issues that may have washed out promising candidates. Take micro-aggression, for example. Many people downplay the seriousness of this practice in the workplace. When BlackNorth was just an ad hoc group, we had a meeting with senior government officials. There were already ten people from our side in the meeting, all senior lawyers, bankers, and entrepreneurs. We gave a compelling presentation complete with analysis and statistics. After the presentation, two senior members of the government's entourage commended us on how "well prepared and articulate" we were. My response: "In comparison to what?" We were senior partners in law firms, senior executives, successful entrepreneurs, yet these representatives were surprised by our collective talents. Once a senior executive gave me the compliment "In spite of the fact that Wes is Black he is doing well." You can see how problematic this statement is right off the bat. McKinsey & Company, in a paper entitled "Racial Equity in Financial Services," define micro-aggression as "small acts of racism whether intentional or not, signal disrespect and lack of belonging, having your judgement questioned unnecessarily, needing to provide more evidence of competence than others, addressed unprofessionally, being mistaken for someone at a lower level, contributions ignored or having demeaning remarks about people who look like you." The paper also stated that Black men are most often the victims of micro-aggressions. I can assure you that every single one of those jabs has been thrown at me during my Bay Street career at one time or another.

The BlackNorth Initiative has its roots in an ad hoc group I formed back in 2018. Initially, BlackNorth was a networking group. The name played off the pride we feel in being Black Canadians. I wanted to change perceptions of Black people in business, particularly in the Canadian financial services sector, providing opportunities for Black people who otherwise would be turned away from the industry.

To get it started, I reached out to my contacts and inner circle. I sent out emails and messages through LinkedIn and Outlook. If I was walking around on Bay Street and saw a Black woman or man in a suit, I would give them my card and tell them I was creating this new group, and would they please be a part of it? The idea was to get together, to share best practices, to find ways to increase Black representation in executive ranks and in every other area of society. I thought it was important that we as Black leaders control our destiny and create a smoother path for the next generation of Black leaders in Canada.

I hosted our first meeting in my family home, and about sixty professionals attended. I invited Prime Minister Trudeau to come by and engage in an informal, fireside chat, but he had a scheduling conflict. It was a terrific session. We emerged with a commitment to work collectively to change the conversation around race and combat systemic racism. We began by coordinating what we were doing through an email network. I called it BlackNorth.

In the months that followed, BlackNorth met with the then federal finance minister, Bill Morneau, and with the then minister of immigration, Ahmed Hussen, the first Somali Canadian elected to the House of Commons. Again, we talked about the issues we faced as Black people trying to move forward in business and the inequities that exist in our society. We wanted to work on more than just mentoring and career development; we wanted to bring about social change.

At one point, I met with Toronto mayor John Tory. I told him what BlackNorth was trying to achieve and asked for his support. Tory said, "Wes, you have to tell me what you want. Groups like yours never seem to have something specific they want from the City. Can you get consensus on what you're after?" The mayor agreed to put all the "Black groups" in one room at City Hall and have us all come to consensus on what we needed from the City. The group met, and we eventually reached a consensus, but we were unable to get the City to follow through. We wanted the City to provide dedicated space for a Black cultural centre. However, it was the Schulich Foundation, the philanthropic vehicle for billionaire investor Seymour Schulich, that stepped up with a million-dollar donation earmarked for building such a centre.

We eventually launched the BlackNorth Initiative in June 2020, four months into the pandemic. Ahead of the announcement, I told my leadership team that I wanted to devote 100% of my time to the project. I had the same conversation with clients. It was a huge request, as we were fully engaged on several proxy campaigns and had a full slate of corporate events. During the pandemic, we were still paying rent on offices in Toronto and New York and still paying our staff. My colleagues and clients gave me their full support. I am very fortunate to have built a deep bench of leaders. Take Kingsdale, for example: over two decades, many of us have worked together on Canada's biggest deals, for blue chip clients such as Air Canada, Tim Hortons, Ovintiv, and Suncor, to name just a few. As the economy reopens, takeover activity is taking off. Kingsdale has never been busier, or stronger.

As I write this, leaders at almost five hundred Canadian companies worth more than $1.3 trillion have signed the BlackNorth Initiative CEO Pledge. Just over a year after George Floyd was murdered, the issue of systemic racism remains top of mind for CEOs. We are tracking the number of Black executives on all these companies' boards and in management. Companies and institutions like CIBC, Sobeys, National Bank, Sheridan College, SickKids, and Cisco Systems Canada, among others, are making significant improvements in the representation of Black executives. At other businesses, progress is not as evident. I would like to see companies move faster on diversity, and the pandemic is no excuse for inaction. I also recognize that it is difficult to quickly turn around four hundred years of history—but it is not impossible.

Look at my own experiences with acceptance. I've accomplished a great deal in business. So why is it that I've never been asked to join a blue chip corporate board? Joining a corporate board is like joining one of those prestigious private social clubs in Canada—and every city has one. You must be invited to join, and you must also be endorsed by a current member. Knocking on the door and demanding membership will not grant you access, no matter how qualified you believe you are. Getting on a corporate board is an invitation-only affair, and the invite generally comes from a head-hunting firm that generally has no Black candidates in their pool. Also, like the private social clubs, CEOs tend to invite other CEOs at large companies to be directors at their companies. If you keep using that narrow, artificial criteria for board membership, you will never get guidance from people with a different world view, and with the ability to think outside the box. Why? Because on the TSX 60 only 0.8% of senior executives are Black. Diversity is not just a nice thing to do to help Blacks and people of colour—it makes financial sense. I have experienced this in all my portfolio companies, but one standout was QM Environmental. When I purchased the company, it was losing approximately $20 million annually. The construction industry is notorious for lacking diversity. The leadership team had no diversity when I purchased the business and I immediately set out to change that. When the management team was slow to act on implementing diversity targets, I took the matter up personally and made the needed changes. As of 2020 over 50% of the workplace now identify as Black, Indigenous, women, people of colour, disabled, or LGBTQ+ in all levels of the organization. The company today is extremely profitable and is among the best in the industry. People from diverse backgrounds can offer an entirely different perspective on entrepreneurism, and on managing during a crisis. I am also proud to say that in all my holding companies, as well as businesses where I have a significant interest, the CEOs have signed the BlackNorth pledge.

The pandemic brought attention to all sorts of social issues, including access to health care and income inequality. COVID struck, and we all came together and responded as one in society to deal with the pandemic. Then came George Floyd's murder, and the call to action on anti-Black racism. Again, we were all united as a society. My concern was and remains that this new-found interest in social progress turns out to be another head-fake moment for Black rights. People may say all the right things and then move on without making real change. That is a pattern that we've seen since the U.S. Civil War; like the movie *Groundhog Day*, racism just flares up, again and again and nothing ever seems to *really* change.

If the BlackNorth Initiative is successful, it will become a redundant organization. No longer will CEOs be required to sign a pledge to do the right thing; doing the right thing will be a part of the corporate DNA. But vigilance will always be needed. If you look at the history of civil rights, there was the Civil War, which brought emancipation, only to be followed by the passing of Jim Crow laws, which was a return to systemic racism. We must remain vigilant and will continue to hold our pledge signatories and CEOs accountable.

Part of my motivation for launching the BlackNorth Initiative is to give back to my community. People who know me tend to know my story. I grew up in a tin shack in Jamaica, raised by my single grandmother, came to Canada as a teenaged immigrant, and worked my way up from a mailroom to advising boards. Now, when I look around boardrooms, I still don't see many people like me. I want to put the next generation of Black leaders in a better position as they try to achieve something like what I have achieved.

My motivation is also to make Canada a better place for the next generation. My wife and I have five beautiful children—the oldest is twenty-five and the youngest is ten. My wife is white. When we shop together in high-end stores we get better service if she takes the lead, if she engages with the sales staff. She gets spoken to far differently than I get spoken to. That is just wrong, and it infuriates me, but I believe it can change—that people can look past race and treat us equally.

As a father, I've had to teach my kids life lessons that no white parent considers. Never walk around with your hoodie pulled up. Knock on the front door of your friend's house, never go to the side door. And when you are driving the family vehicle and you are pulled over by the police, be polite and respectful. My children are part of what we are doing at BlackNorth. One of my sons designed a T-shirt that says "I am George Floyd." We printed it up and he sold it online, with all the proceeds going to social causes in our community.

One of my sons has a game he plays with friends when they are driving together and get pulled over. They each try to guess the reason for the traffic stop—the winner of the pool is the one who gets it right. Recently, my son was pulled over by the police after being followed for a few kilometres, and the officer said it was because he accelerated too quickly toward the speed limit. Not speeding. Not exceeding the limit. Just accelerating. None of the boys had ever heard that one before, so no one won the pool.

When the police officer who killed George Floyd eventually went on trial, the prosecutors played the video of the arrest, with sound in court for everyone to hear. You hear a man begging for his life—the sound of his pleas deeply disturb me to this day. You hear bystanders pleading with the police to help him, to stop what they are doing. You hear George Floyd call out for his mother. Then you hear the defence lawyer say the police officer did what he was trained to do, and that he was obeying the rules. When you hear all that, you need to be uncomfortable with where we are as a society.

The COVID crisis has taught and continues to teach us quite a lot about leadership. It highlighted great leaders and exposed weak ones. It taught us how important it is to have the right voices from various backgrounds around the table. Why people with different lived experiences mattered. That when we exclude these voices our society pays dearly. Imagine if ageism wasn't an issue in our society; then we would not have seen the tragic crisis in our long-term care facilities. Imagine if we were not segregated by wealth; then we would not have seen that COVID had a major impact in poor communities. Imagine if we included people of colour at the table; then 83% of the COVID cases in Toronto would not have been among people of colour. Imagine if systemic racism wasn't an issue in our society; then we would not have witnessed the murder of George Floyd. In his book *Value(s)*, Mark Carney put it this way: "Great leadership isn't just effective, it's also ethical, building both value and virtue through its exercise." He went on to talk about the three Cs, the three most significant crises of the twenty-first century: credit, COVID, and climate. This book is about how as leaders we managed through one of those crises, and the lessons we learned. There will be many other crises in our future, but one thing is for certain: we cannot manage through a crisis in isolation.

BROOKFIELD ASSET MANAGEMENT

Brookfield Asset Management is in the business of owning essential assets. Picture hydroelectric power plants, office towers, ports, railroads, cell towers, and wind farms. They are all Brookfield businesses, in over thirty countries, on five continents. If one of these assets shuts down due to COVID-19, certain areas of the global economy could go dark.

Bruce Flatt, Brookfield's chief executive for the past two decades, spent the pandemic keeping the lights on around the world. Remote work simply isn't possible when you run a power plant or unload container ships in a port. And when you own office buildings, and your view is that COVID-19 represents an event rather than a shift in the way we work, it's important to figure out how to make elevators, workspaces and boardrooms safe for your corporate tenants.

Flatt, along with Brookfield's 150,000 operating employees, never slowed down during the pandemic. The Toronto-based asset manager went into the crisis with five major lines of business—real estate, infrastructure, renewable power, private equity, and a control stake in alternative asset manager Oaktree, which focuses on investment in credit markets. Early in 2021, Brookfield launched a new platform, a global reinsurance business. In the summer, the company jumpstarted growth at the business by staging a friendly, US$5.1 billion takeover of a Texas-based insurance company.

Flatt, a native of Winnipeg, also devoted considerable energy during the pandemic to preparing for a greener post-COVID future. In the spring of

2021, Brookfield launched a US$12.5 billion global transition fund that will invest to help businesses decarbonize and will be co-led by former Bank of England and Bank of Canada governor Mark Carney, now a Brookfield vice-chair.

Brookfield's roots go back over one hundred years, to Brazilian electrical utilities built by the company's Canadian founders. The business has weathered challenges, including recessions and government nationalizations of its businesses. On Flatt's watch, the company dealt with the 9/11 attacks that brought down towers adjacent to Brookfield's New York offices, and then with the global financial crisis. However, COVID-19 qualified as the biggest business challenge of our times, a global health crisis that affected individuals, businesses, and governments around the world, simultaneously.

Bruce Flatt

JULY 2021

In January 2020, Sachin Shah, CEO of Brookfield Renewable at the time, had a call with his senior team. He had just participated in a broader Brookfield global update on an unusual virus in Asia. The teams in China, Japan, and Korea were reporting disturbing trends. Sachin told the team, "We need to be prepared."

This weighed heavily on Tom Deedy, chief operating officer for Brookfield Renewable in the U.S. While power plants are mechanical, they need people to operate them; if they don't operate, the electricity grid goes down. He was immediately most concerned about the safety of all the workers who run our power facilities—and the safety of the people in the surrounding communities.

Renewable power facilities can't be operated entirely remotely. Some of the pieces of equipment in hydropower plants are a hundred years old. As a result, they need people onsite to tend to a thousand different mechanical devices—devices that need to be oiled, adjusted, reset, fixed, and replaced. While we use sensors and cameras, they are no replacement for sending someone downstream to look at a dry lake bed—where, just a few minutes after opening a gate, water could rise as high as six feet.

Hydro facilities also need employees manning the desks to make sure operations run smoothly and safely. These experts know how to manage the river flow, and they know how it can affect the areas surrounding the river. They also understand the idiosyncrasies of an individual unit; for example, two pieces of equipment might be able to run automatically, but a third might have to run manually. Learning all these nuances takes time—and experience.

In January, Tom was thinking about the operators who work at our system control building in Massachusetts, which runs all our hydro facilities in the northeast. He and the rest of the renewables team brainstormed scenarios: Where could things go wrong? If people get sick, what should we do? It all kept coming back to people—keeping them safe while keeping everything running.

By April, faced with the uncertainty of a novel virus in the United States that nobody yet understood, the team decided to ask for volunteers to shelter in place at the control centre. Preparations were made—showers were installed in the bathrooms, cots were brought in, and the galley kitchen was stocked with food. Volunteers came forward: twelve people, along with some backups.

The workers ended up quarantining at the site for a big part of the initial lockdown. They worked twelve-hour shifts in the control room, attended video conferences with the management and senior leadership teams, and slept on cots in tents and empty offices. In their down time, they called their loved ones to check up on them—and, like many other people around the world, got caught up in the Netflix show *Tiger King*. Their efforts and willingness to temporarily live their lives on the worksite ensured our assets were able to provide safe, reliable power during a very difficult time.

While operations steadily normalized over the next year, Tom's anxiety level did not. Until everyone was able to be vaccinated, he worried constantly that his people in the control centre would be exposed. As essential workers, they had to show up to work every day—and he and the rest of the leadership team were responsible for them.

Living Through Crises

At Brookfield Asset Management, many of us have been fortunate to have worked together for most—and in some cases all—of our business lives. During that time, we have seen our share of crises: collapses in the stock and real estate markets; the Asian financial crisis in 1997; the bursting of the dot-com bubble in 2000; the events of September 11, 2001, which very directly impacted us; and the global financial crisis in 2007–2008. The COVID-19 pandemic was unique in that it was a health crisis that affected every corner of the world at the same time. Yet our experience as a team has taught us that regardless of the cause, the response to uncertainty and turmoil requires preparation (since crises are inevitable), discipline, focus, good communication, and flexibility.

Since March 2020, we have had our share of ups and downs—it has been a time of high demands on all our people and has required close coordination across the organization, increased communication with investors and employees, and deep engagement with communities around the world. We are fortunate that the impact on our business was temporary, and we emerged from it stronger than ever. Our experience shed light on the things that we've always believed to be the most important: building a business model that supports resilience, keeping a long-term perspective—and remaining calm—through the unknown, creating a collaborative corporate culture, and putting our assets and resources to good use for the community.

There is much to say about how the pandemic challenged us, how it surprised us, and how it changed us. It will likely take years to understand the full extent of its impact. But what I do know is how all of us were able to work together through this difficult time and emerge more resilient, more flexible, and, in some ways, more connected than ever.

The core belief that we all held through this period was "This too shall pass." This gave us an important sense of perspective in the midst of it all. We stayed focused on the path forward.

Initial Response

When we started to hear in January 2020 about a virus quickly spreading in China, we spoke with our Chinese colleagues extensively. This gave us a head start, but nobody knew that it would eventually reach every corner of the world. Nobody knew how it would come to affect businesses, impose a range of demands on families due to school closures, require a sudden shift to remote work, restrict our ability to freely be together, and inflict an emotional toll on everyone.

In the very first days of the health crisis, we were singularly focused on ensuring our people were safe—not only our office-based employees, but the hundreds of thousands of employees of our portfolio companies, many of which provide essential services. We reached out to every corner of our organization to check on our people and their families to see how they were doing, what they needed, and what we could do to help.

We doubled-down on our communications effort. And while we are a global organization, that meant focusing on the local. The virus was multiplying in different regions at different times, so there was no one-size-fits-all approach. Our leadership gathered regularly to stay connected and learn from each other, but our decentralized model meant that our regional teams could quickly and confidently make decisions to protect employees, including a prompt shift to close offices and move to remote working.

All of our corporate operational teams stepped up—and quickly. We leaned heavily on our IT groups, who excelled at seamlessly shifting our office workers from in-person to remote work. We saw a six-fold increase in digital meeting usage; our human resources team tackled a new and wide-ranging set of challenges exceptionally well; and our communications team wrote and disseminated an ongoing stream of internal guidance and announcements, as well as switching instantly from in-person to virtual client events—to name just a few of the groups.

Brookfield's ecosystem also contributed to our success in business continuity. It allowed our leadership teams to connect businesses with each other to help continue operations. For example, at the height of the economic shutdown, our retail business was struggling to get inventory through ports, and we were able to connect them with a Brookfield-controlled port to get better access to information, allowing them to manage around delays.

Tens of thousands of our people across our companies had to go to work every day. Many of the businesses we own provide essential services that simply cannot shut down—including, for example, drinking water and power. Our operating employees worked through extremely difficult situations to keep water and electricity flowing, natural gas for heating and cooling delivered, offices open, goods available in stores, and mission-critical infrastructure operating.

For example, at our portfolio company Enercare, a Canadian heating and cooling business, CEO Jenine Krause ensured that the company's services were not interrupted. She and her workforce worked around the clock to do so. If they hadn't, customers would have been left at home with no heat, in freezing temperatures. And at our Carlsbad water desalination plant and many of our power facilities, employees agreed to quarantine at the work site, moving into rented RVs on the plant property or sleeping on the floor and rotating through shifts to continue to produce water and power for communities.

All these operations had to keep going, but the work environment also had to be safe. To do this, we focused on implementing strong and consistent safety protocols across our operations, adapting these practices quickly as new information became available, and sharing best practices.

For example, in our U.S. rail business, workers camped out in critical locations for weeks at a time to make sure business continued to run. Health—both physical and mental—became a huge concern as COVID fatigue began to set in. Some of those employees were dealing with sick family members in the hospital, and we had to make sure they had the time off they needed—not only for their safety, but for the public's safety. As a result, we implemented mental health check-ins into our already vigorous safety program.

We also worked throughout the organization to help ensure the safety of others outside our companies, gathering PPE and medical equipment to share with healthcare workers and others in need. Our portfolio company Westinghouse sent PPE masks to healthcare workers in Milwaukee, where another of our portfolio companies, Clarios, is based. In Toronto, our office staff was able to gather five thousand N95 masks for their neighbourhood hospital, St. Michael's. In the U.K., portfolio company Greenergy produced bottles of hand sanitizer and donated gloves, masks, and goggles to NHS-related initiatives. And our office in China provided thermometers to Aveo, our Australian senior housing business.

In a Crisis, Culture Matters More Than Ever

At Brookfield, culture is the key to who we are. Our corporate culture was established decades ago by our founder, Peter Bronfman, and ingrained in many of us by long-time CEO Jack Cockwell. It underlies all of our dealings with each other internally, and with our clients as well. We couldn't set our culture aside or let it languish through the long pandemic.

Our culture has been the most significant factor in the ongoing success and development of Brookfield and is, quite simply, written into our DNA. The importance of trust and sharing among us became exceedingly clear during the health crisis, which, in the early days, required a major shift in how we conducted our day-to-day business. Looking back, we are reminded of how deeply and how often we communicated with each other. There were numerous video calls at all hours of the day (for example, I once FaceTimed with our CFO, Nick Goodman, while he was putting his newborn baby to sleep). In our homes, the more casual setting took some getting used to—and some of us never did get used to it. In fact, another colleague of ours refused to be on video calls without his tie—it was the last stand.

While we shared some laughs at the absurdity of our new existence (I'm not sure everyone enjoys a spontaneous FaceTime call from me!), a greater degree of connectivity was necessary. While in more normal times, I tend to step back and allow everyone to handle their own ends of the business, crises sometimes call for a higher touch. Not to micromanage—but to support. We wanted to make sure that everyone felt comfortable asking for help if they needed it, and we wanted to make it clear that our senior team was there to help. And this message trickled down throughout Brookfield. The tone from all our leaders was measured and calm.

We had more scheduled meetings and more impromptu calls. We spent *a lot* of time on the phone. Some of it was just for camaraderie through trying times, others were to handle issues. Through it all, we remained positive and optimistic that this would pass. And yet, looking back, we had no idea how it would unfold, and how getting back to normal would be a long, slow journey.

As a global organization, we were able to see how the virus moved across the world, affecting different regions at different times. Keeping in close touch with our colleagues in China allowed us to inform our people in Dubai, Australia, Europe, and North America in real time of what to expect and how to prepare for the ups and downs of the climb out.

We also spent a lot of time talking to our investors. Understandably, they were worried. They wanted to know about our various assets and how they were managing through it all.

Life Is Meant to Be Lived in Person

If you were to judge on media coverage alone during this time, you might have come to the conclusion that the office and retail real estate businesses were doomed. Nobody was going to go back to the office, and nobody would shop in malls ever again. To me, those ideas were ludicrous. To believe them was to believe that the nature of human beings—something that has been programmed in us since we first walked the earth—had been fundamentally changed by this one experience.

Do not misunderstand, the world is always evolving, and technological advancements have changed the world for the good for centuries. Technology in various forms has become more relevant every year, and that will only continue. But at the end of the day, people are social beings and have increasingly chosen to live with others for centuries. This urbanization trend has been underway for a long time and has only accelerated over the past twenty-five years.

People like to be with others, be close to the action, meet new and interesting people, and exchange ideas. Ideas are most often generated face to face and spontaneously, not by people communicating from a distance or scheduling appointments. The incubation of a company's culture and the development and growth of younger talent also need to happen face to face. Offices and cities have been designed to ensure that people can meet with others and that businesses can grow and thrive.

Some observers argued that video conferencing would allow virtually everyone to work from home, and that would spur people to move their homes away from cities. But besides the fact that many people will never be able to work from home (such as those who provide essential services), it won't work for office employees either. That's because humans learn from cues picked up by seeing, hearing, and being with others. The Internet, phone, and video can be enhancing tools, but each only works well when combined with face-to-face communication.

The same arguments about distanced working and moving away from cities were made when the automobile became ubiquitous, the telephone allowed transcontinental conversations, and the Internet enabled online communication. None of these has changed the fact that people favour being in cities and in offices. In fact, throughout history, these communication tools have enhanced great cities and offices rather than supplanting them. We firmly believe that this trend will continue.

We believe that video conferencing, like the Internet, will allow more people to choose where they work. But contrary to what some say, based on observations of the past, we believe this will only make large cities— and the offices and other urban spaces within them—more attractive, increasing the concentration of people in major urban centres like New York, London, Shanghai, Sydney, Toronto, São Paulo, Mumbai, and others globally. We believe young, entrepreneurial leaders of the future will continue to gravitate to dynamic, energetic cities while using technology to augment their experience and productivity.

The story for retail real estate is similar. While business as usual was interrupted during the health crisis, it was only a temporary challenge. The consolidation of the retail industry is a trend that had already been happening for decades before the pandemic accelerated it. At Brookfield, we own a very high-quality portfolio of properties that will continue to benefit from their premier locations. And while e-commerce has accelerated, retailers are increasingly turning to high-quality real estate to grow their businesses. As a result, major centres are flourishing once again.

The importance of social interaction and the need for meaningful in-person experiences have never been clearer. As a species, we crave community—and offices and retail properties will continue to fulfill this human need by providing spaces for people to connect.

Bringing Our People Back to the Office

Those early weeks of the pandemic and the subsequent shutdown across virtually all of our offices were difficult. We were all keen to get back to the office—to see and support each other, to focus on the tasks at hand, and, most of all, to collaborate and once again allow our culture to thrive.

But we made a highly strategic decision in order to be with our front-line people. Starting in May 2020, the senior leaders all came back to the office where regulations allowed. We did this to get offices ready to welcome our employees back as soon as was practical. And so, office by office—once it was safe and permissible, and subject to individual personal health considerations—we brought our employees back. We were doing this much earlier than our peers, but we believed this was important to support our colleagues in the field; to reinforce our culture of collaboration, which is central to our business; and to enable the development of our younger employees.

We undertook a massive effort to make this possible. We consulted with health authorities and epidemiologists to make sure we would be able to operate our offices safely. Across our investment offices, we moved over 1,500 desks to accommodate partitions and adequate space for social distancing. This represented about 75% of our employees, while in a normal year, we might move 15%. We rebuilt most of our global offices and *added* space. We provided onsite COVID-19 testing at many of our offices and employed tech solutions to ensure contact tracing and adherence to our health policies.

We followed four key principles to accomplish this safely: adherence to local requirements, implementation of strong safety protocols (often exceeding government requirements), mitigation of risk through continuous reviews of changing protocols, and respect for each employee's privacy. The safety measures included installation of glass partitions between workspaces;

access to regular, free COVID-19 testing; and clear protocols for addressing situations when an employee received a positive test result. In the end, our protocols were successful at preventing transmission within our offices. Despite having had people in our offices globally who tested positive, we had zero outbreaks. Our teams running all that did an amazing job, and we are exceptionally proud of how our employees managed through this.

Our success in being among the first companies to reopen their offices allowed us to help others follow in our footsteps. As the pandemic started to ease in certain regions around the world, our tenants began to reach out to us to learn how we were able to open our offices safely, and we shared all that we learned. We also found that demand for office space was coming back as strong as ever, and globally we are back signing leases and doing business again.

Looking back, this decision to open in May 2020 was completed with zero health issues, and as a company, we are all closer for it. We "lived" a pandemic together for a year.

Managing a Business Through a Shock

Of course, managing through this challenging period meant ensuring not only the health of our people but the health of our business. As the health crisis began to really take hold, the markets got spooked. But we realized that what's most important in running our business during a crisis isn't quarterly results, or making great investments, or raising a big new fund. All of these things are important, but they're not the most critical or what really, truly matters. What's most important, as we noted in a shareholder letter at the time, is "liquidity, liquidity, liquidity."

The most damaging thing for any business owner is to find yourself out of business and unable to participate in a recovery, or in the position of needing to issue shares that dilute the owners' stakes, thereby making it impossible to recover from undue dilution at the wrong time. Most businesses survive, but sometimes with new owners, and that dilutive process is one of the most destructive forces for long-term wealth creation.

When businesses don't prepare in advance for crisis periods, it is often too late. As Warren Buffett has been famously quoted as saying, "Only when the tide goes out do you discover who's been swimming naked." The one thing that really matters is that a business can make it through a difficult period intact and without undue harm. That is what counts. And it is usually a function of having made preparations before the tide went out.

So one of the first questions we asked ourselves when this crisis hit was how bad it could get from a liquidity perspective. Would we need to secure additional liquidity? We had been running quarterly stress tests for years and felt comfortable that we were well positioned. Indeed, one of the great strengths of Brookfield is our very large base of permanent capital, which gives us the ability to ride out storms that inevitably occur in markets. We exemplified this during the pandemic, as we had minimal financing issues despite the market stress.

It also helped that we had been expecting a downturn for some time and were well positioned for it. We purchased a 62% share of Oaktree, a leading credit investor, in 2019 because we believed we would benefit from having a distressed debt business in such an environment. We also put more cash on our balance sheets, extended the maturity of our financings, and secured liquidity.

The last major crisis we faced as a company was the 2007–2008 global financial crisis. But unlike the GFC, the COVID-19 pandemic was a crisis of Main Street, not Wall Street. We felt confident having the liquidity in place, but no one knew how long the crisis would last. We had unwavering conviction that things would return to normal. So we decided to manage prudently and with discipline—we would have no knee-jerk reactions. We put substantial capital to work in the financial markets in March 2020. And we continue to benefit from all of those decisions as our businesses were well positioned when demand came roaring back.

We were also fortunate to have been in the markets, issuing investment-grade financing from our balance sheet and from our permanent equity listed affiliates, with an eye toward opportunities that could emerge. In such times, liquidity is the difference between being able to look to the future rather than having to spend time focusing on the past.

Being very disciplined in terms of our financing and managing of the businesses was only part of what we had to do. Another, arguably bigger part, was on the human side.

Coming Together

For me, the biggest thing that stood out during this difficult period was the caring and consideration we showed for each other and our communities. I had a front row seat to see how that unfolded at Brookfield. Some of the things I saw were small acts of kindness, checking in on each other from all corners of the world to see if there was any way we could help. In especially hard-hit areas like India and Brazil, employees started WhatsApp groups to look out for each other and everyone's families. Other efforts were larger; at Brookfield, we invest in the backbone of the global economy, which means we need to step up in times of need. And we found many ways to put our capital and assets to good use.

We offered up many of our properties for relief efforts, such as hotel rooms for frontline medical staff, hospitals for government use, malls for emergency blood drives, hotel and restaurant kitchens for local food banks, and other properties for mass vaccination sites. We also donated to relief initiatives around the world. One notable example was an effort in Brazil to increase the number of hospital beds in ICUs and the amount of PPE available for healthcare professionals while the virus spread widely there.

We also looked for opportunities to strengthen the communities and local businesses where we live and work. At our headquarters in downtown Toronto, during the lockdown, one of the few businesses still open was the small convenience store downstairs. The owner had just renovated his store before the crisis hit, and he was struggling. So we started putting in weekly orders for snacks throughout our office. The appreciation he expressed to us for doing this simple thing was truly heartwarming. For us, it was important to support a local business, and it was also a way for us to show our respect for business owners and others who could not stay home.

Last but not least, we found ways to encourage more philanthropy among our employees. Our global donation matching program provides each employee with the ability to donate to a not-for-profit of their choice and receive a match from the firm. At the onset of the pandemic, we increased that match to two-for-one for employee donations related to the COVID-19 response. In addition, we implemented a capital pool for each office to support philanthropic activities that are important to our people.

This Too Shall Pass

It never feels like it at the time, but these moments always do pass. And, when you're in the middle of it, every such moment always seems like the worst one. It's human nature to think short-term in a crisis. I believe this tendency among the masses gave us an advantage—the contrarian opportunity. It's hard for most people to realize that crises don't last forever. And it's hard to resist the strong pull of overreacting in the moment, and believing that the world has changed fundamentally. But one of the things that has made Brookfield successful is the ability to think long-term and stay disciplined and clear-headed in order to spot opportunities.

People tend to think of extremes, and they can have a hard time keeping a grounded view of the world after upheaval. For example, after 9/11, many people said that nobody would be willing to work on the higher floors of office buildings. We didn't believe it then, and it turned out to be wrong. Of course, some things had to change—for example, security had to step up, and those measures remain in place today. But in the immediate aftermath of the tragedy, a reversion to the norm seemed impossible.

The year 2020 will certainly live on in infamy in many ways. The loss of life is incomprehensible. The health crisis spurred an economic crisis, with GDP in every country dropping precipitously, stock markets plummeting (and then recovering), central banks collapsing interest rates to zero, and money with little risk becoming virtually free. Many businesses were shut down, most worked from home, people were afraid, and travel came to a standstill. On top of all that, we also experienced Brexit, and then a contentious U.S. presidential election followed by a sort of insurrection.

But signs of life and green shoots of hope sprang up as well. Broadly speaking, the crisis served to accelerate a number of trends—some a little, and some a lot. One silver lining to the pandemic lockdowns was a huge decline in global emissions. The year also served as a moment for society to reflect on itself, with momentum picking up for social movements that had been brewing for a long time. In life, we all need to look onward and upward—because what's the alternative? So we did exactly that. Around the world, the impetus grew for economies and markets to transition to net-zero emissions. Commitments to net zero have now cascaded from the country level to the company level—and there are opportunities to help these companies decarbonize their business operations.

We also took the opportunity to establish new Employee Engagement Groups at Brookfield, to ensure we were supporting diversity and an inclusive culture. Both our Black Professionals network and our Asian Professionals network were established in 2020.

We ended 2020 with our best quarter on record. Given the environment and the extraordinary year, that says a lot for our business. Despite the turmoil and disruption, our investment strategies and the strength of our capital structure showed through.

As vaccinations have picked up around the world, so has economic momentum. As I write this, people are becoming more comfortable and, in some regions, governments have allowed life to go back to normal. It appears we are seeing a strong recovery in economic numbers that should last for at least a few years.

Looking back, I realize how much we all learn from managing through crises like (and unlike) this one. Our next generation of business leaders will be shaped by this experience and I know they will be better for it. In some ways, we will be better because of this experience. The future is bright—we just need to dig in, work hard, and experience life (that is, until the next crisis comes along).

CADILLAC FAIRVIEW

Prior to the pandemic, John Sullivan's company ran North America's busiest shopping mall, CF Toronto Eaton Centre, which attracts fifty-two million visitors annually and is the number one tourist attraction in Canada.

In the spring of 2020, during a COVID lockdown, the Cadillac Fairview chief executive toured the landmark property—it resembled a scene straight out of a post-apocalyptic zombie movie. No shoppers in more than two hundred stores, no diners in dozens of restaurants, no white-collar workers in the complex's three towers. Outside, pigeons were the only signs of life on the street. The pandemic shut down a real estate company that owns $36 billion of retail, office, and residential properties around the world, including sixty-nine landmark Canadian developments. As the crisis played out, all eyes at Cadillac Fairview turned to Sullivan, who has run the company for the last decade.

Sullivan joined Cadillac Fairview as head of development in 1998. Prior to that, he was a senior executive in the property arm of Brookfield Asset Management. The Montreal native has an MBA from McGill University and an engineering degree from Concordia, and he attended the Advanced Management Program at Harvard.

Cadillac Fairview got its start more sixty years ago, when three young friends decided to start a construction company, couldn't agree what to name it, and finally opted for the name of one partner's car—a Cadillac.

The company subsequently snapped up Fairview Corp., a rising star in commercial real estate, in 1974. Ontario Teachers' Pension Plan acquired the developer more than two decades back, a landmark transaction in that Ontario Teachers' was the first Canadian public sector retirement fund to buy a real estate company.

Teachers' takes a long-term view on investments; the fund is investing for plan members who routinely retire in their fifties and collect pensions for more than thirty years. Sullivan spent the pandemic working to keep buildings safe, while also pondering the long-term implications of remote work and online shopping for a company that plans to own office towers and malls for generations to come.

Throughout the pandemic, Cadillac Fairview continued construction on a gleaming downtown Toronto tower that's slated to be Teachers' new home. The pension plan is currently located at Yonge and Finch, a thirty-minute subway ride from the city centre. Teachers' employees are looking forward to moving to new, urban digs, and like many other large tenants they're confident that downtown Toronto will continue to be vibrant and the place for businesses to be.

But after COVID 19, will Canadians still be drawn to vibrant, crowded city cores?

John Sullivan

AUGUST 2021

The Leadup

I'd love to say I was the sage who knew COVID-19 was coming.

In January 2020, as news reports began to circulate about a dangerous new virus spreading through Asia and Europe, Cadillac Fairview (CF) had an early omen: rumours about a suspected case of "novel coronavirus" at CF Markville, a mall that's home to over 140 stores and restaurants in Markham, Ontario. While the rumour was never validated, it pinged on our radar. We refreshed our pandemic plan before the World Health Organization (WHO) declared a global health emergency on January 30. But to be honest, we didn't really think this mysterious coronavirus would reach Canada. As I said earlier, I wish I'd been a prophet who could foresee just how bad things would get. In theory, we had a plan of action in place, should the worst happen. In practice, along with the rest of the world, we had no idea what we were in for.

In retrospect, there were other early warning signs. Every year in the third and fourth week of January there's a very well-attended annual real estate conference in Whistler. The gathering in early 2020 was no exception. But on the flight back to Toronto, my peers who attended the conference noticed that multiple people were wearing masks, a contrast to the mask-free outbound flight. That wasn't the norm.

By February, some travel-related cases of COVID-19 had been reported in Canada. A team of our executives formed a coronavirus steering committee and began holding weekly calls to ensure we were prepared—again, for what we thought was the remote chance it impacted us. In the last week of February, we talked transparently with our retail and office property teams. Fortunately, we also communicated early and transparently with our industry peers about our plan of action, and they did the same.

We agreed a cohesive industry response would bode well for our collective people, our clients and their employees, and Canadian consumers.

The Pandemic

On March 3, I toured Bank of Montreal CEO Darryl White through the bank's contemporary new office space at CF Toronto Eaton Centre. North America's busiest shopping mall was living up to its reputation as about fifteen of us walked through the food court bustling with people. We all squeezed into a large elevator together, not at all conscious of how close we were to one another, and went up four floors to check out the construction progress. On March 5, members of the Cadillac Fairview board and executive team gathered at the iconic Toronto steakhouse Hy's for a meal that wound up being my last one in a restaurant until summer 2021. Believe or not, the virus wasn't our main topic of conversation that night—nor was it the following day, at our final in-person board meeting. Looking back at these moments, I'm struck by how unremarkable they seemed at the time. I don't recall anybody being particularly worried or afraid. None of us had a premonition that we were heading into the biggest humanitarian crisis of our lifetime.

That all changed dramatically five days later on March 11 when the WHO declared COVID-19 a global pandemic and the magnitude of what lay before us started to sink in. The NBA suspended its season, and although the latter played out in that day's news as a potential overreaction, the decision now looks like a prescient show of gutsy, decisive leadership. Within a matter of days, a number of retailers at our shopping centres across Canada made the decision to shut down voluntarily. Gap, Apple, Free People, and some others who had operations outside of Canada assessed very quickly that the pandemic could and likely would take hold here. Others began to reduce hours or limit employee hours in store—familiar names such as Hudson's Bay, Tiffany & Co., and Le Chateau.

On March 13, we asked all CF employees who had the ability to work from home to do so. Our property teams stayed in our offices with a much-reduced workforce, and everyone who was able to work from home did. For the first time in more than a decade, we cancelled our annual leadership conference, which would have happened in May. On our last day in CF's Toronto head office, a half dozen of us on the executive team took a poll and bet a bottle of wine: "Okay guys, how long are we going to be out for?" Some predicted we'd be working from home for a week, some said two weeks. The longest prediction was four weeks. Everyone else had a laugh at the idea of spending an entire month working from home.

Within seventy-two hours, we had mobilized eight hundred people to be able to work from home on laptop computers or with desktop PCs that we shipped to their homes. Fortunately, because CF had made some key investments in cloud and cybersecurity over the years, getting up and running was relatively seamless for us, but I know that wasn't the case in all sectors—least of all the public one.

It's safe to say what came after was a little like shellshock. Most of us thought we'd just have to get the business through to the summer and the warmer weather—that this was like the flu. But when COVID started to break out in countries in the Southern Hemisphere during their summer, we realized very quickly that this was something far worse. As a city builder, Cadillac Fairview has always prided itself on making visionary plans for the future. Initially, it felt like our executive team was trying to figure out who was on first base and what we'd need to do to prepare the properties for a possible, but temporary, shutdown.

We landed on an all-out effort to shift everyone's efforts over to operations and safety. Our property teams, operations team, marketing team, and occupational health and safety teams stopped everything they were doing. They began crafting operating procedures and mass signage to ensure measures like physical distancing, updated hours, and new cleaning protocols were communicated quickly to our clients, teams, and guests. We began having weekly calls with our board, which we'd never done before in the life of the company, and twice-a-week calls with our executive team. Every day involved a very robust, collaborative triage exercise to pivot our work—stop, continue, and start.

In those early weeks, we weren't sitting there wondering, "Is our business going to survive?" We're not over-leveraged. We have a strong balance sheet. We have a pragmatic, steady owner with a long-term view. I figured, one way or the other, that we'd find our way through this. However, we were dealing with something new here, a global health crisis. In those early days, it was possible to imagine a doomsday scenario straight out of a science fiction movie, where almost the entire population dies. And at that time, we just didn't know. The lack of hard data on the virus was one of our biggest challenges.

At the beginning, not everything shut down. We had people working in malls and office buildings, there was no public guidance on masks yet—mandatory mask guidance didn't come from the provinces until July—and masks were hard to come by. People were scared. There were so many unknowns. But everyone stepped up, and to their great credit, they did what they had to do until we largely locked down.

For all the preparation we'd done thus far, the shutdown felt like a sledgehammer when it landed. By April, the first wave of lockdowns swept across the country in Alberta, Ontario, Quebec, and New Brunswick; seventeen of our nineteen Canadian shopping centres were closed for all but essential retail. We knew in these early days that we would have to work directly with our clients to weather this storm. In April and May we worked collaboratively with over 850 tenants on rent deferrals.

An Unfolding Crisis

A few years ago, CF engaged in an exercise that examined our corporate purpose—a mission statement, if you will. As business exercises go, it's an existential exercise rather than an operational one, but highly strategic decisions flow from these kind of reflections: As a company, why are we here? Why do we exist, beyond turning a profit? How do we best serve our customers and stakeholders in the communities in which we operate?

After a robust review, we landed on our refreshed purpose: transforming communities for a vibrant tomorrow. After all, a shopping mall has never been just about shopping. Workplaces have never been just about doing work. We're in the business of bringing people together. At CF, we believe human connection is the foundation of vibrant and thriving communities. Our purpose is to create and nurture exceptional places that foster human connection and positive experiences.

We've worked hard to cultivate a great culture for our employees. Fortunately, CF also recognized the humanitarian crisis at the heart of the pandemic very early on. As leaders, we knew it would have a huge impact on our people and our tenants, and that our biggest priority was keeping them safe. We didn't spend a lot of time ruminating about the decisions that we made. We made them fast. We made them in the best interest of our people.

In keeping with our corporate purpose and strong, supportive culture, we wanted to give our more than three thousand employees and third-party contractors as much support as we possibly could. Everyone was operating in unfamiliar terrain. Everyone has parents or knows older people. Many people had kids to care for and help educate at home. As an executive team, the biggest "continue" decision we made early on was to keep paying our employees. We announced that we wouldn't lay anyone off and we would maintain regular wages, benefits, and pension entitlements and would also maintain the fees payable to our third-party janitorial partners, as we had up until that point.

In the meantime, downtown Toronto looked like a cityscape scene straight out of a zombie film. Eerily empty streets. Not only is CF Toronto Eaton Centre the busiest mall in North America, it's also one of the top destinations in North America for tourists. And all of a sudden, the only inkling of life outside on Yonge Street were the pigeons. Over the course of the next few weeks and months, we saw variations of this scene play out in cities across the country, even in downtown Vancouver, where they never really closed malls.

Closing our malls was one thing. Shutting down multiple construction projects in midstream was another. In April 2020, we had more than $3 billion in projects under construction, and within a week only about 10% were still operating, given the closures in British Columbia, Ontario, and Quebec. As COVID-19 made a deadly advance through Canada, we had to shut down those sites and do it quickly.

The thing is, construction sites don't lend themselves at all well to being shut down. You can't turn them off on a dime and they are never meant to sit static for more than a couple of days. There are walls and steel beams that aren't fully supported. Giant pieces of steel are delivered to these sites regularly, and some were still in transit when we shut down. If you've dug a hole in the ground, that crater extends about four to five storeys below ground level. And if you leave that hole, it will fill up with water and you could wind up with a bathtub the size of a city block. Our people and partners had to ensure that didn't happen. Our construction partners worked extended hours for several days to secure the sites, brace foundations and walls, and make sure projects were structurally sound just to facilitate a shutdown. We were incredibly grateful for their all-out efforts.

Beyond protecting the materials, as many as three hundred to five hundred construction workers are employed at some of these sites. They were also at the forefront of our minds. When pundits talk about the enormous work transformations we've seen during the pandemic, most people's minds go to the work-from-home technology surge, but these are real-life jobs out there in the field. You can't do construction remotely. It would take many months, and several bumpy stops and starts, before we were able to get back to the business of building cities.

While we triaged our way through March and April, my choice of reading material was timely. I'm an avid reader of history. Stories of the past reveal so much about our present. I'd begun reading *The Spendid and the Vile*, Erik Larson's excellent book about Winston Churchill, whose first day as prime minister of the United Kingdom was marked by Hitler's invasion of Holland and Belgium. People were terrified. They didn't know what was going to happen from one day to the next. For the next five years, Churchill had to make decisions and act decisively through an unimaginable crisis. I was struck by his resolve to lead with confidence and persevere until the horror ended.

I can't claim any Churchillian qualities in all of this. But I'm incredibly proud that the CF team did everything imaginable to support our multiple stakeholders through the pandemic—nobody was left behind. Beyond ensuring our staff were paid, it was vital for us to find a way to help retailers and Canadian communities through this siege.

In Toronto, we offered up free parking spaces to local hospital workers and visitors. We also knew Canadians wanted to help the most vulnerable people living in their communities but that they were unable to do so in the usual way through volunteering in person. We launched our Community First program, asking Canadians to submit the names of community charities in need so we could direct our donations there and rally other Canadians to do the same. Through the program, we've supported more than forty charities across Canada.

In April, a coalition of landlords and retailers came together to help the industry find its way through COVID-19. We teamed up with property owners including SmartCentres, RioCan, Oxford Properties, and Ivanhoe Cambridge, as well as more than a dozen retailers, including Indigo and Hudson's Bay Co. I helped come up with the financial side of the plan for us to propose to the federal Ministry of Finance. I had a sense that would take a while to work itself out. Little did I know how long.

Our proposal was for the landlord community to forgive one third of our rent and the government to lend tenants one third of the rent at either zero interest or a low interest rate for ten months. The tenant would cover the final third of the rent. The plan would give tenants a two-thirds discount on rent until the end of January 2021, to give them some room, hopefully, to financially manoeuvre their way through it all. I pushed for that timing—not everyone on the landlord side wanted to agree to a period that long, initially—to take us beyond the most important sales period of the year and out the other side. Even if every single tenant in the country had taken us up on the theoretical offer, the absolute maximum cost to the government, assuming a low interest rate, would have been in the range of $1–2 billion.

The following month, the federal government rejected our proposal. It was a disheartening blow for retail and hospitality businesses across Canada.

Business Impacts and Strategic Shifts

Every part of Cadillac Fairview has been influenced by this pandemic—from our people, to our retail and office tenants, to our strategic decisions about growth, development, and investments around the world. And once we got through those first few weeks and months, the business impact of the pandemic really began to sink in, particularly for the retail side of our business.

For office tenants, their office isn't the source of their primary revenue—it's where they work. But retailers' spaces are where they generate revenue. E-commerce may supplement that revenue, for some more than others, but business depends on being able to keep the doors open for most retailers. When you shut the doors, you pretty much shut off the revenue.

Retail

As part of our all-in efforts to focus on operations, we implemented a number of key measures to help our retailers and customers when things reopened. We kicked off CF's first-ever public safety campaign. We also created retail and office workplace guidelines, both over forty-five pages, for our tenants and created forty-five-page health and safety guidelines for our CF employees.

We communicated frequently with our retailers and worked our way through six hundred abatement requests and also helped them navigate the Canada Emergency Commercial Rent Assistance (CECRA) program, which provided some relief for the smaller businesses who were suffering due to COVID-19. CF submitted more than 1,400 applications on behalf of qualifying clients.

Our investments in technology also helped us navigate the myriad rules at play in different areas of the country. Later on in the spring, we began setting up digital occupancy counters to help our security guard teams at malls assess in real time on their mobile devices how many people were in the building and if the number was close to provincial limits. We invested in things that made sense, like an app to help people find the closest hand sanitizer station in the building, and we temporarily halted ones that didn't, like an ongoing test of an app that finds available parking spaces for shopping centre customers.

I do not want to sugar-coat what this period was like for retailers. This has been incredibly difficult, especially for the larger ones whose businesses were hurting but who did not qualify for any form of government help because of their size. Not everyone has made it, though I'm heartened by the number that have. I think Indigo Books CEO Heather Reisman said it best when she spoke with the *Globe and Mail* about her disappointment with the government's inaction. "Not only do retailers support their communities in all kinds of ways," she said, "but by extension, we support the landlord community—big and small landlords—and retailers are also major payers of taxes that support our cities. Look at all the manufacturers that make things who we support. Government, frankly, needs to step up to the plate in a meaningful way."

That didn't happen. In the absence of government help, CF and other landlords in Canada have become the lender of last resort for some of these businesses. We're proud to help them. And we're happy there appears to be some light on the horizon. Prior to and after the third wave of lockdowns, a number of retailers with open stores were able to perform well and we were back up to collecting 90% of our retail rent. In the worst month, CF collected about 30% of that rent, and since the start of the pandemic we've collected a percentage that has gone back and forth between those two.

As I write this from my home in Toronto, the city is two months out of one of the longest lockdown periods in the world for restaurants and enclosed shopping centres. We know consumers want to support these businesses. We know that when it's safe to reopen everywhere, stability and growth will flow from there. We hope that happens sooner rather than later.

Office

At the start of the pandemic, our office clients hadn't yet perfected working from home. The technology was a complete unknown for many large businesses. But they figured it out pretty quickly. Law firms, accounting firms, banks—all of them found ways to provide their services effectively and efficiently while working from home. Our office tenant properties have operated at roughly 10% to 25% capacity through the pandemic. Most companies have instructed their employees to work from home throughout.

The businesses are surviving, but COVID has had a cultural impact. If there is any upside, it's that while I would never have guessed that in a time of pandemic isolation our working relationships at CF could get deeper, they have. Throughout this time, our people have pulled together to help, to pivot and collaborate, and to get through this as a team. On the executive side, it seemed like everyone forgot what their official title was and had the attitude of "How can I help?" We've seen this at all levels of the organization.

And working from home gives you a lens into people's lives that you don't normally have. Until COVID, I'd never seen inside the homes of all of the people on my team or elsewhere in the company. You see people's home yoga setups and their musical instruments, which sometimes get played! There are all kinds of pets hanging around in the background. There are digital cocktails with colleagues while they're at home making pizza with their kids, or they show you the thousand-piece puzzle they're all working on.

But as much as COVID has proven people can work remotely, it's also proven to us that you can't run a company remotely forever. You can't build a culture remotely. Bringing new employees into a company without being able to meet them face-to-face is simply not the same experience, and we're hearing that across the board from our office tenants. There are learning obstacles and informational black holes. Virtual meetings help us connect remotely, but we also know that when people sit in back-to-back meetings all day on a computer, the majority of them find it mentally and emotionally fatiguing. It's simply not the same as plugging into the energy and culture of a workplace in an office, even part-time.

Cultural and Personal Shifts

Beyond our operational shifts, the pandemic accelerated some long-building societal trends, from a deepening concern about climate change to increased awareness of social justice issues. These issues have been an important focus for us at CF. We know they're important to our team and we know they're important to our communities. We've spent a lot of time throughout this pandemic period to ensure we set meaningful goals and take tangible action in areas such as environmental impact, community engagement, and particularly inclusion and diversity.

Prior to the pandemic, I think we took human connection for granted. Personally, I'd never been in a position where it wasn't there. But I'm luckier than many. My lockdown has been spent in my house with my family around me, and even so, it hasn't been easy. My eldest daughter is twenty-one and only one of her university semesters has been normal. She's on the school ski team, but there has been very little of that. It's been hard on her. My middle daughter is nineteen and graduated from high school in the midst of the first wave without a ceremony. My youngest daughter is seventeen and has significant health issues. God forbid she got this virus. My wife and I were trying to balance work and make things as good as they could be for our kids, under the circumstances. All families have dealt with increased stress through this pandemic. It's impossible to avoid it.

And for many people living through months of isolation in tiny downtown spaces fifty floors up, the isolation has been devastating. COVID has touched every part of people's lives: health and safety, mental and physical well-being, financial security, family security. Some of our people have lost relatives and were unable to say goodbye, which must be heartbreaking. There are so many of these emotional stories in a once-in-a-lifetime event like this, and CF had multiple employee challenges to address.

We began sending out an employee sentiment pulse survey every six weeks to hear how our people were faring and learn how to best help them. We launched an employee resource centre with professional and personal resources and wellness support and updated it weekly.

At the same time, not everyone at our company was working from home. A full 85% of our workforce is on the front line and has remained at our properties throughout this making sure things run smoothly. We had clients with essential workers going in to work and we still had to maintain our buildings from an operations standpoint—there are people who literally keep the lights on in these buildings.

On the front lines amid times of anxiety and uncertainty, they've had their own challenges absorbing ever-changing and sometimes unclear government regulations. Some members of the public—people who were scared or upset or angry about the lack of control they've felt through this pandemic, and a small but volatile segment who do not want to wear masks—have put essential frontline workers on the receiving end of their negative emotions. While all of our workers are trained in how to de-escalate these situations, a peer-to-peer walk for our security staff was also introduced as a resource to a number of CF properties in both retail and office.

The First Wave of Reopenings

As we prepared for the initial wave of reopenings in May 2020, emphasizing safety was our top priority. At CF that involved a tremendous team effort that was part of our pivot to operations. We worked closely with public health authorities in all regions to get clear on messaging and varied regulations in different districts. We developed more than three hundred pieces of creative signage in multiple sizes to ensure our properties were safe and easy to navigate for our clients and customers.

We also developed an education ambassador program through our team in security and guest services, who greeted clients and customers with a smile, educated them on building protocols and the new signage, and made an effort to engage people with empathy. Response from the public was really positive. On live television, Toronto mayor John Tory praised Cadillac Fairview and CF Fairview Mall for good corporate citizenship, industry-leading safety measures, and thorough public communication in our COVID response.

By then, vaccine development had begun around the world, but the timelines for approval and rollout were far from certain. COVID-19 case counts were turning a corner across the country. But that didn't mean the pandemic was done. At this point, guidance on masks was being issued across various cities and provinces. But from our point of view, the inconsistency in rules was a recipe for chaos. We own properties nationwide, and there was no clear national guidance.

In June, the executive team saw each other for the first time in three and a half months, though it felt like a year had passed. We had an outdoor meeting, where we sat six feet apart and did some strategy work. I felt hopeful and utterly exhilarated, like a kid on the first day back at school after summer break.

As summer 2020 progressed, we were hopeful about the future. COVID case counts had dipped across Canada, but we knew there was a lot on the line for the fall—kids were going back to school. For our retailers, it meant heading into the busiest few months of the year without knowing what shutdowns might be around the corner. For most of autumn, it felt like things were getting better. But then the case counts started to creep up again.

The news that we'd have to shut down our properties again right before Christmas was devastating. It's the busiest shopping season of the year. And for many of our retailers, there wouldn't be a way to recoup that lost business, curbside pickup and e-commerce notwithstanding. While most retailers don't talk about it much, the fulfillment costs of e-commerce are very high. They shoulder a lot of that cost in a bid to make home delivery prices attractive to consumers. Store-based sales are much more profitable. And by the end of December, fourteen of our nineteen shopping centres were in lockdown, with a further two operating with 15% capacity limitation.

Once again, CF pivoted in an all-out effort to help our retailers and their customers reimagine the holiday and bring them safe, inspiring virtual and physical experiences. We held holiday drive-thru events, which sold out in less than an hour, and "frozen fairways"—mini golf in our parking lots. We focused on virtual Santa, developing "Storytime with Santa" events for

Facebook Live for kids, and setting up one-to-one video calls with the big man himself resulted in 10,000 visits, far higher than our original estimate of 1,500.

The Toughest Parts

Throughout, some of the things we thought might be the most difficult for us as a company weren't as challenging as we thought they might be. Humans are resilient. They are incredible at adapting to change. We had the safest properties out there, customers were keen to visit us. They wore masks, followed the rules, washed their hands, and kept a safe distance. Mall traffic rebounded in between lockdowns, although overall traffic was thinner by virtue of public occupancy restrictions, so our retailers were not able to operate at full tilt.

What we have found the most disappointing and frustrating throughout this pandemic, frankly, is the lack of clarity from various governments. No uniform criteria ever emerged from governments for safety measures, shutting down, or reopening. We pleaded for answers: What metrics did regions need to reach in order to reopen?

When a construction shutdown was announced, we'd ask whether it applied to residential construction, commercial, or both. We'd hear that "essential construction" could continue. We'd ask for clarity—what construction was deemed essential? And it would take almost a week after each announcement to learn what "essential" meant. The definition changed from region to region and from one lockdown event to the next. When we did get answers, we'd often receive conflicting directions from different branches of government and health officials—even within the same region.

I think there's a better way of handling this pandemic and providing Canadians with a more stable return to a normal life, albeit a post-pandemic one at this point. As leaders, we've encouraged the federal government to do more to expand this country's vaccine manufacturing capacity, particularly in the emerging field of mRNA vaccines. We have a lot to do as a nation in order to put the worst of this pandemic behind us. If governments and businesses work together as allies and partners to fight this horrible virus, we will save more lives and accelerate the restoration of our economy.

Turning the Corner

CF weathered the biggest impact to our shopping centre business in the Toronto market, where we lost 285 days of business. As the country and industry deals with the fourth wave of COVID, I remain optimistic that the worst is behind us. While this period has been a blow to retail, store-based retail will clearly survive. People came back to our malls between the first and second waves, and between the second and third waves. In the U.S., where we have properties and offices and they were initially ahead of us on vaccinations, life has returned to some semblance of "normal" in some areas—and it's happened really quickly.

Our U.S. office is based in Dallas and we've got our team down there flying all over the place, looking at deals, closing on deals. Airports are bustling again. Even better, so are shopping malls. At CF properties, people were thrilled to come back to our centres this summer, restrictions notwithstanding.

It's clear people still want to partake in what I'll call the "theatre" element of a mall, an exhilarating experience that can't be replicated. Humans are social creatures with a thirst for live events and interactions. People gravitate to these vibrant communal spaces—whether it's to eat at a restaurant patio, try on the latest jeans because they burned their skinny jeans in the middle of this pandemic, go to the movies, or participate in community events like Lunar New Year and our annual holiday tree lightings.

While shopping centres will undergo more transitions in the future, that's always been the case for good businesses. At CF, we're endlessly evolving to better meet the needs of our customers, clients, and communities. And COVID-19 accelerated a number of emerging business models and diversified retail strategies.

Retailers that had been making a gradual transition to an omnichannel mode accelerated their e-commerce platforms and capabilities and began extending a number of new shopping conveniences for customers, from pre-orders of items to curbside pickup. New technologies blossomed. Live chats have allowed curbside customers to confirm last-minute purchase details with store associates in real time from the convenience of their cars. Brick-and-mortar retail will clearly survive and thrive because of enhanced speed, convenience, and customer services. They will focus on their top-performing stores that offer customers a premium experience and scale back on less profitable real estate.

The same is true of the brick-and-mortar office. Working from home works well for some people for at least some of the time, and for some roles more than others, but offices will always play a central role in advancing corporate culture and employee collaboration. The evolution in corporate offices will prioritize culture and flexibility. Employees will likely spend fewer days in the office than they used to, and many industries recognize that some of the meetings that once involved flying or driving can be done virtually.

Regardless, our tenants don't believe the head office is going away, not even in the longer term. Some of them are keen to lease even more space. COVID has spurred change on this front, too. Many offices will adjust the amount of workspace they allocate to each person in the future and the phenomenon of sharing a desk with multiple people won't likely happen again. While the office of the future may look different, people will continue to run companies from their offices, not from their homes. For the real estate business, the end result will likely be net neutral.

Ultimately, CF wants to help Canadians get back into the swing of life and feel confident that they can do it safely. I'm very proud of the role our company has played in helping businesses and communities make it through this terrible pandemic. As a city builder, our ultimate purpose as a business is to create vibrant community spaces where people come together—spaces woven deeply into the cultural fabric of cities around the world. Spaces that will play a key role in how people reconnect with one another post-pandemic. This experience has taught us many valuable lessons. We won't soon forget them. And I believe they'll help us emerge even stronger as a society than we were before.

Looking to the Future

By the time this book is published, the vast majority of Canadians will be vaccinated and some will have received booster shots, if required. I'm grateful to live in an era in which we developed the fastest vaccines to market in history. I'm also mindful of the important social contract underpinning our mass vaccination campaign.

A COVID shot is not like a vaccine for chicken pox or shingles—if you don't want to get those, it's fine, and you live with the consequences. With COVID, if people don't get vaccinated, this terrible illness could just keep killing people. It could mutate and stick around with us for a long, long time. In August 2021, CF announced that our mandatory vaccination policy for all employees, third-party frontline employees, and contractors who work alongside our staff would go into effect in September. We remain committed to doing our part to fight COVID-19 and keeping our people and communities safe. It's a problem when businesses and governments aren't able to determine who has been vaccinated and who hasn't.

I'm pretty sure of one thing: we need strong, decisive government leadership to keep us on course. Leadership matters. And as you can probably guess from my earlier observations, I don't believe we have enough of it in this country. Recently, Quebec took a decisive stand in announcing people would be required to show proof of vaccination to access public events, bars, restaurants, and gyms beginning in September 2021, and I'm confident that other provinces will follow suit.

But when it comes to health and safety guidelines and lockdown rules, our cities and provinces have often operated at cross purposes and failed to communicate with one another, sowing public confusion as a result. In my mind, the federal government has failed us on two major fronts—travel guidelines and the haphazard, ineptly managed vaccine rollout. And our chronically underfunded healthcare system has been stretched to the breaking point during the pandemic.

At the same time, too many government actors continue to politicize COVID-19. It is deeply disappointing and wholly unhelpful. Rhetoric and finger-pointing has not in any way benefited essential service workers or those trying get a clear handle on how to contain the spread of this highly contagious, potentially deadly novel virus.

It shouldn't be this way. Collectively, as a society—after we reunite with our families and friends and spend some time celebrating in person what we once took for granted—I think we need to spend time reflecting on how we can prevent a catastrophe like this from happening again. When we look back on the COVID-19 pandemic, what will we have learned about ourselves? How would we do it differently next time? Who do we want to put in charge? Will we elect leaders who will step up and lead? I sincerely hope we do. I think Canadians are resourceful and resilient. And I think we're too smart to let a crisis like this blindside us again.

CANADA GOOSE

Three weeks into the pandemic, Canada Goose posted a series of photos from the floor of its factory in Toronto. The shots showed dozens of workers who normally turn out iconic parkas turning their tailoring skills to cranking out surgical scrubs and gowns. After rejigging its workplace—moving sewing stations a safe distance apart, ramping up cleaning—Canada Goose began churning out more than 10,000 items a week for frontline healthcare workers, at first donating the gear to hospitals, and later providing millions of units at cost to address various Canadian government contracts.

For Canada Goose chief executive Dani Reiss, the ability to deftly pivot his facilities from making Arctic gear to hospital gowns was further vindication of a career-defining decision made two decades ago. In an era when most apparel makers boosted profits by moving manufacturing to low-cost nations, Reiss opted to keep making outwear in his home market and make "Made in Canada" a key element of the company's global identity.

The pandemic tripped up many domestic businesses with global supply chains. COVID revealed that outsourcing cost Canada the ability to produce vaccines and essential medical equipment. In contrast, Canada Goose showed what a dedicated, well-trained 4,000-employee Canadian workforce can achieve in a crisis.

Dani Reiss never intended to stay at the parka business, much less create an iconic global brand. When he graduated from university with a degree in literature, his dream was to be a travel writer. The only reason Reiss took a job for a few months at the company his grandfather founded—which at the time was making outdoor gear under the "Snow Goose" brand—was to earn a little money for a post-university trip.

Back in 1997, Reiss joined a business that sold most of its outwear to people who spent their winters working outside in the bitter cold—Canadian rangers and scientists stationed in Antarctica. As he accompanied sales reps on trips to trade shows in Italy and Sweden, where the company sold jackets under the "Canada Goose" brand because the Snow Goose trademark was already claimed, Reiss realized that European customers associated his company's gear with an idealized vision of the Canadian outdoors. Wearing a Canada Goose parka equated to owning a piece of the great white north.

In 2000, Reiss convinced his father, David, then the company's chief executive, to change the corporate name to Canada Goose and shift the marketing focus from work wear to a luxury brand. The following year, Reiss took over as CEO.

Early on, Reiss made the decision that would define the company's COVID response. From its beginnings in 1957, when his grandfather, Polish immigrant Sam Tick—Reiss's grandfather—founded the business, Canada Goose had made all its garments domestically. A significant chunk of its sales came from making apparel for other brands.

By the time Reiss took the helm, Canada Goose was losing those private label customers to offshore manufacturers with lower production costs. Advisors and customers urged Reiss to move his factories overseas.

Instead, the CEO decided to embrace the company's heritage by keeping production in the home market and emphasizing its Canadian roots. He also shifted away from private label manufacturing, focusing instead on turning out Canada Goose–branded products that boasted far better profit margins. Years later, while accepting an honorary doctorate at the University of Ottawa, Reiss said: "Being Canadian is a strong signal of being innovative, trustworthy, stable and multicultural, and that is unconventional for a country."

Canada Goose used extreme adventures and savvy targeted marketing to cement its brand. When Canadians summited on Everest or won the Iditarod sled dog race, they did it in Canada Goose parkas. When Hollywood stars braved the elements in blockbusters like *National Treasure, The Day After Tomorrow, Spectre,* and *Manchester by the Sea* they sported Canada Goose gear. Its parkas became the unofficial uniform of film crews, then warmed the likes of Rihanna, Daniel Craig, and Tom Cruise.

As Canada Goose sales took off, Reiss enlisted Bain Capital to help fund global expansion. The private equity firm acquired 70% of Canada Goose in 2013 in a deal that valued the company at $210 million. As part of the transaction, Reiss insisted manufacturing remain in Canada.

Four years later, Reiss and Bain Capital took the company public on the Toronto Stock Exchange in a share sale that valued Canada Goose at $1.7 billion. In recent years, Reiss extended the Canada Goose line into lightweight down, knitwear, and rain and wind wear—and later this year, they plan to launch their first footwear collection. In June 2021, the brand announced it will end manufacturing with fur as a part of its increasing commitment to sustainability. When the pandemic struck, Canada Goose was selling $1 billion of clothing annually, making it one of the country's most valuable consumer product businesses, worth over $6 billion.

Dani Reiss

JULY 2021

How It Started

In the last week of January 2020, China shut down. The novel coronavirus had been in the news for about a month already. At first, most people thought it would be like SARS or H1N1—serious viruses of the 2000s that the world was able to contain without incredibly high death tolls or widespread societal disruption.

As a business with robust and growing operations in China, Canada Goose had an up-close view and a somewhat different perspective on what was happening there. We paid close attention when China shut down but the initial details were murky. Many news reports suggested novel coronavirus would be a local issue; it wasn't expected to spread beyond the nation's borders in a significant way.

Believing that at the time, I'm embarrassed to admit how I felt next, given what was to come, but it's the truth: I was disappointed that the lockdown in China would cause us to miss a major fourth-quarter sales milestone there, the January to March period that includes Chinese New Year and is one of the busiest retail seasons in the nation.

Primarily, though, my biggest concern was for our people on the ground. We have hundreds of employees in China and work with many more third-party contractors locally. We closed down major offices in Hong Kong and Shanghai, our network of retail stores, and all of the supporting logistical infrastructure, including a pop-up we were operating at the time in Wuhan, the heart of the outbreak.

Another concern at the time involved potential disruption to global supply chains and any resulting business aftershocks. Many consumer goods sold in the West are made in the East. If China was going to "close" for a month or longer, some companies would be left without inventory to sell. I realized pretty quickly that Canada Goose was one of the few

brands not to be materially affected. In fact, we would be better positioned than most. As a Canadian apparel company that has staked its
business on manufacturing almost all of our products in Canada, we
seemed to be in a great position. We had plenty of raw materials to make
our products for the next few months. Any empty shelves would come
the following holiday season—and that was not going to be a problem
for us. Or so we thought then.

As is often the case when we look back on life-altering times, we replay
certain moments in our minds over and over again and they remain
especially vivid as a result. At this point of the unfolding coronavirus
movie timeline, the plot was thickening, but we were still in the charac-
ter development stage. There was so much we didn't know.

My memories from this period are crystal clear, because during the
brief period in mid-February when coronavirus became "COVID-19,"
I was not on my home turf. I spent the last week of that month in
London, where we have a Canada Goose store and a small sales and
marketing office.

When our team met with investors, I noticed some people were not
shaking hands. Two people from separate companies told me that their
firms had mandated worldwide travel bans. It got me thinking more seriously about the ramifications of the virus. Later that day I called Kara,
our Executive Vice-President of People and Culture in Toronto. I remember hoping she wasn't going to think I was overreacting. We agreed that
she would look into what other companies were doing, and she reassured
me she didn't think I was crazy . . . which I appreciated.

I left London, only to have the U.K. close its borders the very same day.
Italy was clamping down as its case counts soared. Still, I naively didn't
believe the rest of the Western world would soon follow in their footsteps
and mandate varying travel bans within a few short weeks. In the first
week of March I travelled to New York for business, but it was a brief trip.
My mind, truth be told, was on a much bigger journey. It sounds almost
glib or dangerously ignorant to reveal this now, in retrospect, but I was
itching to get to Morocco for a long-desired bucket list getaway.

I've travelled a lot in my life. I like the action. I love the discovery. For much of the past twenty-plus years, travel has been my passion and my escape both for business and in my spare time. Relaxing into an airplane seat en route to a new destination is one of my favourite states of being. It's also helped my business. My wanderlust in the 1990s fueled my belief that the Canada Goose brand would resonate well in other parts of the world. I realize how lucky I am, having had the opportunity to move around, see the world, experience different cultures, and meet new people.

At that time in March, there was only one case of coronavirus reported in Morocco. I figured there must be more, but reasoned, in the way that hopeful people do when they want to make something happen in spite of potential negatives: how many more could there be, really? The risk seemed worth it, within my naive frame of mind. I spent just over a week in Morocco, starting in Casablanca and proceeding east from there to Fez. Things seemed normal, on the whole—normal, at least, for what we're now calling "the before times." People were not wearing masks, everyone dined indoors, and nobody was social distancing.

One moment in the market in Fez, though, is etched in my memory. I saw a middle-aged, heavyset man with a backpack standing on a flight of stairs near me. I glanced at him just prior to a moment that was somewhat grotesque but that looked more like live theatre as it happened. He raised his head to the sky, plugged one nostril, and exhaled forcefully out of the other. A discharge that looked like a misty cloud of aerosol sprayed forth from his nose, covering an area of at least a couple of feet. The sunlight hit his face in such a way that I could actually see the droplets. In that moment it struck me—this is how COVID spreads. And if he by chance had it, he would surely pass it on to others. I was filled with unease, but it soon passed.

In retrospect, I'm still glad I went to Morocco. The trip was one of the most amazing experiences I've ever had, and I've thought about it many times in the months since. Mental snapshots of my time there sate my wanderlust as I dream about the other trips I still hope to take.

At the same time, reality was closing in, both in my business and in the rest of the world. COVID-19 was spreading rapidly in Canada. On

March 12, Canada Goose asked our office employees to work from home for the next two weeks, at least. Many companies did the same, trying to ensure safety for people who were able to work remotely and to contain the spread of the virus. Soon enough, my home city would decree that all non-essential workers remain at home.

I flew out of the Marrakesh airport on March 14. Just like the U.K., Morocco closed its borders later that day. The following week, Canada Goose closed our stores across North America and Europe as well as our factories in Canada on March 17. Canada's borders followed shortly after on March 21. If I'd been oblivious to the gravity of the situation when I was sleeping in a tent in the Sahara desert or shopping in one of the famous markets of Marrakesh, it hit me once I got back to Toronto. Now declared a global pandemic by the World Health Organization, COVID-19 had gone very far beyond China and Italy. Everything had shut down. Borders closed, businesses locked up and stock markets crashed. I realized this wasn't going to be like anything we'd ever experienced before.

All our Canada Goose factories, all of our stores, our corporate head-quarters in Toronto, and offices around the world closed down. Just like that. While it became quickly apparent that many people could work well from home, our people who worked in stores or factories couldn't work. Fear set in. How do you run a business when the whole world is closed? How do you budget for the upcoming year when you don't know what's going to happen from one moment to the next? How do you live a life when life's joys and everyday routines are upended? And, in the wee hours of the morning: How do we get past this, as humans? Will we survive?

From a business perspective, a world in which many things were predictable—signs like wholesale booking orders and online activity that I'd look at as leading indicators of what was coming—was almost all gone and certainly what remained was unreliable. My team and I began trying to come up with our annual budget. It was a seemingly impossible task. What stores would be open six months to a year from now? Would they ever open? Would there be any customer demand? We ran every scenario. Nothing looked good. Fortunately, our balance sheet is strong, so this wasn't an existential threat for Canada Goose. But at the time we had to prepare for the worst.

We came up with what we thought would be our most accurate budget. Even in the best-case scenario, we would have to lay people off. The realization was crushing. In my twenty-five-plus years at Canada Goose, we've only known growth. We've only known expansion. We've only won. Our business had never required corrective staffing action. Personally, letting go more than one hundred employees was one of the hardest things I've ever had to do and, professionally, one of the most difficult days of my career.

I felt like we were dismantling a company I'd spent my life building. We knew we had to do it. We came up with a plan and had to execute it, as we always do, but this time we were doing it to potentially save the company. We couldn't afford to spend like a bigger company if we were going to be a smaller company in the months to come, and we didn't have a clue about how big or small we would be in 2020 or 2021 and beyond. I remember sitting in my home office and looking back and forth between my laptop and my phone as a flurry of emails and texts played an endless scroll across the screens. It felt devastating.

How We Got Through

As I sat through that dark day and the many that followed, three guiding principles got me through, and I know many on our Canada Goose team took them to heart too: (1) Lean into what you know definitively; (2) Be helpful; (3) Get outside.

The executive team realized quickly that we'd likely be closed for longer than the originally planned two weeks. Our conversations turned to ensuring we would take care of our employees in every way possible. We started an Employee Support Fund for our workers who were not able to access government assistance. The executive team seeded the fund through voluntary pay cuts. Watching this unfold was one of the silver linings of the pandemic in my mind and a testament to our close-knit culture at Canada Goose. The response was overwhelming. Many other employees voluntarily contributed without being asked. People gave generously and without any obligation to do so. People with their own families to support were willing to share what they had with those who couldn't go to work. It made me think there was hope for humanity, should we all emerge from this lockdown safely.

What followed next was a long, dark time, during which I imagine hope was hard to find for most people, at one point or another. As a company, we kept up our own hopes by looking outward. There are years and times for everything, and this was certainly not a year to prioritize profit. We were going through some painful transitions and we knew the rest of the world was too. We wanted to help people outside of the walls of our organization. All that mattered was getting through, positioning ourselves well for whenever it would be over, and helping our country, which clearly needed it.

We knew from news reports that frontline workers and essential public and private sector organizations across Canada were running perilously low on personal protective equipment, or PPE—another acronym the world added to its COVID vocabulary in those early months. Canada, a first-world nation with many ostensible advantages, had a clear deficit when it came to our mostly extinguished manufacturing sector. That became heart-breakingly clear as government officials scrambled to secure sought-after PPE from other nations and fell short in their efforts. Staff at nursing homes were reusing N95 masks, and workers across the country desperately needed items like sterile masks, gloves, visors, surgical gowns, caps, and booties. Frontline workers, the people who worked tirelessly through the most terrifying early weeks of the outbreak, were left vulnerable.

At Canada Goose, we saw the PPE crisis unfolding and knew very quickly what we had to do. We came to a decision to make whatever PPE we could. As a brand whose roots lie in making products that protect people from the harshest elements, it made good sense to pour all of our efforts into protecting the people of Canada from this terrifying disease. I have championed our "Made in Canada" commitment proudly for over two decades, and at a time like this I realized just how vital that was to helping hold our nation together. If there was one thing Canada Goose could do with our closed factories and furloughed staff, we could make the PPE that our frontline workers so desperately needed, no matter what it would cost us.

I knew that if we were going to do it, we would have to do it right. We began without contracts, knowing that we were in a position to help. In March, we jumped in. We retrofitted our factories and recalled and retrained our workers. All eight of our facilities worked at full, but modified, capacity to churn out PPE for our dedicated Canadians working on the front lines of the crisis. Canada Goose began by making fourteen thousand units of scrubs and gowns and donating them to hospitals and medical facilities across Canada.

After we reopened our factories to make PPE, I visited our Scarborough facility. It was an incredibly emotional highlight of an otherwise scary time. Every single worker on the floor was filled with purpose. They were all so proud and grateful to be helping. There was no shortage of employees who had been eager to come back and be a part of our PPE effort, and the energy was palpable. It made me incredibly proud to know how many of our people, caught up as we all were in the fear and uncertainty of the pandemic, were prepared to come back to our factories to help our country.

Much like the groundswell of internal support that had poured into our Employee Support Fund, it proved to me again just how amazing the people in our company are. Everybody was united in working together for a cause that was greater than ourselves. To me this was the truest expression of our Canada Goose culture.

Eventually, we inked agreements with the provincial and federal governments as an official contract PPE supplier alongside other Canadian brands such as Bauer, Stanfield's, Calko Group, and many others who had answered the call to meet the immense demand. At the end, Canada Goose made over 2.5 million units of scrubs and L1 hospital gowns, at cost, across our facilities in Winnipeg, Toronto, and Montreal.

Beyond my pride in Canada Goose's effort, this whole experience exposed some of the most troubling gaps in our Canadian supply chain and manufacturing sector. Before COVID-19, Canada had imported all of its PPE and outsourced its contracts to the lowest-cost global producers. But this decision came at a clear cost. When the chips were down, Canada's friendly relationships with other countries didn't help us secure PPE when we needed it. Countries moved to protect themselves first. And the ones with vaster populations—those that had bigger contracts than Canada did with companies like 3M—were at the top of the priority list. Many months later, we saw the same troubling trend play out with our country's vaccine rollouts.

We're fortunate that we still have a handful of Canadian companies with domestic manufacturing capabilities because I'm certain our collective made-in-Canada efforts helped save lives. We need more of them. Did Canadians suffer unnecessarily because of this? These are the kinds of questions we need to be asking ourselves right now. It makes sense to do whatever we can to protect ourselves against mass infection in the future. The quicker, the better. It doesn't get any more serious than when the entirety of humanity is at stake.

Social Change

The pandemic shone a light on other inequities in Canadian society and the world, giving us many moments to pause and think about what matters, such as the progressive climate change crisis and ongoing racial injustice.

In May 2020, George Floyd was killed by a Minneapolis police officer while in custody, sparking global anti-racist protests. The world could no longer turn its back on the prevalence of racism, and neither could we. Canada Goose donated $100,000 to both the American Civil Liberties Union and the Canadian Civil Liberties Association, and we also took a close look at ourselves. What could we do, at Canada Goose, to make the company a more diverse, inclusive, and equitable place?

With that in mind, we created the Inclusion Advisory Council at Canada Goose—a group of leaders across our organization, including me, who focus on matters of inclusion and diversity across our business.

We also created a new management position in 2021, hiring a Director of Diversity and Inclusion to ensure we focus on the right steps toward our goals and continue to do so as we move forward on this important journey.

Our commitment to making Canada Goose more sustainable was in motion long before the pandemic struck. We've put sustainability at the forefront of how we're transforming our business for the future. We released our first Sustainable Impact Strategy report on April 20, 2020. Coming at a moment of crisis that prompted people to reflect on the state of the world, its timing felt especially impactful.

We eliminated single-use plastics in all of our owned or controlled facilities in 2020, and this year we have achieved 100% RDS Certification—a leading animal welfare standard for responsibly sourced down. By 2025, we've committed to net-zero greenhouse gas emissions and 90% Bluesign-approved products, a sustainable textile measure. We've further committed to sustainable design through products like our Standard Expedition Parka, made from recycled, undyed fabrics, responsibly sourced down, and reclaimed fur. It generates 30% less carbon, based on footprint, than our traditional Expedition Parka.

We also continue our efforts to support the people, wildlife, and land-scapes of the North through our ongoing support of Polar Bears International, a non-profit polar bear conservation group. We send Canada Goose fabric ends and repurposed parkas to Inuit communities in the North and Project Agiti, our annual social entrepreneurship project in which Inuit designers create capsule collections for Canada Goose. Our vow to help make society a better place didn't start with the pandemic, and it won't end there.

Our Business

After the first few uncertain months on the business front, we embraced strategies that put us in the best position for resilience and recovery in 2021. We focused on what we knew to be true and what worked for us in the new reality of the pandemic: managing our inventory and responding as quickly as possible to shifting consumer needs, managing our cash flow, safeguarding our people, and ensuring brand health.

We've always aimed to meet our consumers wherever and however they want to shop with us, and through the pandemic lockdowns we saw a massive shift in consumer shopping behaviour. Widespread global lockdowns had shut hundreds of retail stores around the world—both our own and those of our partners—during our most typically robust selling season: winter. Our stores in Canada, the U.S., Europe, and Mainland China were closed for months in fiscal 2021 (from April 2020 to the end of March 2021), including a number of our most significant locations globally throughout what would be their busiest sales periods in January and February.

We saw customers buying goods later than they typically did, and they were doing it with a greater sense of urgency—a "buy it now, wear it now" mentality. Forgoing the typical shopping patterns of fall and winter, people were buying products online and picking them up as soon as they could via curbside pickup, or they'd pay extra to have them shipped express to their homes—all in order to wear them as soon as possible. As a result, our direct-to-consumer e-commerce business, which went into overdrive amid all the store closures, shot up more than 50% year over year (fiscal year 2020–21). We were grateful to see our sales rise substantially—above the level we'd seen prior to the pandemic—and we knew that wasn't the case for many brands or retailers.

Fortunately, we invested heavily in our digital operations when the pandemic began to capture higher online demand. I'm proud to say we delivered on our promise to customers thanks to the investments we made in growing our omni-channel—the "endless aisle" of ways and places for people to shop. We also stayed the course with our plans to invest in Mainland China, which had incredible success in containing the pandemic's spread. In the earlier stages of recovery from the first wave, the Mainland China market was our only store-based growth engine. These successes validated our belief in the incredible global growth potential of our made-in-Canada brand. If Canada Goose sold well when the world was under extraordinary stress, our potential to soar when the pandemic is beaten seems limitless.

Given our resilience, we're even more confident about the future. We're leaning into the expansion of our new footwear business, and we see huge potential there. We're opening stores across China and Europe, and in Southern California. We're optimistic about the rebirth of travel and tourism as people get out there and explore the world. We'll be there for our customers along the way, constantly innovating our best-in-class products.

I'm proud our strong Canadian brand held firm through the horribly challenging COVID-19 period. We took care of our people, we helped communities and causes in need, and our business grew to emerge from this stronger than ever.

Beating the Lockdown Blues

On a personal level, I found the shift to working exclusively from home a challenge. Travelling and wandering through places I've never been—my passion and my escape—is also typically the "place" where I do my best and most creative thinking.

Since I couldn't travel, I started to walk every day. I had a strong drive to get outside, no matter the weather. Some days I'd walk for hours. Anybody who knows me well knows that I have a terrible sense of direction, but through this pandemic I have come to know all of Toronto's network of walking trails. To those who don't live in the city, it may come as a surprise that a place whose centre is filled with concrete and glass towers is also home to a beautiful network of nature walks—hundreds of kilometres of trails, and even more if you include the broader surrounding region.

I'm also fortunate enough to have a second home by a lake outside of the city. When I wasn't taking video calls with my team or poring over spreadsheets and designs through the pandemic, I was able to explore more of the surrounding nature than I'd ever imagined. My family enjoyed the escape as well, my kids getting outside to play in the snow and ride snowmobiles with their dad—another small silver lining. We got to watch the ice come and go and the seasons pass. I even took up ice fishing. I didn't catch a thing, and I didn't care.

The pandemic took a toll on so many people's mental health, and I was no stranger to some dark days myself through it all, but I do think getting outside and experiencing nature saved me to a degree.

As I was going through all of this, I knew our Canada Goose employees were also shouldering immense struggles. Our company attracts people who love nature. During the pandemic we encouraged people to get outside for some nature therapy through an official policy perk—a weekly "Humanature" pass for corporate employees to encourage them to set aside an hour during business hours to connect with nature.

What's Next?
As I reflect on the past year and a half, there is one thought that I can't shake about our future. COVID-19 has given us an incredible opportunity to change the world. We have all had significant time to reflect and we will continue to do so as we eventually beat this horrible virus. As people and as a country, we can decide how we want to improve our lives and how we want society to change for the better out of this time of extreme uncertainty, stress, triumph, and heartbreaking loss.

In my own personal life, it's only redoubled my desire to spend my time engaging with the people who make me the happiest and exploring the world's enriching spaces. And when it comes to the future of my company and of my country, I have an even clearer point of view. Our PPE crisis didn't have to happen. Canada Goose has always seen the value in making our products in this country. We've set up factories with a workforce of skilled sewers and designers as a result. During the pandemic, Canada's access to key essentials like PPE was paralyzed, and that can't be allowed to happen again. As a country, we need to rethink our approach to domestic manufacturing.

I believe Canada should keep its strategic, proprietary supply chain alive and grow it, and not just for safety's sake to get us through times of crisis. Re-establishing domestic manufacturing capabilities will also be good for our economy, if we do it strategically. We need to identify industries that are strategic to our national security—such as PPE, drug manufacturing, food, and technology—and to support the increase of domestic manufacturing capabilities in those industries. We need to elect leaders who support growing our manufacturing economy. Investing in Canada's workers, in sustainable practices, and in innovative technology will make us a stronger, happier, healthier nation in the future.

We also need to double down in our approach to fighting climate change and protecting nature. This planet is hurting, and it's the only one we've got. This is not new. It's a truth that we've known for generations, one that has only grown harsher in recent years with an increasing push for political and business leaders to take meaningful action. Businesses have the ability to move quickly and unilaterally to solve problems, and today the world is full of those. I remember, in my youth, hearing endless stories about the depletion of the ozone layer, that acid rain would impact our lives for generations to come. But, over the past year, it seems we may have finally turned a corner. While the world is more polarized politically than ever, governments and corporations are making stronger commitments, and there has been a massive corporate reset to embrace the imperative of sustainability. It's as though, coming out of lockdown, the blinders are off. It's a change that I'm not sure would have happened without the tectonic shift in priorities brought on by the pandemic.

As business leaders, we need to advocate for people in society who have less power and ensure that our companies do the same. Corporations have a clear role in making this world a better place. Our all-in effort to help the country through its PPE crisis only underscored that fact: helping frontline workers and organizations in need was good for our people's morale, and it made us all even prouder of our vital Canadian brand.

I'm grateful that our company and our incredible Canada Goose employees were able to make it through this devastating time as well as we did. We leaned into what we knew in a time of uncertainty. We helped others. And we got outside.

CANADIAN TIRE

Greg Hicks's first day as Canadian Tire's president and chief executive officer was one to remember.

After more than twenty years in retail, he'd finally landed his dream job—but the celebration would have to wait. The same day he signed his contract, the WHO declared COVID-19 a global pandemic.

Welcome to the C-suite, Mr. Hicks.

Working at Canadian Tire blends Hicks's personal and professional lives. His father was an executive at the family-controlled company, founded in 1922 by brothers J.W. and A.J. Billes and now majority owned by A.J.'s daughter Martha Billes. Hicks's brother is and two of his uncles were Canadian Tire dealers.

Despite the family ties, Hicks built a career in retail at rural outfitter Tractor Supply Co., now part of the eighty-eight-store Peavy Mart chain. He was the company's chief operating officer when Canadian Tire came calling in 2013. Once he joined what amounts to the family business, the graduate of Western University's Ivey School of Business ran a number of divisions, including a successful stint building the company's stable of "owned brands" such as Paderno kitchenware, Woods outdoor gear, and Noma home products. Prior to being named CEO, Hicks served as president of Canadian Tire Retail, the company's largest division.

Hicks took the top job at a time when Canadian Tire faced challenges from traditional rivals—auto dealers, sporting goods stores, and big box home centres—along with the growing online threat of Amazon and other disruptive competitors. The new boss planned to keep expanding a company that, after starting as a single garage in Toronto in 1922, had since grown to include twelve retail banners, a bank, a real estate company, global owned brands, its own digital currency, and more than seventeen hundred retail locations nationwide.

Going in that first day as CEO, Hicks's goal was to strengthen Canadian Tire's longstanding purpose of being there for life in Canada as the brand prepared to usher in its one hundredth anniversary in 2022.

Greg Hicks

JULY 2021

On a Wednesday evening in March 2020, I was on my way to STK, a restaurant in Toronto. It was not a typical dinner out—it was a celebration. I had just signed my new contract with Canadian Tire and the announcement of my appointment was imminent. I was officially the new president and chief executive officer of Canadian Tire Corporation.

After more than twenty years in retail, I'd reached what I'd long considered to be the summit of my career. Over the years, I'd been fortunate to have either met or worked with every Canadian Tire CEO with the exception of our company's co-founder, A.J. Billes. It was an honour to be tapped to carry the torch and the professional milestone felt equally personal. My father was an executive at the company and went on to become a Canadian Tire associate dealer. Two of my uncles were Canadian Tire dealers and my brother, David, is a dealer to this day. My connection to Canadian Tire runs deep—you could say that it's in my blood.

But on that fateful Wednesday evening in March, the celebration did not go entirely as planned. Shortly after I sat down with Gregory Craig, who had taken over as our CFO only nine days earlier, we heard the news that the NBA had suspended their season after a player tested positive for COVID-19. In hindsight, we should not have been surprised: that morning, the WHO had declared COVID-19 a global pandemic.

On a Wednesday evening in March 2020, the ink had barely dried on my contract when I realized that my dream job was not going to be anything like what I'd imagined or planned for. As it would turn out, the COVID-19 crisis would be, for me, nothing short of a masterclass in leadership.

At Canadian Tire, we always plan for the likely crises. It goes without saying that we have a robust enterprise risk process that covers everything from strategic to operational risks. What we weren't as prepared for were the very low probability, high-impact crises. COVID-19 most certainly falls into the second category.

Looking back, my first few days as CEO replay as if they were weeks because of how much we had to do, and fast. On March 12, my first real day as CEO, everything began to unfold very quickly: Premier Doug Ford announced that schools in Ontario would remain closed following the March Break. The province of Quebec declared a state of emergency. The NHL suspended its season. Broadway theatres shuttered their doors. It was a continuous flow of anxiety-inducing news that followed in such quick succession, you didn't even have time to process what you'd heard before there would be another announcement.

The day began to feel more frantic as it went on. Hours into my new role, I was notified that one of our Sport Chek employees had, while on a flight, come into contact with a passenger who had tested positive for COVID-19. The news of this quickly spread through the staff at that store, and by 7:30 p.m.—an hour and a half before closing time—the only person left working in the store was the manager.

Right away, there were myriad decisions that needed to be made with little information and considerable ripple effects. There was so much we—experts included—didn't know. How was the virus transmitted? How long was the incubation period? Could you pass it on if you didn't have symptoms? Would wearing a mask make a difference? The list goes on.

What we did know was that we had to do everything we could to protect the health and safety of our employees, customers, and the communities we serve. That was obvious. So, on March 13—my second day as CEO—I sent an email to employees announcing that our offices would be closed as of Monday, and that corporate employees were to begin working from home. I recall that when I sent the email, many of us—me included—assumed we would be back in the office within a few weeks. Some even thought we might be back in on the following Monday. Many employees didn't think twice about going home that afternoon with nothing but their laptop, leaving behind everything from their computer mouse to the collection of shoes under their desk. Even with everything that was going on around us, I don't think the sheer gravity of the situation had hit home yet. But then it did.

With so much happening simultaneously, it was a challenge to not be pulled in a hundred different directions at once. In addition to protecting health and safety, I felt it was critical that our leadership team remain grounded in five guiding principles: preserving our liquidity; preparing for the worst; not majoring in the minors; protecting our brand by considering what our relationship with customers, vendors, and other stakeholders would be when we reached the other side; and preparing to come out of this stronger than most. Regardless of what we didn't know, our instinct was that the crisis was going to get worse before it got better—I think I can speak for nearly our entire senior leadership team on that front. We began consulting directly with doctors and other health professionals and held daily COVID-19 calls where all leaders provided updates and solutions to problems. It was a think tank with a clear objective: solve the next problem. As it would turn out, our guiding principles didn't just serve to help us navigate the crisis; they fundamentally changed how we work. We didn't know it at the time, but we were at the beginning of our culture change.

Given how much we didn't know about COVID-19, the best way to protect health and safety was by closing our stores. At the same time, we knew that Canadians were relying on us for countless products, many of which were being deemed essential, such as cleaning supplies, bathroom tissue, and hand sanitizer. So we made a decision: we would close many of our stores nation-wide in an effort to protect health and safety and mitigate the spread of the virus while still providing Canadians with the essentials.

On March 19, we closed our Mark's, Sport Chek, Party City, and other banners to the public. And at Canadian Tire Retail (CTR) and Gas+, our teams and the more than five hundred Canadian Tire associate dealers immediately got to work implementing heightened health and safety measures, from installing plexiglass and floor decals to enforce physical distancing, to encouraging customers to use digital payment methods. We sent shipments of masks and gloves to every CTR store for staff to wear and even temporarily stopped the distribution of our iconic Canadian Tire paper money out of fear that the virus could potentially live on its surface. We paused our national paper flyer, a hard but necessary decision. Our flyer is considered one of the backbones of our business, but we knew it was irresponsible to be actively driving traffic to our stores. In its place, we created an e-flyer that drove customers to our website, enabling them to see all the different ways they could shop us safely.

The CTR dealers rose to the challenge and we operated as a united front, focused on upholding our longstanding purpose of being there for life in Canada. But the challenges accelerated and we found ourselves continuously fighting fires. Although our corporate employees were able to safely work from home, this was not an option for our frontline store, distribution centre, and call centre staff, who were hard at work ensuring essential products could get into the hands of Canadians. Mid-March 2020, when bathroom tissue seemed to be at its most scarce, I was told the story of Amanda, a Canadian Tire store employee in Windsor, Ontario. Amanda came upon a customer who was shopping for her elderly mother. The store was, unfortunately, out of bathroom tissue and, recognizing the customer's distress, Amanda went out to her car, grabbed the bathroom tissue that she had bought for herself, and gave half of her rolls to the customer, refusing any form of payment.

Meanwhile in Toronto, a Canadian Tire dealer donated $50,000 in masks to North York General Hospital; hand sanitizer, masks, and wipes to retirement and assisted living homes; and multiple cases of hand sanitizer to the police department. On top of all of this, to ensure the store could continue running as smoothly as possible, the general manager didn't take a single day off for weeks. He ended up spending so much time in the store, he chose to stay at a hotel instead of returning home to his family at night. He wanted to be there for his customers, while at the same time doing everything he could to keep his family safe as case counts continued to rise.

Being there for Canadians was not something embraced only at CTR: it was an enterprise-wide endeavour. In Chilliwack, for example, the store associates at Mark's learned that local healthcare providers were struggling to source enough scrubs. The store team gathered up all their excess scrubs, took the names and sizes of approximately 150 healthcare workers in need, and created care packages for each one of them. Included with the much-needed apparel were thank you cards and artwork created by the daughter of one of the store associates.

These are just some of the many stories about our frontline employees who went above and beyond even though they were no doubt exhausted and concerned about their own health and safety. And yet they continued to proudly show up to work. Simply put, neither our business nor our country could have moved forward without these frontline employees, which is why, on March 25, we announced a special support program of $2 per hour for our frontline employees.

That same day, we launched curbside pickup, allowing a quick, easy way for customers to get their essentials without having to shop in-store. From idea to execution, this came together in days, which is incredibly impressive and a testament to the ongoing collaboration across our company, from the corporation and dealers to our Mark's and Sport Chek teams. This is something that would've taken us months to pull off prior to the pandemic, but one of the things that COVID-19 taught us is how to embrace progress over perfection. We simply did not have time for our old ways of operating: the meetings before the meetings and the multiple layers of approvals that slow us down. Instead, we empowered our people to make decisions and solve problems. Our solutions weren't always perfect, but the solutions got the job done and provided opportunities for continuous learning.

With so much change and uncertainty in those first few days, I made it a priority to communicate frequently and transparently with our people. By no means did I have all the answers—not even close—but I committed to telling them what I did know, along with what I didn't know. I recall writing that email to employees on March 13—the one in which I told them we needed to work from home starting Monday—and I remember a moment when I thought I shouldn't send it. I'd only been CEO for twenty-four hours; did I really want my second-ever email to be about COVID-19? Was this the best time to open up a dialogue and risk frightening people by talking about the global pandemic and the fact that, no, I didn't know what was going to happen?

In hindsight, I'm really glad I didn't listen to that doubting voice. In fact, I went in the complete opposite direction. After I sent the note on March 13, I committed to communicating with employees every forty-eight hours, a practice that was as beneficial for me as I think it was for them: employees began writing me back, and their words of encouragement and support bolstered me on the days I needed it most. The ongoing series of emails to employees would, over time, not only shift how our company communicates, but fundamentally change our culture.

Days soon turned into weeks. Although we were moving forward, the firefighting was far from over. Just when we'd think we'd found our footing, we'd be hit with another big change. On April 5, 2020, our CTR stores across Ontario—approximately half of our CTR store network—were forced to close to the public due to provincial government restrictions. Although our stores were permitted to continue serving customers through e-commerce and curbside pickup, this challenge was compounded by the fact that we were having major issues with our CTR website. You could say that the closure of our Ontario CTR stores was the proverbial straw that broke the camel's back.

Prior to the pandemic, we had not necessarily been known for our e-commerce—which isn't to say we weren't actively working to change that. Our site experience, corporate support, and dealer teams were doing a good job managing about five thousand "click and collect" orders a day, with a small percentage of those being "deliver to home." We were working hard to scale the site and our readiness processes to manage an anticipated thirty thousand orders during Cyber Week.

Then the pandemic hit.

Suddenly, we found ourselves facing upwards of a hundred thousand orders consistently per day. In short, we were hitting goals for customer traffic and transaction volume that we hadn't been expecting for another five years. And our CTR website did not yet have the capacity to handle the pressure. To say this was frustrating for me, our corporate team, our dealers, and, above all, our customers would be an understatement. We urgently looked for ways to expand capacity and reinforce stability, pulling together our strongest IT resources from across the organization and world. The reality was that the issue was deep within the backend of our website, and it was not an easy fix.

But, as dire as it felt at the time, all was not lost. Not only did we have the best possible team who were willing to work around the clock and as quickly as they could to find a solution, but we had a solid e-commerce foundation that had been in the works for several years, which enabled us to respond quickly to the spike in e-commerce demand. By reprioritizing and accelerating our capital investment, we fundamentally improved the capability and capacity of the site. In six weeks, we accomplished what was originally in scope for our e-commerce strategy for the next two years. This was a true testament to the team, who, when facing unrealistic expectations with equally unrealistic timelines, did not crack under pressure and facilitated our quantum leap into the future of e-commerce. Today, our CTR website processes more than eighty thousand orders daily and our e-commerce platform has scaled significantly, with twenty-five times the number of transactions we saw prior to COVID-19. We had a total $1.6 billion in e-commerce sales in 2020—up 183% over 2019—which translates to roughly 10% of the business, and is easily three or four years ahead of where we would have expected to end 2020.

In addition to doing everything we could to provide Canadians with the essentials, we realized that we had an even bigger role to play in the crisis. Across the country, dealers and store staff were already doing right by their communities by donating funds, scrubs, countless units of PPE, and litres of hand sanitizer. They were helping the Girl Guides sell their iconic cookies safely from the shelves of their stores and offering free delivery and reserved shopping hours for vulnerable citizens. Their acts of kindness were endless and inspiring.

There's no question that a company's true values take over during a crisis. For us, that meant being there for life in Canada—no matter what life looked like. So, on April 9, 2020, we launched our $5 million Canadian Tire COVID-19 Response Fund to help frontline healthcare and community workers respond to the pandemic. This fund included two donations of $1 million each to the Canadian Red Cross and United Way Centraide Canada, as well as $3 million in essential products from across our group of companies—including scrubs from Mark's and sports masks and goggles from Sport Chek—to frontline healthcare and community workers.

In the first seventy-two hours, we received more than six hundred requests from organizations in need. In the end, more than one thousand organizations received support through the COVID-19 Response Fund. I'm confident that when we look back on this crisis, companies will be remembered not by the products they sold or the services they offered, but by their acts of kindness and the support they provided when Canadians and communities needed it most.

Weeks stretched into months. As Canadians became increasingly restless, we found ourselves facing a new challenge to our supply chain. Customers were relying on us as the one-stop-shop to meet their needs as they spent more, if not all, of their time living, working, and playing at home. From boredom-busters like toys and games, to fitness equipment and trampolines, we started to see unprecedented demand across many of our categories.

Early on, I had asked my management team in merchandise and supply chain to get on the phones and do everything they could to strengthen our already exceptional relationships with our vendors. Together as a team, we reached out to our vendor community and ordered as much as we could, throwing off all restraints. As unprecedented consumer demand put unparalleled pressure on global supply chains, we quickly adapted our operations. We added seven third-party logistics companies and adjusted all Canadian distribution centres to operate at seven days a week and over twenty hours per day. We even turned CTC's Airport Road storage facility on the outskirts of Toronto into an outbound store-facing fulfill-ment node—in only eight weeks.

Agile as we were, there were some products that were challenging to get, such as trampolines, air conditioners, exercise weights, and paint. Our use of AI technology gave us a leg up in certain categories because we were able to see the surge in demand coming and plan accordingly. For example, in March 2020, we identified early spikes in cycling patterns on the West Coast. Our AI technology allowed us to not only see the trend but identify where our inventory was, where it wasn't, and where it needed to be. To help our dealers meet the incredible demand for bikes at CTR, we tried something new: we redirected inventory from our Sport Chek stores, which were closed for in-store shopping, to CTR. The speed at which we redeployed inventory prevented us from losing customers who would have likely gone elsewhere had the product not been available at their local store. And as demand for bikes continued to surge off the charts, we made commitments with our suppliers to extend the season and gave them more orders to make production runs efficient, recogniz-ing that we would need to carry some inventory over the winter. We also reached out to other retailers who were closed, including a bicycle com-pany in Europe, to procure some of their inventory. When all was said and done, our agility had paid off. By being able to meet the needs of our customers, our bike sales increased by an incredible 400% in 2020.

As the challenges of COVID-19 continued through the spring, other significant events were unfolding, including the murder of George Floyd on May 25, 2020, which led to global protests against police brutality, police racism, and lack of police accountability. Leaders and organizations across the world began speaking out in solidarity with the Black commu-nity. We had reached a point where we needed to begin talking about issues of racism and injustice, and within our company, I knew it had to start with me.

When it came to diversity, inclusion, and belonging (DIB), it was evi-dent that we had work to do. We created a formal DIB team to develop company-wide programs and practices that promote a culture where everyone feels seen and heard and that they belong. We launched Courageous Conversations, an ongoing series that provides a dedicated space and time for employees to listen, share, challenge the status quo, provide feedback, and offer their perspectives on how to create a more inclusive and equitable workplace. Externally, we supported organizations dedicated to helping Black communities by donating $200,000 each to the Black Health Alliance, Black Youth Helpline, and Black Legal Action Centre. We also donated $200,000 that was earmarked for grassroots Black organizations and diversity and inclusion groups recommended by our own employees.

These were just our first steps on what we knew would be a long and important journey. DIB has become a significant priority for me and CTC's leadership team, not only because everyone deserves to feel like they are a welcome part of the Canadian Tire team, but because, as a company that prides itself on understanding life in Canada, the diversity of our organization must reflect that of our nation—that's the only way we can truly be there for *all* Canadians.

As our first pandemic summer came to an end, COVID-19 continued to take its toll on our communities. Canadian Tire's longstanding history of supporting communities is fundamental to our purpose and, since 2005, has been fortified by our corporate charity, Jumpstart. What began as a charity that specifically helped kids in financial need has grown to address other challenges that keep kids out of sport, such as accessibility and gender barriers. True to its mission and vision, Jumpstart could not sit idly by as the pandemic brought sport to a halt.

Recognizing that countless community organizations had shut their doors due to COVID-19, Jumpstart launched an $8 million Sport Relief Fund to help sport and recreation organizations continue to deliver pro-gramming in 2020 and beyond. The response was overwhelming. Even after helping nearly seven hundred organizations, we saw that a significant and growing need for support remained. That's why in early 2021 we com-mitted an additional $12 million to Jumpstart's Sport Relief Fund to help build back sport and play in Canada. As a company, we've always believed in the power of sport. We knew that once we finally reached the other side of the pandemic, access to sport and play would be more important than ever, as it would help kids, families, and our country overcome this trauma and thrive once more.

The one-year anniversaries of my appointment as CEO and the WHO's declaration of the global pandemic came and went. By March 2021, we were all ready to be done with COVID-19—but unfortunately, it was not done with us. For many provinces, the second wave simply seemed to bleed into the third.

Although our people continued to prove their mettle, the sheer persistence of COVID-19 and the ongoing restrictions across Canada were taking their toll. For more than a year, everyone had been navigating not just professional challenges but personal ones as well. Some of our team members, their friends, or family members contracted COVID-19. Others experienced loss. Many had to change, or cancel, the celebration of important life milestones. Those with kids were juggling their jobs, parenting, and at-home learning. I didn't know all the unique challenges people were up against, but what I did know is that it wasn't easy for anyone. By May 2021, the crisis felt relentless.

From day one, the CTC board remained my steadfast supporter, holding weekly calls with management and establishing an ad hoc subcommittee to serve as a resource and critical sounding board on key strategic issues throughout the many months of COVID-19 turbulence. Our teams continued to work together by keeping their eyes on that same North Star that had guided us since day one: being there for life in Canada. Despite their own challenges, our people kept stepping up for our customers and for each other, leading with empathy and collaborating with compassion. We focused our efforts on what we could control, which included contributing to Canada's vaccine rollout. We'd seen first-hand how quickly the virus could spread, as we'd experienced outbreaks in small pockets of our contact centre and distribution centre employee populations. Along with implementing additional safety measures, including rapid COVID-19 testing, we gave all employees paid time off to be vaccinated. We also supported multiple community vaccination efforts, including donating our large exhibition space at Place Sports Experts to be used as a vaccination site by the Laval Region Health Agency. Our teams set up and hosted a workplace clinic for our employees, their families, and the community of Peel at our A.J. Billes distribution centre. We knew widespread vaccination was the best way to reduce virus cases and enable the rebuilding of our communities and the economy. We wanted to help in any way we could.

At the time of this writing, it's been well over a year since the onset of COVID-19 and we have yet to reach the other side. We are, however, starting to see the light at the end of the tunnel, as our country's vaccination rate continues to climb. We are looking to the future with tentative excitement. I think it's fair to say that life will never go back to "the way it was"—but that isn't necessarily a bad thing. We have certainly lost a lot during COVID-19. But we've learned a lot as well.

For me, navigating CTC through the pandemic was truly a masterclass in leadership. Since March 13, 2020, I've sent more than fifty company-wide emails to employees, an exercise that made me realize how critical communication was and is. In rereading some of the responses to my notes, employees' words of encouragement, hope, and resilience are palpable. Despite the challenges we faced, they remained optimistic and maintained their genuine pride in working for CTC. I know company pride is something that can neither be forced nor manufactured. Pride is fostered by aligning to common goals and believing in a collective purpose. It is cultivated when we feel connected to something greater than ourselves. In a year marred by social distancing protocols and rampant disconnection, arguably our greatest feat was the fact that we were so connected: to each other, to our customers, and to our communities. That is what enabled us to achieve the results we did.

In confronting the unprecedented, we learned so much about our business, how we operate, and what we need to do to grow. But above all, we learned who we are as people and what it means to truly be there—for our country and for each other. Long after the last mask has been discarded, we've finally hugged our extended families and friends, and we've returned to restaurants, concerts, and sporting events, we will still carry with us the lessons we've learned through this crisis. Because of this, I'm confident CTC will emerge from the pandemic as a different company. A stronger company. A better company.

My dream job did not turn out to be what I'd imagined or planned for. It turned out to be better.

COUCHE-TARD

COVID-19 does not care if you are a CEO working on one of the biggest deals of your career. When a global pandemic gets rolling, it spares no one in its path. Just ask Brian Hannasch, chief executive of one of the world's largest convenience store operators, Montreal-based Alimentation Couche-Tard.

At the start of 2020, Hannasch was deep into a stunning growth opportunity in the Asia-Pacific region, close to shaking hands, on the company's largest acquisition to date. The CEO was hearing the first global concerns about a potentially deadly new flu in China while working on that US$5.6 billion transaction in Australia. Only a few weeks later, Couche-Tard walked away from the deal due to pandemic-induced uncertainty. The opportunity no longer made sense—it was shut down by the impact of COVID.

At the start of 2021, COVID-19 shut down Hannasch. The virus turned the leader of a company with 124,000 employees at more than 14,200 stores in 26 regions into another healthcare statistic—a guy who tested positive, felt pretty awful for a few days, and spent two weeks in quarantine. It was a humbling experience for a CEO and a company with great pride in its humble roots.

Couche-Tard, which operates convenience store brands such as Circle K and Scandinavia's Ingo, traces its roots to a single corner store in Laval, Quebec. Couche-Tard means "night owl" in French. Over four decades, founder Alain Bouchard built the company partly through a series of acquisitions. One of those takeovers saw Couche-Tard make its initial foray into the U.S. in 2001 by snapping up 172 Midwestern convenience stores under the Bigfoot banner.

Hannasch was Bigfoot's vice-president of operations. A native of farm town Carroll, Iowa—population ten thousand—Hannasch started his career in the oil business after graduating from Iowa State University. By age thirty, he was one of the youngest vice-presidents at British Petroleum. Reluctant to uproot his family for a job at the U.K. head office, he opted to quit the company rather than keep climbing the ranks. He joined Columbus, Indiana–based Bigfoot shortly after, and his family home— he and his wife have two adult children—is still in Columbus, a city of fifty thousand.

Over Hannasch's seven years as CEO, Couche-Tard has become an increasingly global player. The COVID crisis may have kept Hannasch uncharacteristically home in the U.S., but it has not stopped growth at the chain, nor has it slowed down Couche-Tard's ambitions. What it undoubtedly did give Hannasch is an even deeper faith and gratitude for the culture of one of Canada's global champions, a chain that anchors neighbourhoods from thousands of street corners.

Brian Hannasch

JUNE 2021

It was only May 2020—a few months into the coronavirus pandemic—
and to me, it already felt like a year or maybe an eternity. It was time to
write my letter for our annual report, and this is how I started:

> This year has clearly been one for the record books. In my almost 20
> years with Couche-Tard, I could have never predicted these last twelve
> months, in particular the last three, when an invisible threat evolved to
> challenge our businesses, our communities, and our families. We started
> this historic year as a strong company—and through the compassion,
> care, and dedication of our team members and customers—ended it a
> better, stronger company.

Maybe I should not have been surprised about how well the company
was dealing with the crisis. After all, I had been CEO for nearly six years
and witnessed first-hand how resilient and strong we could be. But this was
my first pandemic. Most of all, I was already deeply proud of our teams. I
went on to write in that same letter:

> If we measure a company by how it responds to challenge and contro-
> versy, then I must say that Couche-Tard is succeeding in ways we never
> imagined. Our store employees have become frontline heroes, we are part
> of the solution in the communities where we work and live, and, with our
> customary financial discipline, we are positioned to continue our growth
> journey. I have never been prouder to be CEO of this company!

In hindsight, that spring we were only at the starting line. As the virus
persisted month after month, we kept getting better and kept getting
stronger, both as a culture and a company, and my pride kept growing.

Let me back up a little to January 2020. We were coming to the end of our third fiscal quarter (we report May to April), and we were on track to have our strongest fiscal year on record. We were hitting milestones of our five-year strategy, driving organic growth, expanding our network through new builds, growing our fresh food program, rebranding at a rapid pace both at our stores and on our fuel courts, and improving the customer experience through innovative solutions. This real progress on our strategic plan reflected the committed teamwork behind it. I was also expecting an exciting period of growth ahead. In fact, in February 2020, I was on a trip to Australia as we were well on our way to signing a deal to buy Caltex (now known as Ampol). It was poised to be one of our biggest acquisitions ever and to mark our long-awaited entry into the Asia-Pacific region.

Before the trip began, I had heard bits of news about a killer virus in central China. However, as Alimentation Couche-Tard did not have a presence in China, it seemed quite far removed from me and from the business. As I said, I was in Australia to ideally begin our Asian journey. Yet I kept getting emails and calls from Ina Strand, our chief people officer in Charlotte, North Carolina, saying I needed to make some decisions (i.e., "now") about how the company should react to that virus in China, and that I needed to put out a company email talking about our approach to travel, remote work, and more. I must be honest here—I thought Ina was overreacting. I did not get back to her quickly, figuring it could wait until I returned to the U.S.

By early March 2020, it became all COVID all the time, and on March 3, 2020, I sent my first company email on the virus, where I wrote:

I know all of you, like me, are concerned about the news and warnings regarding the coronavirus COVID-19 and are looking for updated information on what it means to you and your family, your community, and your work. In this letter, I want to outline what we are doing as a company as we anticipate the spread of the virus. Please know that we are committed to getting you timely information.

The information we put out at that time was pretty low key—follow the guidelines of the World Health Organization and the Centers for Disease Control, do not travel to China, minimize non-essential travel, and wash your hands frequently and maintain proper hygiene. We naively believed, at that time, that we could treat the coronavirus like the flu, and truthfully, I felt a little silly giving our 124,000 team members advice about washing their hands properly. I ended the note by saying: "As of today, it is business-as-usual in our offices and stores." That was the last time for a long time that I referred to business-as-usual.

The rest of March and April hit Couche-Tard and the world with a tsunami of bad news about what was turning into a once-in-a-century pandemic. Stories of illness, death, and communities on lockdown overtook our business and our neighbourhoods. As CEO, I knew I needed to lead with compassion, care, and consistency: I had hundreds of thousands of scared team members relying on me to keep them safe and shareholders depending on me to protect their investments. I also knew that millions of customers around the globe were counting on us. So I did what I have done for so many years as a leader: I trusted my people and I trusted our decentralized model. I knew that if I gave them the authority to do so, our local leadership and teams would know how to take care of each other and our customers. I just needed to trust them and allow the entire company to learn from each other.

A little context is important here. The convenience industry is often at its best during natural disasters. Over and over again, during countless hurricanes and other life-threatening natural disasters, we have shown our importance to our communities and customers in need. Our store team members have been endlessly brave and inventive in order to keep stores stocked, fuel available, and support given to first responders and healthcare workers. Now, for the first time, we needed to take those lessons and apply them on a global scale. As a company, we take pride in making things easy, but have no doubt, getting our more than fourteen thousand stores prepared for this epic disaster was not easy.

We had to do things we had never done before. Frankly, that list of things still looks quite crazy. Some decisions mirrored those made by companies around the globe. For example, we too had to set up our support team members to work remotely as offices and towns were closing down at a rapid rate. Our global tech team had to figure out how to get computers to thousands of office support team members (most did not have one at home) and how to set up mechanisms to do our accounting and payroll work remotely, supplies ordered, benefits administered, and emergency procedures created and in place. Most of us, including myself, had never worked routinely from home. Back in March 2020, I had never heard of Zoom calls or Microsoft Teams meetings. This was a completely new way of working for me and for our relatively small group of office-based employees who support our stores.

At the same time, we had to figure out the even harder part—how to keep our stores operating. I had spent almost my entire life on the road and in our stores. I began working as a teenager in a convenience store pumping fuel, and I care deeply about the team members who are at the heart of our operation. Now I was asking them to go out to work while so much of the world was figuring out how to stay home. In fact, most of our areas were under strict curfew. In order to keep our stores operating, we needed our store team members to be officially recognized as essential workers. That way, we could provide them with official certification to show to local law enforcement, keeping them from being arrested or fined while on the way to their shift.

Only three weeks after that "business-as-usual" email, I wrote the following to all team members, and I was now calling the situation a crisis:

> Across the company, and around the clock, we have an army of employees working hard to get through this crisis and serve our customers and communities. I know it feels like this virus has been with us forever, but we have truly accomplished an incredible amount in just a few weeks. In most regions where we operate our stores are part of the designated critical emergency infrastructure, and our communities and customers

rely on us more than ever to provide needed emergency products, fuel, and everyday necessities. In some areas, we are among the only remaining providers of these necessities.

Our store employees are on the frontline, and we will support them. In some areas where we operate, there is not the same government safety net for healthcare and temporary layoffs. For our North American hourly store employees, we have implemented an emergency appreciation pay bonus and emergency sick care pay plan. And, we are quickly putting together solutions to make our locations safer, from cleaning procedures, separators at the registers, and social distancing signage.

I have interesting stories of how we put together some of those safety and cleaning measures. Before the start of 2020, we had never considered how to supply massive amounts of masks; how to close, clean, and reopen infected stores within hours; or how to set up social distancing and safe payment methods. Like I said, I needed to trust local leadership to come up with solutions. Our franchise folks in Hong Kong alerted us to mask production in China and suggested we fly one of our corporate jets to that country and load it up with masks. So we did. Early on, we were able to distribute masks across the network for our team members to wear and customers to purchase. Of course, these were not N95 masks, which were in notorious short supply for healthcare workers.

Next came the issue of social distancing. This time our solution came from a team member in one of our Poland stores, who had the idea of hanging plexiglass between the cashiers and customers, basically as a huge sneeze guard. Pictures of the invention were sent to me and other members of our leadership, and I made it clear that by the end of the week I wanted this in every one of our stores. I cannot prove it, but I believe we were either the first company, or one of the very first, to have this kind of a store guard.

It was the beginning of April, and I felt strongly that I needed to visit our store team members. I could not ask them to be out in society and serving our customers unless I too would take that risk. Granted I travelled by corporate jet, as public air travel was not possible, and I journeyed only to U.S. stores as international travel had already been banned. One month after my first email on the topic, my tone had become more urgent:

> I visited many stores last week in North Carolina and Indiana. Other members of the executive team have been out visiting locations in other states, Canada, and Europe. Wherever we go, we are **truly inspired by the incredible care we see from our store employees**— they are cleaning down surfaces every hour, helping guests stay safe with social distancing, and showing customers where to find emergency needs. We are hearing great feedback from our customers— customers who also just need a kind conversation in an increasingly isolated world.
>
> I have made it clear to the entire leadership team that **at all cost, the health and safety of our employees and customers is our first priority**. We will have cash register barriers up across the network this week, supplies are on the way, and we will do all we can—working harder and smarter than ever before—to support our stores in making it easier for our customers. And, we will continue to rely on the army of thousands of support office employees who are giving all they can to the business to create impactful solutions for our communities.

I also shared at this time that Alain Bouchard, Couche-Tard's founder and chair of the board of directors, and I were forgoing all of our salary for a period of time, and that each member of the executive leadership team was giving 20% of their salary to seed a COVID-19 ACT Employee Assistance Fund. It was important to show our team members, especially in our stores, that we were in this together, and that we would help our most significantly impacted everyday heroes move through this pandemic. We opened the fund to contributions from across the company and generous donations poured in. With the fund, we have been able to help many families of team members who have passed from complications around the virus. My heart breaks when I think about the team members we have lost to this deadly virus. I try to find some consolation knowing that this fund has been of some, at least financial, help to their loved ones.

We also had communities that were hurting, really hurting, and we took a hard look at ourselves and our services to see how we could help. We asked ourselves, "What are we most known for?" Safe to say, beverages and fuel. So we started with an idea from our Ireland business unit to give away free coffee to first responders and healthcare workers. It was incredibly well received by our customers there and made our store team members feel like they were making a difference. From there, we expanded it across our network and enlarged the offer to giving away hot and cold free beverages. We also gave them out to our own store team members, who had clearly become frontline heroes as well. Over a million free beverages were given out over the next few weeks.

Looking at the growing issue of food insecurity, we recognized we could use our fuel business to do good. The global marketing team under chief marketing officer Kevin Lewis had an idea to team up with Feeding America to give a free meal for every gallon of fuel purchased at our locations. I agreed, again trusting my leadership with the idea, and within a week—or maybe it was just a few days—we had a campaign across all our U.S. business units to give twenty-five million meals to Feeding America. Soon after, we decided that was not ambitious enough and upped it to forty million meals, and we set up a similar campaign to give five million meals in Canada. We stopped officially counting after giving away forty-five million meals, though it was more, and it fills me with immense pride to know that we were truly part of the solution in the communities where we work and live.

Of course, we also had a business to run, and it was a business under threat with societies under lockdown and fuel volumes, essential to our bottom line, drastically down for months on end. Every week, I had a meeting with my top leadership team to look at business continuity plans, and along the way we made some tough decisions to cut capital expenses and make small staff reductions. We also had to walk away from what we once considered growth opportunities. At the beginning of my story, I shared my excitement about acquiring Caltex in Australia. By the end of April, we had to walk away from that deal, and I wrote the following to team members:

> This was not an easy decision, but a necessary one that I am proud of as it both reflects our disciplined approach to acquisitions as well as the difficult times surrounding the COVID-19 pandemic. We have been excited to bring Caltex into the family as we have seen it as a strong strategic fit and instrumental to our Asia Pacific growth journey. However, the COVID-19 situation has created a high level of uncertainty, especially to the outlook for many businesses globally including Caltex. On top of that, it is important that at ACT, we remain focused on managing our own business through this period and continue to put the health, safety and well-being of our employees, customers and the communities at the forefront of our financial planning.

Stories kept coming in from across the company about how local teams were keeping their local business going and taking care of our customers. In Caribou, Maine, one of our newest team members made headlines around the world with her unique delivery system. Hannah Lucas took it upon herself to deliver supplies from our stores to vulnerable members of her local community by using her husky dog sled team. I loved hearing about how Hannah and her dogs galloped across snowy fields in sleds filled with Circle K goods. In Ireland, which was under some of our strictest confinement orders, stores decided to introduce new outdoor products and sell them outside the store. With garden centres closed and more time spent at home, customers started coming to Circle K Ireland to purchase gardening and BBQ products. Again, local leadership was empowered to make it work. They did not need to ask permission, and as a result we were able to innovate and execute quicker than ever before.

Spring turned to summer. By now, masks were required by everyone at all of our global locations, COVID procedures started to become strangely routine, and there were momentary flashes of hope that we were turning a corner in the pandemic. These hopes were quickly followed by setbacks, new strains of the virus, and new lockdowns. Along the way, we decided to check in with our team members with a quick "pulse" survey. We wanted to know if they were getting what they needed in terms of communication and support during these difficult days. The first pulse survey, as well as our annual Gallup engagement survey done every spring, showed overwhelmingly that team members were more engaged at work than ever before. This bolstered my confidence that we were on the right path, as can be seen in this email:

> These survey results show us **doing a lot right**—especially in terms of having and communicating a clear plan of action and keeping our teams well informed and well prepared. If there is a silver lining to this crisis, it is that it has brought out the best in our culture and in our people. We have seen caring leadership across the network and our teams working closer together, which will only further strengthen our commitment to grow together as ONE TEAM.

As the weeks rolled into the fall, we worried about how we could keep up that ONE TEAM spirit. By now, I had sat in more digital meetings than I'd ever imagined possible. My spirits were sagging, and I knew we had to look hard at how to keep our culture motivated and not let COVID fatigue get us down. I shared my concern with team members:

> What is on my mind today is the continual and lasting impact of COVID-19, both the physical toll that it is taking on team members and customers and the emotional toll of what has become known as "COVID-fatigue." Almost nine months after we first learned of this virus, many of our store team members continue to wear face masks throughout their work day, many support office team members continue to work remotely without the joy of interacting with colleagues, friends and loved ones, and parts of our network have returned to

lockdown conditions. Unfortunately, instead of the numbers declining, covid infections are going up across the globe.

Recently, I asked the leadership to present concrete plans to combat COVID-fatigue. I know COVID and fun do not usually go together, but I truly believe we all need a little laughter to get us to the other side of the pandemic. During our executive leadership meeting earlier this week, I heard some really encouraging and engaging ideas, and I know that you will hear soon from your local leadership about plans for your team.

Honestly, in some ways, keeping our team spirit up often felt more challenging than running the business. Many members of the leadership are operators at heart, and putting together team-building activities and supporting mental health on this level was uncharted territory for us. As always, we trusted that local leadership knew their teams and customers best: we took our cues from them and shared their best practices across the organization.

We also dedicated ourselves to communication campaigns centred on not letting our COVID guard down and promoting the promise of the vaccines. I never expected the resistance to COVID vaccinations that became evident around our network. However, I firmly believed from the beginning that mass vaccinations were the only way through this pandemic, and I asked my entire management team to reinforce this message. I wrote the following to explain my position to team members:

Believe in the vaccine: I do. The leadership does. The company does. We believe that vaccines are the best and safest option to protect your health and the health of your family and friends and that we need a vaccinated workforce to continue being part of the solution in the communities we serve. We will not mandate vaccines at this point, but we highly encourage you to get your vaccination as soon you can. We have a dedicated team looking into when the vaccine may become available in your area, how you can receive it free of charge, and how we will prioritize our frontline workforce. We want to make it as easy as possible for you to get the vaccination. Please know that we are carefully reviewing the science behind the vaccines to make sure they hold the same promise for all our diverse communities. If you have any questions, reach out to your HR representative, and we will get your further information as soon as available.

As we all waited for vaccine drives to begin, and as I tried to not let my COVID guard down, I too contracted the virus in February 2021. I immediately went into quarantine and consulted with the executive leadership team about next steps. My illness never rose to the level of needing to inform shareholders, but I knew I needed to let my team members know:

I am writing to you today to let you know that I recently tested positive for COVID-19. While I have had classic symptoms of the virus, I am now feeling better and am optimistic that my case will be a mild one. I want to share this with you because—as I have said many times—we are all in this together, ONE TEAM. It is important that together we do not let our COVID guard down and together we get to the other side of this pandemic.

A few things that are important for you to know: first, I have not had any contact with other team members in the days prior to my diagnosis or since my positive test. I am in quarantine now and will remain so until I am symptom free and have isolated myself for the required amount of time. Also, over the last several days, I have been working remotely and will continue to do so. For the leadership team, it has been business as usual, and if there are any changes in my health that warrant attention, I will inform all team members.

One year into this painful pandemic, I know many of you—too many—have either been ill, spent time taking care of others suffering from the virus, or have grieved over the loss of loved ones. As we wait for the promise of the vaccine and brighter times in the future, we must continue to commit ourselves to not letting our COVID guard down.

I was touched by how many reached out to me, to see how I was doing. As leaders, when the pandemic entered its second year, we kept focusing on the business, innovating for the future, and keeping the health and safety of our team members and customers at the forefront of all our decision making. When that Gallup survey came around again, we broke our record of the previous year with engagement over 90%. This score was higher than almost all our retailer peers. Once again, it was time for me to write that letter for our annual report, and again, the pandemic was front and centre:

> Have no doubt—this year was not easy. A year ago, when I wrote this letter, we were only three months into the pandemic, and it had already made us a better, stronger company. Now, twelve months later, the virus not only persisted, in many areas it worsened—impacting our lives, our neighborhoods and our business. Incredibly, it also prepared us for the future as we grew stronger together, searched harder and quicker for solutions, and spread our wings into Asia to serve new regions and customers. Along the way, we strengthened our financial foundation, securing the way for future growth.

My main message this time could be summarized in a single phrase:

> When I look back at this year, one word comes to mind and that word is "gratitude." My gratitude goes out to all our team members for their continued commitment to each other and the business during this difficult year. It is only because of their hard work, engagement, and courage that our company culture and balance sheet are stronger than ever before, and that we are ready for the future—a future beyond the pandemic, where we can continue to make our customers' lives a little bit easier every day!

As I finish writing, a year and a half after the pandemic began, I am watching with concern the rise of the delta variant, especially in our U.S.

market. There is an uncomfortable sense of déjà vu as we once again institute a mask mandate in the U.S. and continue to push the promise of the
vaccines. Yet I am cautiously optimistic that brighter days are ahead.
Vaccination rates are especially strong in our Canadian regions and progressing well in our European markets. As I am vaccinated, I have been
back on the road, visiting stores and long-time team members. I am eagerly
looking forward to trips to Canada and Europe as well as an opportunity
to meet our new team members in Hong Kong. With this new wave of the
virus, as so often before, I am also reflecting on what I learned as a CEO
during COVID. To be honest, what I learned was actually nothing new to
me—trust your team and say thank you. I learned once again that this
simple formula works. It has for us during COVID, and we are now a
better, stronger company.

FINNING

For those who spent their childhood playing with sandbox toys, working at Finning is a dream. The Vancouver-based company is the world's largest Caterpillar equipment dealer. It has thirteen thousand employees who get their hands dirty selling and servicing bulldozers, excavators, dump trucks, and a host of specialized machines for clients in sectors such as mining, construction, and forestry.

In normal times, Finning president and chief executive officer Scott Thomson is a road warrior, working with teams and customers in the U.K., Ireland, Chile, Argentina, and Bolivia, along with Western Canada. However, there are no normal times in a global health crisis.

Finning, a company founded in 1933, was among the first wave of Canadian businesses to experience the business impact of COVID-19. In the winter of 2020, the company's executives in England warned that customers were shutting down projects as employees called in sick and authorities locked down communities. For Thomson and his team, the pandemic meant balancing the needs of clients who needed equipment for essential work with the healthcare needs of a workforce on three continents.

Finning recruited Thomson to be CEO in 2013. The native of British Columbia's Okanagan Valley started out on his corporate journey after earning an undergraduate degree from Queen's University and an MBA from the University of Chicago. Thomson spent the first part of his career in finance, with Royal Bank of Canada and Goldman Sachs. In 2003, he decided running companies would be more satisfying than raising money for them and joined the executive ranks at Bell Canada Enterprises. In 2008, he returned to Western Canada as chief financial officer at Calgary-based Talisman Energy.

Scott Thomson

AUGUST 2021

The Uncertainty at the Beginning

When people ask me to describe how I felt at the outset of the pandemic when it hit Canada in early 2020, I immediately remember the fear. The kind of fear that you feel in every fibre of your being, that consumes you and leaves you feeling helpless, almost paralyzed. My fear at the time was due to the vastness of the unknown. I, like so many others, had no play-book, no precedent, and no case study to navigate the immediate and life-threatening issues we faced. What I did know is that the leadership team and I were going to have to make decisions that would impact thousands of people's lives.

My concerns started percolating in January, as we, like many others, were keeping an eye on the situation in China related to potential supply chain constraints post–Chinese New Year. Not long after that, the leader of our U.K. and Ireland business, Dave Primrose, started updating our leadership team about how COVID was impacting our operations and the broader community in Europe. It was becoming very clear that it wasn't just an issue in China and that Europe would become the global early warning system for just how immense COVID would be. In hindsight, the pace and force of the challenges we faced were far beyond the "worst-case scenario" we imagined.

"Scott, things aren't letting up," said Dave Primrose, who had called me very early one morning in March. Dave was just over a year into his new role, moving overseas from Canada to take up a new challenge with enthusiasm and energy. I knew the situation must be bad for him to call me at this hour. Dave said, "Employee health and safety is a growing concern for us here now and customers are pulling their purchase orders, cancelling service appointments, and declining sales calls. There is a major hesitation to do anything at all right now. It's time. We need to start taking significant actions around what we do about protecting our employees, as well as cost and inventory management."

Dave's conviction around the seriousness of the situation resonated with me. Hearing him tell me we needed to act, now, really hit home. This was a pivotal moment. A worry that was just beneath the surface earlier in the year, when Dave started updating us, began to grow. We were scheduled to have our weekly Finning leadership team meeting in a few hours. I realized that session had to include the first step in our response to the pandemic, primarily ensuring employee health and safety, and then getting a granular understanding of our outstanding capital and inventory commitments across the global business.

Triaging a Global Business

Our regular meeting agenda was discarded, and our sole focus became COVID and our preparedness. We aligned around the fact that this was a situation that would eventually come to Western Canada and South America, a reality that was hard to grasp given the lack of cases and the lack of concern from the local media and health authorities. The word "pandemic" was yet to be used.

The meeting was peppered with questions, as each country was at a different stage when it came to COVID impact and response, yet every question raised was legitimate. I knew we did not have the luxury of time to spend on the unknowns, so I took a firm line. We wouldn't be expending any additional capital until we had data to review.

We discussed the fact that most of the important variables were out of our control, like market conditions, customer reaction, and supply chain performance. We also had a keen awareness that each of our teams in the different regions would have to adapt within rapidly changing health authority and government regulations. As the U.K. and Europe were being devastated by COVID in the spring of 2020, the effects had yet to be felt by our South American employees, who would bear the brunt of COVID much later.

We all knew we were dealing with a difficult issue in the U.K. and

Ireland, but we weren't all convinced we had to make the tough calls yet. Part of the challenge was getting the whole team aligned around the concept that this was a severe situation, a global health crisis that would ultimately spread to Western Canada and South America with the same force that it was currently having in the U.K. We also had a new executive team that had not worked together long, and in some cases we had not even all met in person. In addition to Dave, Greg Palaschuk was our newly minted CFO; Kevin Parkes, the head of our Canadian operations, was a year in his role; Juan Pablo Amar, our leader in South America, was mere months in his role; and our general counsel, Jane Murdoch, had just formally joined our leadership team. We hadn't gelled as a team yet, hadn't found our rhythm around trust and expertise of each leader, so the debate on solutions was fragmented. I couldn't fault anyone for this—I can't imagine being new in an executive role and being thrown into a crisis like this. I knew I needed to be firm and clear in our way forward. We settled in and started framing out the core elements of our plan.

Step one, we agreed we would stop any further ordering of equipment until we had a clear understanding of our outstanding commitments with our suppliers. Fortunately, we had already reduced our inventory purchasing as we entered 2020 because of our expectation that the market was slowing based on the insights we were getting from our connected machine utilization data. But stopping our equipment ordering in its entirety until we had better information was a monumental decision given that our business is based on selling the machines used in sectors such as construction, mining, infrastructure, and forestry to our longstanding customers. The key for us was the lack of clarity around whether customers would still take the equipment they had ordered and whether they would put in any additional orders in the coming year. An aggressive outreach plan with clients was essential to fully understand the pipeline of orders and our customers' willingness to deploy additional capital in the face of emerging concerns around the pandemic, and we were also going to have to rely on our ability to manage relationships all along our supply chain. Difficult conversations were inevitable, but fortunately our sales and supply chain teams had strong relationships, and we were determined to find win-win solutions for all stakeholders.

Step two was to stop any non-critical capital investment and double down on the cost reduction work we had already started in 2019. We knew this was prudent for the business itself, though we did worry about the concern it might raise for our customers, suppliers, partners, and of course, more than anyone else, our employees. All discretionary spending, travel, and investments were immediately stopped to conserve our cash flow. This decision was one of the easiest from a common-sense perspective, and our employees and customers were gracious in their understanding given the uncertainty.

Step three was to reach out to our credit partners and ask for an extension of our credit facility just in case we ran into financial difficulties if our sales dried up for an extended period. We knew we might not need it but didn't want to be scrambling at the last minute. I was relieved when we made that call and received a positive and supportive response from our bankers. We were ready to have this conversation thanks to the hard work and efforts of our finance team, who, under Greg's leadership, had been running a variety of scenarios to see how long we could keep our thirteen-thousand-person global business on track. We were able to expand our credit facility from $1.3 billion to $1.8 billion in twenty-one days from first call to close, which was incredible velocity at a critical time.

Step four was to put our chief human resources officer in charge of COVID emergency response, which would include daily early morning leadership team meetings, followed by daily afternoon meetings with our health and safety team to review COVID cases across the business. We kept these efforts up until the end of the first wave, and this commitment helped us manage the nearly eight hundred cases that we tracked through the global business during the first, second, and third waves. We made the decision early to ensure each action we took would always consider our employees first. We knew if we took care of our employees, our employees would in turn take care of our customers.

And finally, in an unprecedented move meant to ensure the safety of our employees, we landed on a plan to ensure those who were not customer-facing were sent home to work, a decision that required a huge amount of trust and the hope that we wouldn't lose productivity and connectivity. Like what we planned as a global leadership team, we would encourage all our leaders to have start-of-day and end-of-day virtual meetings with their teams to set a new cadence at the beginning of work from home. Nothing concerned me more than ensuring our employees remained healthy and well. Some of this decision was to be made for us quite quickly when the U.K. government mandated furlough for most of the U.K. workforce. But for Canada and South America, the directive from governments was not as immediate or as clear, so we had to make the decision ourselves, one that would require a delicate balance between maintaining essential service levels and the health, safety, and mental well-being of our thirteen thousand employees.

At the end of the meeting, we sat in a moment of silence as the realization sank in that no sector or industry was going to be spared. The meeting was difficult as we had made some material decisions that we knew would impact on business and people without a clear view on how or when the pandemic would come to Canada and South America. It was at times a very challenging conversation, but it's important that I recognize and give credit to the team as we came out of that meeting aligned and ready to execute, which I am convinced set the stage and tone to help us navigate through the pandemic.

We're All in This Together

Prior to the start of the pandemic, we had been working diligently on cost reduction initiatives across the entire business. COVID impacts made it clear that we would quickly have to accelerate these plans. Sooner than we had planned, we would have to make the very difficult decision to revisit our business structure and do the reorganization and headcount reductions in our South American and Canadian oil sands businesses. In Western Canada we would soon be dealing with the double impact of COVID and lower oil prices. Instead of easing these impacts in over a year we now needed to expedite them in just one month. This decision, more than any other, made me feel sick to my stomach. Letting employees go with so much uncertainty out there didn't sit well with me and weighed heavily on my mind. Our South American colleagues were navigating pandemic uncertainty on the back of social unrest, and many of these employees had no government safety net. It was an extremely complex situation. We started with mandating our employees to take vacation to manage costs, but it was not enough. I recall numerous difficult conversations on headcount reduction between me; our head of South America, Juan Pablo Amar; and our board of directors, with whom we were meeting regularly. The board prompted us to think through alternative scenarios, challenged our assumptions, and ultimately provided us unwavering support in our decisions. We decided to go ahead with reducing our workforce in South America. As difficult as it was to announce layoffs in a time of uncertainty, I am proud that we treated employees with respect and compassion.

In Canada, we had to find other ways to manage through and save the highest number of jobs. Sitting down with the executive team, we talked through many, many other options.

"What if we asked every employee in the Canadian operating business, including the board, to take a decrease in some way—everyone contributes so it is fair and equitable?" asked our CFO, Greg Palaschuk. "This would go a long way to helping us keep as many people employed as we can." I knew that move could be unpopular and increase fear and uncertainty among employees, but we were quickly running out of other viable options. And we were fresh from negotiating new collective agreements in Canada, so our union partnerships were improving but not in an ideal place to have this kind of conversation.

Fortunately, we had recently hired a new labour relations director, a talented negotiator with an exceptional track record, by the name of Manny Galan, who came to us from Canadian National Railway. He agreed that we should be up front with our union partners and ask them to be part of the solution through encouraging flexible work weeks, early retirement options, vacation use, and job sharing for their members. From there, the union would vote on the proposed approach and we were hopeful they would rally behind what was needed for the benefit of the enterprise.

We embarked on developing a plan in Canada to proportionally decrease salaries of the board and the executive and to offer all salaried employees the choice of accepting a salary decrease, moving to a reduced work week with a corresponding decrease in pay, using up their vacation allotment, or taking an unpaid leave of absence. Luckily the union was game and took the idea to their membership. We got support for a ninety-day plan with a variety of options. This approach, while rocky at first, was a show of solidarity.

Taking the time to educate employees about the options, we held remote Q&A sessions to help employees feel comfortable, and by mid-April we had activated our plans and employees showed us that they were in it with us, which gave me a sense of reassurance.

Around the same time that we implemented the salary reductions and ninety-day plan with our union employees, the Canadian government announced the Canadian Emergency Wage Subsidy (CEWS) to help support businesses in keeping as many employees as possible. The decision to apply for this subsidy was one of the more challenging ones we faced. While we qualified for the program, as we had already seen a drop of significantly more than 30% of our revenue, was it the right thing to do? Taking CEWS would not reverse the headcount reductions and the other cost-saving measures we had already taken in March and April, but it would help us preserve more than five hundred of our highly skilled technician-level roles, ensure we could continue our apprenticeship programs that help us guarantee our future workforce, and put us in a good position to rehire quickly when we started to see market recovery. We would continue paying shareholder dividends but not increase them and stop share buybacks to ensure we remained true and transparent in the decisions we were making to achieve our goal of maintaining as much of our workforce as possible.

The leadership team ran scenario after scenario, talking through the optics and reputational impacts of taking a subsidy, and made the call to make our application in June, which we continued to do for the balance of 2020. We were transparent in all our reporting and proactive in indicating we had taken the subsidy, being completely upfront with our employees and other stakeholders about the how and the why. In hindsight, I am glad we made that call and I stand by that decision. As bumpy as it was for a while—we got negative press and pushback from employees for accepting the funds—in the end, it protected jobs and helped us rebound much more quickly by keeping as many skilled workers as possible who are so essential to Finning's success.

The Importance of Communication and Embracing Technology

On top of the Finning leadership team's daily meetings, we made efforts to communicate with our employees and customers, constantly. We held virtual town halls to tackle tough questions around financial viability and contingency plans, and every executive, including me, called their senior leaders often to check in and ensure employees had what they needed to be successful.

We also worked hard to ensure our shareholders and stakeholders stayed informed. We issued public corporate updates in late March and mid-April to share the news that we had activated our business continuity plan, were open for business with a functioning supply chain, and were executing on our approach to immediately reduce costs including top-down compensation reductions. This went a long way in settling down investor and stakeholder fears.

Looking back, Finning was positioned better than most companies to transition to a remote work environment. Thanks to the foresight of our chief digital officer, Dave Cummings, and his team, we had invested a significant amount of time and money in 2018 and 2019 as we worked to lay the right foundation to digitize our business and engage with our customers differently, whenever and however they needed us. We had made great progress in connecting customer machines to better understand data for parts inventory and predictive servicing, and we'd revamped Finning.com to accelerate online ordering. Thanks to that early-stage investment, much of our salaried workforce had the right tools and access to be able to continue to serve our customers from home.

Enabling employees to communicate effectively and effortlessly was also key. We had a strong relationship with Microsoft and had started to migrate to the Office 365 suite of products, including Microsoft Teams, which we started using for collaboration in mid-2019. Moving to a model involving more work being done remotely meant we needed to ensure secure, reliable channels to engage with one another, and many in the business were waiting to transition to Teams from older platforms like Skype and BlueJeans. By summer, every employee in Finning who needed to had access to an Office 365 email and Teams on their company mobile device for meetings, chats, and collaborations, which was no small achievement during a pandemic.

As important as adapting our remote workforce were changes for our frontline staff, who were essential in keeping our business going while we figured out what varying degrees of normal looked like. Our priority was determining our "skeleton crews"—who needed to be "in facility" for the business to keep running, despite the fact our face-to-face customer business had significantly decreased in the first six months, from March to August of 2020. We developed strict protocols for all staff reporting into a facility, including sanitization and hygiene requirements, daily health checks done through an app, booking of workspace ahead of time if employees needed to report to corporate offices, as well as processes for potential COVID contacts, including our own internally developed contact tracing program. We made a commitment to support employees if they contracted COVID and could not work, allowing for sick days and longer-term vacation use as needed to ensure they didn't face financial hardship.

In the early days of the pandemic, we engaged at all levels of government across our global footprint to ensure we would qualify as an essential service. Our people undertake critical work like maintenance on backup power systems for airports, hospitals, and wastewater treatment facilities. In addition, our machines are used in the maintenance of important infrastructure like roads and bridges and for mining of materials, including in the oil sands. Our local relationships facilitated getting us our essential service designation, which gave us incredible peace of mind knowing we would be able to continue to serve our customers.

Juggling Safety, Mental Health, and Wellness

One of the things that quickly became evident to me was that, unlike any other crisis I have faced as a leader, COVID would be all encompassing. COVID was something that you couldn't get away from, no matter if you were at work or at home. I worried constantly about employees and their families getting COVID and getting very sick. The fear that we could lose people was on my mind from the moment I woke up, every single day. I was hell bent on ensuring we had zero fatalities, and I wanted our people to feel that our leadership team was committed to the highest standards of safety during this difficult period.

After a year and a half, in a team of thirteen thousand members, we tracked just over eight hundred cases, with the majority occurring in Chile. With deep sadness, I report that we lost two South American colleagues to COVID. Even though neither of those cases was contracted at work, it was devastating, demoralizing, and deeply painful to lose two valued members of the Finning family.

Despite the challenges we were facing with cases, our employees in the office and on the front line continued to show up for Finning, every day. Our leadership could see, however, that COVID was starting to take its toll. Our employees were experiencing a greater level of stress and fatigue, which led to an increasing number of safety incidents on our front line and a higher level of burnout among our work-from-home employees.

We immediately began outreach programs for employees, using resources from our benefits providers. We created online training for our leaders to help give them the tools and resources they needed to hold safety talks with the front line and identify signs of stress or mental health issues among their teams.

On the front line, we reinforced employee accountability, reminding our employees it was okay to say no to a job that was unsafe to perform if they were tired, stressed, or not focused on the task at hand. We reminded our teams to speak up if they saw a better, safer way to deliver on a job, not only for themselves but for their colleagues as well. I am convinced Finning's safety culture was a differentiator, as our employees followed guidelines closely, took changes seriously, and adjusted as necessary to stay on top of updates. We received feedback from our customers that they appreciated our commitment, and we saw a material increase in customer loyalty scores throughout the year.

Light at the End of the Tunnel

We started to see a turning point in late October 2020 across the business. Customers were reaching out and engaging with us again, reactivating projects, and planning for 2021. Notable improvements in our connected machine utilization data gave us the confidence to start ordering inventory again.

Thanks to these insights, we got out in front of many of the supply chain issues that some of our competitors are now facing. This early window of enthusiasm, plus the work we had done to keep the business running lean and focused, was the green light we needed to restore salaries and begin hiring particularly frontline technicians. We would continue to control what we could control and keep an eye on global markets to guide us in making our next moves. The proof was in our financial results for the first half of 2021, which highlighted higher earnings than in the pre-pandemic period despite still seeing revenues significantly below these levels.

Vaccinations were starting to make the rounds in each of our regions, kicking off in the U.K. and Ireland, which also helped our confidence in getting back to work with a more normal cadence. Despite this, we remained cautious on the health and safety front at our facilities and offices, continuing to follow local restrictions, and those who could continue to work from home did so. This proved a wise choice, as we saw an aggressive third wave in the winter of 2020–2021, a fourth in the summer of 2021 with significant variations in cases, and government and health authority response across our global footprint. There was a great deal of continued uncertainty and variability in each of our operating areas, so we focused on controlling what we knew we could control—namely, keeping our employees, customers, and communities safe.

Learnings, Realizations, and Growth: The Road Ahead

Managing a business through a crisis like a global pandemic, is, I hope, a once-in-a-career experience. What I do know is that, as a leader, my perspective on what really matters has ultimately changed and so much learning and growth came out of this experience. I can't adequately express the range of emotions I felt daily—like being on a psychological roller coaster and not being able to get off the ride. Through all the challenges and decisions we navigated, I have an overwhelming sense of pride in our leadership group. Finning is fortunate to have a diverse team with different experiences and from different geographies. This global perspective was critical in producing a better outcome for all stakeholders. I am also humbled to lead an organization with thirteen thousand employees around the globe who were committed and who stepped up every day, despite challenging personal circumstances. Their performance was inspiring, and I will forever be in awe of the stories of compassion and support they showed one another, our customers, and our communities.

First, a key business reflection for me was understanding that we made the right call in staying calm and making difficult decisions quickly, using the data and information we had. There were processes we needed to implement and improvements we needed to make that were not received well by everyone. I remember getting phone calls and emails from shareholders, partners, and employees questioning the reasons why we made some of the harsh and abrupt decisions we did. There was no lack of criticism or, in some cases, borderline hysteria. As a leader it is difficult to be unpopular and it's a heavy weight to carry when your decisions impact people's lives in times of uncertainty. But being a leader means you must make decisions that find a balance, for both the short-term and long-term viability of the business. Fear of how you will be judged cannot hold you back, particularly when decisions need to be made quickly and decisively. It's crucial to realize and come to terms with the fact that some things are out of your control and that your efforts need to be focused squarely on those things you can control. Controlling what you can is a message I have emphasized, and will continue to emphasize, within my organization.

Second, in a crisis, relationships matter, and you quickly find out who you can rely on. As an eighty-eight-year-old company, Finning has spent decades building trusted partnerships with suppliers, customers, lenders, shareholders, and our employees. Whether it was having the trust and confidence that I had the right people internally in the right places giving the best guidance, or our customers trusting that if they came to us we would find solutions for them, or our major suppliers and lenders trusting and backing us when we had to ask for support—our trusted relationships at all levels have come out of this pandemic even stronger than when we went in, and for that we can be truly grateful.

Third, staying close to the business, in terms of really understanding the day-to-day granular work that is being done, is crucial to being able to understand the impacts of your decisions and gives you the ability to move with more velocity. Normally, I would say that, as leaders, we could operate with a high-level overview of the business and delegate as needed. But this situation was anything but normal. We needed to have leaders spending time intimately understanding the details and the impact that each decision we would make would have on the business, both immediately and in the long term. It was exhausting poring over data, running scenarios, checking assumptions, and getting feedback in real time from the business, but it was so necessary. For us, I believe it has changed the level of accountability and visibility into the how and why we do what we do as a business, for the better.

Finally, I cannot understate the importance of embracing innovation, thinking differently, and enabling the business through technology. We benefited early through the groundwork we laid on digitizing our business and offering flexibility for our customers when it came to parts, service, and support. We also made the right call in investing in the needed technology to enable our employees to work remotely, which set us up to have the continuity we needed to keep the business moving when the status quo was no longer an option. We also allowed flexibility in how we worked with our customers during this period, understanding clearly that the way we had always done things wasn't going to work in many cases. Permitting client relationships to evolve in unorthodox ways made a major difference in how we were able to support our customers. This is the kind of thinking we will carry forward as we continue to serve our customers, permitting and empowering our workforce to think about how to get the best outcome and move to action.

Personally, I learned a lot about the importance of work–life balance that I don't think I embodied or modelled well in the past. Working from home with two children under six years old proved to be challenging, but the time spent at home strengthened my relationship with my wife and children. Being present was a critical realization for me and is something that I will keep pushing down into the business, both with my direct team and every employee at Finning. Sometimes we wear our busy schedules as a badge of honour, and what COVID really landed for me is that while work is important and gives me a sense of value, it should not be what defines us. Make time for yourself, and make time for others. Time is a precious commodity and cannot be replaced.

Moving forward, I'm excited for the future of our company and for the continued growth and development of our people. Although we weren't completely unscathed, we navigated the pandemic admirably and are thriving during the recovery. Although revenue is still 15% below pre-pandemic levels, we posted record quarterly earnings in the second quarter of 2021. Our employees have recognized our leadership through the pandemic, and we are stronger and more connected than ever as a team. The future for Finning is bright as we are even more committed to delivering the best solutions for our customers in a way that benefits all stakeholders.

FOUR SEASONS HOTELS AND RESORTS

John Davison started 2020 with a lengthy "to-do" list. Just over a year into his tenure as chief executive officer at Four Seasons Hotels and Resorts, the world's leading luxury hospitality company, Davison and his team were capitalizing on record growth with plans to open new properties in Madrid, Bangkok, Sicily, New Orleans, and more.

They were also driving forward the continued expansion of one of the fifty-nine-year-old company's fastest growing businesses—attaching the Four Seasons luxury brand and service ethos to private residential developments.

And then there was the Four Seasons Private Jet—first launched in 2015 to fly guests between iconic Four Seasons hotels on bespoke itineraries in a style unmatched at thirty thousand feet. With sold-out itineraries and newly announced plans to build a brand-new luxury Airbus aircraft to replace the initial Four Seasons Private Jet, the company was flying high.

But then hotel managers at Four Seasons properties in China began calling the Toronto head office in January, warning of a serious flu outbreak, centred in the city of Wuhan. Within weeks, the company's hotels in Beijing and Macau shut down. Davison was among the first CEOs in Canada to confront COVID-19.

Four Seasons ranks as one of the country's most global companies, operating more than 120 hotels in 47 countries. It is a business that is greatly dependent on travel and in the winter of 2020 Four Seasons went into survival mode.

Davison joined the finance team at Four Seasons in 2002, after a fourteen-year stint at big-screen movie chain IMAX, where he was president and chief operating officer. Three years after his joining, Four Seasons named the former KPMG accountant its chief financial officer. Davison became CEO in 2019, after serving as interim leader for several months. The father of three is also on the board of directors at iconic apparel company Canada Goose and IMAX China Holdings.

Leading Four Seasons means building on the legacy of Isadore (Issy) Sharp, who launched the company in 1961 with the Four Seasons Motor Hotel. Located in what was then considered an undesirable area in downtown Toronto, the hotel, which offered high-end service to business travellers, became an urban oasis that attracted locals and travellers alike.

Sharp, one of Canada's great entrepreneurs, presided over the first phase of his company's global growth. In 2007 he partnered with Microsoft founder Bill Gates's personal holding company Cascade Investment and Saudi billionaire Prince Al-Waleed bin Talal's Kingdom Holdings to take the company private. In the summer of 2021, Gates's company increased its stake in Four Seasons to 71% by purchasing half of Kingdom Holdings' interest. Sharp, through Triples Holdings Limited, retains his 5% stake in the company and remains involved in Four Seasons operations as chair and founder. He is mentioned, fondly, in any executive discussion of the company's strategy and values.

To carry on the journey that Issy Sharp started, Davison and his team would need to lead Four Seasons through an unprecedented global health crisis.

John Davison

JUNE 2021

I remember it was a Thursday. It was March 12, 2020—the day after the World Health Organization declared a global pandemic. I shut down my computer, left my office, said good night to colleagues on my way out, and drove home. We—the members of the Four Seasons Executive Leadership Team—had decided to temporarily close our global head office in Toronto, for two weeks at most, we thought.

It has been an impactful exercise to reflect on all that has occurred since then. As I did, I realized that this is not a story about leadership or about the pandemic. At Four Seasons, this story is about the strength, resilience, and dedication of our people. Our success and our ability to overcome this challenge is a testament to the incredible, compassionate people we have working at all levels of the organization. While we highlight certain people in the pages that follow, the true heroes were, and still are, our 40,000+ team members across our entire portfolio of hotels and resorts globally.

Every day I am inspired by the extraordinary efforts and creative ingenuity of our people. Some efforts were large scale, such as the opening of three of our hotels to house frontline workers in the early and most uncertain days of the pandemic; in other cases, our people quietly took action to help where they could, such as in Paris, where one of our chefs personally bought groceries and cooked meals for healthcare workers and first responders. Even as our people were caring for our guests and their local communities, they were looking out for each other too. In Bogota, a group of employees formed a spontaneous aid committee to support each other in smaller gestures, such as delivering groceries or lending a laptop for at-home learning. In Chiang Mai, employees opened a community pantry, offering surplus ingredients from the resort and even their own kitchens and gardens to those in need.

These stories are what motivated and inspired our leadership team during the pandemic's darkest days—the call to duty, the sense of urgent action, the skills and expertise tested and brought to bear, the tireless work effort and incredible energy of our people further define our company and our brand.

At the time we made the decision to close our head office, Four Seasons had just come off our best year ever in 2019. We were in a strong position and poised for even greater success. The company that Isadore Sharp founded with a single hotel in downtown Toronto in 1961 had grown to more than 120 hotels, resorts, and residences in more than 47 countries. We had an additional 50 projects in our pipeline, and our development team was continuing to evaluate opportunities to extend our global footprint into new and existing markets. We had tens of thousands of employees spread around the world at our hotels and resorts from Tokyo to Paris to Hawaii, including about 700 employees in our corporate offices in Toronto, New York, London, Dallas, Dubai, and Singapore.

Four Seasons is a hotel management company; under the Four Seasons brand, we operate hotels and resorts that are built and owned by investors. In all, we have about seventy owner partners, and we also have a committed group of long-term shareholders who are represented by our board of directors. Their unwavering, visionary support of our brand and culture, and of me personally, is critical to our business, never more so than during pandemic when they offered guidance during monthly and even weekly calls beyond our quarterly board meetings.

Our business model is complex and with many involved stakeholders: owners who trust Four Seasons with management contracts averaging eighty years (far above the industry norm), tens of thousands of employees who bring the Four Seasons experience to life every day, millions of guests who stay with us, and homeowners who live with us in more than 4,200 Four Seasons Private Residences. We also have a loyal following in our local communities among people who patronize the hundreds of restaurants, bars, and spas located within our hotels.

As someone who was used to spending each workday in the office, or on the road visiting our properties around the globe, it was an adjustment to a full work-from-home schedule, connecting with my colleagues on video conference calls but unable to see anyone in person. As the crisis unfolded, our schedules became all day, every day, and sometimes well into the night as we surfed the time zones virtually with colleagues worldwide. My three children are adults, and at that point my youngest son moved back home to join his older brother in living with us; so we now had virtual offices for three different companies in our home, with audit, tax, and advisory services firm KPMG operating out of the top floor, Four Seasons on the ground floor, and PricewaterhouseCoopers in the basement. For many others, makeshift "offices" on kitchen tables had suddenly become classrooms too, and we were all doing our best to adapt and make it work.

The pandemic was spreading fast and the challenges to our business were growing exponentially, but I remained confident. Our company was strong and so was our executive leadership team, having welcomed two new members in early 2020. We were working together better than ever before—and we were staying ahead of the pandemic-related challenges as best we could—even as our hotels started closing for extended periods.

The virus was spreading as borders closed, but many of us thought it could be contained, that here in Toronto the stay-at-home situation would perhaps last a few weeks at most. As weeks became months and months stretched to well over a year, the more vividly I remembered that last day in the office and my fateful prediction of a short duration.

For Four Seasons, the situation had already started to have a serious impact months earlier, at the beginning of January 2020.

There are currently eight Four Seasons hotels in Greater China, and we are in various stages of development with additional locations expected to open in the next few years. China is also a critically important outbound market. While we don't have a presence in Wuhan, we certainly paid close attention to those first reports of a new, fast-spreading, and deadly virus.

Almost immediately the virus had a direct impact on our business in the form of cancelled reservations. There was a scramble for information—so many questions and so few answers about this virus that did not yet have a name. Our president of hotel operations in the Asia-Pacific (APAC) region, Rainer Stampfer, started providing regular updates, keeping the rest of us informed of the latest developments, while here in Toronto we supported our hotels in the APAC region in any and every way we could.

Although so far the virus was contained in China, Christian Clerc, president of global operations, was paying particular attention from the beginning. With operational oversight of our global portfolio, he was concerned for all our properties, especially as the first cases outside China were reported. It was only a matter of time, he thought.

On January 23, the Chinese government shut down the city of Wuhan, and we had our first possible case, a guest in Singapore. Four days later, our hotels in Hangzhou and Macau were the first to close. Each of our properties in the region was experiencing its own challenges, based on local government and health agency directives, increasing numbers of cases, and the impact of border closings. Christian knew we needed to do more, so he assembled a cross-functional global response team and asked Rainer to provide a broader brief via conference call to this team of employees around the world.

On February 2, we issued new directives, this time to our entire global portfolio, apprising them of what we were doing and providing operational guidance, including updated health and safety protocols and cancellation policies as well as continually updated materials to help them communicate with guests and other stakeholders. It was alarming, no question, and there was also a precipitous drop in new bookings. But in early February at least, we did think the situation would be contained to some degree, at least in duration.

After all, we had been through this before. We've survived other viruses, like SARS, which was felt so acutely in Hong Kong and here at home in Toronto. We've had unexpected closures of hotels and resorts due to hurricanes, earthquakes, and other major weather events. And we persevered through the recession of 2008–2009 and 9/11. We know how to evolve business plans and adjust budgets when new hotel openings are delayed, or when we temporarily close an existing hotel to conduct renovations.

Our business was still in a very optimistic position. We were profitable and well capitalized; we had good cash flow and liquidity and the strong support of our shareholders. Our president of global business development and portfolio management, Bart Carnahan, and his team were signing new management contracts for new hotels and residential projects all over the world and we still had plans to open new hotels, resorts, and residences in the year ahead. Over the years we had expanded our business with the introduction of the Four Seasons Private Jet Experience, online retail, and more.

Yet by late February, as the virus began to spread more rapidly, I knew we had to start planning ahead—preparing for the worst but hoping for the best.

In January 2020, Allison Keppy joined us as chief financial officer and a pivotal member of our leadership team, filling the position I had previously held for fourteen years. We had armed her with a solid financial standing and an ambitious business plan for 2020, and she had already hit the ground running.

Soon enough, I was running alongside her as we rapidly adjusted business plans to respond to the pandemic's devastating impact on the travel and hospitality industry. We modelled and remodelled for every possible scenario. Region by region, country by country, hotel by hotel. And then we did it again and again in the coming weeks and months. We responded to new and daily developments, evolving direction from governments (not just in jurisdictions where we operate but also in those where our guests travel from), and emerging data and guidance from health authorities.

Our hotel owners were doing the same. After the 2008–2009 recession—until the pandemic the most challenging period in my career at Four Seasons—we worked with each of our hotels to put a plan in place that was meant to prepare for the possibility of dramatically reduced business levels and extended hotel closures for any reason, along with a plan for reopening and eventual recovery. This was the foundation for what we were able to quickly pull together as hypothetical scenarios became harsh realities.

Much of our work during this time focused on operations and finance. Both depended heavily on the counsel and guidance of our legal team, led by Sarah Cohen, our general counsel and corporate secretary and a critical member of our executive team. Working closely with Bart Carnahan, who oversees our global portfolio, the team held daily and then weekly calls during the early pandemic months to guide and support hotel teams and owners through myriad challenges unique to their properties and locations, helping them solve problems and manage their hotels in the short term without disrupting our long-term commitments and strategic planning.

After several of our hotels in China closed, the next big hit came in Italy, beginning in late February. We had two hotels there at the time, including in Milan, the capital of one of the earliest hot spots, the Lombardy region. Thankfully, we were already well versed at adapting the procedures and protocols we had created for our Asia Pacific properties by the time the virus began spreading throughout Europe.

As is so often the case at Four Seasons, lessons learned at one hotel will benefit many others. We encourage our people to make connections with colleagues around the world through job transfers, temporary assignments, and our employee travel program—all of which contribute to a broader sense of team, never more so than during the greatest challenge we've ever faced.

By February we knew that impacts to our North American business were imminent. We have more hotels in the United States than any other country, and critically, more than half of our guests worldwide come from North America. Our hotel and corporate teams were in overdrive, adapting our operating procedures, communicating with guests, supporting our employees working in the field, coping with massively reduced or no revenue, and so much more. Throughout March, our hotels were closing one after another, falling like dominoes.

As we witnessed the devastating impacts of the virus in Italy and other parts of Europe, it became clear that we would be in this for the long haul.

Our executive team was conferencing every day, seven days a week, working through countless micro-decisions as we reviewed every possible indicator in an effort to not only get through this but prepare the company and our hotels to emerge in a strong position. Breaking off into smaller groups in partnership with our board members, corporate colleagues, owner partners, and hotel teams battling it out on the ground, we were putting out fires everywhere.

Along with all of the minute-by-minute decisions, we were confronted with the overarching dilemma of being a travel company in a world where no one could travel. Our guests were having to cancel their travels—long-planned adventures abroad, family vacations, honeymoons, weddings, important business travel, meetings, events, and more. And so were we. All of us at Four Seasons share a love of travel and exploration, and whether travelling for work or through our employee travel program, we were stuck at home wondering what this all meant for our company.

It was at this time I knew we had to face one of the worst aspects of this crisis—the inevitable reduction of our global workforce. It was already happening in our hotels as it became clear that for some at least, closure would be extended for months. As a company, we'd been through this only a few times in our history, but that certainly did not make it any easier.

The Golden Rule—*treat others as you would like to be treated*—has been the guiding principle of Four Seasons ever since it was established as a core philosophy of the company by our founder, Isadore Sharp, early in our history. To this day, it is a mantra that every Four Seasons employee not only understands but lives and works by. In the same way we offer a warm welcome, personalized service, and the best possible experience to our guests, we strive to do the same for our colleagues. We are deeply connected by our culture. When asked what makes Four Seasons special, I share this as the key element. Many might assume my answer to be the physical hotels and resorts, which are wonderful too, of course.

With revenue reduced to near zero and plans for reopenings moving further and further into the future, as CEO I knew that we could not responsibly maintain a full workforce, much of which is funded by hotel owners, in the hopes that it would somehow all work out. These were the most difficult decisions I've had to make in my time as CEO.

Coincidently, and thankfully, we had just hired a new chief people and culture officer. Anna Filipopoulos had barely set foot in her new office—she and Allison had been in the midst of a global orientation tour—when we had to call her back home to Toronto, where her extensive experience in corporate restructuring and deep commitment to principled change management was required. Having Anna on our team was a godsend.

I knew the longer we waited to act, the more difficult it would become. We were holding regular "town calls" with our full corporate team, and I and other members of the management team were in constant contact with our people—colleagues who were working around the clock to take care of our guests and each other even as they were dealing with the personal stresses of the pandemic. We started to see more cases among our guests and employees, including in several of our employee housing facilities (in more remote locations, as well as locations with a more multinational staff, Four Seasons offers housing for employees). For all of us, the pandemic was now dominating our lives, our work, our families, and our communities.

We recognized we needed to act swiftly and with both precision and care. These were the principles that our executives, with the support of our board, agreed on. Anna took the lead.

We started with our very DNA, something we talk a lot about at Four Seasons. We take great pride in our corporate culture and we thrive because of it. We absolutely had to do this right. Openly, honestly, fairly, and with as much empathy as possible. As is often said, it's easy to lead during times of prosperity, but it's the challenging moments when our principles, values, and leadership skills are most tested.

And so we viewed these hard choices through several key lenses: guided by the Golden Rule, we worked hard to ensure that any colleague who had to leave us was supported and treated well. For those who remained, we made sure communications were clear and transparent, providing them with empathetic supports as much as possible.

Another lens looked further ahead. We thought about the people who would help bring us out of this and drive our recovery. Even further ahead, we thought about what we would need for the future we had been planning before the pandemic. We thought about tomorrow's leaders, and how they would learn and grow from this unprecedented challenge.

It was very important to me that we do this only once. I didn't want our remaining employees to have to look over their shoulders even as we asked more of them. We knew it would be painful, heartbreaking. But we thought and hoped that if we moved as quickly as was responsible and could tell them with confidence that this was it, we could begin the arduous process of moving forward.

Over a period of about a week in mid-April, we said farewell to nearly 20% of our corporate employees in Toronto and regional offices. As of this writing, there have been no further corporate layoffs at Four Seasons.

Meanwhile, in late March, the governor of New York tweeted the news that our hotel in Midtown Manhattan would offer free housing for frontline healthcare workers in what had rapidly become a pandemic hot spot. It was a wonderful offer by the New York hotel's owner, but we knew that it would be a complex operation requiring detailed scenario planning and training for employees to ensure everyone remained as safe as possible. Our already stringent hygiene standards and stepped-up protocols were scrutinized even more thoroughly, knowing that a vulnerable group of people would be staying together in one single building. We worked closely with Ecolab—a global company specializing in cleaning and disinfecting products, on-site support services, and public health expertise that we partner with in hygiene products—and International SOS, a health, security, and logistics company under the leadership of Professor Robert L. Quigley, MD, DPhil, senior vice-president and global medical director. I remember looking at floorplans that mapped out traffic patterns in public areas and inside guest rooms, as well as hospital-grade screening procedures with nursing staff at the hotel's entrance. The learning was extensive, so when our hotels in Riyadh and

Mumbai also opened to healthcare professionals later in the year, we were well prepared.

Concurrently, with about 70% of our portfolio of hotels and resorts temporarily closed, it was time to begin preparations for reopening plans. As a luxury hospitality company, we already had the highest of standards, but as we continued to enhance and adapt our protocols, we knew that our guests and our employees needed more. Our employees needed to feel confident returning to work, which in turn would help reassure our guests that they would be safe and well taken care of with Four Seasons. And so Lead With Care, our enhanced global health and safety program, was launched.

We also knew that our efforts had to be grounded in scientific and medical facts in a time of so much confusion. Christian Clerc, who is based in Washington, D.C., where he has also spent much of his more than two decades with Four Seasons, leveraged his network to search for an external consultant to help guide our efforts. He found a credible, internationally recognized academic institution that could help us confidently navigate the complex path ahead, with an emphasis on science and accuracy.

Within a few weeks of Christian's initial discussions, and in large part thanks to Sarah Cohen and her team, Four Seasons entered into a consulting agreement with the institution.

It has turned out to be a deeply impactful relationship, with experts knowledgeable in facilities, infection control, epidemiology, and viral infections. An advisory board was formed, with formal webinars monthly and countless direct consultations in between. These webinars proved to be vital touchpoints for our global teams and we provided them to as many employees as possible, understanding the need for all to benefit from the experts' knowledge as well as an open forum to ask detailed questions. Experts spent time observing guest and employee processes and protocols at our hotel in Baltimore to identify detailed steps where we could elevate our health and safety program. This included evaluating and enhancing protocols to prepare for reopening, taking our already high standards to another level entirely.

In addition to leading epidemiologists, the consulting institution has experts in areas such as ventilation and surface transmission, information that would be critical not only in our operations but in explaining to our hotel employees and other stakeholders why certain policies or policy changes were necessary. We set up an "Ask the Experts" tool on our internal portal, and our people did—more than four hundred questions were answered in the first year alone.

I've been asked if there were moments when I doubted our ability to get through this, when I was secretly more worried than I let on. There were certainly dark days when we had to let go of many valued colleagues, even though we had done the very best we could under the circumstances. But for the business itself, its survival and continued success, the truth is, I remained confident.

Having joined Four Seasons nearly twenty years ago and having been CFO since 2005, I knew the business intimately. We are a profitable company that has many checks and balances in place to protect us from the unexpected. Our RevPAR—"revenue per available room," an all-important measure in the hotel industry—is enviable.

The Four Seasons experience—what it's like to stay with us, to host events with us, to dine in our restaurants and relax in our spas—was very much on our minds throughout the pandemic. So much of what our brand stands for is personalized service. Genuine caring, a real dedication to making others happy, making important personal connections, which we do, thousands of times every day. But what happens when the guest can't see your smile?

We went through a similar reckoning when we launched the Four Seasons App in 2015. There was some question about how well the personalized service we are known for might suffer. Guests were already used to booking rooms on our website, but now they would also be able to make restaurant and spa reservations, order room service, arrange luggage pickup and airport transfers, all things you'd normally call one of our people to do for you. Worst fears were never realized as our guests loved having us in the palm of their hands. We added a live, real-person chat function two years later.

Like so many trends that were accelerated by the pandemic—the idea of open space as a luxury, for example—the app was so important in reshaping the Four Seasons experience for our guests as we followed physical distancing guidance. The extent to which our employees adapted was impressive, and the way our guests embraced this new world was astounding. In 2020, app traffic grew to more than six million chat messages exchanged in more than one hundred languages—incredible in a year when the bulk of our hotel rooms were unoccupied.

I remember some of the early language we used in countless internal memos, letters to guests and clients, and notes from our regular town hall calls. We used the word "pause" a lot, but in fact we never did. We kept going. There was never a day when all our hotels were closed. Even at the worst of it, somewhere someone was staying at a Four Seasons and we had to make sure it lived up to our brand standard. We operate forty-five branded residential properties, and our Four Seasons residents were also staying at home and looking to us for our usual service and care. Our restaurants, some of which had been offering free meals to furloughed staff and others in need in their communities, tapped into the award-winning creativity that our teams are known for, offering takeout packages, meal kits for pickup, and wonderful holiday menus to enjoy at home.

It's worth noting that even when people aren't staying with us, they stay in touch. The extent of the Four Seasons digital ecosystem is incredible—we currently have more than 14 million followers across about 630 active social media channels. Filled with dreamy images and travel inspiration, our social media channels became a lifeline as team members went live with everything from cocktail how-tos to online meditation sessions.

An occasionally overlooked segment, but a critical business driver in urban hotels, comes from corporate accounts and what we call MICE—meetings, incentives, conferences, and events. In other words, business travel. We have always put great effort and care into creating a home-away-from-home for business travellers, and to setting the stage for productive and memorable client events. And while there was indeed a significant pause on this business, a number of U.S. properties were entrusted with creating professional sports team "bubbles" for various tournaments and playoff games, including housing MLB players for the World Series at our hotel in Dallas. To us, this signalled that when the time is right, our properties will be well equipped to support companies looking to reconnect with their colleagues around the world. I'm completely convinced that business travel and meetings are not a thing of the past, but like so much post-pandemic, it will be different, and we will be ready to meet these evolving client needs and expectations. Business people want to connect with colleagues, business partners, and customers as much as leisure travellers. I share this desire—strongly.

At Four Seasons, we are deeply connected by our culture, and it was critical to me that throughout it all, we stayed in touch. Our leaders had to be visible and accessible. Regular town calls built in open forums for questions, discussions, and ongoing communication on all manner of related topics—including sharing stories of success, innovation, and even failure. I insisted that our corporate teams take their vacation days, and we also created new wellness days globally, encouraging our hard-working team members to take a break from work and spend time with their loved ones. Understanding that the pandemic also took a tremendous toll on mental health, we knew we had to support our employees through this difficult time as much as possible.

In 2019, we had sponsored a study by Harvard Business Review Analytic Services on the topic of emotional intelligence, or EI. It's something we've always felt strongly about—that began with our founding as a company and continued to thread its way through just about everything we do. Four Seasons hires for attitude and trains for skill. We know that many hard skills can be taught, but when it comes to self-awareness, social skill, self-control, and empathy, it needs to start from within. The study confirmed what we knew intuitively—that a strong commitment to EI can be a driving force in organizational success.

It's also what gets you through challenges, both professional and personal, never more so than in 2020. And in the middle of everything, we continued to progress our work on diversity, inclusion, and belonging, recognizing that this is an ongoing, important journey for our company and future workforce. As always, we turned to our core DNA, our own culture as a company and as people. Even as we were all working hard to manage the crisis, we took time to listen, to respond to the needs of our employees, and to lead with empathy, compassion, and care.

Looking ahead, I remain incredibly optimistic about the future of travel. The turbulence of the pandemic solidified that travel is such an important part of our lives. The pandemic has redefined what is most important in life—connecting with others and getting out in the world as materialism shifts to authentic experiences. Even during the very difficult last year, we opened four new hotels and we're on track to open four or five more by the end of 2021—a sign that the insatiable need to explore the world remains.

Some segments of our business have done better than others. Not surprisingly, we saw increased demand for our Private Retreats (luxury home and villa rentals), and the Four Seasons Private Jet has waiting lists well into 2022. Our online retail business—offering up our signature Four Seasons bed and a range of bed and bath linens at the core of a growing product assortment—outperformed 2020 projections as people brought a little bit of Four Seasons home with them, as they were spending so much time there.

As we embrace and increasingly rely on technology, we also value personal connections and in-person experiences more than ever. Never before has the entire world been united in a single experience as the pandemic touched us all. Even though it was different for each of us, as one of my colleagues said, "We're all floating in our own little lifeboats, but it's all the same sea."

As the pandemic concentrated all aspects of our life into our homes, it forever erased what was already becoming a blurry line between business and leisure travel, two aspects of our industry that, with the invention of workcations and schoolcations, have become one. Aside from continuing to ramp up technology capabilities, our operations and design teams have been thinking a lot about things like creating spaces throughout our hotels where guests might take a private call in the middle of a family dinner, or quietly work by the pool with their laptop for an afternoon. Another area that the pandemic has put into greater focus is design. At Four Seasons, it means beautiful hotels, resorts, and residences of course, and beyond that, how people use and move through the spaces we create. The pandemic and its changing rules on physical distancing and size of gatherings has us thinking about our spaces more than ever.

Lead With Care, the program we created last year in response to the pandemic, has quickly become an umbrella for a much broader range of health, safety, and security programs within our hotels. Among many other aspects of the program, we now have a dedicated Lead With Care ambassador in every one of our hotels and resorts, and it's a permanent position. This is about more than committees and protocols, though; Lead With Care is an integrated program with complex operational, legal, and communications implications, and we are deeply committed to it.

Our leadership team also continued to grow, with the addition of Marc Speichert in March 2021 as the company's first ever chief commercial officer. Marc oversees Four Seasons integrated commercial strategy, including brand marketing and communications, data and analytics, and our digital ecosystem. His extensive global experience and vision is critical to our recovery efforts. The pandemic challenged our team like never before, and through our collective efforts it created even stronger bonds that give me great hope for our future.

So, even as we are continually problem solving in real time, we keep moving forward, knowing that people love to travel; that they miss spending time with their friends, family, and colleagues; and that they want to not only see but actually experience the world. At the same time, the importance of community is never more in focus than when we face challenges together.

Getting together with friends or pitching in to help others in our communities, supporting local businesses, these are things we might have taken for granted before. For those of us in the hospitality business, we look forward to welcoming those who come from afar, as well as opening the doors of our restaurants, bars, and spas to our friends and neighbours in the community.

We've done and continue to do what we can, always at the highest level possible. In a world of uncertainty, we remained connected. We focused on the things that were within our control—our business and, perhaps most importantly, how we care for our employees and our guests.

Again and again, and often under enormous stress, our people have shown agility, resilience, innovation, and compassion.

I know we can all be proud.

GOODLIFE FITNESS

David Patchell-Evans spent the bulk of the pandemic feeling like he needed to do more to help people take care of their health.

Patch, as he is known to friends, has first-hand experience with the healing power of exercise. When the founder and chief executive of GoodLife Fitness Centres was in his first year at Western University, he was in a serious motorcycle accident. Patchell-Evans broke bones and tore muscles in his chest and shoulder.

Rehabilitation took months, and it played out in the university's gym, where the London, Ontario, native watched elite athletes working out before competitions or working to recover from their own injuries. The whole process fascinated Patchell-Evans, prompting him to switch majors from business to kinesiology. By the time he graduated from Western, the former biker was a world-class rower. After graduating, he used savings from a snow-shovelling business to buy his first GoodLife gym. That one location launched an empire that now numbers 400 locations, 11,000 associates, and 1.5 million members in the GoodLife family of clubs, which includes Fit4Less and Éconofitness. Patchell-Evans is walking proof that a commitment to fitness can carry anyone through tough times. That's why the CEO is beyond exasperated over decisions by governments of various stripes to shut down gyms during the COVID-19 pandemic— an era that's tested the mental and physical health of every Canadian. GoodLife, working with other fitness businesses, presented policy-makers with a number of options for opening gyms safely. By and large, they were rebuffed.

Along with Canada's largest chain of fitness facilities, Patchell-Evans's private company owns a network of forty-two clubs in New Zealand, under the CityFitness brand. During the pandemic, CityFitness began opening gyms in Australia—it now has four in the country. Running a trans-Pacific business gave the Canadian entrepreneur a unique view of how different countries dealt with the same public health challenge. Without giving away Patchell-Evans's COVID-19 story, it's safe to say he's a big fan of New Zealand prime minister Jacinda Arden and is far less impressed with Canadian politicians.

Now based in Victoria, B.C., Patchell-Evans is a father of four, including one daughter who has special needs. He is married to former Olympic rowing champion Silken Laumann, who is also a testament to the rehabilitative power of exercise: Laumann won a bronze medal in the Barcelona Games weeks after her leg was torn apart in a rowing accident.

"Patch" is a passionate Canadian who believes that everyone should have the right to access opportunities for fitness and health. The pandemic has reinforced his determination and fuelled his desire to bring fitness to everyone in Canada.

David Patchell-Evans

On March 15, 2020, I sat staring at my computer screen with a terrible sinking feeling in my stomach. I was trying to write something that would reassure our team and members that closing our fitness clubs to protect our communities from the emerging and scary virus was "the right thing to do."

Can you imagine how it felt? I'm sure many of you can relate to this, given the uncertainties and sacrifices that we all were presented with in the initial hours and days of the pandemic. For me, after forty-two years of building a company to help people take care of their health, and all the trials and tribulations of doing that, I was actually considering closing the entire business down for everyone's benefit. It was so counterintuitive and painful. There were many questions and considerations. Was it the right thing to do? Was it enough, or maybe too much? Did we even need to do anything? Was there anyone I could ask for an opinion or for advice? Were there other examples in history?

Like many leaders, I had no reference points to help me make a decision. We were all faced with an onslaught of contradictory information and opinions from global experts, the people and institutions we can usually look to in a time of crisis to set the record straight. I thought about what would happen if one of our employees got sick, or possibly even passed away. My brain kept switching gears. I also worried about how they would afford to live and take care of their own health and families if I had to close all the clubs.

There were simply no easy answers available.

In the final analysis, it was a gut feeling, one that shook me to my core, but I knew in my heart it was the right thing to do. I knew my job as the leader of this organization was to be decisive. I used the best information I had at the time and relied on GoodLife's core values—caring, trust, integrity, happiness, peak attitude, passion, and personal fitness. Throughout my life, I've tried to follow three rules:

1. Always aim to do the right thing.
2. Surround yourself with caring, intelligent people who have the highest integrity.
3. When you're not sure what to do, go back to rule #1.

"Our purpose has always been to give everyone in Canada the opportunity to live a fit and healthy good life. There is no moment in our history when that purpose is more important than today," I wrote back in March 2020. And yet, as I sit here well into the pandemic, I'm realizing our purpose might be even more important than ever in our collective recovery as a nation.

At the very beginning of the pandemic, our team took the important step to proactively close all our clubs from coast to coast to protect our communities, even before it was mandated by government. As Canada's largest fitness club chain, we knew we had to be a role model for others. Because of all of the uncertainty, we had to set the standard. It was critical to find ways to stay connected and take care of our employees and members, and really to help anyone who needed it to look after their mental and physical health.

Early in the pandemic, the U.S. Centers for Disease Control and Prevention and the World Health Organization positioned gyms as dangerous environments where COVID-19 could easily spread. But they failed to account for the physical, mental, and emotional damage of inactivity. Although they had to make decisions based on limited information in a high-pressure situation, the result proved to be a uni-dimensional approach to a multi-dimensional issue. Unfortunately, these public health authorities did not update their positioning as the pandemic went on to reflect the incredibly low transmission in gyms globally. They never acknowledged that, with a significantly modified environment like the majority of gyms implemented, the risk of transmission was almost zero if all procedures were executed correctly.

That approach meant gyms were considered unsafe from the outset and that we could not reverse that association, no matter the extent of our COVID-19 safety protocols or our clean record with no transmission at a GoodLife club in regions where facilities were open. As governments and public health leaders learned more about how COVID-19 could be spread, we saw some inconsistent policies about which businesses could stay open. Although these decisions were frustrating and difficult to understand, my goal as a leader was to do everything I could to support my team and act as a beacon of hope.

We resolved to continue to lead our industry in how we introduced, managed, and implemented COVID-19 safety protocols. Long before provincial governments gave the green light for gyms to reopen, GoodLife consulted safety, medical, and healthcare experts in COVID-19 response, infection prevention, and control and sanitization to ensure every club would align with or exceed the recommendations and standards put forth by all levels of government.

Our team built a comprehensive health and safety plan focused on four main areas: ensuring physical distancing, reducing capacity levels in our clubs, requiring masking and enhanced cleaning, and strengthening sanitization practices. The plan was introduced as The GoodLife Standard and acted as a guide for reopening our clubs across the country. In fact, different government agencies used The GoodLife Standard as an example in how they operated. Public health units thanked us for our efficiency.

But that was just the first step. We brought in two emergency room physicians to test our COVID-19 safety protocols against real-life scenarios to identify and fix confusion points and blind spots, as well as eliminate friction associated with compliance, before clubs opened. In spring 2020, with very little information, GoodLife and Fit4Less worked closely with the provincial governments and regional public health authorities to prepare clubs to open as safely, responsibly, and efficiently as possible. We prepared our gyms in every province so we could open our doors to members as soon as we had the green light.

Each member of our team spent months on end working to get us through this very difficult time. We have paved new roads together and taken risks we never would have otherwise. Together we were able to go where no one has gone before (yes, I guess I am a fan of *Star Trek*) and the company has emerged stronger and ready to face the next phase.

Caring for Employees and Members

When the pandemic started, our foremost concern was our more than eleven thousand employees who had to go on temporary layoff. How would they survive without income? What would happen to them and their families? We gave employees two weeks' pay and continued to pay their benefits after we closed all our clubs. People needed to pay their mortgages and buy groceries. It was a huge financial hit for the company, but it had to be done to take care of our people.

In the first months of the pandemic, we identified three main priorities. The first was to get our physical clubs ready to open again by maximizing COVID-19 health and safety protocols. The second was to keep highly trained, highly motivated employees focused and energized in a brand-new environment. The third was to invest even more in digital to keep members and staff active.

With strict safety protocols and processes to enforce, it was tough to keep staff members connected with their passion for fitness and helping people. Our staff are the trained athletes of the fitness world. If an athlete doesn't use their skills, they lose their edge. If we wanted our employees to come back 100%, we had to invest in their management and leadership skills to keep them connected to their purpose.

I decided my top priority was connecting with my employees whenever I could, and learning how they were doing and what they needed from me. I had the opportunity to speak with many of our team members at different phases of the pandemic, and I tried to provide information, reassurance, and hope.

Our employees' responses started with disbelief, then shifted to fear, and then turned into confusion, uncertainty, and frustration as our industry came more under fire and was increasingly misunderstood as the pandemic progressed. Things were changing quickly, and the messaging was beginning to feel confused and ill-informed in some areas of the country.

In the face of so much criticism of the fitness industry during COVID-19, my job was to remind people that their profession is vital to the health of the population. They needed to remember why they got into the fitness industry and how much they could help people. Even when government, media, and others were telling them they were optional, it was critical that they knew how integral they were to the overall health and wellness—both physical and mental—of society.

I invested weeks of time doing virtual calls with GoodLife employees across Canada to hear how they were doing, update them on plans for the business, and reconnect them with their passion for the fitness industry. I wanted to thank them for their dedication and get them to think about what they love about helping people live healthy active lives. My job has always been to make GoodLife team members feel successful. I believe that management should work for the employees. Even if I didn't love the rules of the road we were on, my job was to follow the speed limit and support our team through this incredibly tough time.

And then there were our loyal members. Whenever our clubs had to close, we were profoundly aware that the health of our 1.5 million members was in jeopardy. Most of our members count on fitness to take care of their mental and physical health. Going to the gym offers a connection to community, a chance to invest in yourself and build your self-confidence and a sense of accomplishment.

To have indoor fitness facilities taken away so abruptly was, and still is, absolutely detrimental to people's health. It's like being in a car accident that someone else causes but you have all the injuries. Add to that the uncertainty and panic we all felt, especially at the beginning, and it was a recipe for disaster. Our members lost the ability to take care of their health through exercise at a time when they needed it most. This just drove me crazy.

It was even more frustrating that the people who were making the decisions in many cases likely had the resources and opportunity to exercise at home or outside, if they exercised at all. These decisions hurt those who are most vulnerable. They were blatantly unfair to the heath and well-being of a large section of the population, while others barely felt it. It should not be allowed to happen again.

The GoodLife team knew we had to find ways to take care of these people, and to deliver fitness options so members could take control of their health and wellness. The solution we arrived at wasn't as good as going to the gym in person, but it was way better than doing nothing. We amplified our existing resources to deliver online content and tools for members to work out at home. Shortly after gyms closed, GoodLife launched its new digital gym, GoodLife At Home, to give all Canadians free access to a weekly schedule of free workouts, wellness tips, and free live classes on GoodLife's social channels (@GoodLifeFitness). Then we had to think about the financial hardships so many Canadians were beginning to face. Understanding that some members were not ready to return during the pandemic, we offered to freeze membership fees for the worst part of the pandemic. Again, we took a huge financial hit, but it was the right thing to do.

As governments enforced and changed restrictions, the member experience team managed high volumes of inquiries and requests. Just imagine ten provincial governments and multiple provincial health authorities all making different rules. It was difficult for people to understand what to do. We tried to be as supportive and accommodating as possible to ensure members felt comfortable and safe. And when the time came to reopen for the first time in spring/summer 2020, we made sure members understood the new normal, including health and safety protocols, cleaning requirements, and what to expect during their workouts.

The key leadership issue here was to let people know we were doing our best, that even under this scenario we were leading the way to deliver the best and safest fitness experience, and that we would continue our efforts even when the pandemic was over. It's like being an athlete. You have to prepare your training program to win the championships, but you still have to strive for the little victories along the way. Work hard in every workout! We used the same psychology and theories in adapting to this crisis.

With so much contradictory COVID-19 information and noise, we had to be clear and confident with our messaging. We used as many channels as possible: email, social media, our website, and more. In many cases, media outlets worked with us to get the word out about GoodLife's safety protocols, what to expect at the gym, and the extensive measures we took to keep our staff and members safe. From our end, we also made sure Goodlife and Fit4Less team members were equipped to explain the new protocols and answer questions from members.

Adapting Our Business to Pandemic Conditions

I knew nothing would derail our efforts faster than a case of transmission in one of our clubs. We saw it happen with some other gyms, and the negative repercussions affected the entire industry. We needed to keep our people healthy and our communities safe.

In preparing and testing The GoodLife Standard, our team recognized we needed a bulletproof process to manage when someone who had been in one of our gyms tested positive for COVID-19. We also realized we would need to be faster than public health teams that were overwhelmed with cases across the country and were trying to figure out how to respond in real time.

We established our own assessment and reaction protocol, as well as a solid contact tracing system, in order to stay ahead of COVID-19 contagion and ensure our clubs would be as safe as possible, as quickly as possible. Without established guidelines about what to do, we resolved to do our best with the things we could control. The best approach during times of uncertainty is to do what's right in front of you.

How the Pandemic Affected Me Personally

It totally sucked.

The extreme measures at the beginning of the pandemic were stressful and frustrating. Being immunocompromised with my arthritis, doctors told me I would probably die if I got COVID-19. I've always been active and spent most of my time travelling across Canada running my businesses. All of that came to an abrupt halt. Government, medical professionals, and the media were constantly warning us of the risk, and that risk was amplifying exponentially. The uncertainty and sense of panic was mentally exhausting for everyone.

I was told to send my special needs daughter Kilee to live somewhere else for her own safety, since people with severe autism are at risk for serious complications from COVID-19. It was the first time we had been truly separated, and that was extremely difficult for her and our entire family. It's very tough for a person with severe autism to have their entire routine upended and to be taken away from their familiar surroundings and people. It was heart-wrenching.

I also wasn't allowed to visit my 101-year-old mother and didn't know if I'd see her again. I had to close the business that I'd spent my life building. And I was incredibly worried about my employees and their futures. If it was rough on me, imagine what it was like for them!

I have faced adversity in the past, but this pandemic is different. This time, no matter how hard I work, I've been prevented from doing what I'm good at—helping people take care of their health through fitness. It's frustrating for all of us in the fitness industry. We know we can help, but we're being held back.

I firmly believe that life is 10% what happens to you and 90% how you react to it. So I decided to take steps to do whatever I could and make the best of my situation. I was motivated and encouraged by my wife, Olympian Silken Laumann, who runs the non-profit organization Unsinkable, a platform for youth that is focused on mental wellness and building mental resilience. I realized early on in my career that being a leader can be physically and emotionally draining. You need to refill your tank, especially during tough times. You have to practise self-preservation. You can't lead your team if you're physically weak and emotionally burned out.

By investing in my own mental and physical health, I could replenish my strength to lead GoodLife. I resolved to start with that and pass along what I learned to others who are facing huge challenges. Shortly after the pandemic hit, I published the *21-Day Leader's Guide to Resilience* to share my experiences and what I'd learned about taking care of your mental and physical health during tough times. The world often asks for a lot from us, so my plan was to ask people to invest just a little time in themselves in order to get the biggest rewards.

I got up at 5 a.m. every day to practise what I preached. I spent two hours filling my own tank so I could be the leader people expected. I knew twenty-one days is all it takes to form a habit. I wanted to offer suggestions for small things people can do each day to take care of their own health—like drinking more water, meditating, exercising, eating healthfully, and getting proper sleep. COVID-19 reminded me it's not self-indulgent to take time for yourself. It's like putting on the oxygen mask first on the plane. Take time to exercise whenever you can. The benefits are huge in terms of productivity, stress release, and greater balance. Plus, you're setting an example for your team.

The pandemic has been a time of personal growth for me and so many others. To get through it, I remembered something my mother told me as a kid. She always said, "Never give up. Hang in there." She spoke as someone who has been forced to deal with formidable challenges. Our family picked up the pieces of our lives and got moving again after my father died in a car accident when I was only eight years old.

When people are having a tough time, I always tell them: Believe in yourself even if no one else does. Believe in what you're doing. Be patient and remember it's an active decision to be happy, to look for what's right, to look for opportunities. These are the most important decisions you can make as an individual and a leader. People want leaders who believe. Positivity is contagious. Negativity sells newspapers and gets clicks, but positivity breeds success and happiness. I believe that to be a good leader you have to be a realistic optimist.

Getting through a crisis like this pandemic is like running a marathon. The first mile is exciting, and the last mile is exciting, but the miles in between can be hard. Anyone can run a marathon, but you have to train for that steady state in the middle where you put one foot in front of the other. The middle part is all about persistence and believing you can do it. You have to train and build the mindset to be persistent. The mindset is more important than the physicality. That's how a leader can get through the peaks and valleys.

My Approach to Managing Through This Crisis

In my career, I have always tried to put people before the business. I often tell people I'm not a businessman, I'm a fitnessman. I want people to experience the benefits of being healthy and active, and the fitness business is a way to achieve that purpose and to truly take care of others.

If I'd put my business first, I would have found a way to keep every cent. Instead, I did the opposite. I borrowed a whole lot of money to let as many people as possible keep their jobs, and hopefully to give people a place to exercise. In the past, there have been companies that used a crisis to make money, even if it meant taking advantage of the situation. I chose to use this crisis to create hope.

We knew our employees weren't able to work in our gyms, so wherever possible we used that time to provide them with ongoing learning and development opportunities. Our leaders engaged in regular management training to advance their skills, and employees were offered mental health training and at-home workout options to keep their minds and bodies healthy and strong. The goal was to keep our people connected, engaged, and thinking about the future, and to help them advance during a time when they were forced out of work. We wanted them to feel appreciated and to be excited to come back to the clubs.

With gyms open again, I believe we'll see a renewed focus on fitness and health. People had this time to realize how important health is to quality of life. Without your mental and physical health, you have nothing. Let me say this again: If you don't have health, you have nothing. Are you getting my point? COVID-19 has proven that. The more out of shape you are in a healthcare crisis, the more danger you're in. Your health is everything.

Members will appreciate the opportunity to get back into the gyms to get into better shape and to look after themselves—to recover their health after the pandemic. More and more people are starting to realize the hospital's job is to help them with sickness. I'm here to teach people how to look after their own health.

Our team has used this time to get better. We've dedicated our energy to making GoodLife an even more extraordinary experience for members and employees. It's not just a gym; it's a community, and a place where you can work with experts to improve your health and live a better life.

I used my leadership position to connect with fitness leaders around the world to learn whatever I could that would help us in Canada. I did regular phone calls with fitness club owners from around the world—every country operated differently. I kept thinking it would have been so much better if we could have learned from each other and followed the same universal approach on a global scale. For most fitness club leaders, this was a toughening experience. Every region was affected at a different time, but I was able to learn from their experiences.

Keeping the Business Viable Despite All the Odds

With 365 GoodLife Fitness, Fit4Less, and Éconofitness clubs across Canada that were required to close and reopen over and over with no end in sight, and roughly 11,000 employees on temporary layoff, we were faced with some very serious financial decisions from the outset of the pandemic. Luckily, we were in a good position before this crisis, with minimal debt and strong relationships with partners. In simple terms, we built on the relationships we established over more than forty years.

When it came to working with landlords and banks, we relied on our longstanding partnerships. I have always believed in doing the right thing and giving more than you take when it comes to business. If you do business in a way that is fair and equitable, people remember that you're a solid, successful partner. You have to be the partner they want to work with now *and* in the future.

In more than four decades of business, I've had to rely on my partners for support and flexibility to move through tough times. The important thing is that when you operate strategically and with integrity, they know you'll recover and continue to succeed. When I got started, I relied on others for advice and opportunities. I remember the partners who helped me along the way. It's a matter of trust and of loyalty.

GoodLife has paid its rent for more than forty years. That track record has paid off. The same with banks—the lenders know our business is solid and that we always pay back our loans. We had no revenue because you can't charge members when you're not open. So we reached out to banks and landlords and asked for help. It's important we come out of this together and that we shoulder the difficulties as partners. That's how business should be done, and we're lucky we have such longstanding and solid partners.

The Role of Fitness in Pandemic Recovery

I believe Canada can be the healthiest nation in the world. To make that a reality, we have to continue to give everyone options to be physically active. Access to spaces and programs for physical activity should be considered a basic right—something that cannot be taken away. It should just be part of living here, like going to school or accessing health care. Fear of COVID-19 has made more people than ever aware of how important health is to our quality of life. Regular exercise contributes to better health, so it follows that access to physical activity should always be available to everyone. It's an essential way to take care of your health.

It's always been my mission to give everyone a chance to experience the incredible benefits of exercise. In Canada, our inactivity rate scares me, and COVID-19 has made the problem so much worse, as unfortunately we're more sedentary now. The pandemic has also exposed the inequities that exist in our society when it comes to accessing physical activity. COVID has made the situation even more difficult, especially for people in vulnerable communities. People in Canada are 40% less active than pre-pandemic, which means we're at greater risk of chronic diseases like diabetes, cancer, obesity, and cardiac problems.

I am committed to helping people realize the connection between health and fitness and quality of life. If you don't tell people the benefits, they're not going to know. In the same way that people have adapted to quit smoking and to stop driving while impaired, we can help people change their behaviour patterns to exercise more. A lot of people don't believe it can happen. My job is to make people believe in themselves and what's possible. I'm even more driven to make this happen now that I've seen our country face COVID-19.

Nearly half of Canadians reported that their mental health has worsened since the beginning of the COVID-19 pandemic. Anxiety, depression, and substance abuse are at an all-time high. Inactivity has become a crisis. It's urgent that we allow people to take care of their health and wellness because our options to be physically active have been radically reduced. Months and months of inactivity and isolation have eaten away at our collective physical and mental health. Our quality of life has declined, our lifespans are shorter. Canada's healthcare system will be overwhelmed for generations to come as we deal with higher rates of chronic diseases. Fitness is the answer to the healthcare crisis.

We need a forward-thinking approach to support safer, more accessible opportunities for physical activity that will reach people during the pandemic and into the future. Let's not just target healthy people who live in optimal conditions. Everyone should have the right to look after their health through more opportunities to exercise. It's going to take a shift in mindset.

I'm in the business of making people believe in themselves and believe in their own capabilities. One of my personal affirmations is "Don't let the things you can't do stop you from doing the things you can." With that mindset, GoodLife has done everything we can to support people to find ways to be active for their health.

We've evolved GoodLife digitally to enable people to work out at home and at the gym—we want to give people as many resources and supports as we can to help them keep moving. GoodLife launched live and on-demand group fitness on Instagram. The GoodLife app features workout programs and on-demand content. We have remote personal training that can be delivered virtually or outdoors; we introduced outdoor fitness classes at some clubs to help more people get active while their province kept gyms closed. If the pandemic did one positive thing, it expanded the options for people to work out.

But I know gyms will be back stronger than ever. We've seen traffic at our clubs increase after lockdowns, and we know people will have an appetite for the gym once we're out of the pandemic. It's like when you're thirsty—all you can think about is water!

Government Leadership During the Pandemic

Governments have been working tirelessly, day and night, for months and months with no end in sight, trying to get this virus under control. COVID-19 is a sneaky and changing beast that keeps showing new sides, and while the most brilliant scientific and medical minds have committed countless combined hours to finding the cause and the cure for this thing, it is a formidable task, and the solution will not come quickly or easily.

I see what we do in the fitness industry as an integral part of the health-care system—a continuum to take care of people's health. The fitness industry aims to get people to take responsibility for their own lifestyle choices in order to stay out of the healthcare system as much as possible. And when they do have to seek medical care, I hope they've been investing so much in their own personal physical and mental health that they don't have to stay too long and drain precious and finite resources.

When I look at the resources that governments and businesses have spent to control COVID-19 as much as possible and keep people safe, I can't help but think that we missed the opportunity to help prepare the health of our population *before* the pandemic. Then, during the pandemic, we could have provided better medical facilities and found innovative ways to help people stay healthy and connected, but we didn't, because we thought it would be over in a week.

At the start, we gave our leaders a break. We all said, "They're doing their best." Political leaders and public health physicians in many provinces and municipalities have shown real leadership. They had an extremely tough job and had to make judgment calls that were often not popular. But it seems like some leaders are making decisions based on the polls—what they think will get them re-elected. I hope that's not the case, but I'm frustrated by this limited and two-dimensional approach. I worry we'll feel the negative impacts for months and years to come. I hope we learn from this experience. I'm going to make it my job to show leadership in this area and not to let people forget they need to work out for their own benefit.

I own a chain of fitness clubs in New Zealand called CityFitness, and I can't help but compare how New Zealand handled the pandemic with how we did it here in Canada. When the pandemic started, New Zealand acted decisively, closed its borders, and enforced a national lockdown. Every business was required to close. They did not play favourites. They threw everything at COVID-19 from the start and aimed for total elimination. As a result, the country was able to lift some restrictions and get back to a relatively good quality of life sooner than in other countries. Gyms could reopen much sooner there.

Here in Canada, I believe we took too long and came at the situation in a fragmented way. There could have been more decisive, centralized direction. A tough approach across the board, like what we saw in New Zealand, might have saved us some of the pain of dancing with COVID-19 for months and months on end.

If we're going to rebound from this pandemic, access to physical activity needs to be the first step, not the last. Millions of Canadians already depend on being physically active for their mental and physical health, whether it's simple activities like walking or cycling, or exercising within the more structured environment of a gym or fitness studio.

Throughout the pandemic, nearly every province in Canada has recognized that access to physical activity is essential. Most provinces have only closed fitness facilities during the strictest lockdowns and have prioritized access to fitness early in their reopening plans. Clearly these provinces understand the positive impact access to exercise can have on the mental and physical health of people in their communities.

We can't change what has happened, but we don't have to react to subsequent waves the same way as we did to the first four. As a country we have to be better prepared. Fitness clubs are a vital part of the preventative healthcare system. If gyms can operate safely, they should be used to keep people healthy.

All we can do is prepare for the future and focus on caring and providing for our communities and our people. The fitness industry will stand ready to help people recover their health and do what we can to undo the damage.

Emerging on the Other Side

As in a marathon, I'm ready to keep running and to support people as they get their health back. While this has been a difficult time for me and my team, I continue to be inspired every day by the people who weren't allowed to stop—our nation's essential workers, who faced unknown risk and rapidly changing conditions to keep society going. I'm especially moved by our nurses, doctors, and other caregivers, who I'm sure have been significantly affected by watching so many people suffer. But they've just kept going through the chaos. They've persisted, they've shown compassion, and we owe everything to them.

Every day, I make a point to exercise for my physical and mental health. I also have gratitude for what *is* working as we move through the pandemic. These pillars of strength—time spent being physically active and in investing in my own mental resilience—enable me to plan for the future and support everyone I can. I encourage you to do the same for yourselves and the people in your community.

I hope that, like me, other people are inspired to just keep moving. The entire GoodLife family is ready to continue helping people get active, get fit, and get healthy as a nation. We're ready to take back our health and start focusing on what really matters—people.

GOOGLE CANADA

How many people can say their business is one of the most recognizable brands in the world?

As vice-president and country manager for Google in Canada, Sabrina Geremia leads the strategic direction of Google's business strategy in Canada and Google's advertising business in the market. Google Canada has grown to be more than 2,000 employees and continues to invest in new offices and tech talent across the country.

However, if we want to look up something quickly—these days, probably to find out if your favourite pre-pandemic restaurant is still open—we open Google on our phone or laptop and search. You could say to someone "Google that" and they will know exactly what you are talking about.

When Canadians found themselves living online during the pandemic, Geremia and her colleagues at Google were there to host us, to teach us, to connect, to comfort and entertain us. Imagine weathering this crisis without YouTube. Impossible.

A business graduate of Wilfrid Laurier University and the University of Pavia in Italy, Geremia started her career working in Italy for Procter & Gamble. P&G is something of a boot camp for aspiring marketing executives. She moved to the U.K. to jump into the tech world, first with a mobile startup called Incirco, followed by the search engine Ask Jeeves, and then helped global health and CPG (Consumer Packaged Goods) company Reckitt Benckiser lay their foundations for digital marketing globally.

In 2006, Geremia joined Google, launching the tech company's consumer product and healthcare businesses in the U.K. A year later, she moved back to Canada, leading a series of businesses before being named Google's country head in 2017.

Geremia and her team made sure one of the world's most valuable technology companies kept humming and being helpful to Canadians during an unprecedented global crisis.

Sabrina Geremia

AUGUST 2021

The last big in-person gathering we held at Google before the pandemic was in February 2020, when our global chief financial officer, Ruth Porat, came to Toronto. We did ordinary things, having no idea they were about to come to an end for the foreseeable future. Our local employees gathered in an energy-filled room to hear an announcement about our plans to build new offices across Canada and that we were making new investments in digital infrastructure and skills to help prepare Canadians for a digitally driven workforce. We met with our client and non-profit partners in person. We shook hands. We sat side by side. We shared food and stories with our friends from the Toronto–Waterloo tech corridor. It was an exciting time filled with promise for the tech ecosystem in Canada. But quickly, the clouds of the pandemic rolled in.

When we hosted a fireside chat with clients and Ruth, someone asked her during the Q&A what she had learned during her time at Morgan Stanley and in the 2008 financial crisis that could be applied to a potential pandemic. She talked about the importance of leadership driven by courage that's grounded in experience and instinct. She also explained that in a crisis, events move so quickly that sometimes the best option is the "least worst" option.

That was a prescient question, as we were about to find ourselves in the midst of the biggest crisis any of us had ever faced. Our first step, as we were tracking the early days of the pandemic and its progression through our global counterparts in Asia and Italy in February 2020, was to start a cross-functional Canada Incident Response Team (IRT). We had formed our first IRT several years prior because we knew that in times of crisis a coordinated and nimble response team that shares information and can make fast decisions is critical. So we had worked together before in times of crisis, but never in a situation like this one.

Our IRT was led by our regional security leader, Maria, a whip-smart straight talker with a big heart. Maria gathered the right people in the room and set the agenda and the tone. We met daily to review the data and give roundtable updates. And Maria made sure these were concise updates—if you went on too long she would gently nudge the conversation back, discuss options, and make fast decisions.

Witnessing Maria take on this leadership role, and truly excel at it, I realized we could find a silver lining in all the bad news of the COVID crisis with emerging leaders stepping up to all-new challenges. The following months have proven that to be the case. I've seen countless people across Google Canada step up, take on new responsibilities, and find creative solutions to help us adapt and respond to an ever-changing crisis and do everything we could to help our partners and customers through such a challenging period. Their leadership has been inspiring.

Our first decision was a major one—to send our people to work from home in early March. The message we sent was short and clear: Working from home reduces the density of people in offices, which experts suggest may slow down the spread of COVID-19. That reduces the burden on the local community and health resources, freeing up support for those in need to get quicker support.

What we can easily forget today is how new and uncertain so much of this information was at the time. I gathered all the managers in a room to share the news with them first. It was important that they understood and internalized it. Afterward, I sent the email and walked the floors to see people face to face, answer their questions as best I could, and talk with them about their uncertainties. People were clearing their desks and packing bags and boxes. Some looked shocked as they processed the news. There were so many questions and very few answers. How bad was it? When would they come back? One person asked me if anyone would be in the office to water their plant. We hugged, said our goodbyes, and hoped that we would see each other back in the office in a few weeks or months.

The shift to working from home for many Canadians was hectic and chaotic. In 2019, only approximately 39% of Canadian workers were set up for remote work. Now every business needed to shift to digital. Work itself quickly transformed, and for many of us, work was no longer a physical place we went to, and interactions that used to take place in person were (and still are) being digitized. Office workers no longer had impromptu discussions at the coffee machine or while walking to meetings together, and instead turned their homes into workspaces. We flipped a switch to a world where frontline workers, from builders on a construction site to delivery specialists, kept critical supply chains moving with digital tools and turned to their phones to help get their jobs done. A world where many Canadians ordered groceries online for the first time and visited their doctors from screens while sitting at their kitchen counter. The first months of the pandemic witnessed the most accelerated shift to digital in history.

In our own work environment, we were in the fortunate position of being already plugged in to the enterprise version of Google Workspace, our suite of collaboration and productivity tools for businesses. Even prior to the pandemic, our Monday to Friday was largely spent in a hybrid state—a mix of face-to-face and video meetings with Googlers and customers across the world. For me, the shift to remote work involved clearing a small back room of our house in Toronto, setting up a comfortable chair and a monitor and plugging in my work laptop. Many of my team members set up shop in their bedrooms or at their kitchen tables. A few garden sheds got a lick of paint. For me and my teams, the technical shift to working from home wasn't a huge hurdle because of where we work and the type of work we do. But we knew that this was not the case for most businesses in Canada.

With the onset of the pandemic, every business needed to shift to digital fast. To help with this, we launched global, free access to our video conferencing service, Google Meet, and expanded access to the already free suite of Google for Education tools, enabling students and faculty to interact seamlessly. One of the many notable challenges of the past year has been the transition to online, remote schooling for children, educators, and parents. As a working parent I felt it too. Just before the March 2020 break, when we were already working from home, my husband and I went to our kids' community school to help them pack their bags. When we told our ten-year-old kids that they would be learning remotely for a few months they were uncomfortably excited. Living in downtown Toronto, we were fortunate to have access to fast Internet and to be part of a school that offered loaner Chromebooks to students. The entire class was online within days.

In the first inning of the pandemic I was running on adrenaline and trying to keep up with the chaos. I cancelled my March Break plans and put all my energy into pandemic preparedness for my family and at work. I tried to get an early start at setting up home-schooling and I made a daily schedule for my kids on a cork bulletin board in the kitchen. It included things like math, independent reading, and virtual music lessons with Grandpa. It was not pretty or sophisticated, but it was an attempt to create structure for my kids while I also worked in a critical week.

The cork board was almost immediately ignored by everyone in the house and I learned that home-schooling for young kids was going to be harder than I had hoped. When we officially went "back to school" it was a relief to have them connect to their class virtually. At first my husband and I needed to help them log in and get connected. But within a week they were teaching us how to use Google Classroom, showing us the command keys on Google Docs, and stumbling out of bed to join the Jamboard kick-off with their grade four class. At first it was tempting to romanticize home-schooling, but soon we learned that juggling working full time and home-schooling is just plain hard.

For one thing, it turns out that kids in virtual school, especially young ones, need a lot of supervision and help to keep on task. What would've been a fifteen-minute coffee break in between meetings at the office became a fifteen-minute tutoring session with my kids in the kitchen. I've talked to tapped-out parents who have been brought to tears from the stress of working and home-schooling, especially frontline workers who didn't have the luxury of digitally working from home. I've also talked to teachers who went the extra mile to check in with parents when kids seemed distracted and were doing things like turning off their video or falling behind in math. It's no surprise that the pandemic caused a peak in anxiety and depression among caregivers, and its after-effects are still being felt.

One of the silver linings of working from home has been the sight of everyday life in meetings, from the mundane (my favourite was a colleague folding his laundry while participating in a meeting) to the unexpected video bombing from kids and pets. In the first weeks of working from home I was having a virtual conversation with a senior leader of my leadership team when I noticed the wardrobe door behind him moving. It burst open and out popped two of his kids, who were either playing hide-and-seek or looking for Narnia.

But even as we were adapting to the new ways of working from home, it was also very apparent to us, from the first days of the lockdown, that our work at Google Canada had never been more important to the customers and partners we serve. People and companies needed to make the transition to digital in a matter of weeks, rather than months, or more typically, years.

We found ourselves living in a once-in-a-generation digitization moment and understood the importance of helping Canadians, our communities, and the 1.2 million businesses in Canada who needed to shift fast to digital. In the early weeks of work from home, we gathered a cross-section of leaders from across our organization to brainstorm the answers to one question: How do we support Canadians and Canadian businesses as we navigate a global pandemic?

In our brainstorming session we discussed ideas big and small for the economy, from testing to mask distribution to volunteering in our communities. No idea was too small, but two conversations stuck out. First, our finance leader, Sue, presented an overview of the Canadian economy with one stat that stopped the clock. Ninety-eight per cent of businesses in Canada are small and medium-sized businesses (SMBs), and they employ close to 70% of working Canadians. In other words, the backbone of Canada's economy is SMBs. But at the start of the pandemic, very few of these businesses were digitally enabled. We knew that 50% of SMBs did not have a website and an even smaller percentage had e-commerce capabilities. How could we help SMBs come online fast?

Second, our community STEM (science, technology, engineering, and math) education lead, Sandy, a former principal at a public school, pressed upon all of us the importance of getting teachers trained in how to use their new virtual classroom. In just a matter of months, we helped more than ten thousand teachers adapt to teaching from home with Google Workspace for Education training. We also partnered with non-profit digital skills trainers NPower Canada and ComIT to broaden and further build the technology workforce in this country.

Most importantly, we focused on providing Canadians with reliable and authoritative information about the pandemic. Colin, our public policy lead for Canada, was already working closely with governments and healthcare authorities across the country to surface the most accurate and up-to-date information on Google Search and YouTube. His team were also supporting provincial and federal government partners in rolling out official exposure notification and vaccination apps. The entire Google team was concentrating on how to make our products more useful for healthcare officials—for example, by using location data to produce mobility reports that demonstrated how social distancing measures were having an impact on our personal behaviours and on our communities.

We formed core working groups across our business teams in Canada, and one of the lead workstreams was to find new ways to support small businesses and help with economic recovery. Our small business workstream, led by Elana and Tristan, worked fast and furiously to bring Canadian businesses online. A digital presence brings businesses enormous opportunities for growth, innovation, and jobs. However, digital skills and tools can still seem out of reach to many. In Canada, many small business workers were laid off as companies closed. According to the OECD, closures hit SMBs the hardest.

To help Canadian independent businesses, entrepreneurs and artists built a digital presence to minimize the economic impact of the COVID-19 pandemic. In May 2021, Google Canada announced a million-dollar commitment to scale Digital Main Street's ShopHERE program, and "ShopHERE powered by Google" was born. In the weeks to follow, FedDev Ontario and the Ontario provincial government announced a $57 million investment to expand the program across Ontario.

We quickly began to see the impact of our work. Businesses came online and adapted their services to use the free curbside pickup and takeout features in Google My Business. We helped train eighty thousand Canadians in digital skills that employers are looking for, free of charge, through Grow with Google. This includes Google Career Certificates that are helping Canadians grow digital skills that can help them land high-demand careers in growing sectors in under six months, with no degree or relevant experience required.

One of the most inspiring things was hearing feedback first-hand directly from Canadians. I met Laura Freel of 22 & Lou on a dark evening in November in a Toronto alleyway. That might sound ominous, but there's a very bright ending to the story. Laura was making and selling jams and marmalades out of her home kitchen in Toronto and I was eager to buy local for the holidays. It was my first purchase from her online store and I walked to her home in Leslieville to pick up my goods. After she handed me my bag of jalapeno jams and fig preserves, we stood masked and socially distanced and talked. She told me that she had just moved to a new home and lost her job. The jam business was a side gig that she ran with spreadsheets until she saw an ad for ShopHere. She clicked on the ad, signed up, and a few weeks later was paired with a student who helped build her a Shopify web store and bring all of her inventory online. The web store helped change the game for her business and the jams were flying off the shelf.

Laura wasn't the only one who was discovering the power of an e-commerce-enabled business. One year after ShopHERE was launched, twenty-five thousand Canadian businesses signed up and started communicating with and selling to their customers online. One of the most encouraging things about these business owners is how diverse they are.

Sixty-four per cent of these new online shops have owners that identify as women and 33% that identify as BIPOC. Additionally, over 780 university and college students have been hired and trained to build websites for the businesses and provide digital marketing support.

Here's another example. Lululemon is a fitness apparel and lifestyle company that's a made-in-Canada global success story. Faced with the pandemic-driven lockdown, they didn't just pivot to digital—they went all in. They repurposed store staff for the new realities of the digital world by bringing in virtual appointments and virtual waitlists to help customers. They started YouTube exercise classes. They bought the in-home fitness company Mirror, which turns a mirror into an interactive home gym. This was a perfect shift as people all over the world swapped more formal work clothes for comfortable leisurewear and looked to stay fit at home.

The pandemic pivot to digital also accelerated a flurry of innovation and growth for Canadian technology startups. After shifting their offerings to virtual, Ashley and our Google for Startups team launched two incubator and accelerator programs for Canadian entrepreneurs in 2020 and have rolled out even more in 2021. Some of my favourite virtual roundtables in the past year have been the conversations with the smart and ambitious Canadian entrepreneurs who participate in these accelerator programs. These are companies who are building technology and solutions for the world, based in Canada. Companies like AccessNow, a social enterprise developing smart technology that connects people with disabilities, as well as governments and corporations, to accurate, up-to-date information about the accessibility of places around the world. Or nesto, who offer a positive, empowering, and transparent home financing experience, simplified from start to finish.

We have learned so much since the beginning of the pandemic and there's still so much to learn. We know that the focus on growing the mindset of a curious continuous learner is here to stay. My lens is that the road to the future of work is paved with right-brain creativity paired with left-brain critical thinking and powered by digital skills and collaboration. I was passionate about STEAM (science, technology, engineering, arts, and math) and digital skills before the pandemic. Seeing our world turn upside down has only reinforced my commitment to empowering people of all ages and backgrounds to engage with technology. Not as an end in itself, but as a means to an end. I've worked in technology for two decades, but what I and my team are really in the business of is helping people to succeed, to stay informed, and most importantly, to stay connected.

Here's a very personal story. My father lives alone on our family farm. He is an Italian immigrant in his nineties and, partly because of his rural setting, at the start of the pandemic he had never accessed the Internet outside of his mobile phone base plan. But to keep him connected with his family and the grandkids he loves so much, one of our first priorities as a family was to set him up with home WiFi access and a Google Nest Hub. It has been a lifeline for him and for so many seniors in Canada who have been isolated during the pandemic. Our partnership with Best Buy to donate Google Nest Hub Max devices to more than three hundred private and public senior living residences across Canada was something that hit close to home. Even now, one of my favourite parts of my day is calling my dad at night to check in and then passing him on to my kids to share stories and say prayers before bed. He has also discovered YouTube (he calls it "the YouTubes") and tells me about all the things he's watching and learning.

The drive to make a difference is why we at Google came together at the start of the lockdown and challenged ourselves to meet the moment. One of the biggest challenges we faced as a group was building our team culture in a virtual environment. Before the pandemic, our ritual was to meet in person as a team first thing Monday morning to share updates, celebrate successes, talk frankly about roadblocks, and learn from one another.

As we moved to virtual we shifted the format entirely online and doubled down on storytelling. Our goal at Google is helpfulness. Helpfulness to Canadians, to Canadian businesses, and to the community we operate in. Every Monday we shared virtual coffees and stories about the businesses that were rapidly transitioning to digital and how we could help them go further, faster. In the first months of the pandemic, our auto team met with four hundred dealers of a major auto manufacturer to teach them how to open digital showrooms on YouTube when physical ones were shut. Jamboards—digital bulletin boards—became a huge hit as teams found new ways to connect to one another and innovate in a virtual setting.

We shared stories about our challenges. One of our best weekly Monday meetings was when Mary Deacon, chair of the Bell "Let's Talk" initiative, joined us for a frank conversation about mental health. She reminded us of the importance of checking in on a personal level with everyone we meet. It struck a chord. I noticed that more and more people would start a one-on-one or group meeting with a "How are you?" Sometimes the answer would be "Fine" (or "COVID-fine," which became a bit of a buzz word in the peak of the third wave). Other times this question unlocked a conversation that was very real and very raw. We shared grief over loved ones in hospital or living far away, worries about family members working on the front lines, and concerns about team members who were struggling. These shared stories brought us closer together and created a web of support in the most difficult time many of us have experienced.

The interesting thing about taking our weekly Monday meetings virtual is the sustained attendance. Rain or shine, the attendance always hovers at more than 80% capacity. In a period when we've intentionally been pruning internal meetings to create space for focused work, this one has been a staple that we will continue as the world evolves to a new hybrid normal.

One other aspect of our pre-pandemic work that we did not let go of is our commitment to diversity and inclusion. Diversity in the workplace is something I'm passionate about and is a priority for every Googler. My journey began in the early days when I started the first Canadian chapter of Women@Google. We've also opened chapters of our global employee resource groups that provide community, personal, and professional development opportunities for Googlers from underrepresented communities. To name just a few that are operating in our Canada offices, Pride@Google, GAIN (Google Aboriginal and Indigenous Network), and BGN Google (Black Googler Network) all work hard to drive grassroots awareness and action. We saw the impact of that work during the summer of 2020, when it felt like the world had paused during the terrible moment of George Floyd's death and again when the first of what would turn out to be many mass graves were uncovered at the site of a former residential school in British Columbia. Leaders cleared their agendas and made room to listen and create safe places for open and honest conversations. People shared stories they had never shared before, and eyes were opened to the work that must be done to improve.

Change is a process, and we still have more work to do. However, at Google we are committed to continuing to make diversity, equity, and inclusion part of everything we do—from how we build our products to how we build our workforce. We're supporting a more diverse workforce at Google by changing the way we hire people and how we work to retain them. We've increased our focus on meeting the needs of people with disabilities. And we've created more ways to help Googlers support themselves and others, which has never been more important than during the last eighteen months.

Moments of crisis are moments of loss but also of learning. As of this writing, Googling "pandemic business learnings" yields more than two million results. While we are not yet through the other side of this pandemic, I have learned so much from my team and from the partners we work with every day. Since the pandemic began, I think a lot about resilience and about what that means at a personal level but also at a business and community level. Canadians are resilient. I hear stories of courage and adaptability from the grocery delivery frontline workers who made it possible for so many of us to stay home and stay safe. I read stories of heroes who run Toronto vaccination clinics that break global records delivering twenty-six thousand vaccines in a day. Our businesses are resilient thanks to the Canadian leaders, workers, and creators they employ. I've been so inspired by all the people at the businesses we collaborate with who worked tirelessly to adapt to the largest economic and social disruption of our time by harnessing digital to recover and, in many instances, thrive. I'm extremely proud of my Google team and colleagues who went the extra mile to share insights and help accelerate the digital capabilities of Canadian businesses large and small in the most critical of times. Our communities are resilient. The pandemic has made us more aware of the importance of community and of the positive impact a small act of kindness has in a difficult time.

As we look to the future and ask ourselves "What comes next?" we must not forget everything we learned during and through the pandemic. Collectively, we have to take all of the good and bad of the past year and put those learnings to work building a better, stronger Canada and stronger communities. We saw Canadians connecting, learning, and thriving this past year, in spite of so many hurdles before them. And this was made possible by their unflagging spirit and by technology closing the distance when everyone was separated. I am a technologist at heart and I believe that technology, when thoughtfully applied, is a tool to build a better world.

INNVEST HOTELS

They are the hotels that anchor downtowns in Canada's biggest cities. Vancouver's Hyatt Regency, Calgary's Palliser, Edmonton's Hotel Macdonald, Toronto's Royal York, Quebec City's Hilton, and Ottawa's Marriott are normally hubs of activity, welcoming travellers and hosting celebrations.

All these iconic properties belong, in whole or in part, to the country's largest hotel owner, InnVest. And it was chief executive Lydia Chen who made COVID-19 calls on InnVest's portfolio of eighty hotels in all ten provinces.

Along with its landmark downtown properties, InnVest's collection includes Canadian hotels operating under a number of familiar banners: Fairmont, Marriott, Hyatt, Hilton, Kimpton, Comfort Inn, and Holiday Inn. The company also acquired the financially troubled Trump Hotel in Toronto and rebranded it as the St. Regis, the first St. Regis in Canada.

Formerly listed on the Toronto Stock Exchange, InnVest became a private company in 2016 when it was acquired by Bluesky Hotels and Resorts. Chen led Bluesky's friendly takeover and became CEO at InnVest the following year.

Chen was born in Beijing, China, where her father was an engineer who did research on semiconductors while her mother taught music. Electronics were part of her childhood, and Chen learned English in the 1980s in part from programming an IBM personal computer. She went on to earn an undergraduate degree in computer engineering and a master's in management. Prior to joining Bluesky and InnVest, Chen spent two decades in executive roles at finance, pharmaceuticals, and real estate companies.

Going into the pandemic, Chen's mandate at InnVest was to expand the portfolio by acquiring more properties, to upgrade existing hotels, and to grow its third-party-owned hotel management business. Once COVID-19 arrived, the focus was all about running a collection of large, expensive, and eerily empty buildings.

Lydia Chen

AUGUST 2021

Every January, I attend the hotel conference held by the Americas Lodging Investment Summit (ALIS) in Las Vegas. ALIS is the largest hotel investment conference in the world, and more than four thousand top industry leaders attend every year. In 2020, the event went very well. I remember that one conversation I had was about the possible impact of COVID-19 on the hotel business, as the virus was spreading quickly in China. However, at that moment in late January 2020 a worldwide pandemic still seemed a faraway possibility.

On that same trip, I flew to San Francisco from Los Angeles, and the airport was full when I arrived. I waited a while before the Uber driver showed up. His car approached me slowly and the driver spoke to me through a half-opened passenger-side window instead of opening the trunk and helping with my luggage. He asked me, doubtfully, which city I was arriving from, and if I had been in Wuhan. I was very surprised by his direct questioning. I answered that I was from Canada. I sensed that he was hesitant to give me a ride, so I added, "Technically, I spent the last few days in L.A. before arriving here." He conceded and let me in his car.

During the ride, the driver told me the first COVID case in California had just been confirmed and that people were beginning to get very nervous. I realized the virus was spreading to North America. It was the start of a worldwide, long-lasting pandemic.

To say that the past eighteen months have been challenging is an understatement. The time has been stressful, demanding, and taxing while at the same time strangely stimulating and inspirational. At InnVest, the early months of the pandemic were full of uncertainty and our path forward was unforeseeable, as was the case for many businesses worldwide. As I reflect, I realize this extended crisis has been a journey full of turmoil and hardship as well as surprises and innovations. As a business leader and parent, I had to find new ways of working, new ways of doing things, new ways to think. I had to face fears and problems that I have never faced before and hope never to deal with again. I had to be bold, decisive, and firm as well as empathetic and compassionate at a time when everything around me was unpredictable and unprecedented.

After the outbreak of the first wave of the pandemic, there were divergent opinions on the trend of the economic impact and ultimate recovery. Every conference or seminar presented a different recovery curve. Some industry analysts predicted a short downturn followed by a slow upturn, while others predicted a sudden drop and a sudden upswing. As time passed and we went through two waves of the pandemic, it became clear that everyone was just guessing and that nothing was predictable for the hotel and travel industries.

Compared with industries like technology, the life sciences, and others that continue to grow stronger in the pandemic, the hotel industry faced, and continues to face, its most challenging time ever. In 2020, the tourism contribution to global GDP plummeted to US$4.7 trillion, cut almost in half from US$9.2 trillion. Nearly sixty-two million jobs were lost. Airlines, hotels, tourism, resorts, restaurants, catering, and other entertainment businesses were hard hit.

InnVest is one of largest hotel owners, operators, and employers in Canada. In January 2020, more than 6,200 people were employed at our 84 hotels. During the three years between when I assumed leadership and the start of the COVID crisis, I am proud to state that InnVest was growing revenue at a pace higher than that of the Canadian hotel industry. We created a new business model to integrate hotel management, capital management, and procurement functions into core InnVest corporate functions, instead of outsourcing to third parties. We started 2020 with very strong liquidity capacity. Performance in January and February exceeded budget. Our hotel management team worked on several promising new opportunities, and our capital management group was focused on the Comfort Inn revitalization renovation program and several other key projects. We were doing well!

Then the pandemic hit, hard, and hotel bookings fell off a cliff early in 2020. We needed a rescue plan. The InnVest team and I, together, had the gear—we had the ropes—but we had no idea how to start a rescue. We went back to basics.

On March 1, 2020, I read a market insight that compared the impact of COVID-19 with the effects of other recent epidemics over the past twenty years, such as SARS, cholera, and H1N1 influenza. The article questioned whether COVID would impact a strong global economy, because at the time the numbers were relatively small and mostly limited to the countries where the epidemic struck first—South Korea, Japan, and China. Under the header "Will COVID-19 become a global pandemic?" the answer provided was "WHO still undecided, as there has been no sustained community transmission yet." At InnVest, I remained cautiously optimistic.

On March 2, we issued an impact tracking sheet to all hotels to measure the impact of COVID on our hotels, and at the same time I informed the company that travel arrangements were being suspended until further notice, starting with the quarterly general managers' conference. I also postponed several celebrations and in-person team-building events, such as our annual celebration dinner.

By March 3, as the cancellation of reservations escalated rapidly, our large city centre hotels were very heavily affected. Many large companies had begun to issue travel bans and we were in communication with all of our hotels almost daily at this point. We started discussing preparedness plans and business contingency plans and immediately reviewed all capital expenditure projects. We postponed all renovation activities. It would be fair to say I was no longer optimistic.

On March 9, at our regular Monday morning executive meeting, we had a heated debate about whether to cancel the upcoming general managers' conference scheduled for June 2020 in Winnipeg. We had chosen Winnipeg because one of our Winnipeg Comfort Inns was the prototype in our Comfort Inn revitalization renovation program, and we wanted all our Comfort Inn GMs to see the first newly renovated Comfort Inn. We were still in business, after all.

There was one compelling argument in favour of still holding the conference—it would look very negative to the hotel industry for InnVest to cancel a conference, and we would potentially be viewed as not supporting the travel industry. Nevertheless, we decided to cancel the conference because we just couldn't take the risk of our conference becoming what months later would be referred to as a "superspreader" event. The winning argument was simply that we couldn't take the chance of our people contracting the COVID-19 virus and carrying it back to numerous Canadian communities across the country.

Two days later the World Health Organization announced that COVID-19 was a pandemic. The following day the NBA announced that their season was being halted until further notice. The NHL's announcement quickly followed, as did the cancellation of almost every upcoming scheduled sporting, entertainment, and business event. The seriousness of the situation hit home that week and we went into pandemic survival mode.

Our main objective during this time was liquidity preservation. No one knew how bad business would get or how long the downturn would last. The timing of the pandemic could not have been worse for the hotel industry, as we were just approaching the spring-summer season, a time when a significant portion of our annual cash flow would be generated. A pandemic that started in October might have been much more manageable, but I didn't get to decide the timing. I was in reaction mode to preserve our business and safeguard our people.

The week of March 16, we sent the following message to our mortgage lenders:

> We are busy working through the Coronavirus pandemic impact on our business. The travel restrictions implemented or recommended by various Governments are severely impacting the travel industry. We cannot put an accurate dollar amount on this impact on our business and the impact to the hotels financed by your institution because it is changing day-by-day, however we do know that the impact is and will be material in this unprecedented time.

The good news is that our overall leverage is currently low, and we entered 2020 in a very strong liquidity position. We and our industry partners are taking steps to ensure that we can financially survive this crisis and come out the other side remaining in a strong financial position.

All lenders agreed to our request of a principal-repayment holiday of between three and six months and we saved a significant amount in cash outflows. One of our lenders indicated that our request sat under consideration for about a week, until similar requests started rolling in from their other hotel borrowers.

During the month of March, Canadian hotel occupancy was at 31.5%, down 47.6% from the same month in 2019. In April, it fell to 14.1%, down a disastrous 77.3% from April 2019. InnVest suspended operations at twenty-five hotels, representing half of our rooms. We were proactively preparing a business recovery plan for each hotel in late May. Our sales teams continued to have some great wins in this difficult environment and were also continuing to book business for future years.

In late September 2020, with the second wave of the pandemic officially upon us, all the provinces reinstated stricter health measures. Ontario, Quebec, and Alberta were in total lockdown again. Our hotels were facing the second wave of cancellations, extending to the middle of 2021. The lockdowns made it even more difficult for us to plan for the coming year. Fortunately, the good news about the pending availability of a vaccine brought us hope. We worked closely with operators to finalize 2021 business plans, assuming travel would start to recover in the summer of 2021.

During the second wave, cash-flow monitoring and liquidity planning continued to be our top priorities. At end of 2020, InnVest successfully secured a credit facility with a new lender. Several of our lenders agreed to advance additional funds against the hotels that they had financed for us. Some of our hotel brand companies took quick action to defer cyclical renovations. We are so thankful to have such understanding and supportive partners.

Like many other businesses, we also benefited from various government support programs. It is not hard for us to imagine how many of our hotels would have been shut down without the government support. Indeed, across the economy, many businesses would simply have closed their doors.

In January 2021, the third wave hit in Canada and pushed the hotel industry into another long waiting period. Fortunately, by spring, the vaccine rollout was in effect in Canada. Although we had not yet seen a significant uptick in bookings, as hoped for in our business plan, I continued to hear good stories from our hotels about how our service made our guests feel special at this difficult time. Each of the stories demonstrated the value of our company.

For example, back in February 2021, one guest checked in at Comfort Inn Sydney, in Nova Scotia, planning to stay there while attending her treatments at a local cancer centre. The guest would have to travel over several mountains, traverse a large bridge, and take a ferry ride in the middle of winter during a pandemic just to receive her chemo treatments. Our staff wanted to do something to make her feel secure and supported, so they went to a local store and picked up fuzzy warm slipper socks to keep her feet warm, along with herbal teas to help ease her nausea from her upcoming chemo treatments. All items were placed in the guest's room with a handwritten note. This guest deeply appreciated the gesture and has since become a repeat customer.

During the height of the pandemic, many hotel properties in the city weren't permitting reservations from essential workers or guests from outside of the province. Our team tried to capitalize on this issue by promoting our property for self-isolators, offering long-term stays for our essential workers.

In P.E.I., essential workers were not permitted to go to restaurants or to patronize drive-thrus and were forbidden to have social interaction after the workday, week after week and month after month. So our hotel team decided that they would try to make a difference to these valued guests. Our team in Comfort Inn Charlottetown asked our guests what they missed most about being on the road during the pandemic, and they all replied, "Home cooking." In response, our team planned various events, including the Ham and Scalloped Potatoes Fall Event, Chili Nights, and Holiday Roast Chicken Dinner. Our team enjoyed doing these events as much as the guests enjoyed the time chatting and eating and feeling somewhat normal again.

The response from guests was incredibly heartwarming on each occasion. Our hotel team was able to do something, with relatively little effort or cost, that had a huge impact on these guests. We are finding that, across our portfolio, these acts of kindness built loyalty to our hotels.

As we continued through this unpredictable situation, we realized that transparency is key to our success. Throughout the pandemic I hosted regular update calls with all of our hotel leaders and our corporate offices. I communicated key priorities and major decisions as soon as possible, and I encouraged our team to share their concerns and ideas. During the first few calls, I stated clearly that we should prepare ourselves for a marathon. That meant we needed to set a sustainable pace and plan that would conserve the precious energy and capacity of the team, both collectively and as individuals. Most importantly, I led by clearly stating and explaining our base expectations and I tried to set realistic goals during the crisis.

Stretch goals in areas such as revenue growth were no longer viable. With employees, and with lenders, the board, and leadership teams, we celebrated the smallest wins during the crisis. We exceeded our 2020 COVID reforecast that was set very early in the pandemic. This was a significant achievement, as it showed we were capable of managing through the crisis and that we wouldn't need to reset our strategy every month.

The hardest decision that I made was to suspend hotel operations. Twenty-five of our hotels, which represents half of hotel rooms, were closed for five months. We had to lay off almost 80% of our workforce during the pandemic. One of our long-service hotel staff emailed me to share her sadness at leaving, noting that the hotel she worked at had never been closed since the day it opened.

The night before some hotels closed, several of the hotel teams intentionally left room lights on in a heart-shaped pattern that could be seen from outside the buildings. Many people in the community were touched by this. At the most difficult moment, our hotel team shared their compassion, caring, and enthusiasm with the community and that inspired everyone at InnVest. At that moment, I was exceptionally proud of our company and humbled to be allowed to lead such a compassionate team. This ordeal has demonstrated to me that it is easy for a fast-growing company to attract and retain people in the good times, but it is more precious to have dedicated people willing to stay and work through the troubled times.

In July and August 2020, most provinces started to see a slight reduction in COVID virus cases, and we gratefully and gradually reopened all our InnVest hotels. During the eighteen months that followed, we focused on three priorities: First, we emphasized health and safety. Our hotels were mandated to strictly follow the highest standards for hygiene and cleanliness provided by our various hotel company brands to ensure the safety of our guests and staff. And we closely monitored health department updates and local government guidance on business operation regarding COVID-19. When travel rebounds, our new elevated expectations regarding safety, security, and cleanliness will continue to influence booking decisions.

Second, we transformed to a more efficient operating model. Labour is one of the primary areas where a business like ours begins looks for savings as it forms a significant portion of hotel operating expenses. But costs don't tell the full story. In the last few months, many staff had extra responsibilities as the hotels kept a minimum staffing level. However, we don't want to be caught short-staffed, with stressed employees and unhappy guests. This has inspired us to rework our staffing models. For example, we plan to introduce technology to optimize labour scheduling, which will allow us to forecast staffing needs and plan accordingly. We are also looking into ways to lower utilities and service costs at the individual hotel level. And I am challenging our green and sustainability committee to work on an initiative to collect more benchmark data and identify more potential cost-saving opportunities that will also benefit the environment.

Finally, we reduced our capital spending, focusing on completing renovations that were started pre-pandemic. This included the Hilton Quebec hotel project, one of the largest capital projects in InnVest history. In late 2019, Hilton Quebec, a renowned landmark property in Quebec City, closed its doors to the hotel's loyal guests and associates to embark upon a transformational renovation. The planned year-long multi-million-dollar renovation would be comprehensive in nature, involving upgrading the exterior, all public areas, restaurants, event spaces, and guest rooms.

As COVID-19 took hold in North America in March 2020, most hotels across North America shuttered operations in their initial response to the safety threat as well as the significant downturn in demand. Some would see a pre-existing closure for a year-long renovation as a fortunate coincidence. However Hilton Quebec was not without its challenges. The pandemic shut down construction in Quebec for seven weeks, and as restrictions eased and contractors returned, our InnVest team faced recovering from a seven-week hiatus in the face of new health and safety protocols. Working with our partners—Garoy Construction Inc. and Lemay Michaud Architecture Design—we reset our strategy and set out on a path toward finishing the project during the pandemic. On January 1, 2021, Hilton Quebec successfully and safely reopened. I am incredibly proud of our team and partners for their ability to navigate through this incredibly challenging period, working collaboratively to safely complete the renovation on schedule.

The global pandemic of 2020–2021 has been the ultimate test of our adaptability. I was in uncharted waters at both the business and personal level. For my family, the pandemic hit prior to the March shutdown in Ontario. Our children attended a Chinese-language school on weekends to help them learn my mother tongue and an important part of their heritage. In January 2020, fears of COVID-19 shut down the in-person classes and the kids started online learning. That was the start of the whole family working from home.

My husband was often asked how he liked working from home, and he would reply, "I've been working part-time from home for a few years, and

I enjoy it. I just don't enjoy everyone else in the house working from home too!" This experience of having our entire family working and living together, 24/7, was one of the biggest personal challenges to overcome, along with keeping our kids entertained and off their digital devices.

Along with thousands of other Canadian families, we had to adjust to the new ways of working and schooling. We were fortunate that we were able to pivot quickly to the at-home model, which many families were not able to do as easily. I donated our hotels' retired laptops to families who could not afford to buy new devices for their kids.

At the start, it took our kids some time to follow their daily agenda and to learn how to use Google Classroom. Technology was not new to our family, but we now needed to use it in different ways, including as a way for the kids to attend virtual school. There were months of challenges in keeping our children in their seats, focused on school, doing homework in their own rooms, and not surfing on their laptops or watching YouTube. And we adapted to being teachers, tutors, and parents all day long. As the pandemic dragged on, we adapted. I found more online activities for the kids to enjoy and sites that allowed them to interact with other kids and learn while they played online.

For me, there was some escape in work. I found myself with no commute, but the downside was that I was not just working from home—I now lived at work. I ended up working later in the day, taking breaks as needed, but lunch breaks were not just for me—we had to feed the kids too. Over the past eighteen months as a family, we became closer. Yes, there were, and still are, challenges—being together too long can be stressful, and it can be depressing at times. But we tried to be considerate of each other and for the most part we were successful.

I started walking more. My goal became to rack up ten to fifteen thousand steps per day. I found I enjoyed the beautiful views along the shoreline of Lake Ontario. The birds flying low above the water in mist amazed me; watching the beautiful sunsets made me think that no matter what happens, every day can end beautifully. My mind was calm and more focused after my daily walk.

At the time of writing, the Canadian government had recently announced that we will begin allowing entry to Americans who are fully vaccinated on August 9, 2021, and will open the borders to any fully vaccinated travellers beginning September 7. Air Canada resumed seventeen international flight routes and re-established the network of connections between Canada and the world. The employment numbers for the tourism industry in the U.S. increased rapidly in July. This news is exciting and encouraging. The vaccine will take some time to be distributed, and variants of the virus pose a potential setback to our economic recovery. However, the restoration of travel and the upturn in business activities means hotels are coming back.

I am encouraged by signs that we are recovering, however slowly. We have adapted, we have overcome, and I have the same hope I had when the pandemic started—that we will survive, we will flourish, and we will stand strong as a team. Being resilient was how we managed unpredictable challenges and changes. Whether that team is our families, our companies, our neighbours and friends, or people across the world, we will adapt and we will end this pandemic standing together.

KRUGER PRODUCTS

You'll find a roll of Kruger Products' toilet paper in one of every three Canadian bathrooms. Unless you work at the 117-year-old Canadian company, you likely never gave much thought to how it gets there. You run low, you go to the grocery store and buy more. There's always toilet paper on the shelves.

That is, until COVID-19 hit in March 2020. Suddenly, people began hoarding bathroom supplies. Grocery stores and big box retailers were running out of staples such as toilet paper. Family-owned Kruger Products faced a run on its brands—Cashmere and Purex—just as governments began to shut down businesses. It was up to Kruger Products chief executive Dino Bianco to figure out how to keep toilet paper on the shelves while keeping 2,700 employees at nine plants safe.

Bianco joined Kruger Products in 2018 after a twenty-eight-year run at Kraft, where he ran the food company's Canadian business and its beverages unit, which is headquartered in Chicago. A PricewaterhouseCoopers accountant by training, he first learned the consumer products business at cookie maker Christie Brown—remember "Mr. Christie, you make good cookies"?—during a summer job while a commerce student at the University of Toronto.

Kruger Products is owned by the fourth generation of Joseph Kruger's family. The New York native moved to Montreal in 1904 and started a fine-paper-making business. The second generation moved into newsprint, packaging, and sawmills. In the past two decades, Kruger moved into renewable energy, spirits, and specialized paper products.

While the company has diversified, it remains close to its roots. In the midst of the pandemic, Kruger Products opened a new state-of-the-art tissue facility in Quebec that can turn out six hundred million rolls of toilet paper annually, with a single mill able to supply every Canadian household with over forty rolls per year!

Dino Bianco

JULY 2021

It was March 2, 2020, when I received a text from a good friend saying Costco had run out of toilet paper. *That can't be*, I thought. *Costco always had lots of inventory.* I had to see this for myself. I got in my car and drove to my local Costco, in the Toronto suburbs. I could not believe my eyes. People were pushing shopping carts filled with toilet paper. The floor pallets, normally piled high with Kruger Products' Cashmere and Purex brands, were empty. In that moment, I knew that life was about to become very different.

On March 12, I received a call from a *Globe and Mail* reporter who wanted to do an article on toilet paper based on hearing of the short supply. *That's odd*, I thought. *With all the challenges going on with COVID, why do they care about toilet paper? Nobody ever cares about toilet paper.* Until, of course, you don't have any. So I did the interview. I took an upbeat tone. I reassured *Globe* readers that our toilet paper was made in Canada, we had lots of supply, and what consumers were experiencing was short term and the shelves would be stocked again soon.

Well, I was only partially right. We were shipping toilet paper at record levels to retailers, but as soon as an order got to the store, it was gone. Panic-buying had set in. Under Maslow's new hierarchy, toilet paper ranked near the top, right after food, water, and shelter! Suddenly people realized that this product that everybody used but never really thought about had become the beacon for the COVID crisis. If you run out of pasta, you have rice; run out of oranges, you eat apples; but run out of toilet paper, then what?

After my interview with the *Globe* I received dozens of calls from various other news outlets across Canada, all wanting to talk about toilet paper. As the Canadian market leader in the category, at a family-owned, Montreal-based company with one hundred years of history in this country, I realized I had a responsibility to ease the mounting uncertainty around a basic household staple. I told the outlets that our production came from Canada—many people thought most of our toilet paper came from China. I informed them we had lots of capacity to produce and encouraged them not to hoard and to buy only what they needed so that more people could get toilet paper.

My message didn't get through. From the first Canadian lockdowns in March right through to July, we could not catch up to the panic-driven demand. Our plants were running at full capacity, day and night. Not only were we short on toilet paper, but demand for paper towels and facial tissue spiked. People were stuck at home and clearly decided to clean anything and everything. In the first months of the pandemic, we were running out of not only toilet paper but also our SpongeTowels paper towels and our Scotties tissues. Kruger Products had never experienced anything like this and neither had any of our peers. Across North America, tissue producers were running full out to meet surging demand and selling every roll they produced.

As I reflect on the time before the pandemic, I had always thought that, as a leader, I was prepared to handle pretty much anything that could come my way. Over the past thirty years, I've worked in finance, sales, and marketing. I'm a CPA, and I've been fortunate to have executive roles in large, well-run U.S. and Canadian consumer product companies. I'm at the stage in my career when I thought I'd seen it all.

Then came COVID. Early on, it felt like none of my previous experience was relevant to what was happening in our business. I didn't know it at the time, but as I reflect on the journey, even though I was not specifically prepared for a pandemic, the leadership experience I had gained over the years had provided me with the foundation, framework, and courage to manage through the huge uncertainty and disruption that came our way.

Let me take you inside the situation at Kruger Products as COVID began to sweep across North America. In the early weeks of March 2020, with COVID lockdowns in place and life radically changing for all of us, my leadership team and I faced several issues that would have been a challenge under normal times, let alone in a pandemic, when none of the old rules applied.

Demand for our consumer products surged by 30 to 40%. However, demand for our commercial products were declining by similar amounts as restaurants and hospitality shut down. We were trying to shift the mix of paper products we produce, while at the same time we had to lock down and reconfigure our production facilities to keep our people safe. We were in the middle of building a new, state-of-the-art $575 million tissue manufacturing facility in Quebec. And to top it off, we were set to move to a new corporate head office in early April.

Kruger Products' executive team was also in flux. I had just lost my senior vice-president of operations in February and hadn't begun the search for a replacement. My new chief marketing officer had just started. And as if this weren't enough, in early March we had implemented an IT upgrade. That change to our systems meant we had reduced technology capability well into the fall as we upgraded our network and hardware, just at a time when working from home created a huge demand for increased bandwidth and IT support.

As I reflect on these challenges we were facing, a few things stand out from a leadership point of view that ensured we would succeed as a company and as individuals. The three key ideas I want to spend time on are centred on (1) providing clarity of goal; (2) making decisions based on values; and (3) communicating openly, honestly, and often.

Clarity of Goal—"Keep our people safe and keep the business running!"

In early March, prior to government-imposed lockdowns, I established a crisis management team of key leaders who met at least weekly to manage through COVID. We quickly mandated pandemic protocols for our manufacturing teams, who work at nine facilities across North America. The measures included masks, physical distancing, pre-screening, no visitors, and increased cleaning.

We also implemented a wage top-up program so that if one of our employees couldn't work because of COVID, they knew they were covered financially. We closed our offices and had people work from home. The protocols we implemented were aimed at doing everything we could to make people feel safe and supported, while trying to alleviate any financial stress or uncertainty if they couldn't work.

On this front, I'm proud to say we did quite well. We had employees who got the virus, but our numbers were below the infection rates in the regions where we operate and we had no internal COVID transmission. The actions we took seem commonplace now, but in those early days they were ground-breaking. It was also clear to me at this time that although COVID was a humankind event, affecting everyone on the planet, it was a very personal experience. Everyone was dealing with it in their own way, with varying degrees of anxiety, stress, and uncertainty.

As the weeks of pandemic living became months, we introduced several mental health and emotional well-being initiatives, including taking the pulse of our workplace with employee surveys. We could see and hear the stress the pandemic was creating in people's lives. Even though I was going through my own journey, every time that Teams camera came on, I worked hard to project focus, calm, and hope. I knew people were counting on me for reassurance. They needed to hear that we were doing the right things to keep them safe at work, both physically and emotionally.

We work in an essential industry, so yes, running the business was critical and I talked openly about this. However, I tried to always balance the message that the show must go on with my concern for employee health, with the goal of maintaining a sense of trust and an unwavering commitment to our people. This was a responsibility I did not take lightly. The CEO—decisive, confident, empathetic. This wasn't fake, it was the real me and the only me I know how to be, but after ten back-to-back meetings a day while keeping up with the rapidly evolving changes in our local environments, when the Teams camera went off, I was emotionally exhausted! At this stage I also realized I had to look after myself. So I increased my workouts at my home gym, I began running—and I hate running—and I worked from my cottage as often as I could. This helped clear my mind, recharged my emotional batteries, and kept me physically active.

On the business continuity side, we purchased four times the raw materials we needed to keep our business running, to be prepared for any supply disruptions. We made quick, bold operational decisions. For example, we eliminated 50% of our product lines so we could focus on the fast-moving ones and produce more goods with fewer change-overs. We delayed non-essential shutdowns and maintenance so our facilities could run longer. Also, about a year prior to the pandemic, I had brought in an operational excellence program to increase the output of our machinery. Using a lean manufacturing approach, this "OpEx" program set the foundation for how we run our plants and drove increased capacity. The timing of this program could not have been better, as we were able to benefit from improved output just when we needed it most.

Being Guided by Values Makes Tough Decisions Easier!

I knew that we would be forced to make decisions on issues that we had never encountered before. I committed with my leadership team that we would evaluate our actions against our vision and mission through the lens of our values with the focus on delivering. When you have a framework for how to respond to the uncertainties using values, it makes tough management calls easier. This allowed us to make sure we were making decisions not just for the short term but also for a post-COVID world. This principled approach shaped the way we moved through the pandemic. For example, we openly stated we were not going to take a price increase just because demand was strong. We allocated our tissue supply fairly across our customers; we were transparent about who got what. We made sure that, even with tight supply, we provided free tissue packages to our employees. We saw many of our people pay this forward with kindness, sharing their supply of tissue products with family and neighbours. On the marketing front, we decided not to cut our advertising despite the surge in demand because we wanted our brands to be right there alongside our consumers during these challenging times. We also changed our advertising campaign to be much more emotional and connected to how our consumers were feeling with the launch of our award-winning "Unapologetically Human" campaign.

Early in the pandemic, one of our employees read a story about a nurse who was in tears after an eighteen-hour shift because she could not find toilet paper at her local grocery store. We decided to act. We partnered with Mercedes to deliver our toilet paper directly to frontline workers at some hospitals across Canada, so they at least had one less thing to worry about as they were keeping us safe.

Also, in response to the increased spotlight on social injustice issues, we amplified our strong commitment to our diversity, equity, and inclusion strategy to ensure all members of our team felt connected and proud of the culture we were building at Kruger Products. During a time of uncertainty, I wanted to reassure everyone that they were all part of the Kruger Products family and that, despite what was going on around us, they could feel welcome and proud working for our company.

Being guided by values and doing the right thing is also what drove our decision to provide each of our hourly manufacturing team members a special one-time monetary bonus in December, right before the holiday season. This was a thank you in recognition of the incredible work they did during a period of turmoil, when everyone had to adapt and do their jobs differently.

Communicating Honestly and Often!

I pride myself on being able to connect with people at all levels of the organization. I learn a great deal from these connections, I truly enjoy these relationships, and I feel that talking to our teams creates a more open culture. With COVID keeping us physically apart, it was more important than ever for me to connect with people. I needed to keep the organization engaged and also track the mood and rhythm of our company. I continued with regular virtual town halls where I, along with my leadership team, would discuss what was going on with the business and answer any questions. I wanted to assure all our employees that, despite not being together, the business was running well and that they each had a critical role to play in our success.

Apart from the regular town hall meetings, early in the pandemic I also held special COVID update meetings for all our employees. My objective was simple. I wanted to remain visible and accessible during a time when people were experiencing a great deal of uncertainty and significant change. I must admit to feeling somewhat vulnerable going into these meetings. They weren't scripted, and I knew I wouldn't have answers to all of the questions on people's minds. However, what I quickly learned is that people found comfort in coming together and that these meetings kept us united during this crisis. Even if there were a lot of questions no one had answers for, hearing how we were thinking about things and staying connected as a team was critical to building resilience.

In my quest to somehow try to replicate the spontaneous in-office interactions, I made a point of virtually dropping in to team meetings, so that I could personally thank our colleagues in a smaller setting and open up casual discussion to hear how people were doing, what they needed help with, and what was on their minds. I made a special effort to reach out to our newest employees, those who started with us during COVID. It was so important for me to welcome them and to make sure they felt part of the broader team. I can't imagine how I would have coped while starting with a new company, virtually. It impressed and amazed me to see strong connections forming from online gatherings. The communication flow was amplified by what my leadership team was doing with group meetings, cocktail hours, and birthday and anniversary celebrations. Our goal, right through the company, was to try to create a sense of normal in the un-normal, and also have a little fun.

I have two closing thoughts on our experience during COVID. First, I found that tasks that may seem impossible become possible through the dedication of people and the strength of a team. I saw this first-hand when we opened a brand-new tissue facility in the middle of the pandemic. At maturity, this site will be able to produce six hundred million rolls of toilet paper, which represents 25% of all consumer toilet paper sold in Canada in a year! Starting up a new site is an extremely challenging undertaking in the best of times. It was enormously daunting during a pandemic.

Let me provide some context. Building this plant required over one million construction hours and involved hundreds of suppliers and contractors on site at any given time. Highly specialized technical professionals flew in from Italy, Sweden, and the United States, and parts and equipment were also coming in from all over the world. All of this was happening at a time when borders were closed. The recruitment, onboarding, and training of 180 new employees was all done virtually. Against this backdrop, we completed the project safely, on time, and on budget with a seamless and successful assimilation of team members. Production started up in February 2021. The only way this happens is with a committed team, a clear plan, strong collaboration, and a safe environment, along with a commitment to removing barriers by empowering the team on the ground and backing their decision making. With our new facility rolling, we now have 15% more tissue capacity to serve the needs of our North American consumers.

My second thought is that success is a team sport and the differences that each member of the team brings to the group make us stronger. Our organization would not have succeeded without the guidance, courage, and compassion of my leadership team. They all recognized that we needed to work as a unified group, leveraging one another's unique strengths to achieve success. We would discuss and debate, but once a decision was made, we would move forward as one.

In a strange way, COVID has made our team and organization stronger. Supplying toilet paper during a time of incredible need gave us a renewed sense of purpose. It showed us that the organization we built could withstand the challenges thrown our way and that we would emerge stronger. Most importantly, it brought us closer together even though we were further apart. To each and every one of my colleagues, thank you, it is an honour to lead such a talented team. I am so proud of this group and will always look back at this time knowing we did the right things for our employees, customers, and shareholders.

The COVID pandemic created a time in my life that I will never forget. In years to come, when I'm retired and sitting on my dock with a scotch, I will look back at a crisis that started with a trip to Costco and reflect on a job well done.

LIFELABS

Charles Brown is no stranger to high-profile, high-pressure assignments.

When the winter Olympics kicked off in Vancouver in 2010, Brown was the Bell Canada executive responsible for the five-hundred-person team who wired the Games so the world could watch.

When hackers stole customer information from LifeLabs Medical Laboratory Services in the fall of 2019, Brown was the chief executive who had to deal with the fallout from one of Canada's largest data breaches.

Those assignments pale beside the challenge facing LifeLabs' CEO and the 5,700 employees at the country's largest lab testing network when the pandemic hit. COVID-19 tests and contact tracing were health workers' primary weapons in fighting the pandemic, prior to the development of vaccines.

LifeLabs went into the healthcare crisis with the ability to run more than 100 million medical tests annually. In the earliest stages of the pandemic, the company ran 600 COVID-19 tests each day. Within weeks, the volume exploded to over 10,000 daily tests. Those nasal swabs were administered at select sites redesigned on the fly to prevent spreading the coronavirus, by LifeLabs frontline workers who pulled on personal protection equipment to start each shift.

LifeLabs became Canada's dominant testing facility in 2013, when the Toronto-based company acquired two rivals, B.C. Biomedical Laboratories and CML HealthCare. One of the country's largest pension plans, OMERS, owns LifeLabs. The fund manager invests the retirement savings of Ontario municipal employees, including fire fighters, police officers, and healthcare workers.

Brown has spent his career at the intersection of technology and customer experience. He held senior roles at a number of upstart telecom companies, developing a reputation as a fixer by winning subscribers for the likes of Clearnet Communications and Wave Wireless, which competed with deep-pocketed incumbents Bell, Rogers, and Telus.

Bell recruited Brown in 2009. After running the Olympic project, he spent six years as president of The Source, the electronics retailer acquired and turned around by the phone company after U.S. parent RadioShack filed for bankruptcy. In 2018, Brown joined LifeLabs with a mandate to instill a customer-centric culture. The job description also ended up including dealing with cyber criminals and a global health crisis.

Charles Brown

JUNE 2021

I have to confess, when I first began hearing about the coronavirus and its impact abroad, I was in denial about the potential of it directly affecting our lives in the same way here in Canada. In an early meeting with my executive leadership team, I recall them asking all the right questions about preparedness. But I couldn't go there. When I reflected on it later, I realized my worry and fear had been taking over. As an organization, we were just coming out of another crisis, having been the victims of a cyber-attack in 2019; I knew that our people were still reeling and rallying to get through that crisis, so I was worried about what a global pandemic—which would be a marathon crisis, not a sprint—was going to do to the resilience of our teams and the spirit of our people. Just a few days later, when the global pandemic was officially declared, I had to eat my words; I apologized and thanked my executive team for being focused and determined during such a critical moment in our history.

The devastation that we have seen around the world in terms of loss of life, mental anguish, and economic hardship has been astounding. After COVID-19 hit, our team knew we had a responsibility to Canadians to continue our essential work and adapt to any challenges that came from the pandemic. I truly believe that the resilience of LifeLabs was the result of a combination of elements, including our strong partnerships, our investments in innovation and technology, and, maybe most importantly, the fact that as a healthcare business resilience is in the fabric of who we are.

Right from the start, the pandemic blew up our business model. We had to reassess our busy waiting rooms, in-person blood collections, requisition form processes, and open-plan offices and labs. Our frontline teams—phlebotomists, mobile lab technicians, couriers, and lab staff—kept us open and running, doing their job under very difficult circumstances. New protocols took the little joys out of each day—masks made it harder to communicate, colleagues had to eat lunch apart, and every cough or sneeze became suspicious and a potential threat to exposure.

Thanks to the learnings from our experience with the SARS outbreak in 2003, we already had a pandemic plan in place. This allowed us to react swiftly and to immediately put our frontline employees in full personal protection equipment (PPE), which some questioned as being overly cautious. Looking back, I'm glad that we went above and beyond from the start; we wanted to do everything we could to give our customers and employees the assurances they needed to feel safe.

Our procurement team made sure that we had a good amount of PPE stock available for our employees. While some organizations were facing shortages and backlogs, we were able to support others by temporarily lending out essential equipment to supplement their supplies. At a critical time in 2020, we were able to organize a loan of around 225,000 N95 masks and 200,000 isolation gowns to help with the PPE coverage for Ontario. Around the same time, we also provided approximately 200,000 isolation gowns to support organizations in British Columbia. We were not alone in supporting others; the mobilization and response to the pandemic has been nothing short of extraordinary. It has truly been remarkable to see the amount of collaboration and teamwork across all industries as many of us coped with the unexpected.

Early on in the pandemic, we were asked to be part of a serology study—the first of its kind in Canada. The collaboration between our company, the B.C. Centre for Disease Control (BCCDC), the University of British Columbia, and public health scientists was required in anticipation of a possible SARS-CoV-19 transmission in the province. The study looked at anonymous blood samples collected at our locations (for reasons unrelated to COVID-19) in March and May 2020, before and after public health measures were introduced. On our side of the study, we assisted with specimen collection, de-identification, and secure transmission. Because we have a large network of labs across the province, we were able to gather all of the specimens needed in a short time period. As a result of the study, health officials were able to determine that there had been a "successful suppression" of community transmission in B.C., and possibly the lowest rate of infection in North America. It was determined that fewer than one in one hundred people in the Lower Mainland were infected during the first wave.

Although we were involved with important work like the serology study in some segments of the business, we were also facing an overall loss of revenue due to lockdowns. But, as they say, necessity breeds innovation, and COVID-19 had us quickly rethinking how we could deliver our services. In many ways, we were given the opportunity to reconsider our standard practices and move toward exciting, customer-centred solutions supported by technology. Under normal circumstances, these advancements would have taken years, but during COVID-19 they were taking place in a matter of days or weeks.

The team was regularly accomplishing tremendous large-scale projects in timelines that were previously thought impossible. After being asked to help with testing COVID-19 samples in our British Columbia and Ontario labs, our laboratory operations, medical science, and logistics teams jumped into action immediately to increase the capacity in our labs. I can't stress how monumental this was—our team was able to get the process up and running in just five days. This was only possible thanks to the tremendous collaboration between our government partners and several teams across LifeLabs. To give an idea of the significance of this timeline, under normal circumstances it can take around six months to one year to get a complex line of testing up and running.

At launch, we were running six hundred COVID-19 molecular diagnostic tests per day. At our peak, we were able to run an average of about ten thousand tests per day, and our team continued to work diligently to push and challenge themselves to help increase the capacity. We have always been a 24/7 operation, but during this time it felt like we were running 48/7. We were so busy that we did a call-out to friends and family to assist our specimen management teams with receiving, counting, packaging, and organizing samples for transportation in one of our B.C. labs. In one case, a team member's son volunteered to help out with specimen packaging. At eighteen, he was the youngest member on the team and was honoured to help out, expressing his privilege to give something back to the community and to assist during the pandemic. Another team member's daughter shared that she was thrilled to be able to contribute to the community during the pandemic and was "thankful to work alongside those who were guiding us through the difficult time."

In June 2021, we celebrated a major milestone of completing over two million COVID-19 molecular tests for Canadians and their healthcare providers. I am still blown away by the LifeLabs team and their remarkable efforts that played a role in saving lives, protecting communities, and keeping the economy running. On top of all this, we were still in full operation with our other lab testing and diagnostic work.

While our team of healthcare heroes continued working diligently on the front line, our management and professional teams had the opportunity to explore unique business opportunities and ventures. I would say that the pandemic awakened our entrepreneurial spirit. I have a theory that all the problems in the world have already been solved—just outside of your professional or personal bubble. I have spent the majority of my career in the technology and retail industry, from entrepreneurial startups to large corporate entities like Bell and The Source. The move into health care definitely required a switch in mindset for me, but my technology and retail background, which fuels my curiosity and relentless pursuit of putting the customer at the centre of everything that we do, proved to be a valuable asset. Historically, health care has been an industry with tremendous potential for creative innovation but one that also faces countless regulatory obstacles and barriers. COVID-19 gave us a chance to take on new challenges and had us all thinking outside of the box. The pandemic also helped transform LifeLabs' culture at the leadership level and challenged people's mindset in a push to be more agile. And as president and CEO, I believe my role is to support my leadership team and help keep things moving along by removing barriers and, ultimately, getting out of the way.

With this new line of thinking, we were able to move beyond the lab into some great new ventures. We were proud to provide our services to the NHL as the testing partner for its Return to Play plan. Daily testing allowed the hockey season to resume in late May, after being suspended in March. I think that allowing hockey to come back brought some normalcy to Canada, which was good for everyone's mental health and well-being.

With COVID-19 molecular testing successfully running through our labs, we were able to turn our attention to helping Canadians get back to some sense of regularity and routine. Through our WorkClear and FlyClear services, we partnered with several high-profile companies in the airline, film, and energy industries. In December, we even tested Santa's elves and reindeer before the big man's big night on Christmas Eve! (Obviously, Santa was immune to COVID already.)

Our entrepreneurial mindset helped us get involved with several exciting initiatives across the organization. Our digital technology and strategic partnerships team got us involved with a very exciting new project with the UBC Faculty of Medicine in collaboration with First Nations and healthcare partners to use drones to fly healthcare supplies into rural and remote communities across B.C. We used one of our collection centres in Mississauga, Ontario, to offer asymptomatic COVID-19 testing and ran a pilot program to determine the accuracy of rapid testing kits. When vaccinations began to appear, like a beacon of hope, our Saskatchewan logistics team (who are seasoned experts at driving cautiously with precious cargo—even in snowstorms) were able to help with the distribution of vaccines across the province.

And as schools began reopening in Ontario, we were asked to conduct asymptomatic testing for our youngest population. I have volunteered with the Kids Help Phone (KHP), as well serving as the former board chair for several years, and I empathize with the uncertainty and fear that children must have been feeling while navigating school closures, social isolation, and dramatic changes to their daily routines. According to KHP's Impact Report, young people connected with Kids Help Phone over 4.6 million times in 2020, a 137% increase over 2019. It's no doubt that the impact on children's mental health will be longstanding after the pandemic is over.

To help provide peace of mind to students and their families, we worked with the Ontario government to create hub collection sites in high-priority areas for asymptomatic students and their families. This testing was useful in identifying cases early and potentially managing outbreaks to ensure that schools remained safe. I also like to think that this increase in testing helped to reduce any stress or anxiety that teachers or students may have felt about returning to the classroom setting.

In addition to the clinics provided in schools, we were asked to participate in a pilot project to bring COVID-19 testing to students and families in hot spots in the greater Ottawa area. As part of the pilot, LifeLabs' staff travelled to locations in a paramedic bus and delivered testing from within the bus itself. This was a truly mobile solution that helped to provide testing where and when it was needed most.

All of these opportunities were possible thanks to the agility and professionalism of the LifeLabs team. I can say with great certainty that almost everyone's role in this company has been altered in some way in order to help support our efforts during COVID-19. And I have no doubt that we will continue to redefine our roles as we come up with more ways to support Canadians through COVID even as restrictions and protocols are removed.

It is very humbling to work alongside healthcare heroes who risk their lives every single day, and I've spent a lot of my time in the last year saying thanks. While the LifeLabs team may be more behind the scenes than nurses or doctors, there was a strong sense of purpose in being on the front lines of the pandemic.

One especially bright spot in the pandemic came just before the holiday season, when we decided to recognize our frontline teams with a healthcare hero recognition payment. I had been asked about pandemic pay almost every day in 2020, but due to the drop in our regular business revenue we were never able to make it happen without recovering some of this loss. When we announced the one-time payment, it was incredibly moving to hear the stories of joy and excitement from those who received it. Employees responded with heartwarming gratitude, sharing that they were "shocked and thrilled" to receive the payment and expressing how they appreciated the management and leadership teams for making it happen. That was one of my proudest moments of the past year.

As a leader, saying thank you is one of my favourite things to do. Even in normal, pre-COVID times, I regularly asked my leadership team to share the names of employees who had worked especially hard and I would then find out what they did and how it impacted the organization. From there, I would set up phone calls to personally acknowledge these team members and their work. I always find it hard to get going on Mondays, so I would reserve time in my calendar to make these calls and start the week off on a positive note. Having an authentic one-to-one conversation with an employee energizes me. I don't take myself too seriously, but I realize people feel valued when the CEO calls them. For them too, it sets up their whole week. Sometimes I'd talk to them a second time and they'd tell me that they had told their family or their spouse about the call. There's nothing I like more than thanking my employees for their great work, and I really felt that having this type of positive human connection was more important than ever during the pandemic. It kept me going.

Many of my phone calls went to frontline employees who worked tirelessly to support and serve our customers. When the public was asked to stay home, our teams came into work every day to provide Canadians with access to essential healthcare services. They donned PPE, guided our customers through new protocols, and made outstanding contributions to the broader healthcare system. At the same time, emotions and anxiety had intensified. People were stressed and began behaving differently, and we started seeing an increase in rude and offensive behaviour from customers at our collection centres.

Physical distancing protocols meant that we had less space in our waiting rooms, which sometimes resulted in lineups outside. Because many of our customers are elderly, ill, or vulnerable, we had to take special considerations in how to manage these lineups and customer expectations. We introduced a concierge role to direct the flow of customers, implemented appointment booking (we've always been a walk-in operation), and started accepting electronic test requisition forms. Despite that, I still regularly heard stories of verbal and even physical abuse of our staff.

In one disappointing case, I had to phone a fellow CEO to tell them that they were no longer welcome at any of our locations. They were shocked that I was calling about it and stunned that they were banned. They didn't offer an apology, which just made it worse. I'm sorry to say that as a result of this incident the employee who experienced the brunt of the verbal abuse ended up leaving LifeLabs. I still regret that they were made to feel attacked; our client services and logistics team will always do everything they can to make sure our collection centres are welcoming and safe for employees and customers. LifeLabs has zero tolerance for abusive behaviour at our collection centres, and I always ensure that our team knows we have their back. When I called the employee to let them know about the action that had been taken, they appreciated the support but maintained that the incident was too traumatizing for them to return to work.

Despite the increase in negative confrontations, we have been delighted by the humanity and kindness shared by our communities and customers. We have received many positive messages from customers and clients. Teams were regularly surprised with appreciation letters, gift cards, flowers, food deliveries, donuts, "ear savers," and handmade healthcare hero medals—and there was even a remarkable batch of handmade quilts from a Saskatoon customer. These quilts were dropped off anonymously with a note to explain that they were made by a local resident who donates close to two hundred quilts for charity and special gifts each year. (In the note, the resident shared they had made a total of two thousand quilts so far!) What truly stood out to me was the thoughtfulness and dedication that went into each quilt—it took about ten to twelve hours to complete each of these personalized and heartfelt pieces of art. Needless to say, our employees were blown away by this act of kindness. We made sure to highlight this story and others in our internal weekly newsletter to share the appreciation across the organization.

The past two years have presented us with a lot of learning that we can leverage into the future—particularly at the leadership level. We are getting to a place where people are challenging each other, which I see as a sign of confidence. We've got a team now that has a lot of confidence in itself; they are speaking their mind more and feeling empowered to do so. A great lesson for me as a CEO has been that if you give people the space and support they need to do their jobs, they will deliver. And when you do that it not only strengthens confidence, it also cultivates a deep, trusted relationship with your people—and that is the most rewarding part of being a leader.

I can't say that I've changed much as a leader as a result of COVID-19, but I've certainly learned a lot. Mainly, I've begun to show my appreciation more openly and have made an effort to always prioritize it in my communication. I've realized how important it is to over-communicate; the amount of change and uncertainty we faced made this a necessity. When any organization is facing great change and a crisis, visible leadership is so important, especially with a large part of our team working from home. I found that the team wanted to know that I was there and that I had their back. I began recording weekly "Catching up with Charles" videos—a series dedicated to providing key updates and answering employee questions. I'd also invite guests on to discuss updates in our business, and frontline employees to share their stories about what they were facing on a day-to-day basis. We also implemented an employee recognition segment called "Lifey's [our unofficial mascot] feel-good moment," showcasing excellence in performance and customer service from across the organization.

During the pandemic, I also had to adjust in order to dedicate a few moments for myself each day. I would book time at the end of meetings to get outside, even if it was just for five minutes. A breath of fresh air would do wonders and I found that allowing myself these little mental breaks really helped. When possible, I would organize my calendar so that I would start off my mornings with meetings that I found intellectually stimulating to help carry me through the rest of the day. Other times, when I was feeling worn out, I would focus on articles or video clips that brought humour and levity to the day. For the wider organization, I made sure that my leadership team was equipped to have the necessary conversations in order to support each other in coping with fear, anxiety, and isolation.

An important element of a positive mental health and well-being program is making sure that employees are able to bring their best selves to work. As part of the monumental shift in the social justice movement that sparked international dialogue, we re-examined our diversity, equity, and inclusion initiatives and launched our Stronger Together program to reinforce that all individuals—no matter their race, gender, beliefs, preferences, age, abilities, and so on—are accepted, respected, and valued at LifeLabs. As I write this, I would like to acknowledge that I do so from the traditional territory of many nations, including the Mississaugas of the Credit, the Anishinabek, the Chippewa, the Haudenosaunee, and the Wendat peoples, and that is now home to many diverse First Nations, Inuit, and Métis.

While there is a lot more work to do in this space, I believe we've made a positive and meaningful step forward. We are continuing to work on this initiative to allow for meaningful, permanent changes throughout our organization. I feel that an important part of my legacy is to leave an organization stronger than it was when I first joined, and celebrating the diversity of our people, their opinions, beliefs, and experiences is a big part of making LifeLabs a better place to work.

We have been involved with a tremendous amount of important work in the past two years, and our success is a result of the tireless efforts of the entire LifeLabs team through these challenging times. I am proud to share that we were recognized on Forbes Canada's "Best Employers of 2021" list, which truly reflects the pride felt by our employees.

Looking ahead, we still face uncertainty and will require a strong culture and mindset to navigate the way forward. Our resilience is thanks to a team that is agile, collaborative, and innovative. Building on the momentum of the past two years, we are in the midst of an internal culture transformation, with an updated strategy that will guide our decisions and actions moving forward. I can feel the energy and excitement across the organization as we focus on delivering long-term solutions for Canadians. Nothing would be possible without the expertise and enthusiasm of this team—my LifeLabs family.

LINAMAR

In 1966, Frank Hasenfratz started a machine shop with a metal lathe in the basement of his house in Guelph, Ontario. He called the business Linamar and built it into a Canadian industrial champion.

In the spring of 2020, Linamar chief executive Linda Hasenfratz showed that her father's entrepreneurial zeal and deft touch with machinery still permeates the company. As part of a pivot to combatting a global health crisis, Linamar retooled manufacturing equipment in a matter of weeks. The company began cranking out multiple different types of ventilator parts and assemblies for critically ill COVID-19 patients.

As the leader of an unabashedly traditional industrial company with sixty-one plants and twenty-seven thousand employees, Hasenfratz comes out of the pandemic as a passionate advocate for a vibrant Canadian manufacturing sector as a part of the prescription for a healthier economy.

Linamar—which the founder named for daughters Linda and Nancy and wife Margaret—turns out everything from auto and truck parts to farm equipment and aerial work platforms. The company calls its specialty "advanced manufacturing." To survive in the face of changing consumer tastes, increasing competition, and the occasional economic downturn, Hasenfratz stresses responsiveness, flexibility, and balance as key components of the corporate culture.

A science and MBA graduate of Western University, Hasenfratz started her career at Linamar in 1990 as a machine operator. She went on to hold management roles in a number of divisions before stepping up as president in 1999 and then taking over as CEO in 2002. In her first year as chief executive, Linamar sales were $800 million. The company's revenues were $7.4 billion in the year before the pandemic. Linamar has come a long way from the founder's basement, yet has maintained the versatility of that one-man machine shop.

Linda Hasenfratz

JULY 2021

In February 2020 I took a ski vacation with my family to Italy. It was a wonderful trip. We were driving back to the airport in Venice to fly home when we heard on the news that five villages in the area we were literally travelling through were being locked down due to the spread of COVID-19. That really brought the situation to an immediate and personal level. It was the moment that I realized this was going to have a bigger impact on us than I had originally expected.

The next week, I visited New York City for business meetings and a gala event, the Maple Leaf Ball, an annual event put on by the Canadian Association of New York. I wasn't feeling 100%, so over the course of the trip I declined to shake anyone's hand, out of fears that I might have picked up a bug. A week later, New York City was shut down, Broadway dark. Thinking back, I recall people in New York were taken aback that I didn't want to shake their hand. What a difference from how we are interacting with each other just eighteen months later. . . .

The last eighteen months have been an experience none of us would have predicted and none of us wish to relive. The enormous global impact of the COVID-19 pandemic on human life, business, families, society, economies, and day-to-day interactions has been profound, and in some cases is leaving long-lasting impacts. How companies approached and dealt with the situation revealed much about company cultures and resiliency. At Linamar we approached dealing with this pandemic as we would any crisis.

Crisis 101

Our first step was to assemble a team and make sure it had all the resources to drive decision making. We established our COVID-19 Task Force in early March, right after I returned from that trip to New York and before the World Health Organization actually formally said we faced a global pandemic.

At the lead were me and our president and chief operating officer, Jim Jarrell, one of the best business leaders I have ever met and exactly who you want by your side in a crisis (or any time for that matter!). Everything we accomplished in the last eighteen months Jim and I did together. Crisis management is a team sport, not an individual one. Our team included our other most senior executives as well as HR, of course, and operational representatives from around the world.

Next step: gather data. We were constantly gathering the latest in data from all possible sources, both broadly around the pandemic and more specifically for Linamar in terms of the impact to our own workforce and team and the impact on our customers. We are still gathering data regularly and using that to make fact-based decisions, not emotional ones. Frankly, this is how we have always approached running our business.

Gathering information, then using it effectively drove every element of our business, from how we ran our factories to our finance department. Our chief financial officer, Dale Schneider, and his team changed the way we managed our balance sheet, putting additional emphasis on gathering real-time information on our liquidity. Dale later described the shift this way: "The need for data was critical, notably around cash management, to ensure that we had the liquidity needed at the height of the pandemic and ongoing. The team understood the need, pulled together, and developed a weekly cashflow forecasting process for every facility globally. It was an amazing effort which paid off in spades as the increased transparency on our cash and cash requirements was critical. I am so proud of the entire team for pulling together, overcoming all obstacles and having great success!"

Next step: make a plan addressing the needs of all of our stakeholders, follow up, and execute on that plan daily. Our plan at Linamar was called the Linamar Health First Plan—that meant the health of our people, our health financially, our customers' health, and our communities' health. In keeping with our culture at Linamar, we approached the situation in a balanced way, considering the needs of all our stake-holders.

Most importantly, at all stages: prioritize communication. Our rule is to communicate frequently and ensure every conversation is fact based. We reached out to our employees first and foremost but of course also stepped up our dialogue with investors and customers. We communicated every couple of days in the early weeks, then backed off to weekly, monthly, and quarterly as the urgency of the crisis started to regulate. The frequency of communication in a crisis should be directly correlated to the urgency of the crisis. Jim summed it up by saying, "A leader must always create hope, encouragement, teamwork, and act immediately. Ensure everyone knows they are not on an 'island.' We are here for each other and there is nothing we can't achieve!"

We held a series of meetings with shareholders to make sure they knew what we knew and could have confidence in our plans and outlook. And of course, we maintained close connection with customers to understand their needs and help them solve their problems as they arose. We tried to communicate in a balanced way to ensure the urgency of the situation was clear and the need to follow the plan, without instilling panic.

I think an important point around communicating is that you should do so whether you have all the facts yet or not. Communicate what you know and what you are still working on, and admit what you don't know yet. Don't wait. That is key, because in the absence of fact, emotion and speculation thrive. People don't know what is happening, so they start guessing and making decisions based on conjecture. Keep all parties informed as you go, make sure they have all the facts, and you will reduce panic.

The tone of the messaging is important as well. Staying positive is crucial, but it is also extremely important to deal with the reality of the situation *as if it will continue for some time*. I feel like we did a good job of that. Hope is not enough. Hope is important—critical, really—but hope has to come with a plan. Blend optimism with being brutally realistic and strategic about how you will cope and succeed.

Ventilators

One of my daughters was living in the U.K. at the time COVID-19 began spreading globally. The U.K. was several weeks ahead of us in terms of the pandemic unfolding, and my daughter told me the U.K. was having a big issue with a lack of ventilators, equipment that was essential to keeping patients alive in the rapidly filling hospital wards.

Our team immediately jumped on the idea—if the U.K. was short, Canada would be too. We started researching Canadian ventilator and life support manufacturers, reaching out to see if we could help. We contacted provincial and federal governments to see what the need was. We also talked to companies outside of Canada that were building ventilators, including one of our automotive customers, General Motors, who had partnered with ventilator manufacturer Ventech to launch ventilator production in Michigan.

We pivoted rapidly to launch projects to manufacture ventilator parts and full ventilation and life support systems for five different companies. In some cases we were up and running in a matter of days—ten days from our first phone call to our first sample parts. In other, more complicated programs, launch took a little longer, but still, within about six weeks, we were in production on all programs.

Many folks have asked how we managed to start producing ventilator parts, something we had never done before, in such record time. The answer is simple: we have a flexible and incredibly skilled team of people at Linamar who are responsive, determined, and focused on execution in a way rarely seen. We involved multiple plants with multiple teams in the projects to spread the workload.

Our equipment is purposefully flexible, a strategy we employ to help us maximize asset utilization, which meant we didn't need to buy new equipment to launch the ventilator parts, just reprogram and build new fixtures. We had daily update calls with everyone involved to gauge progress and solve on the spot any issues popping up. Skilled, capable, accountable people; flexible equipment; and a solid plan and communication process were the keys to success.

The most complex product we made was a full life support system—basically an intensive care unit in a box, inclusive of ventilation systems, with more than 1,700 different parts—for Thornhill Medical, in Ontario. Thornhill's unit was a great example of Canadian-developed innovation in the biotech sector. It uniquely used ambient air to extract needed oxygen, allowing life support to happen anywhere, including in transit, without the need for oxygen tanks. Our supply chain experts jumped on the job to work with a global supply base to get quantities ramped up fast for this complex project. "During tough times, be alert and look for the opportunities for growth," said Jim. "Growth for leaders, growth for the team, growth for business, and growth for yourself. Take some calculated risk. Like Gretzky says—'You miss 100% of the shots you never take!'"

Our people around the world rallied in a myriad of other ways to support local communities with needed personal protective equipment, food deliveries, and many other support programs. In the end, we delivered nearly one million ventilator parts or systems during the pandemic. I am incredibly proud of the Linamar team for doing that at the exact time the entire world was shutting down.

Global Shutdown

As we entered the back half of March, we had to react quickly on a global basis to government mandates to stay at home, shelter in place, and shut down production. Although manufacturing was considered essential in some areas of operation, all of our customers were required to shut down, giving us no choice but to shut our operations down too, and to instruct all our people to work from home if they had work to do and lay off the ones who did not. This was a devastating moment for us as leaders. At peak, we had 16,500 of our 26,000 global employee base laid off; even in the depths of 2009 we did not have that level of layoffs.

Thank goodness for the government programs swiftly installed to help laid-off employees access funding quickly and help employers like us to bring people back to work at a full wage way before we needed them. There has of course been criticism of governments for their actions, and of companies for taking the subsidies, but the bottom line is that it made a big difference to employees and employers in the darkest days. Bringing people back to work was critical, and those programs made it affordable to do so.

We thought our operations would be down for two weeks globally, as experienced in our Chinese facilities when the pandemic first started; in the end it was two months. Finally, shutdowns were eased, and facilities started back up around mid-May 2020. The restart varied in different countries, but in North America it felt like we went from zero to a hundred overnight.

Restart and the Long, Bumpy Road to Recovery

Getting everyone back to work safely and managing a rapid relaunch with best quality and precision were top of mind when we got the call to resume production in May 2020.

Our first priority was to create effective protocols to protect the safety of our people, protocols that have proven to be very effective at ensuring no transmission of the virus in our facilities is occurring. This included screening pre-entry, including temperature testing, masks for everyone, social distancing (and plexiglass dividers where that wasn't feasible), assigned seating to allow traceability if needed, and extra cleaning and disinfection. We were able to work together, in the office and on the shop floor, without transmitting the virus. Even during the highest peaks of infections, we were able to keep our people safe at work. That was incredibly important to us.

Managing the relaunch in North America was a huge challenge. Our customers had seen demand stay at a much higher level than noted in other countries throughout the pandemic, and as business started to resume, demand surged. That meant a big decline in inventory levels of finished cars and therefore a need for production to resume, and fast.

Of course, this put pressures on supply chains. Suppliers were having issues getting production ramped up quickly. This was particularly true in the electronics sector, where increasing demand from the automotive and industrial sectors was compounded by surging demand for consumer electronics for a shuttered world. Reduced investment during 2020 meant supply was constrained, and surging demand and constrained supply caused big disruptions to production levels.

The impact of this was felt mainly in 2021, as more and more of the world starting ramping back up and supply of semiconductor chips just couldn't keep up with demand. Just when we thought we were on track for a great year, our customers were forced to shut down operations again due to lack of chips.

Supply chain issues were not limited to the electronic sector. Shortages of shipping containers caused shipping costs to spike. Shortages in other commodities, such as plastic resins, also began impacting production. In short, investments in general had ceased in a world very focused on cash generation, and when demand rebounded sharply, as is often the case post-crisis (unlike post-recession, when demand grows less sharply), shortages abounded.

The bottom line is, just like we learned in grade twelve physics, when something big stops, it takes a lot of energy and effort to get it going again. "It is important we all understand that during these times we have been on a little journey; it was not a trip," said Jim. "A trip is predictable, a trip is planned, a trip can be a little boring. A journey has all types of new discoveries! What we have been through, what we have seen, was unpredictable, never contemplated, never anticipated, and certainly not planned. We need to be ready, flexible, adaptable, and to continue to expect the unexpected!"

We became heavily engaged in testing to help reduce community spread and vaccination programs to advance the move toward herd immunity and a return to a more normal life; these efforts are ongoing. We believed testing to be absolutely essential to reducing the spread of the virus. People are most contagious in the one to three days *before* they show their first symptom. That means they don't know they have it yet and are actively spreading it. Learning that was what tipped the scales in my mind to how important testing is. We started testing employees in nearly half of our facilities regularly, using rapid tests.

We also believed vaccinations were crucial for keeping our loved ones safe and getting back to a normal life. In February 2021 we decided to launch a vaccination clinic in Canada to help get our community vaccinated as quickly as possible. In just four weeks, we had established a highly efficient vaccination clinic at our customer care centre for our Skyjack business. We had capacity for two thousand shots per day and a team of Linamar and community volunteers on deck to deliver them. I am so proud of our team for another flawless launch, this time literally saving lives in the process and giving people the chance to start to interact again.

A complicating factor was the surge after surge in COVID infections globally. Notwithstanding the incredible work of the pharma sector in getting excellent, highly effective vaccines developed and approved in record time, the vaccines weren't coming fast enough to stop the infection waves of winter and spring 2021. This was difficult to deal with, both mentally and emotionally, after a wrenching 2021.

Lessons Learned

As with any crisis, I think it is important to spend some time reflecting on what we have learned, what we could have done better, and how we can take that learning to be better prepared for the next crisis.

At Linamar we have a history of effectively managing crisis situations. We also have a rich history of long-term success. Our thirty-year and our ten-year growth rates for sales and earnings are at double-digit levels, a fact we are incredibly proud of. The full range—short-term, medium-term, and long-term success—is what you will see with Linamar. How did we achieve that? Reflection has taught us these lessons: be fact based and really understand all sides of an issue before acting; don't just follow the lead of others before questioning and challenging the validity of the direction; be flexible; and be responsive and opportunistic. From a business perspective, we believe three things are needed for long-term success:

- a strong, effective culture;
- the desire to always seek out and create opportunity from any situation; and
- the will to always be competitive by virtue of a devotion to innovation and efficiency.

We have spent a lot of time thinking about what has made Linamar successful, specifically in managing through highly uncertain times, in a crisis, and in a rapidly changing industry and environment. Our clear conclusion is that our culture has been crucial to our success. It includes five distinct and equally important components:

1. We Are Strong Communicators
   - We consistently keep employees, shareholders, and customers informed regardless of the challenges being faced.

2. We Are Balanced
   - We have always run our business as a balance of customer, employee, and financial satisfaction. Long before this was a trendy thing to do or anyone had thought about sustainable businesses, we were doing it.
   - Our Linamar Health First Action Plan, developed at the outset of the pandemic, focused on employees as well as financial health, the health of customers, and the health of our community, and is a great example of real-time living that balance.

3. We Are Responsive, Fast Moving, and Focused on Execution
   - We have always been entrepreneurial and quick to jump on an opportunity. We are not bureaucratic, meaning we make quick, insightful decisions and get things done fast.
   - We quickly created and implemented cost teams, flexible financial models, and highest-level cash controls to manage the pandemic crisis.

- We saw an opportunity to help with ventilators, went after it, and made it happen.

4. We Are Decentralized with Autonomous Profit Centres Run by Full Teams
    - We don't rely on centralized groups to launch or run business. We rely on our entrepreneurs and full management teams in our plants, which are autonomous and run as profit centres. (Other businesses have struggled on launch and oversight as central staff do this work.)
    - Our plants and groups are self-contained, capable, and accountable.

5. We Are Flexible
    - Our flexible equipment means we can quickly reallocate equipment to scale lines and tool up new jobs.
    - Our flexible workforce, accustomed to change, quickly adapts to a new reality.

Manufacturing Is a Critical Sector for Every Country

I think the pandemic has served to shine a light on the importance of the manufacturing industry in any country. As evidence, look at what this industry did during the pandemic. Linamar shifted production to make ventilators. Woodbridge, another Canadian auto supplier, started making masks. Canada Goose was making medical gowns instead of cozy parkas. I think we learned it is critical to have a manufacturing industry in our country for just that type of crisis.

Now to be clear, I don't think we need to have the *capacity* to make absolutely everything in place at all times, but we do need the *capability* and the skill set so those companies can pivot to make what is needed. The auto industry is actually a great example of where a lot of manufacturing capability for a lot of different processes and materials exists.

Metal, plastic, fabric—all are manufactured in the auto industry, so it by definition has the skill set and capability needed to make almost anything. That is important! I think the pandemic highlighted the fact that industrial businesses remain essential in a modern economy. I'm confident the manufacturing sector's impressive performance during a global health crisis will help attract more talent to the industry. Hopefully, what Canadian companies such as Linamar, Woodbridge, Canada Goose, and many others achieved will highlight to government the importance of supporting a thriving manufacturing sector.

The Importance of Being Together

At Linamar we were fortunate that the vast majority of our employees were able to come back to work on site quite soon after the initial lockdown. As I write this, fully 98% of our workforce is back on site in our facilities and have been so for more than twelve months. We really only had two months in the very early days when all who were working were doing so remotely. We still have pockets of folks working from home as we enter the summer season, but we hope to see everyone back in the office by the fall of 2021.

I know many companies are thinking through their plans for return to work. Some want to stay remote, some want everyone back, and some are looking at hybrid solutions. At Linamar, our belief is that we are better when we are physically together as a team. We are more creative, we are more innovative, we are better aligned. Frankly we are just kinder and nicer to each other. We understand that we need to be flexible and we expect our leaders to manage this issue situation by situation, but we do want to see the majority of our people working on site the majority of the time. Why? Humans are social animals, not solitary ones. It isn't mentally or physically in our DNA to be alone, to not interact with others. Ultimately, isolation takes a toll on us.

We think we are stronger, happier, and healthier when we are together, and that five key results are achieved.

Innovation

So much innovation, creativity, and problem solving happens in informal discussions—when you are walking past someone's desk and start chatting about what you are working on and suddenly find the solution that has been evading you.

Talent Development

When we are not together, I worry that good leadership, development, and coaching of others just isn't happening. Again, much of that coaching is informal, a reflection of something happening in real time, not during a scheduled sitdown to discuss challenges and problems. Those are important too. But possibly more important is the informal day-to-day reinforcement of good leadership and teaching of others.

I know a lot of people who say they are more productive working from home, and I don't doubt that they are. The reason they are more productive is that they aren't being interrupted by people asking questions or needing help with something, as happens every day in the office. The problem is that those questions still exist; they just aren't getting answered. That help is still required; it just isn't being offered. I worry there is a price to pay for that productivity, that those who are more productive are sacrificing coaching and development time to get all that work done so efficiently.

That isn't leadership. We are leaders and coaches, not doers. If you just want to "do," stay home. If you want to lead, go where there are people to lead.

Teamwork and Team Alignment

In a remote environment you just can't get the collaborative camaraderie of building a team like you do when you are together. You can't read body language and non-verbal clues as effectively when all you can see is faces on a video call. You tend to be focused on the speaker, not the rest of the team. You miss a lot of the dynamics that turn individuals into a team when you aren't in a room together. You miss the chats on the way out the door or as you gather.

Being together is how we build relationships, start to care about each other. Being together we are nicer and kinder to each other than we are when technology shields us. Relationships are suffering from primarily technology-based interactions, in which we tend to be more direct, less friendly, and more critical than we would ever be in person.

I also think it is important to be cautious about creating an occupational divide in businesses where there are a bunch of people who are *not* able to work from home if you allow those who can work from home to do so. It could create a sense of entitlement in those who can and a sense of resentment from the ones who can't. It creates an "us and them" divide. It can also put undue pressure on those that are at work to carry out the duties of the work-from-home crew that can't be done remotely, which can also create resentment and destroy a business's team culture.

Culture Development

Culture is learned much more informally than formally. New employees will have no clue what company culture is if they haven't been immersed in it physically. Culture is reiterated in small ways, over and over again, in informal interactions. It is how you learn about what matters to the leaders in your business. About the company's values and philosophies. The very definition of culture is that it is a way of doing things developed by a group of people living and working together.

Appeal to Young Talent

Young talent, in large part, don't like remote work. They are generally living with other people or in tiny apartments by themselves. They are either fighting for a place to work remotely or are desperately lonely and alone. I know quite a few young people actively seeking new jobs solely because their companies are choosing to continue to work remotely (if that describes you, perhaps you would like to apply at recruiting@linamar.com).

Looking Forward

Our business and our society has never faced the degree of uncertainty we encountered in 2020. It was an incredibly tough time. However, the pandemic hit after what I feel were the most uncertain few years in my professional life, when we had faced challenges that ranged from speed-of-technology changes to the emergence of vast amounts of data to drive our business to uncertain political situations shaking up international trade.

My reflection on all this uncertainty is that it has been a real lesson in the importance of staying flexible and responsive in every facet of business. When uncertainty turns into a crisis, what I've realized is there is a dangerous tendency toward underestimating the impact of that emergency. Conversely, it is enormously important to prepare for the worst, to have a plan in place that can see you through difficult times, and to constantly update that strategy in the face of an evolving reality.

Create a Strategy Plan for Uncertainty

When the outlook is uncertain, and you don't know what is going to happen or when, don't bet the farm on a guess of what the future will be. That might sound pretty obvious. However, it is surprising how much companies have been doing that the last few years. The management team makes a guess as to what the future will be and then fully aligns their strategy to that projection. What if they guessed wrong? What if they didn't challenge the assumptions generally made and really understand the facts in an end-to-end-life-cycle way?

In contrast, I think you need to create a strategy that will allow you to be successful within as many different outcomes as possible. Our auto business is a great example of that. No one knows what the evolution of electrification will look like. Which technologies will win and when? So we developed a flexible strategy—we built up our product portfolio to ensure we have an equivalent level of value for every type of vehicle propulsion—battery electric vehicles, fuel cell electric vehicles, hybrid vehicles, and traditional internal combustion vehicles. We are ready for whatever comes, whenever it comes.

Stay Flexible

When risk and volatility levels are very high, we as a company need to stay as flexible as we possibly can in every way. Flexibility applies to every element of the business. It's critical to strategy and tactics, but also to people, property, and equipment, as well as debt levels and cash. As a manager, you have to ensure your flexibility is directly correlated to levels of risk.

To me, that has been an indispensable lesson from recent years—the higher the risk and uncertainty the more flexible you must be, in every way. Organizations, large and small, need to be nimble and responsive; they have to be ready to pivot quickly when necessary.

Be Realistic

A final key point is you don't know when that uncertainty is going to end, so be careful not to overpromise and underdeliver. What played out in 2020 is a great example of that. All year long we were underestimating the number of cases, the number of deaths, certain it would all be over by June . . . September . . . maybe December.

That creates management challenges in how you are communicating with your people or your investors. Stay positive but have a plan to deal with the reality of the situation. Provide hope and a plan. Be realistic.

We told our folks over and over, "Tough times don't last. Tough teams do, and we are one tough team." The tough times that came with COVID thankfully look to be ending, and we can proudly look to our tough team and say, "You did it!"

LULULEMON ATHLETICA

For the millions of people who worked remotely during the pandemic, the dress code was all leisure, all the time. What to wear to that important Zoom meeting with the boss? A freshly ironed shirt for the screen, over your favourite lululemon pants. Gathering online with the team or friends? lululemon gear from head to toe was the default fashion decision.

The increasing demand for the brand's product continued to drive its business to new heights during the pandemic, built on the strength of the brand's functional, athletic apparel and the growing trends of well-being, active and healthy lifestyle, and connection. Vancouver-based lululemon athletica sales rose by more than 80% a year after the first lockdowns in 2020, while its stock price more than doubled. For a business that started in 1998 out of a building that was a design studio by day and yoga studio at night, it was a heady run.

Which is not to say lululemon chief executive Calvin McDonald had an easy, straightforward pandemic experience. Keeping employees safe across a global network of more than five hundred stores, managing supplier relationships, dealing with social justice campaigns, and ensuring customers (whom lululemon refers to as guests) stayed happy were leadership challenges for the ages.

McDonald took the reins at lululemon in 2018, recruited from high-end cosmetic company Sephora Americas after five years as president and CEO. Sephora is a division of France's LVMH group, which owns a stable of luxury brands. Earlier in his career, McDonald spent two years as president and CEO of department store chain Sears Canada and seventeen years at Loblaw, Canada's largest grocery retailer.

A native of London, Ontario, McDonald earned a science degree at Western University and an MBA from the University of Toronto's Rotman School of Management before launching his career in retail. An ardent triathlete, McDonald found that working from home during the pandemic took away one of his preferred ways to build exercise into his daily routine: prior to COVID, he often ran or biked to or from work.

Calvin McDonald

OCTOBER 2021

Leadership is an ongoing journey with tremendous learning and growth at every turn. If there were ever any doubt about this, the events of 2020 proved it in ways that have altered how I now define leadership and development. It's hard to imagine a tougher or more challenging year. Yet at the same time, I can't think of a year that was more transformative on many levels—for leaders like me, for companies adapting to the changing world, and for the employees and guests who love brands like lululemon.

As I reflect on 2020, I see three clear and distinctive paths in my own leadership journey, triggered by two momentous events—the COVID-19 crisis and the social justice movement.

First, facing an unprecedented global pandemic, the speed of decision making, the need for more ideation, and the complexity of the challenges were amplified beyond anything we had faced before. It had that adrenaline-rush sense of tackling a challenge, this time at hyper speed with no playbook. Each of us as leaders knew we were facing something entirely unparalleled in our lifetimes. From the earliest days of the pandemic onward, it has become clear that any company or leadership action must stay true to their culture and values to maintain and encourage the trust and confidence that is foundational to the relationships of all stakeholders.

Second, less than three months into the COVID-19 pandemic, we collectively faced the explosive, emotional impact of the social justice movement. Throughout my career, I've been proud to lead diversity, equity, and inclusion (DE&I) changes in organizations, particularly in my previous role as CEO at Sephora Americas. Even with my commitment to DE&I, I was struck by the depth of what the conversation around systemic biases exposed on multiple levels in business and society. This historic inflection point elevated and heightened the need for progress, and I embarked upon my own professional and personal journey to fully understand my role in creating the change that has been far too long in coming.

Third, in the last eighteen months, people have reassessed their lives and are looking at what is important, meaningful, and fulfilling to them and are seeking work that is connected to purpose and impact—it is an era of disruption and choice. Business leaders are often accustomed to the speed with which consumer behaviours can shift; it's why we obsess over innovation and are constantly looking for advantages and threats. What has emerged from employees over the past year is this same intensity and urgency—about the role their organization plays in their well-being, in social justice, in personal and professional development. Following months and months of working from home, employees now have an especially strong focus on remote work. More than ever, the need to innovate and the potential benefits of leading and disrupting can drive talent management strategies. Similarly, doing nothing or being slow will disrupt your business as it crushes your ability to anticipate the needs of your guests.

The pandemic unquestionably revealed that none of us can be static in our leadership approach when the environment is constantly changing. This reinforced the fact that compelling leadership must be equally adaptive and agile in our increasingly dynamic and competitive environment.

Over the next few pages, I invite you to share in my learnings along this journey. My intent is not to create a "how to" guide for leaders. Nor will I offer a chronological summary of what occurred or detail the many amazing leaders across lululemon who helped us evaluate, navigate, and lead through this time. My intention is to speak about some of the lessons I learned as a leader and my realization of how leadership within business has changed in important ways.

The Earliest Days of the COVID-19 Pandemic

Looking back, from day one, faced with the global challenge of COVID-19, one of the most critical decisions we made was establishing a clear compass, given how priorities were shifting by the hour.

In what felt like a blink of an eye, the spread of the coronavirus demanded that decisions be made, and be made quickly. We knew this couldn't be done in a vacuum. We needed a critical filter that enabled us to make decisions at a rapid speed and to communicate clearly to our people, customers, and shareholders. As problem solvers who are driven to find a solution, we first turned to our existing toolbox. Some of our tools worked. Others didn't. When they didn't, I was ready to make the bold choices necessary.

Knowing that we would face uncertainty, I wanted to establish guidelines, reducing the risk that we would lose our way in the heat of a decision. In the first days, I drove the conversation with our management team to create three guiding principles for our COVID-19 response, which were then distilled down to (1) supporting our people, (2) maintaining a balanced share of mind, and (3) continuing to invest in our future.

These guiding principles became our compass to navigate the unexpected. We knew the road was not paved, and we would have to adjust, but the compass would help guide us in this journey. As our employees and shareholders faced a world of ambiguity, establishing this framework enabled us to explain some of the trade-offs that were going to be absolutely critical, not only to survive an unparalleled pandemic but to come out on the other side in a position of strength and opportunity.

Considering the enormous scope and serious nature of the crisis, I knew our choices had the potential to be industry-leading decisions, given our strong financial position, our tremendous guest loyalty, and the passion of our people. I committed to taking what could be considered courageous measures, understanding the necessity to re-evaluate and reprioritize our pre-pandemic plans within the context of the changing behaviours of people and the fundamental desire to further strengthen our guest and employee relationships.

My remit was to plot our path to aggressively address this emergency across our organization worldwide, while maintaining our focus on priorities to set us up for future success. Our guiding principles meant we would act decisively and protect our people—lead now through balanced decisions as well as for the long term—while being true to our values.

Staying Focused on What Matters the Most During a Crisis

In the earliest days of COVID-19, we asked ourselves a fundamental question: What is the most important asset that we need to protect above all else? And it became immediately clear that our overarching priority was protecting our people and our community.

This informed our decision to be among the first major retailers to close stores across all markets worldwide and our early commitment to provide pay protection to our employees as we worked to reassure our employees in an uncertain and stressful environment.

Following through on our first guiding principle, we prioritized taking care of our people. The question of whether to furlough our employees or keep them on our payroll was a critical early test for us. How would shareholders react to the cost and the expenditure? How long would the closure last—two weeks, four weeks, six weeks? What were the government programs offering to employees who had lost their jobs because of the pandemic as compared to what pay protection would provide?

Weighing what would be the best thing for our people, and aligned to our values, we knew only one decision was right for lululemon: paying our people, and offering them the security of knowing they had a job and a salary. We first provided store employees with paycheques for the hours they were scheduled to work and later revised this to minimum base pay for six weeks, whether stores reopened or remained closed. This was a very different path than nearly every one of our competitors, but we wanted our employees—full time and part time—to remain our employees.

The decision was important for a number of reasons. First, this was the right decision for our employees and our company. Our employees could be confident in their short-term financial situation and in the company's support during a very trying time. We were standing up for our values, including our commitment to courage, entrepreneurship, personal responsibility, connection, and inclusion. And most of all, our commitment to being a people-led organization.

Our stores initially remained closed for two and a half months, and we offered pay protection during this entire period. Some markets and stores continued to be shut down for many more months; pay protection continued in those locations until our stores could ultimately reopen.

As demand through our e-commerce business grew, we set up stores for distribution and brought back employees to serve our guests in a new way. At our distribution centres, our employees were responding to increased workload due to store closures and online demand. We established enhanced bonus opportunities, shift flexibility, and special relief pay consideration for those who needed time off to deal with the disruptions from the pandemic. In addition, we introduced a hardship fund that all employees could tap into as unexpected difficulties occurred.

Importantly during this time, we knew that we also had an opportunity and, in fact, a responsibility to ensure that we continued to invest in the development of our people. Our People and Culture team rapidly created a calendar of global offerings to keep us feeling supported—from virtual group sweats to meditations to development and resilience training. More than two thousand employees took part in the very first week, and the numbers exponentially grew from there. And the training evolved over time to help us prepare employees for new responsibilities that emerged to serve our guests, such as our virtual educators.

It was critical that the principle of supporting our people was not limited to our employees. It also meant protecting our stakeholders and our collective. We paid rent to our landlords. We maintained our orders to our vendors who make our products. Many of our global ambassadors, who operate their own studios and are a key part of our communities, were forced to close their operations. We created the lululemon Ambassador Relief Fund, a $4.5 million global program to provide grants ranging from $10,000 to $20,000 to help sustain their businesses.

I believe that by supporting our collective and helping them navigate the day-to-day realities of this period, we built even stronger relationships and increased trust during this most stressful of times. My advice for any leader in a similar situation is to stay true to your values. The decisions that are made and how they are executed should be done through the lens of protecting the most important assets of the company—and for us, this was our people and our community.

Maintaining a Share of Mind About Near-Term Opportunities and Challenges

From the moment we closed our stores, we knew that at some point they would reopen and communities would come together again. We needed to be prepared for whenever and whatever form that took. The challenge was to balance our share of mind so that we could address the immediate crisis, consider the steps necessary in the mid-term, and build for the long term. It's easy and quite natural to let your share of mind shift to be overly focused on the crisis at hand, but it's critical for leaders to keep that equilibrium between the short, mid, and long term.

It's particularly important for leaders to consider the mid-term area of focus during a period of crisis. Immediate decisions tend to consume the focus of management teams; it's often easiest to address what's most urgent in the short term. Conversely, the longer-term decisions that are more related to the distant future are often relatively easy to evaluate.

My view is that the mid-term period is the most pivotal. The decisions that affect what's three, six, or nine months ahead can actually have the most significant effect on the business. It was essential to plan for what we knew would eventually happen—our stores would reopen and guest behaviours would evolve or stay in place. Taking these strategic steps in the mid-term can kickstart the momentum of your business and shorten your recovery. Failing to do so will only prolong the impact and extend it well past the actual event.

Looking beyond the immediate crisis, decisions had to be made even while the world was shutting down in the moment. We made digital investments to support holiday online shopping in the event that closures and business disruption continued through the end of the year. This had an outsized impact on the business. We developed our store reopening plan, which included training our teams to operate under health and safety constraints. These decisions, and others, required time to implement. Losing sight of the mid-term, due to the focus on crisis, would have extended the impact on our business.

The pandemic required that we re-evaluate our operating model, reprioritize our initiatives, and make some immediate choices. We made some bets, like accelerating our digital investments further, and reset plans for our strategic priorities, managing expenses, and inventory. Initially, the focus was on the present, but as a leader you are always learning from the past and creating the runway to potential opportunities.

Across the globe, our e-commerce business spiked, maintaining a double-digit growth trajectory through the year. We harnessed the power of our distribution network to ensure our guests received a high level of service and leveraged and built upon our sourcing capabilities that use machine learning and artificial intelligence to route e-commerce orders through our distribution network in the most efficient way. Our pre-pandemic investments in our sites and our mobile app paid off, improving functionality in checkout, navigation, search, browse, and speed across sites.

We followed our principle of balanced management to speed up the enhancement of our omni-channel guest experience through virtual channels that offered online workouts and a digital educator service through which guests and educators could chat via video to discover new products and answer questions. The winning formula lies in creating a distinctive and unique experience, with physical and fully integrated digital offerings. It's just one of the many reasons we are continuing to invest, test, and learn.

As the pandemic stretched into months, the juxtaposition between major milestones and the new normal of working virtually was stark. We felt stuck, like we were in the movie *Groundhog Day*. And this makes it incredibly important to over-communicate so that we could manage the crisis at hand and also maintain that share of mind that was so essential. In a company that values connection, our physical separation challenged me and our leadership team. How you connected with people became fundamentally different. We had to balance how we were managing the business and ensure we were communicating clearly and often. We as leaders are maintaining our own share of mind, but balancing our messaging is equally important so people are consistently engaged. This kind of focus helps everyone realize there is a light beyond the crisis, and we are focused on preparing for what needs to be accomplished in the mid-term.

As a leader, especially during a crisis, one of your most important roles is being the lead communicator for your organization. People will gauge their confidence in the future through not only what you say, but the way you connect. I adjusted my approach, almost overnight, with more emphasis on smaller group calls to listen, learn, and create more personal dialogue. I also began recording weekly videos on my iPad, where I shared updates and offered visibility into different areas of the business in order to encourage connection with our global teams. Not the best production values for sure (and I avoided sharing just how many times I had to re-record some messages), but they were honest and real, which I hoped would create authenticity and trust. If you think as a leader you are communicating enough, say more. The members of my leadership team welcomed this philosophy, and it has permanently changed the way we all communicate.

Keeping Your Eye on the Future

Times of crisis often accelerate change within business and consumer attitudes, when new behaviours can be adopted overnight and other initiatives must be accelerated to meet the emerging demand. Crisis offers new potential for innovation, as leaders continue to evaluate the environment and changes in guest behaviour that create opportunities. The key is to lean on your purpose and vision. Ours was to be an experiential brand that ignites a community of people living the sweatlife. As the crisis creates or accelerates shifts, you review, assess, and apply those to your vision and decide if there is an opportunity.

All leaders have a vision of the future they are creating or hope to create. It's essential during a crisis to evaluate the risk and reward related to both the challenges you're facing and the opportunity of the moment.

And I applied this filter in what would be considered a huge decision for any CEO even in ordinary times: making the first acquisition *ever* in the company's history.

Prior to the pandemic, we began discussions that would lead to the acquisition of MIRROR, a two-year-old startup that enabled at-home training and classes, with a review period that coincided with the first four months of COVID-19. Working on finalizing the agreement at the same time we navigated the complexities of a global pandemic required us to carefully consider the pros and cons. Yet through the many long discussions with our board of directors and my leadership team, debates in my head about how to make it work, and more than a few sleepless nights, we knew this acquisition was the right decision and would set the stage for future growth.

Even before the pandemic, I was interested in the opportunity of in-home connected fitness. It was a good fit with our vision at lululemon. We could see strong potential that was quickly being realized in our work-from-home environment. This behavioural shift was going to be a permanent change, and we committed to acquire MIRROR.

Moving forward is part of the essence of being a leader. It brings together the combination of confidence, courage, and timing—all fundamental to strong leadership. We were confident in the momentum of the business, assured that our stores would reopen, and in where we were going as a brand and business. We had demonstrated the courage to innovate and grow again and again to fulfill our vision. Naturally, the question of timing came up. As a leader, I knew we still needed to move forward. We were going to be smart and timely.

My conviction to make the acquisition was based on a number of factors. This being our first acquisition, my initial consideration was how MIRROR strategically fit into creating the future we envisioned. Second, the timing was right in relation to our strong financial position. The third factor was the ability to integrate and develop the synergies that the investment thesis was built upon. I believed the investment thesis was strong and there was real momentum behind this category as COVID lingered.

Consumer buying behaviours, which accelerated during the pandemic, were shifting for good. Lastly, even if one of the highest-degree-of-risk scenarios played out, we were not betting the firm with this acquisition. It was a right-sized opportunity for our first acquisition, and it made sense before the pandemic and even made sense during the pandemic as well.

Still, there were considerations to assess and obstacles to overcome. Other companies were in cash conservation mode. No one had been making acquisitions at the time, and we seemed to start a trend when we moved forward. In the midst of our due diligence, our chief financial officer left the company, and we tapped finance leader Meghan Frank (who was later promoted to be CFO herself) to step in. And I was also unable to travel to meet the MIRROR leadership team in person, making integration and synergies more challenging with negotiations over Zoom and via texts.

Grounded by our guiding principles, and the importance of each one of them, I was excited and proud to share, on June 29 of 2020, the first acquisition by any company in our sector during the pandemic as we welcomed MIRROR to the lululemon family in a $500 million transaction.

Recognizing the Power and Importance of Social and World Events

There are moments in time when the world stops and all eyes are focused on a particular situation. Despite all that was happening, the social justice movement in 2020 was one of those instances.

As I took on leadership roles in my career, I always aspired to make a positive impact on diversity and inclusion. I take pride in the changes I've made to create more diverse and inclusive organizations, at Sephora and elsewhere. The Black Lives Matter movement ignited a conversation and a call to action within lululemon and across our collective, serving as the powerful catalyst to critically examine our culture and practices.

The murder of George Floyd in May 2020 opened the floodgates for candid discussions of what systemic discrimination, social injustice, and inequality feel like. The deeper the conversations went, the more I became committed to my own journey and how we could transform the company. I focused on taking action dedicated to searching for and breaking down embedded social injustice within the company and in our communities. We continue to confront uncomfortable truths—lululemon currently does not reflect the diversity of the global communities in which we operate, and our practices and policies need to evolve to address inequities and discrimination across our communities.

Across our company, we are asking if we truly live up to our intentions, and if our language and culture are inclusive. We realized our practice of hiring for "culture fit" led to less diversity, and we immediately shifted our language to hire with the lens of "culture add" to better reflect our communities. This process enabled us to identify the impact and bias inherent in the practice of hiring as we make clear our intent going forward to hire with a more inclusive mindset and practice. I have no doubt that if we are truly grounded in our purpose and values, we will obtain our unconditional commitment to take actions that support inclusion, diversity, and equity, so that everyone can truly realize their full potential.

Taking the time for self-reflection is critical. I believe every leader—and, perhaps especially white, male leaders like me—need to be willing to learn and teach themselves about racism and biases that exist, both in society and within their own organization. Being vulnerable, willing to make mistakes, and having the courage to be in conversations without knowing the answers opens us up to new possibilities and pushes our boundaries in ways that can create lasting change.

Frankly, I had to go through my own journey to feel comfortable with the term privilege. And I plowed myself into reading every book I could find, such as *Caste* and *White Fragility*, to better understand the context and history contained within privilege and the caste system around us. My advice to any leader is to have the courage to admit what you know and what you don't know. And to spend the time necessary to become educated so you can lead others.

Creating Lasting Change That Transcends One Moment in Time

A leader has the responsibility to recognize the past and to chart a new path forward that lasts beyond the tenure of any particular executive. After taking time to listen, learn, and understand the specific challenges in our company, our senior leadership team co-created and delivered five commitments to stand up and fund Inclusion, Diversity, Equity, and Action (IDEA). These are actionable commitments that are shaping how we work and how we interact.

To accelerate our actions and create accountability, we hired a global head of IDEA; filled nearly twenty roles on the team; and brought together an executive steering committee, advisory committees, task forces, and many work streams dedicated to the work. We held our first virtual IDEA Summit in June 2020 for our people and our ambassadors to provide tools and resources for creating behaviour change and inclusive environments, continued to deliver localized training throughout the year to our global employees, and launched global on-demand coaching.

Since then, we have established eight employee-led resource groups that provide equity-centred spaces for connection and development, and a global advisory committee comprising of lululemon ambassadors who bring diverse knowledge and skills to inform our actions and collectively drive meaningful change around the world.

I continue to hold monthly listening sessions with our racialized employees, fostering ongoing connection. These are no-holds-barred discussions, where my job is to listen and learn rather than speak and solve. It can at times be a humbling experience of just how much more we have to do, but it's inspiring to know that these spaces have emerged through the courage of the participants.

Those leading others today must know that the onus is on you to fully understand and appreciate your role to drive change within the organization or community. You cannot fake it to lead. This is now a lifelong journey to equip leaders—particularly white, privileged leaders—to continue to learn and understand. It is an essential journey that will be ongoing for me throughout my life.

Living into the "New Normal" That Is Right for Your Company and People

The third path I am taking on my leadership journey is a growing understanding of the post-pandemic world, and how the way we work and operate has undeniably been changed by COVID-19. Earlier I described how crisis drives changes in guest behaviour and creates opportunity for the business. Equally, this crisis, more than any I can remember, is transforming the way that corporations function and grow. The pandemic is having an enduring impact on how we work and the expectations of employees.

Much has been said about the shifting consumer behaviours that are continuing, and there's no doubt that lululemon is prepared well for the trends of health and well-being that are more top of mind for everyone. Yet an equally and potentially more powerful trend that's taken hold is how the expectations of employees have evolved in many ways. Employees expect leaders to be more vulnerable and to connect with their people in human and authentic ways; the veil of leadership has been lifted. Employees expect companies to be more proactive and take public stands on social and civic issues that are relevant, which can feel like a steady cacophony on any given day. And, importantly, the expectations for what constitutes a place of work have evolved.

This new wave of working is a global revolution, which will fundamentally change the future of the workplace. Leaders must identify how to blend remote, hybrid, and in-person workplaces to support their business priorities. Remote work and its impact on talent retention is accelerating the battle for the best talent. The work-from-home experience of so many people has shown how remote work can allow them to be productive from anywhere. There are a growing number of companies that are prioritizing remote work as an incentive to recruit and hire people. With so many factors outside of our control through the pandemic, one of the things people feel they can change in life is the context of their work. This is opening up a perfect storm of loss of talent on a scale I have never seen before in my career.

Leaders ultimately need to decide the role that in-person work should play in their organization and culture. At lululemon, our culture is rooted in connection—to each other, to our guests, to our communities. Being face to face with one another unlocks our core value of connection, facilitates deeper relationships and understanding of our guest and product, and enables teamwork to flourish across our collective.

There is no denying that, during the pandemic, I missed the visceral, tangible aspect of being physically together and the spontaneity of creativity. I restore my energy from being with others and feeling the energy build in a room. I have always felt drawn into our culture for that reason—it is very much in line with my own leadership style.

Any leader must weigh the benefits and disadvantages of remote work. The learnings from the pandemic provide insights into hybrid work and the flexibility it provides for people to manage their responsibilities as caregivers to their family and their community. The benefit of doing so allows people to bring their whole self to work, which, in turn, leads to enhanced productivity and makes a positive impact on the workplace and the collective. This complex shift poses big questions for productivity, policy, and culture and will require bold decisions.

And, finally, we continue to acknowledge the challenge of leading our people through the transition to the post-COVID-19 world. Being in a state of action is second nature to me and to all of us at lululemon, given the fast-paced world of retail. When the crisis began, adrenaline kicked in as we confronted the challenges in front of us, and the urgency of the situation jumpstarted innovation in a matter of days and weeks. This led our leadership team to consider our expectations in this environment and what we needed to provide our people in order to sustain this innovation.

With so much uncertainty around us and the potential for burnout, it was crucial to be clear in our approach and expectations. We spoke to our people about what mattered most and why, which created purpose and meaning behind our goals. We adjusted our approach to remote work and implemented spot bonus programs across our frontline leaders in our stores, distribution centres, and call centres to ensure people understood how much we appreciated their resiliency. We worked together to practise slowing down in order to be able to speed up. And we reinforced the power of saying no to ensure we were actioning against our defined priorities.

Six Leadership Lessons in an Unprecedented Year

Leaders are taught to convey strength, conviction, and certainty, but there were so many points in 2020 when my job as a leader was to convey how much we as a company didn't know. To build confidence in how we were navigating what was in front of us across the divergent crises of COVID-19 and the social justice movement.

Just consider all that we didn't know at the time—how to run a business and support our people during a global pandemic; how lululemon needed to stand up for inclusion, diversity, equity, and action. I had a responsibility to our people and communities to provide answers when I didn't always have them. What came out of the year was that many leaders, me included, recognized the need to add more skills to lead organizations forward.

Reflecting on the year, I've identified the following six key learnings that I'll take away with me as the unexpected continues to occur around us.

Establish Your Compass Early

You may just have a few hours or days to do so, but your organization needs to understand the objectives you're driving toward and that they're consistent with your culture and values. In a frenetic time, your key stakeholders need to know how they can hold you accountable as a leader and if your decisions are sound. Establishing a clear compass builds trust and clarity during times of both crisis and opportunity.

Act Decisively and Protect Your Greatest Asset

At lululemon, employees are our greatest asset, and it was critical for us to maintain that asset intact post-crisis. Employees have so much choice today in where they choose to work, and managing a crisis can bring out the best in some people and the worst in others. From the moment we announced our pay protection for our employees, the wheels were in motion for all that followed and for the nimbleness we were able to display. It's only when your people have confidence in their own future that they can begin to turn to creating confidence through your company or firm.

Maintain Your Share of Mind About the Near Term

The pendulum can swing back and forth in a business environment rapidly—from a period of opportunity to a period of uncertainty. It is easy for leaders and employees to get so consumed by the crisis at hand that they can't see what's ahead in just a matter of months. So when you're ultimately making the toughest of calls, make sure that it's grounded in a sense of balancing the immediate needs in the business with creating a share of mind about the opportunities ahead, in the near, mid, and long term.

Keep Your Eye on the Future

Whatever we faced in 2020, we had to recognize in the moment that we would get to the other side. We didn't know exactly what we would learn or how we would grow, but we knew that some type of new normal would emerge. By continuing to stay true to our vision and by continuing to build and maintain the relationships with our guests and collective, we were confident that the future within sight would emerge through the turbulence we were navigating.

Create Lasting Change

Looking to the playbooks of the past won't allow any of us to keep up the rapid pace of change around us. So as we each face whatever challenge lies ahead, it's important to recognize the moments that call for a higher level of leadership, when fundamental change is required, such as the social justice movement. It's when leaders step forward and are able to bring others along through vulnerability and inspiration that lasting and meaningful change can truly occur.

Listen and Learn

The most important thing, no matter where you are on your journey, is to always continue listening and learning about how employees are evolving and the impact that has on your corporate culture. When your culture is about serving guests, the changing expectations of employees due to the remote work experience may affect your ability to successfully meet the goals you are trying to achieve. As a leader, you will need to make decisions based on who you want to be as a business, and what you are willing to give up or stand for as part of your culture.

In closing, it's crucial to realize that CEOs and companies are now measured by new expectations of the role a brand and a CEO play in social conversations. It's no longer acceptable to stay silent. Part of your responsibility as a leader is to figure out how you and your brand will meet these expectations. As leaders, we need to be eager and willing to be in the conversation—seek out what we don't know, to be curious, listen, and learn. It's a vulnerable position, and it may feel counterintuitive as a leader, to open yourself up to making mistakes or being uncomfortable. But we can't move forward if we don't move forward together, and we can't drive change if we don't understand what we need to change.

Based upon the life-changing experiences of the past year, I am committed to continuing to develop and grow as a leader, to listen and learn, and to connect and adapt. And my hope is that each of us as leaders can continue to open up the conversation about how we can transform the leadership landscape for the better.

The pandemic ultimately brought more clarity, focus, and coordination to our organization, and allowed us to identify more areas of opportunity for us in the near and long term. Following on our success in 2020, my job is to ensure that we maintain the same level of clarity across the organization and carry forward an inspiring sense of focus and meaning.

The work is never done, and I am constantly learning on this journey; it can often require that we each take time to adjust our own expectations. But what's important to recognize is that we are moving forward.

MAPLE LEAF FOODS

For years, Michael McCain has fought for action to address the crisis of food insecurity. As president and CEO of Maple Leaf Foods, he has championed the need for structural solutions to end hunger, with one in seven Canadians struggling with food insecurity. Through the Maple Leaf Centre for Action on Food Security, McCain and other board members lead work that includes advocacy, capacity building, and funding of innovative approaches, with a goal to reduce food insecurity in Canada by 50% by 2030.

In the wake of the COVID-19 pandemic, food insecurity took on a whole new meaning, as the economic shock resulted in job loss for thousands of Canadians and food bank usage surged. Confronted with a global health crisis, Maple Leaf Foods faced the monumental task of maintaining production at over two dozen facilities across North America and adjusting its supply chain to ensure store shelves stayed stocked, all while safeguarding the health and well-being of its thirteen thousand employees. For a company that processes 1.8 billion pounds of food annually, the challenges were daunting.

Born in New Brunswick and educated at Mount Allison University and Western University's Ivey Business School, McCain has spent over forty years working in the food industry. The first leg of his career was at McCain Foods, a global frozen food business built by his father and uncle, Wallace and Harrison McCain. The disciplined and high-performance operating culture at McCain Foods had an indelible influence on Michael's leadership style.

In 1995, McCain Capital acquired controlling interest of Toronto-based Maple Leaf Foods, a century-old Canadian food company. Alongside the leadership team, Michael has built Maple Leaf Foods into a high-growth protein company with leading brands, a deep values-based culture, and a commitment to building an enduring enterprise through shared value creation.

In 2008, Maple Leaf faced a devastating *Listeria* contamination at one of its prepared meats facilities, resulting in the death of twenty-three Canadians. This tragedy deeply tested the company's leadership values. In response, Maple Leaf leaned into transparency and placed consumer safety ahead of legal and financial interests. McCain's authentic approach and public face throughout the crisis saved the company, with improvements made over the years that have established Maple Leaf as a global food safety leader. This experience led to the establishment of a quickly deployed crisis "playbook" that proved invaluable as the management team later confronted the challenge of a global public health pandemic.

Over the past ten years, McCain has been at the helm during the transformation of the organization's supply chain, involving significant capital investments to streamline the business and scale its core protein operations while exiting non-core businesses. In recent years, the company has pivoted to driving organic growth as it pursues a vision and purpose to become the most sustainable protein company on earth by raising the good in food.

Michael McCain

JULY 2021

Leading through crisis is not new to my colleagues or me. But as the COVID-19 pandemic gripped the world in early 2020, we at Maple Leaf Foods could not have imagined how events that unfolded would impact us and our business. The all-encompassing and sustained nature of the pandemic affected every aspect of our working and personal lives, fundamentally changing how we live and work.

I'm a person who gets immense energy from people, and I really missed the contact and camaraderie of being with others. Meanwhile, the majority of our people faced the ongoing responsibilities of working in our plants, and it was incumbent on me to do everything possible to keep them safe. As leader of an organization with over 13,500 people trusted with a mandate to produce the essential, nutritious food people need, and also as a son, father, and grandfather, I felt an extraordinary responsibility.

We are a company rooted in our leadership values—they define our behaviours and what we expect of each other. We also have a deep commitment to safety leadership, which is foundational to our operating culture and decision making. Early on in the pandemic, we committed to following the science and the recommendations of the world's leading health organizations. That said, we knew we would need to act swiftly, taking extra precautions to protect our people and the security of the food supply chain before we had perfect information. In responding to this crisis, knowing when and how to be agile, and how to empower teams to pivot and collaborate in creative ways, was essential. I believe we navigated this crisis successfully because we had the common grounding of our values and our safety promise.

In confronting the challenge of COVID-19, we stayed true to the core values that have guided us for decades and upon which we have built Maple Leaf Foods. Among these, doing what's right, disciplined decision

making, accountability, transparency, and creating shared value were
critical drivers underlying our response. A crisis tests what exists in a
company, the strength of its culture, and the resiliency of its values. When
you're in the midst of an emergency, you can't create these foundations;
they need to be well ingrained in an organization's ethos, and you need to
build on them. This is one of the most important lessons we've learned
from leading through crises.

Safety has always been ingrained in the culture of our organization, but
since the listeriosis outbreak at one of our plants in 2008, we have committed to being world leaders in safety, including our people's safety and
that of the food we make. Our Safety Promise is something we've collectively built into our operating environment; it's integral to our culture.
Safety is first on the agenda at our executive meetings, where detailed
reports on safety metrics and risks are provided, so that we stay deeply
involved as a leadership team. Beyond the formal reporting, I make it a
priority to be engaged in ongoing discussions about all aspects of safety
with people throughout Maple Leaf. We invest heavily in safety training,
the essential base of a safe culture, including our Safety Foundations
course, which has now run more than forty-five times, creating internal
advocates for our Safety Promise. This culture has been a rock in our
journey through the COVID-19 pandemic.

Quickly Responding to Early Signals

Because of our existing strict food safety protocols, we regularly procure
large volumes of sanitation supplies and personal protective equipment
(PPE), including items like masks and face shields. Even before our pandemic response, many would have likened the prevalence of PPE on our
production floors to that in surgical rooms. Before COVID-19 turned the
world upside down, our procurement team detected an early red flag
when one of our mask suppliers speculated on the potential for increased
demand for masks due to "a virus" that was hardly mentioned in Western
media at the time.

While the team couldn't predict what would soon come, to decrease the risk of downtime due to a shortfall in a vital piece of safety equipment they started to secure additional mask supplies. I distinctly remember a meeting back in December 2019, when the team mentioned increasing our mask orders due to a potential supply risk. At that time, I wondered if this was an overreaction. It sure wasn't! This team was the first in the organization to feel the impact of COVID-19, months before it hit main-stream consciousness. And their quick responsiveness meant we were well equipped with essential supplies to protect our frontline workers.

Early in 2020, our view of the risk associated with COVID-19 was evolving. In late January, it became an important topic at our executive-level meetings. By that time, case counts were rising in Asia, and we knew there was a chance of significant global spread. Part of our awareness was aided by the decades-long business relationships we have built in Southeast Asia and China. And our science-based approach meant we already understood the increasing risk of zoonotic transmission of disease from animals to people as population densities increase worldwide. We have dealt with this risk, from "bird flu" in chickens to MERS and African swine fever in pigs, in a very proactive way. As many in our industry were taking a wait-and-see approach, we immediately began educating our people about the potential impact of COVID-19.

As intensity and uncertainty increased throughout February, we knew quick and potentially drastic measures would likely be required. We engaged our safety team, appointed a COVID incident commander, and equipped our teams with the available resources to take a fact-based approach. By the first week of March, we had implemented screening questionnaires, established a mandate to self-isolate after international travel, and held company-wide educational town halls. We were also acutely aware that we had to manage supply chain risk. We thought we were ahead of the game, but we didn't know how fast and intensely the game would play out. Our company is significantly vertically integrated, meaning we control much of our raw material supply, but we still rely heavily on third-party suppliers for livestock and other inputs. By March, it was clear that we were facing global supply chain uncertainty. During the week of March 9, the risk shifted from somewhat abstract to all too tangible. Personally, I was losing sleep thinking the situation was moving faster than we had prepared for.

At the core of the Maple Leaf management process is a monthly all-day meeting with our entire senior leadership team. On March 12, at the start of our regularly scheduled meeting, we threw out the agenda to focus on the risk of COVID-19. We dove deeply into what actions we had in place and what more we needed to do to protect our people and our business continuity. After a day of intense debate, we decided to dial up all measures significantly, including the call for a lockdown—a hard, fast lockdown. Close our head offices immediately, implement our emergency protocols at the plants, gear up the already established crisis team . . . we were in full crisis mode. No one knew how the virus was transmitted or how to effectively treat people who were infected. What we did know was that this virus was unlike any we had ever experienced.

We had to make hundreds of decisions with little information, but we knew we had to act quickly and decisively. In many instances, we had limited data to work with as government decisions and direction were not coming fast enough. We drew on the available data and our experience in implementing effective safety programs to move with pace to implement immediate actions, while diligently following directions from Canadian public health authorities and the U.S. Centers for Disease Control (CDC).

Looking back, it is shocking but understandable how little information we all had, but a period of information and "misinformation" overload was about to begin. We knew that it was time to fully engage in our COVID-19 response playbook. When we face a crisis, quick decision making and responsiveness are key even without full data. We started gathering what facts we had, with dedicated external experts to inform our decisions as we began to act with what can best be described as "hair on fire" urgency!

Maple Leaf is a vital part of the Canadian food chain. We had to work through highly complicated decisions: how best to protect our people, maintain the well-being of our animals, reliably produce the food that feeds Canadians, and meet our strong social commitment. In our industry, the complexity and time sensitivity of fresh meat inputs means that every moment counts, and every decision can have both near- and longer-term consequences. Every decision we had to make that day came with a tremendous amount of risk, as we had little certainty of all the variables and the future. I am incredibly proud of the team leading this effort and the judgments they applied in balancing so many complex considerations.

At the end of that leadership meeting back in early March, I emailed the entire organization outlining the incremental steps we were taking to protect our people. The impact was relatively easier on our office workers. Starting immediately, everyone would work remotely if possible, no visitors were allowed on our properties, all business travel was cancelled, and mandatory self-isolation was required after international personal travel. But we had a more significant challenge to work through. The decision was *much* more nuanced in our network of farms and in our processing and distribution facilities. There was no work-from-home option—the livelihood of these people depended on a safe work environment, and our customers and consumers counted on us to continue to provide the food they needed.

We immediately took the actions we thought were best. Yet it was clear we needed expert opinions and a system for live and ongoing decision making to act on the most recent, best available information. We followed the CDC guidelines, both the medical and scientific advice, but there was still a significant amount of grey space, and discretion was required. Starting the next day, we instituted a daily COVID-19 safety call with our leadership team, COVID safety team, and key members from across our manufacturing network and appointed an expert external medical advisor. This daily call became the core place to assess the issues and make major daily decisions based on the experts' recommendations and the learnings and challenges brought forward by our operations leads.

We put tremendous efforts into delivering consistently high quality with all our products, supported by robust standard operating procedures that govern all elements of our food production, including maintenance and sanitation. We took the same disciplined approach in planning for our first internal cases by building out our COVID-19 playbook for use in the event of a positive case within our network. This playbook became a living and breathing document that was constantly updated based on the evolving CDC guidelines and our internal learnings. It became foundational to our management through the crisis and also took on a life outside Maple Leaf.

As an organization, we never use safety as a competitive advantage. We have invested heavily in implementing best practices and we share our safety expertise and learnings with the broader industry or whomever it can help. *The Maple Leaf Foods COVID-19 Playbook* was no exception. When we published the first version on March 24, we quickly shared it with public health authorities. It was recognized as best-in-class by the Public Health Agency of Canada and shared across industries as a model for others to follow. To this day, I am so incredibly proud of this body of work and its role not only in keeping our people safe but also in helping to improve workplace safety broadly in Canada.

The early signals about potential mask supply shortages prompted us to explore alternative paths to reduce risk and supply chain disruption. We moved some of our science team members into a new project, with the objective of safely sanitizing masks for reuse. This team developed the creative solution of leveraging some of our smokehouses to heat the masks to a sufficient temperature to sterilize them completely. Fortunately, the global production of masks increased sufficiently to keep up with demand.

We also decided early on to introduce a weekly bonus for all our frontline workers while there was still a high degree of uncertainly around how the virus spread. We actively encouraged our people *not* to come to work if they felt sick by letting them know their jobs were safe. We also implemented a top-up program to ensure our people were still being paid while taking time to deal with their health. To us, these investments were a no-brainer and the right thing to do, encouraging and supporting our people to stay home when sick.

Supporting our communities was our other immediate priority. We made a $2.5 million founding donation early in the pandemic to establish the COVID-19 Frontline Health Worker Fund, which provides important support for healthcare professionals across Canada. We also significantly increased our efforts to address the surge in food insecurity, as people lost their jobs and emergency food organizations struggled to meet a 39% rise in demand. The Maple Leaf Centre for Action on Food Insecurity, a charitable organization founded in 2016, mobilized our action with over $2.5 million in healthy food donations and $2 million in funding to projects that reach vulnerable people. The centre also played an important role in connecting the private sector to organizations in need of support and in liaising with government to ensure that emergency food aid was distributed quickly to reach the most vulnerable. While food insecurity is a structural problem requiring policy solutions, not charity, the pandemic required the centre and the food security sector to immediately pivot their focus to emergency food relief. Having this well-established organization with existing strong connections enabled us to quickly participate in these efforts.

In the Thick of It

During this time of great uncertainly for our people, I went into over-communication mode. Our culture values transparency and abhors politics and hierarchical thinking. Importantly, I believe direct, honest communication with our people needs to reinforce this. For twenty-five years, I've been sending a weekly note across our organization, which is a reflection of my week and where I share what's on my mind. Given the level of uncertainty during COVID-19 and the relative isolation of our office people with the move to a work-from-home policy, I shifted to daily communication. I wanted to keep everyone informed as frequently and best as I could, given the enormous change and uncertainty in our work and personal lives—and in the science around the virus.

Similarly, we strove to be open and transparent with media, who were critical sources of information for so many Canadians. We posted regular updates on our website; shared information and photographs describing our actions, challenges, and incident rates; and engaged in interviews whenever possible. Early in the pandemic, I focused a considerable amount of my effort on cutting through the clutter and clarifying what the risks associated with COVID-19 were according to the most recent science. I felt our governments weren't doing enough to lock down our communities to slow the spread, and I used this platform to help protect our people, both inside and outside work.

While the transition to working from home went relatively smoothly, our business shifted significantly. Before the pandemic, roughly 25% of our business served restaurant and food service customers. With institutional and restaurant closures, this demand dropped by over 70% overnight. At the same time, our larger retail business increased drastically as people began to panic-buy and load their pantries with food and other essentials. Our manufacturing and supply chain teams had to respond rapidly, cutting back on food service production and gearing up retail. While we pivoted rapidly to find creative solutions to meet the abrupt shift in demand, our finance team sought to understand and manage the volatility in the financial markets on critical commodities in our business. It took a lot of quick thinking and creativity to keep our operations consistently producing the food people needed in a world of shutdowns and isolation.

While there were initial scarcities as grocery stores and suppliers transitioned to this new environment, we should be proud of the resilience of the Canadian food system. One of the biggest challenges we faced was how to deal with a significant volume of food stored in fridges and freezers that were destined for restaurants, when some grocery store shelves were empty and many people were facing food insecurity. We worked fast to move as much product as we could to emergency food relief organizations, yet this effort was highly challenging, as they often don't have the scale and labour required to separate and distribute what were all the large format products. Together with our trade associations and the Canadian Food and Inspection Agency, we developed a creative solution to move restaurant products through the retail channel, even though they didn't meet the labelling normally required for consumer products. Although it may seem like a small step, it helped get more products onto store shelves and into homes while supply chains adjusted to the new mix between eating at home and restaurants.

The consumer shift from restaurants to grocery stores did not impact all products consistently. One interesting trend in the early stage of the pandemic was a return to "comfort" foods. With so much uncertainty, we saw people returning to traditional and well-known categories and becoming less adventurous eaters. As a result, sales declined for some of our newer and more innovative products, while consumption drastically increased in longstanding categories such as bacon. Within grocery stores, we also saw a shift from products consumed on the go to foods consumed at home. With kids at home taking classes online, parents were no longer packing lunches to send off to school. Instead, they were looking for easy, nourishing lunches to make at home that their kids would devour.

This movement between categories required very nimble planning with our supply chain and operations group, as we shuffled raw materials and people to produce as much as we could in the categories with rapidly increasing demand. Along with a shifting market, we also had to modify our marketing strategies. Early in the pandemic, we significantly pulled back on our marketing campaigns, as it didn't feel right to be advertising during such uncertain times.

Responding to the pandemic required agility and creative problem solving across our organization. It also meant we had to weigh our priorities carefully. Our Project Management Office compiled an inventory of all significant projects underway and made decisions about what could be paused so that we could focus on keeping our people safe and our supply chain moving. We continued to review this list periodically, adding and removing projects as managing the risks of COVID-19 became less about crisis management and more integral to how we operate our business.

The pressure on our information solutions (IS) team to support the rapid pivot to working from home was intense. They quickly sourced increased network capacity to support our foundational business applications. Office phones were replaced with computer-based software so our customer service teams could maintain contact with customers and suppliers. Many people needed hardware updates to function in the new world of video calls. To safeguard us from cybersecurity risks that came with new ways of working, our IS team ramped up our security software and protocols.

At the same time, a whole array of technology and procedural challenges arose in our facilities. We adopted new processes to enable increased social distancing to protect our people. We installed protective barriers in lunchrooms and production areas. We rolled out advanced screening protocols, such as thermal cameras and "Internet of things" technology to manage occupancy and capacity in high-risk areas. As a self-proclaimed tech nerd, I was fascinated to see how we quickly transitioned from ideas into execution. This crisis helped push our adoption of new technologies that will long outlast the pandemic.

I will always remember April 6, 2020, the day we had our first confirmed case of COVID-19 at one of our poultry facilities. While we had implemented the first iteration of our playbook, we saw gaps as we transitioned from theory into practice. Out of an abundance of caution, we temporarily shut down the plant, using the time to build out the critical skill of contact tracing and executing full-plant deep sanitation.

Implementing this decision was anything but straightforward, as it affected the supply chain and the welfare of birds being raised for processing. As chickens grew, barns risked becoming overcrowded, with the increased potential for diseases to spread. Our poultry team immediately shifted the flow of chickens into our other poultry operations, which then strained the network. As we increased processing at these plants, we stopped producing much of our value-added products that take more time, such as boneless, skinless chicken thighs, and shifted to whole birds and bone-in, skin-on cuts. This decreased profitability came when poultry prices were already low from the drop in food service demand. Shutting down this one facility had upstream and downstream implications all through our supply chain. But it was the right call.

At the same time, the CDC was changing its guidelines to recommend wearing masks while indoors. Over a few days, our operations network shifted to 100% mask-wearing internally and doubled down on our plexiglass installations where we couldn't guarantee six feet of separation. We also rolled out changes to our shift structures to limit the interactions between people, bringing in trailers to increase square footage in areas where we didn't have enough space to socially distance, such as lunchrooms, and increasing sanitation requirements throughout our facilities. This was an intensely busy phase throughout our operations network, as we continued to implement changing workplace safety requirements while still producing high volumes of product.

Having our first positive case allowed us to learn and enhance our COVID-19 playbook, including fine-tuning our safety protocols and building out the contact tracing skills that allowed us to trace the root cause of future cases. We quickly learned that community spread posed the most significant risk to our people. In response, we ramped up communications to help them understand not only the importance of following all plant safety protocols, but also the precautions we all needed to take in our personal lives. In some instances, we had to manage temporary increases in absenteeism, but these were overcome through our efforts to provide a safe work environment, through increased communication, and through working collaboratively with unions.

And as the pandemic extended from months to years, we knew we risked complacency. Awareness, education, and safety culture are the primary means of establishing a safe workplace, but enforcement and accountability need to underpin these. We had to get even better at finding at-risk areas in our facilities, which included utilizing GoPro cameras to monitor our workflow processes and people to ensure we adhered to six-foot distancing requirements. Studying countless hours of footage helped us continually refine our safety processes and guide where investments were required, such as in expanding lunchroom space with trailers.

Rules and policies mean nothing if they are not ingrained into behaviours and embedded into an organization's culture. This was our approach, setting the tone from the top that compliance with our COVID-19 protocols was expected 100% of the time, emphasizing that safety came before any commercial or business interests, and cascading that expectation throughout the organization.

Looking back, I'm incredibly proud of the daily examples of leadership and creative problem solving that allowed us to continue operating safely and reliably meet our customers' needs. The results are clear: to date there has been no recorded transmission of COVID-19 in our facilities. While this is a significant accomplishment, we feel deeply for our people who have been infected by the virus, including one tragic death. Everything we do at work helps raise awareness and knowledge that our people can bring home to help protect their families and communities.

I have been a vocal advocate for vaccinations. As they became available, we worked closely with public health authorities to support vaccination efforts and make them readily available and accessible for our essential frontline team members. We organized on-site vaccination clinics at many of our plants, offered flexibility for people to attend off-site vaccination appointments, and donated to support community clinics. We also provided people paid time off to get vaccinated! Just as we communicated extensively about the risks of COVID-19 and the protective measures we needed to follow, we also ramped up communications about the benefits of getting "the jab."

Reflections

During the pandemic, I had the wonderful experience of having one of our frontline people reach out to me to thank our leadership team for how seriously we were taking our employees' safety. I received many notes from team members letting me know they felt safer at work than almost anywhere else besides home. This was the most important validation that we were living our values and our commitment to putting safety first. While this crisis has created so many work and personal challenges, it has also reinforced and strengthened the best of who we are as a team and company. To me, these were some of the most fulfilling moments as we managed through the pandemic.

We are an organization that is committed to creating shared value—delivering profitable growth through confronting and addressing critical environmental and social issues. As part of living this commitment to creating shared value for all stakeholders, we sought to make a broader difference in flattening the curve, feeding the nation, and offering support to those who found themselves in unprecedented situations. The efforts we invested in initiatives such as mask giveaways in local communities, support for hog farmers, donations to help fight food insecurity, a contribution to the Front Line Workers Fund, and sponsoring vaccination clinics, all while continuing to safely deliver food for our customers and consumers, are a testament to the spirit and values of Maple Leaf Foods. I am both proud and humbled by the extraordinary, sustained efforts our people have expended to make this happen.

In 2020 alone, we invested almost $60 million in response to COVID, to protect our people, supply chain, and communities. This equates to over $12 per team member per day over the year. In 2021, our level of investment continues. The pandemic has taught us so much about the safety of our people and the vulnerability and inequities within our society. As a result, the enhancements in our safety protocols, our increased outreach and communications on issues affecting our people, and our ramping up of the important work of the Maple Leaf Centre for Action on Food Security will increasingly contribute to shared value creation.

While we did an amazing job of transitioning our business, this new way of working brought other challenges. Increasingly, the mental health of our people was a concern as they dealt with the pressures of a global health threat, working from home, social isolation, home-schooling, and elder care. We significantly increased the mental health supports available, from online resources to counselling. We launched a speaker series, featuring mental health experts who gave practical advice on how to deal with the stresses created or exacerbated by the pandemic. Providing a safe space for people to share their concerns and know they aren't alone has proven to be incredibly important. Destigmatizing mental health issues is a focus of our commitment to provide a supportive and inclusive work environment, and COVID really accelerated our efforts. We encourage our people to invite family members to any talks of their choice—hopefully spurring

their own conversations about mental health at home. Attendance continues to be high. We're clearly meeting a need, and we'll be continuing these
events as part of our people programs.

But these are not the only ways the pandemic will change our business
over the long term. We are working through what the future of work will
look like for Maple Leaf. This experience has shown that productive work
does not require full-time physical presence and that virtual meetings can
often be more efficient and certainly more sustainable. Yet it has also highlighted the importance of physical proximity in giving and receiving energy,
enabling collaboration, and fostering connections. We know we will return
to a form of hybrid work model, and we will optimize the office design in
support of this shift. We want to ensure that whatever path we take forward
is flexible enough to work for people while supporting the in-person experience we believe is essential to foster creativity and connectedness.

As an organization, we have a vision of being the Most Sustainable Protein
Company on Earth. While COVID temporarily paused some initiatives,
our vision and strategies are stronger than ever. If anything, this pandemic
highlighted the importance of being a purpose-driven organization. We
have a broad vision of sustainability that includes our environmental
impact, the treatment of the animals under our care, our profitability, and
the people and the society in which we operate. Our core commitment to
creating shared value guided our response to the pandemic. I think about
the organization's sustainability in terms of lasting for generations, not just
for my tenure as CEO.

As we make it through the COVID pandemic, I hope our learnings help
us collaborate on other monumental threats facing humanity, such as global
warming and social justice. Like fighting COVID, it will take a tremendous
amount of collaboration between countries, governments, companies, and
civil society. As the world rallied to meet this crisis, we have shown we can
direct our collective will to meet the global challenges of our time. I know
that Maple Leaf will be at the leading edge of these efforts.

McKESSON CANADA

Ask Canadians to explain what McKesson Canada does, and you will likely get a blank stare. Yet in the pandemic, we found out the healthcare company is essential to the country's well-being. McKesson Canada forms part of the backbone of Canada's healthcare system. The Canadian business is a unit of Irving, Texas-based McKesson Corp., one of the largest U.S. healthcare companies.

Behind the scenes, the more than 12,000 employees at McKesson Canada run the largest drug distribution network in Canada, responsible for safely delivering a third of the medications administered in the country each year. One area of expertise is transporting medication that must be kept cold, or frozen in the case of vaccines, across a vast nation.

McKesson Canada supports a family of independent pharmacy banners including Guardian, I.D.A., and Medicine Shoppe and owns the Rexall drugstore chain. The company also operates a national network of clinics under the Inviva brand that administer complex therapies to people with chronic illness.

In 2017, McKesson acquired online health and wellness e-commerce company Well.ca to expand its digital business. The deal also landed the company the CEO who would eventually guide it through most of the pandemic, Rebecca McKillican.

After earning a shelf-full of honours as a student—she has an MBA from Harvard and undergraduate business and engineering degrees from

Western University—McKillican started her career, first at consulting firm McKinsey, then in New York City at pioneering private equity shop Kohlberg Kravis & Roberts. She worked with the firms' retail and consumer products businesses. Living in Manhattan transformed McKillican into an online shopper, picking up packages from the doorman in her building, and she realized Canada's digital retail experience lagged the revolution playing out in major U.S. cities.

In 2012, McKillican joined Guelph-based Well.ca, and in 2013 she was promoted to CEO; she took over from the founder and continued to build a leading national online retailer. When McKesson bought the company five years later, McKillican was first asked to run both the retail banner and e-commerce divisions of McKesson Canada, then promoted to CEO in August 2020, six months into the COVID-19 pandemic.

Rebecca McKillican

FEBRUARY 2020

"We need to stock up our freezer," my husband said to me, showing a video on his iPhone one evening with people in hazmat suits disinfecting the streets of Wuhan, China. It was late January 2020. "Are you serious?" I responded, thinking he was overreacting. "Yes." And then he asked, "Do you think we need to invest in a bigger freezer?"

Over the coming days, he was scanning the shelves of our local grocers and filling his cart with frozen and shelf-stable foods. As it turns out, so were many other Canadians—increasingly anxious as Canada confirmed its first case of COVID-19, and news of the virus sweeping through Italy brought worry to Canadians across the country.

By February 2020 it was starting to become clear that the virus was already with us, and I was on the constant lookout for community transmission, which would mean a significant change in the trajectory of the virus. We had to be ready. We needed to stay ahead of it. What I thought would be a brief sprint quickly turned into a months-long marathon that would test our leadership, our people, and the resilience of Canada's pharmaceutical supply chain.

February/March/April 2020

As we entered the first week of February, my family's own freezer was filled with frozen food and my pantry was stocked. My family typically likes to run our food with a "just in time" model, which made seeing this amount of food, in what is usually a very lightly stocked freezer, overwhelming. Was my husband overreacting, or was I missing something?

Early in the pandemic, as chief retail officer I was primarily responsible for overseeing our retail assets, including the strategy and operations of our community pharmacies, as well as our growing e-commerce offering in Well.ca, Canada's leading health and wellness e-commerce retailer.

I was racking my brain about what this meant for our business. Should I urgently contact the team with the alarm bells ringing? Or should I wait longer and see if my family was an anomaly? I thought about it long and hard and finally came to the conclusion that something about this felt different. So I called Erin Young, our president at Well.ca.

"Erin, I think we need to buy a lot more food inventory at Well.ca—and we need to buy now."

"Are you sure about that?" she asked.

"I'm sure. We need to buy deep."

If my family was stocking up, there had to be other families out there doing the same.

Erin turned to general manager Nicole Flynn, asking her to buy a significant amount of food inventory for our Well.ca e-commerce customers and greatly exceed our planned inventory budget. Nicole bought what she thought was a tremendous amount of inventory in mid-February 2020, but it turned out it wasn't nearly enough and delivery was too slow to meet our demand.

By late February 2020 hoarding was well underway across Canada and in other parts of the world, with the images of bare grocery and store shelves in Italy and Australia plastered all over the news. People around the world were fighting over toilet paper. But at McKesson Canada, while we struggled to keep food and toilet paper in stock across our various retail assets like Rexall, Well.ca, I.D.A., Remedy'sRx, Medicine Shoppe, Guardian, Proxim, and Uniprix, our minds immediately went to "What happens if the same customer panic translates to their prescription medications? And what if hospitals start to panic and start to stock up on medications? How are we going to ensure the toilet paper problem doesn't translate to prescription medications?" Our team started to plan scenarios of how we would manage through and ensure continuity of medications to Canadians. We may be able to get by without toilet paper for a while, but we certainly can't afford to forgo our critical medications.

By mid-March 2020, it was clear our customers had begun to panic. And who could blame them? Presidents and prime ministers were on the news daily talking about supply shortages with countries and ports shutting down, so Canadians were doing their best to plan ahead. And our worst fears started to materialize . . . the panic began to translate to all facets of Canadians' lives, including their purchase of prescription medications.

Hospitals and pharmacies began stocking up on medications in ways we'd never seen before. Our year-over-year customer demand from March 2019 to March 2020 for a variety of products had risen, almost instantly, by 50%. Generally, the supply of medications is a fairly steady and predictable business and the supply chain around them is extremely fine-tuned. A shock of 50% is something neither we nor our manufacturer partners had ever seen. Our teams were quickly overwhelmed. Every predictive statistic built over years of experience, everything we thought we knew about consumer trends and behaviours, changed overnight.

Our portfolio of businesses makes us unique in the healthcare space; McKesson Canada has a stake in every aspect of the Canadian patient journey. We are one of the largest medication distributors in Canada with over twelve thousand employees across the country who help us deliver to ten thousand pharmacies and hospitals each and every day. This translates to us delivering one third of all medications in Canada, daily, with approximately ten million Canadians interacting with our retailers each month.

Prior to joining the healthcare industry, I can't say I ever gave much thought to the pharmaceutical supply chain and the intricacies behind it. I can't imagine many of you have either. That's the sign of a robust system that works. A steady and reliable hand that makes sure life-saving medications are there when you need them—even if that means chartering a bush plane to get insulin to a community in Yukon's interior, or driving through an Alberta forest fire to deliver a drug for a rare disease to a hospital in need.

If I had to picture it, I'd say the pharmaceutical supply chain is sort of like an electricity system—constantly buzzing in the background, a complex, finely tuned machine pulling and pushing electricity, managing demand and supply on an almost instantaneous basis to ensure that when we flip on the switch, anywhere, anytime, the lights come on. We don't give it a moment's thought—until the electricity is out and we're scrambling to find flashlights, candles, or blankets.

The Canadian pharmaceutical supply chain is a vastly complex, global network of manufacturers, logistics providers, and cold chain protectors spanning dozens of countries and regulatory environments on a daily, often hourly, basis. It sources, stores, delivers, and administers essential medicines to our pharmacies, our homes, our hospitals, our doctors' offices, and our clinics. Our industry prides itself on being reliable partners to government, biopharmaceutical manufacturers, healthcare providers, and patients. That's the way we like to operate—we're low maintenance and we are constantly planning to ensure that today, tomorrow, or in three, six, or nine months, our supply is strong and healthcare is available to Canadians. We are always on.

In addition to our pharmacies and our Well.ca e-commerce business, we provide technology services and support to our customers through our pharmacy management technology systems and pharmacy automation businesses. Both of these businesses are critical in offering pharmacists the highest quality technology solutions, which allow them to spend less time behind the counter and more time with patients delivering health services.

And lastly, we support patients on complex therapies with our specialty health business, including our Inviva patient infusion network, which provides infusion and injection services in over ninety clinics across Canada to patients who need chronic medications with challenging access and administration requirements.

We have experienced natural disasters before—our teams and distribution centres are well equipped to deliver in forest fires, floods, and power outages. But there was no playbook for what COVID-19 wrought—a pandemic that would affect all of our distribution centres, all of our pharmacies, all of our partner hospitals and doctors' offices and clinics, at the same time, for months on end. However, with all crises come opportunities to step up for Canadians—and in this case, we used COVID-19 to build up stronger than ever before.

Mid-March 2020

I couldn't help but wonder, "Are they overreacting or am I overreacting?" On March 10, I was in Mississauga in our corporate office for an all-day team meeting. I was completely consumed by what to do to protect the health and safety of our employees, and also how we would keep supplying medicine to Canadians. The team meeting carried on as normal, yet I found myself unable to focus, stepping out to make calls to key team members over the course of the day, asking questions and stepping into unknown territory.

"How can we protect our employees?"

"Can we mandate temperature checks?"

"What about health screening questionnaires?"

"Can we ask our distribution centre and retail employees if they have travelled?"

"Can we mandate masks?"

"What happens if employees don't want to come into work?"

I left that meeting with a comment to the team that I hoped they would stay safe and well, and that I didn't think I would see them in person for a long, long time. I remember the expressions on their faces. Some clearly showed some fear while others feigned a small smile as if to say they thought I was joking. But I knew that day, when I was walking out, that we weren't coming back for a while. I thought months was extreme but in the realm of possibility. But I didn't think years. . . .

On March 11, the World Health Organization declared COVID-19 a pandemic. Within hours, borders were closing, only essential businesses remained open, and schooling became remote.

At the beginning of March we had planned a pilot to test working from home at scale. The test was to be executed on Monday, March 16. It ultimately turned out not to be a pilot. The test that day became our blueprint for the next eighteen months and counting. Our IT teams worked around the clock to prepare monitors, laptops, keyboards, and other equipment required for a secure work-from-home environment.

We decided to make a distinction within our organization almost immediately, and we closed our offices on March 13 for non-essential-onsite staff. This designation of "non-essential" was meaningful—in terms of not just where you worked but what your role was. We immediately saw a cultural shift in the organization. We promoted the notion that our "non-essential" office employees were entirely engaged in supporting our essential, frontline employees, who in turn were directly supporting Canadians through their healthcare needs of this unprecedented pandemic. Our essential employees needed to continue to show up for Canadians. These were our heroes. The frontline workers who never stopped.

Being a pharmaceutical distributor and frontline healthcare provider, we couldn't shut down our distribution centres, close our Inviva clinics, stop our technology field technicians, or restrict our pharmacies. Thousands of employees across the country needed to remain working to keep the supply chain moving and we needed to keep delivering life-saving products to hospitals and pharmacies. And to boot, our customers—those hospitals and pharmacies—were acting just like patients and consumers, ordering huge quantities of products, completely overwhelming our teams and our operations. The strain on our teams was never higher than at this time, and the personal and professional stress felt by all our employees was something we had never experienced.

As we tried to implement safeguards in our frontline teams, we learned that we weren't necessarily able to ask detailed questions about travel or health history or take employee temperatures. So we were in a difficult situation in the early days—we needed information to keep our teams safe, but the regulatory environment was so grey that we were unsure of the path forward. No one had ever experienced a pandemic. Ultimately, we were able to balance the risks involved and build a solution within the proper legal and regulatory framework. And so emerged a common theme of the pandemic—we needed to be flexible, bold, and decisive when protecting our McKesson Canada team, our customers, and our communities.

We placed health and safety at the centre of everything we did, in order to best support our distribution centres, infusion clinics, and pharmacy retail employees. This included rolling out an enhanced employee support program with financial, social, and healthcare support initiatives.

We introduced robust health and safety sanitization measures in our distribution centres, working to disinfect gel cooling packs, blast freezers, totes, clerical areas, and products, and also ensure access to quality PPE for all our employees. Our frontline pharmacy staff, nursing teams, distribution centre employees, and IT teams continued working throughout the surging case numbers. Our absolute priority was on keeping these employees safe and we are proud that we were able to maintain continuity of our operations throughout the pandemic.

Regardless of how much we prepared for the worst-case situation, it became a reality—I vividly remember our first case of an employee testing positive for COVID-19 in one of our distribution centres. We agonized for hours over how to disinfect the entire distribution centre. We asked ourselves questions like "Should we disinfect each individual bottle, product, or case?" and "What are the standards we should follow to set the benchmark for future cases?"

At our Inviva infusion network, which consists of clinics that infuse specialty medications to patients with chronic or rare illnesses, it wasn't as simple as protecting just our own—we had patients who were immuno-compromised and needed their life-saving treatment.

Typically, a patient comes into our clinic and sits comfortably for hours as they receive their treatment. They can have a snack, chat with others, listen to music, or just relax as they receive their treatment. The remarkable team at Inviva had seventy-two hours to change our entire patient and employee experience—manually moving chairs around the room depending on how many appointments we had, and in some cases renting trucks to bring chairs from one clinic to another to ensure we didn't lose a precious chair required for patient infusions due to social distancing measures.

This posed significant challenges for us—ensuring physical distance between people meant we could only treat so many patients per day. The conversations with patients and guardians were often difficult, as treatment schedules were interrupted and, in some cases, prolonged to protect the health and safety of our immunocompromised patients. What we were most proud of, though, is the fact that through both the early days of the pandemic and onwards, we did not miss a single infusion treatment. Our nurses, through their creativity, hard work, and determination, found a way to ensure patients were safe and socially distanced and that they received their treatment.

Our retail pharmacy teams were one of the first among healthcare companies to implement pandemic pay for our employees, who were there every day, around the clock, making sure Canadians had access to the medications they needed. The very act of going to work, despite the strictest precautions, could potentially put them and their families at risk. It was the right thing to do.

March/April 2020

"Let's be transparent. Let's overcommunicate." This was one of our first critical decisions. I believe the more people know, the more they can understand. Never before in our more than one-hundred-year history in Canada had we experienced supply shortages across hundreds of medications from hundreds of manufacturers. This was more than unusual. This was unprecedented.

Dimitris Polygenis, a pharmacist himself but more importantly a deep veteran of managing the pharmaceutical supply chain for McKesson Canada over the past decade, was stunned by the situation we had rapidly found ourselves in. Overnight, we went from a consistently strong in-stock position across all areas of medications to red flags blinking across all of our systems, with hospitals and pharmacies ordering mass quantities of every type of medication you can imagine—sometimes a year's worth of supply in one daily order.

Dimitris, other critical team members, and I held an emergency meeting the week of March 16 to make some precedent-setting decisions in order to ensure continuity of the pharmaceutical supply chain. Canadians needed their day-to-day prescriptions, hospital ICUs needed medications, and treatments for patients with complex medical needs could not be disrupted. We strategized around all the options in front of us. We knew we needed a clear plan, we needed to move fast, and we needed to drive impact, immediately. The decisions we made in those critical moments together would help shape our management of the crisis going forward.

The pharmaceutical supply chain is truly global, and at this time we saw various countries—such as India, China, and others that typically export active pharmaceutical ingredients (API) used for producing common pharmaceutical products—in various states of lockdown. They had halted their pharmaceutical exports over fears about how they would manage the health of their own populations. Countries became protectionist, and it had immediate implications for us in Canada.

Our customers at McKesson Canada are some of the largest retailers and hospitals in the country. Both our own retailers and our customers were placing incredibly large orders from us each day and understandably calling into our customer care centre at unprecedented volumes. We needed to give our customers reliable information and provide it often. Wherever Canadians decide to get their medication from, there is a very good chance it came from McKesson Canada. This underscores my point: We needed to be the calm in this storm. We needed to discourage hoarding by our customers. So on March 18, 2020, we issued our first of what became a daily customer update across a number of key businesses at McKesson Canada—touching thousands of healthcare endpoints across the country. These updates went to Canada's leading hospitals, pharmacists, nurses, and all levels of governments.

We knew there would be questions. Our message was that everyone needed to order only what they needed and stick to their regular ordering patterns, for the sake of all Canadians. Understandably everyone was in fight-or-flight mode—and they were all fighting for what they thought was limited supply of product for their patients. The calls flooded in, with an average of 2,500 customers a day—an increase of more than 60% almost overnight. Although we were communicating information daily, it did not stop customers from contacting us to ask about orders, supply, sanitization measures, and service levels, even as many were ordering a year's supply for their stores. We knew almost immediately that we needed to segment our inquiries into urgent and non-urgent calls. We built a critical call line, which managed approximately 10% of our incoming customer calls every day. This phone line was intended to be solely meant for urgent patient situations—where pharmacists or hospitals needed a specific medication or there would be serious health impacts.

This was when our primary leadership principles became clear, almost naturally, as we delved deeper into the crisis during that first critical week of the pandemic. We knew we needed to first and foremost protect the health and safety of our employees, so that they could continue to deliver for the healthcare supply chain in Canada. Second, we had to do what was right for patients and the broader healthcare community in Canada— even if it meant managing upset customers. Thirdly, we had to urgently align our employees with the common mission and purpose of improving health outcomes for all, through rallying around a plan centred on over-communicating, being transparent, and supporting our frontline staff. Finally, we had to partner more closely with government—more closely than we ever had before—to be sure they understood what was happening on the ground to ensure the best possible outcomes for all Canadians.

Once we landed on our principles, we made a second critical decision— we implemented product ordering limits on our customers. It was very rare for us to implement such a measure, and a very frightening decision for all involved. We had to be bold. When order restrictions do happen, a manufacturer will contact our team, tell us they are experiencing a challenge related to a product, and we will in turn look at our inventory and forecast how much we need to hold back to ensure we can stretch it out for as long as possible. We do not want to be left in a situation where a certain drug is unavailable for an extended period of time—that may have direct implications on the health of our communities. Often times, we are the only distributor for a certain drug in Canada, so if we allowed a few eager customers to order the product in large quantities, there would be nothing left for other cities, provinces, territories, hospitals, and pharmacy retailers.

By the week of March 23, we knew we were going to have to run the business in a much different way than we had ever before. We knew we would need a cross-functional team meeting every day to bring the best solutions to Canadians. On March 24, we made the critical decision to look at the historical weekly demand of each customer, and adjusted their allowable order limits based on their historical demand. We calculated this would provide a reasonable buffer for customers—a chance to get extra product and serve the healthcare needs of their patients. We knew that, outside of COVID-19, there were no different illness patterns related to chronic or acute care in the country, so historical data should be sufficient in predicting forward-looking demand. It seemed the most equitable thing to do, and it would ensure patients across the country continued to get their medications.

That is easy to say but hard to do when faced with healthcare professionals across the country working under very stressful and unknown conditions. Try telling hospitals urgently needing medication that we're going to have to monitor ordering behaviour and scale back if we notice unusual activity. Yes, exactly. Predictably, people were *not* happy. We received hundreds of concerned calls every hour from governments and customers alike.

Through my previous retail experience I was accustomed to having to occasionally communicate to customers that their favourite shampoo or food item was out of stock. However, being in a situation where we had to communicate to some of the largest retailers in Canada, or our own healthcare teams at pharmacies like Rexall, Guardian, IDA, and Uniprix that we were holding back pharmaceutical products or tempering their orders—that was a whole new world for me, and for our teams.

Our goal at the time was to gradually continue increasing access to product over a few days or weeks, until we were able to remove these historical filters completely. A few days or weeks turned into almost eight months before the system and pharmaceutical supply chain was stable enough to fully lift the filters. For over six months we worked with the manufacturers of these products, who had their own challenges and were continually directing us to slow down the distribution of their products.

Ultimately, our measures had a positive impact on medication supply in the country, and we were successful in stabilizing customer behaviour throughout the early days of the pandemic. Medications continued to flow, largely in the same manner as they always had.

Our third critical decision was building a personal protective equipment (PPE) task force. Our first meeting was on March 16, with a cross-functional team. We needed to secure PPE not only for our frontline staff but also for our customers—retailers and pharmacies from coast to coast. And if that wasn't enough stress on our relatively small but growing medical supply business, we also had government at all levels contacting us to access PPE for hospitals and public health units across the country. Even some of our manufacturer partners who supply us medications wanted to know if we could provide them PPE for their employees.

In normal times, having high demand for a product is a problem we love to have. But during mid-March, it felt like we were just set up to fail. Call after call after call resulted in little to no available PPE from the factories we work with across the globe. And even when we did secure product in those early weeks, there was zero luck in securing air or ocean freight to get the product into the country.

But we didn't give up. We tried every angle. Our employees, our customers, our communities and the government needed us more than ever before. We developed overnight expertise in airspace logistics for medical supplies, enhancing our skills and learning when product was quarantined on a tarmac, how long it would take for it to be released, and who we needed to call to ensure it came to our distribution centres and ultimately into the hands of Canadians. Our efforts were successful—so much so that we were able to donate supplies of PPE to governments, customers, and charitable organizations.

These were decisions made with a speed only an unprecedented global pandemic could dictate. We did not have time to engage in the type of research, analysis, and sober second thought that came with multi-million-dollar expenditures. We weren't perfect. But we got more right than we got wrong. We did not compromise on quality, and we leveraged our global relationships, supply chain infrastructure, and strict quality control procedures and did what was right according to those four principles we set out early in the pandemic

July/August/Fall 2020

As the anxiety-filled days of spring 2020 morphed into summer, life seemed to be returning to something that felt more familiar. On August 10, 2020, the City of Toronto was entering its second week of Stage 3 reopening. Kids could play in previously cordoned-off playgrounds, we could dine inside restaurants, and we could put our kids in summer camp. Some normalcy had returned.

August 10 was also the day I was named CEO of McKesson Canada. At the time, our operations and protocols were largely stable, and we were in the glory days of lower COVID-19 case counts that summer. The crisis had strengthened our relationships with customers, patients, and government alike due to the incredible work of team McKesson.

The summer of 2020 allowed us to take a step back from the crisis and think ahead. We asked ourselves three key questions: What market opportunities or threats had COVID-19 created for us? How could we ensure continued employee safety and business continuity? And how could we support our government partners in the distribution and administration of COVID-19 vaccines that we were all anxiously awaiting?

In the fall of 2020, we were hyper-focused on the upcoming flu season—getting ready to distribute and administer that vaccine to millions of Canadians. And we were monitoring developments around any COVID-19 vaccines. We knew we had an essential role to play.

The call came in September. It was Ontario premier Doug Ford, calling to talk to me about a pilot program for COVID-19 testing in pharmacies.

With approximately 25% of all pharmacies in Ontario counted across our brands, such as Rexall, Guardian, I.D.A., and Medicine Shoppe, we were here to help. Without hesitation, I responded with a resounding yes. Our pharmacy services team, with the support of our distribution operations and government affairs teams, managed to have that up and running within ten days.

We also knew the COVID-19 vaccines were coming. We just didn't know when. Our goal in the interim was to continue to build trust with our customers so that we could be a strong partner to government and make significant commitments to support Canadians. Then on December 9, 2020, came the news so many Canadians had been hoping for—Health Canada authorized the emergency use of the Pfizer vaccine.

Soon after, I met with General Rick Hillier, chair of the Ontario COVID-19 vaccine task force, and Ontario health minister Christine Elliot. We toured our Brampton distribution centre and talked about the role McKesson Canada could play in distributing the COVID-19 vaccine across Ontario. We were having similar conversations with other provinces across the country. They weren't clear yet on when vaccine would be available. We weren't exactly clear on how it would work. But we knew the government—and Canadians—were relying on us, and we knew, just like with the pharmaceutical supply chain stability, or PPE availability and access, we could figure it out.

Our relationship with our government partners became much more strategic and collaborative. Governments across the country were seeking us out and looking for strong public–private partnerships across many areas of COVID-19, and we were focused on bringing the best of McKesson to the government and to Canadians. We became a trusted source of information with our customers and suppliers. This meant communicating in advance when we knew there would be a medication shortage, delivery delays, or impacts from government regulations. We wanted to arm our partners with the information they needed to improve health outcomes.

The power of this approach came with a call from the province of Alberta on January 8, 2021. The government asked if we could distribute the Pfizer vaccine to 1,500 pharmacies across the province. Without hesitation, we said yes.

May/June/ July 2021

How do you feel about your relationship with your pharmacist? Do you consider them a trusted healthcare partner, or is your relationship solely transactional? I can tell you that Canadians who have complex or chronic illnesses rely heavily on the advice and expertise of their pharmacists. When doctors' offices closed and hospitals halted elective surgeries, community pharmacists became one of the few trusted healthcare providers still open to serve patients. Our teams across our retail pharmacy brands sprang into action.

I think most Canadians will vividly recall the situation that occurred in our long-term care homes across the country. Residents were fully locked down for months without visitors, experiencing extreme isolation. Many also became ill with COVID-19. During that time, one of our Rexall pharmacies was dealing with a customer who was in a senior's residence and had been unable to see friends or family. It was her one hundredth birthday. Her daughter lived in Halifax and was unable to come visit, which was absolutely heartbreaking for her. So, without skipping a beat, the pharmacy team, who had heard this story, drove over to the long-term care residence with balloons. They gathered outside the home at the woman's window to wish her a happy one hundredth birthday on her family's behalf. These are the moments, hundreds of them, from the McKesson Canada team and also many other businesses and communities, that brought Canadians together during this time.

Pharmacies were one of the few retail establishments permitted to remain open, giving them a unique perspective living through COVID-19 with their patients and customers. Going through the same emotions—fear and uncertainty—together. Trying to reassure one another that we would be going back to normal and everything would be okay. Supporting one another became a constant theme throughout our organization. Over the course of the pandemic, pharmacists felt an immense sense of privilege and purpose, being able to contribute to the solution via the administration of COVID-19 vaccines. We heard stories of patients expressing relief, hope, and gratitude from their local pharmacist—an experience that brought positivity to the front lines.

In this vein, Saint-Michel, a community in northern Montreal, was one of the areas hardest hit by COVID-19. For us at McKesson, it was personal. This was a neighbourhood in which we had a distribution centre. This was our neighbourhood and we wanted to help. McKesson, along with four other corporate leaders in the area, joined forces to open a hub to provide easy access for vaccination. The clinic would be open to the general public, including the employees of the partner companies. McKesson, for its part, also provided nursing expertise and staff from our Inviva infusion clinics.

It was a beautiful warm day in July 2021, and Jean-Philippe (JP) Blouin, who leads our pharmaceutical distribution operations across the country, was in the Saint-Michel neighbourhood in northern Montreal. That day, Saint-Michel had a very special visitor—Prime Minister Justin Trudeau—who wanted to show his support for the community and all those involved. After the event was over, JP shared some light-hearted moments with the prime minister. They had both spent a lot of time strategizing how to serve the expansive regions that we have in Canada and discussed how each province had such unique needs when it came to health care and medication. Prime Minister Trudeau had also been vaccinated at one of our Ottawa-based Rexall pharmacies along with his wife, Sophie Grégoire Trudeau, and he spoke about the welcoming experience they had with some of our McKesson team members.

They say necessity is the mother of invention. What I learned—what we learned at McKesson—was that we could make the seemingly impossible possible.

We ensured the equitable and stable supply chain of life-giving and life-saving prescription medications and drugs.

We kept our frontline workers safe and in pharmacies and pharmaceutical distribution centres across the country.

We built a medical surgical supply chain bringing large quantities of PPE into the country overnight.

We quickly mastered the ultra-frozen supply chain to deliver and administer life-saving vaccines.

We answered the calls from governments across the country day and night and creatively.

We retooled our technology in pharmacies to best serve our customers.

We rapidly responded to changes in consumer behaviour and attitudes.

We became a work-from-home company overnight.

We changed and we grew. The pandemic was a baptism by fire. It made us stronger. It made us better. It made us braver. But more importantly, it made us more human.

I would say that we at McKesson Canada, and society as a whole, took a very short-term view of this pandemic, at least in the beginning. We all collectively tried to get through the day or the week, hoping that cases would stabilize and normalcy would return. The pandemic was relentless. I felt as though I was in a war zone, and so I reacted. I saw problems and I wanted to dig in and solve them right away. As urgent as some of those problems proved to be, there was an even greater challenge—stepping back.

It's hard to do, especially when you're in the midst of a global pandemic. It's not something one industry or one country was experiencing. Every last one of us was affected. This is where incredible skill and mental strength is needed to take that thirty-thousand-foot view. Right now is important. So is tomorrow. But what about next week and next month and next year? As leaders, we must find that space. If you're anything like me, you will need to force yourself, with your team, into taking the space for long-term thinking. In that space, we must bring the power of focus to our teams.

The pandemic also challenged our notions of risk. Like many large corporations, we engage in due diligence. We strive to make informed, responsible decisions. The pandemic didn't care. We needed to make decisions quickly, often in an information vacuum, truly not sure of what was coming the next hour, much less the next day. We've learned that we can be far more agile.

And finally, the greatest lesson for me has been the power of our collective humanness. We're not just part of this company. We are not part of a machine. We're humans who have experienced this pandemic personally and professionally in many different ways. But we have all experienced it together. This pandemic has exposed our vulnerabilities as individuals and as a company. It turns out, when you acknowledge this, you don't get weaker, you get stronger. And there is always someone there to lift you up.

I'm privileged and humbled to have been able to share our McKesson Canada story with you as CEO, on behalf of our over twelve thousand employees across Canada. This story is not about me, but about the phenomenal team who were able to deliver for our customers and patients across the country during this unprecedented pandemic. Our response to COVID-19 wasn't easy, but it was made possible by the unbelievable teamwork, agility, speed, and unity we showed across the company. Thank you, Team McKesson.

NATURE'S PATH

When you spend your entire working life trying to keep people healthy, a pandemic is a call to arms.

Ratana Stephens and her husband, Arran, built Nature's Path into one of North America's largest organic food producers out of a passion for nutrition. It all started in the 1940s, on a Vancouver Island berry farm owned by Arran's father, an organic farming pioneer.

Inspired by that organic approach to produce, Arran opened Vancouver's first vegetarian restaurant in 1967, then travelled to India to study yoga and meditation. He came back with a wife—Ratana was a university professor in New Delhi prior to meeting her husband and moving to Canada in 1969. The couple opened several Vancouver restaurants. In the 1970s, they launched Canada's first natural food supermarket, then built a flour mill and distribution business that was sold in 1981.

In 1985, the Stephens began making organic breakfast cereal out of the back of one of their restaurants under the Nature's Path brand. They were among the first to stress the importance of the farm-to-table process, highlighting the company's sustainable approach to agriculture and organic ingredients on every cereal box. Over time, Nature's Path added granola bars, oatmeal, waffles, and snacks to the menu.

By the spring of 2020, Nature's Path was running three factories in North America and Europe, with 750 employees. The couple's two adult children also hold senior roles in the business—Arjan is general manager, and Jyoti is VP of mission and strategy.

COVID-19 lockdowns prompted families to revisit their relationship with food, putting a new emphasis on healthy options at the breakfast table. As a result, Nature's Path saw demand soar during the pandemic, and the company faced the challenge of producing far more food while at the same time reconfiguring its facilities to ensure employees stayed healthy. The balancing act was fraught—at the start of one shift, workers at their facility in Sussex, Wisconsin, walked off the job over safety concerns.

Looking back, Ratana said solving the labour issues and keeping store shelves stocked simply reflected the company's founding philosophy—that Nature's Path isn't in the cereal business, it's in the people business. This CEO makes a unique claim to fame on the corporate website. Ratana would like the world to know that she gives the best hugs at Nature's Path's head office in Richmond, B.C., something she is looking forward to getting back to doing in a fully post-pandemic world.

Ratana Stephens

JULY 2021

February 8, 2020. My husband, Arran, and I were at the tail end of a trip to India and ending it in the loveliest way possible. We were invited to Canada House in New Delhi, to attend an event in honour of our dear friend Rakesh Bakshi. Rakesh was affectionately known around the world as the "Green Maharaja." Born in London, he moved to India when he was young and became one of the world's most prominent climate activists, pioneering India's renewable energy revolution. He was also one of our closest friends.

It was a pleasure to see one of our friends celebrated by the high commissioner. Rakesh was such an incredible connector of people and was in fine form that night—happy and healthy and full of joy and zest for life. Arran and I would fly home to Vancouver the next day, still basking in the glow of the evening. It was a magical end to a wonderful trip.

Two and a half months later, our dear friend would be dead. One of the world's casualties of COVID-19. It still shocks me to write these words.

I often think of that night—how beautiful it was, and how little we knew then. I think about how much we miss Rakesh, and I think about all the other people who have lost loved ones during this pandemic.

Before we travelled to India, we of course knew about the virus. We researched extensively, but all the research we did and the advice we received indicated it was still safe to travel. In retrospect, that is hard to believe, but of course we didn't know then what we know now. During our trip at the beginning of February, we still felt safe.

After we returned home, things changed. By late February the coronavirus was all anyone was talking about—first the spread of the virus in China, then its spread from China to the rest of the world. It began dominating the news cycle. The focus was, would it come to Canada? And if it did, how bad would it be? At the time it was still business as usual in our country, and in B.C., where Nature's Path is based, although the fear and speculation seemed to be growing by the hour.

I remember the week of March 9, when things really started to escalate. That week, it felt like matters were changing by the minute. What I remember most from that week was the pervasive feeling of instability. Then, on March 11, I was at home, sipping a cup of chai and watching the news on CBC, when the head of the World Health Organization officially declared a global pandemic. The unthinkable was happening, and I knew Canada would not be immune.

We are all presented with challenges in life. They are inevitable. The test is how one will handle these challenges. When presented with a challenge, I tend to jump into action. I need to feel like I am doing something, and the best thing I could do in the face of the pandemic was to make sure my family, which also means my Nature's Path family, was safe.

I called my husband and my children. To my son Arjan, who is the general manager of Nature's Path, I said, "Have you heard? It's a pandemic. We have to do everything we can to look after our people." I believe that the purpose of power is to protect. When we are in a position of authority, we have some power, and we need to use it to look after our people. As the head of the organization I have a duty and responsibility to look after all the members who make up the organization. It's very important. I feel very strongly about this.

That Monday morning I called an emergency meeting of our executive leadership team (ELT). This was the start of March Break, so some of our people were already out of town, while others were frantically cancelling plans. I remember that our head of manufacturing was supposed to be in Hawaii with his family, but he stayed. It was all hands on deck.

Those of us who could gather in person met in the office, and we had video calls with the others. Remember, video calls weren't as commonplace then, at least not for our office. That call was the first, but it soon became the norm. From that day on, we implemented the daily 9 a.m. COVID call with the ELT. We kept that daily call for well over a year.

That first day, the main topic was plant safety. We talked about bringing in temperature screening, but of course that doesn't happen overnight. We reviewed the COVID numbers in the areas in which we operate, and we got down to business, but these were extremely stressful days. I have to say, we also turned to each other for support. We were all trying to react and get things done, and so much was changing. I could not have made it through those weeks and months without this exceptional group of people. That same day, Monday, March 16, like so many other companies, we also shifted everyone at head office to work from home. We quickly ordered monitors, keyboards, headsets, whatever our people needed to be effective in working remotely. But that was the easy part. Clearly, we are in food production, and the majority of our team members cannot work from home. They have to go to the plants, working the front lines, making our food.

We have three manufacturing facilities, employing a total of about six hundred people—one in Delta, B.C., another in Blaine, Washington, and the third in Sussex, Wisconsin. Sussex is our largest facility. To give you an idea, it's three hundred thousand square feet, the size of five football fields. Our Sussex plant produces forty-five to fifty million pounds of food a year. At all hours of the day it is alive with activity. At every moment, there are about sixty to seventy people on the floor. It has four processing/baking lines, four pack lines, and a chip line. Some lines are working, some lines are being sanitized, and supplies are being run in and out, feeding all the lines. There is always something happening, things are always moving. The lines are moving, the ovens are on, the machines are moving, and there are forklifts all over the place. It's pretty chaotic on a typical day, and trying to juggle it all during the start of the pandemic was—as my grandchildren would say—"next level."

We immediately started investigating what we needed to do to keep our frontline team members safe. My son had heard that progress was made against the coronavirus in China, partially through mask wearing, and immediately we started searching the globe for as many masks as we could find. As I write this, we are now very used to masks, and only recently is it no longer mandatory to wear them indoors in public spaces. But in March 2020, few people in North America were wearing them. We were still two months away from Canada's chief public health officer, Dr. Theresa Tam, finally recommending Canadians wear non-medical face masks. And it wouldn't be until June that the World Health Organization would make the same recommendation. This is so hard to believe, as we are all so used to them now.

Sourcing masks at the start of the pandemic was not something everyone was doing. In that sense we were lucky, as we were slightly ahead of the curve. Masks were still hard to find—my son reached out to everyone he knew on Facebook, consulted friends around the world, made so many calls—but it was not impossible. Finally, our VP of manufacturing reached out to one of our vendors who gets us pumpkin seeds from China and was able to procure about forty thousand masks for us. I will be forever grateful to Sunshine Produce for sourcing these for Nature's Path. But forty thousand masks ended up not being enough. Thankfully, they then connected us with a supplier, and we jumped on the opportunity. While we were able to get our hands on masks, at this point we had not yet decided whether we should mandate them. We just wanted to be ready.

We had all the masks shipped to our facility in Delta, B.C. We decided the easiest way was to bring them all to Canada and to distribute them to our two U.S. facilities from there. However, the freight piece of the puzzle was interesting, as things really slowed at the start of the pandemic. But we managed to get them and to send them on to the plants. We provided masks to all our frontline team members, but initially there was a lot of pushback, as people didn't want to wear them. To be honest, I think much of the world felt like that at the start of the pandemic. At this point we had not yet made mask wearing mandatory.

Now that I felt we were taking tangible steps to protect our team members, my next thought was product inventory. How much stock did we have? This was in the days just before the panic-buying pantry loading started, but I knew it was coming. I could feel it. I knew there was going to be a need the likes of which we had never seen before, and I wanted to be prepared.

I looked at our inventory and we didn't have enough to last even for a few months. Our fiscal year ends in February, and our new year starts in March, pretty much coinciding with the start of the pandemic. At the end of the fiscal, we were trying to get as much inventory off our hands as possible—of course, we didn't know that the pandemic was coming in a matter of weeks. So we started the new fiscal year off with very low inventory. And almost immediately, sales went through the roof. That first month sales were up 25% to 30%. Our limited inventory was entirely wiped out, and we couldn't manufacture product fast enough to replenish.

We were scrambling to source raw materials and to find co-manufacturers; we were going full tilt trying to recover. My team was under immense pressure. It was a very tough situation involving a lot of balancing and innovation to solve our various challenges. Nature's Path is the world's largest producer of organic cereal and snack foods, so there are a lot of people who depend on us—both customers and team members. The increased demand was a welcome challenge, but all I could think of was, what if we couldn't continue manufacturing? What if we were shut down? In mid-March this was a very real possibility. We had to do everything we could to reduce the chances of that happening, everything we could to keep Nature's Path team members safe.

So we hired two public health nurses as consultants. They advised us to install plexiglass partitions between team members, to ensure physical distancing. Again, we were lucky—we ordered the plexiglass fairly early, before there was a worldwide shortage. We reconfigured the manufacturing floor at our three facilities to allow more distance between people, and we introduced mandatory temperature checks. At first, we had a nurse on site taking temperatures, but eventually we installed state-of-the-art technology that takes people's temperatures as they walk into the building and displays it on a TV monitor. We still use it today. If your temperature is above normal, the door to the manufacturing floor will not unlock, and an email will immediately be sent to the supervising manager on duty.

We drastically increased our cleaning protocols and hired an extra cleaning crew to constantly wipe down all machinery, surfaces, doorknobs—everything that people might be touching. We reconfigured the lunchroom, allowing just one chair per table. And in the lunchrooms, where wearing a mask is pretty much impossible due to eating and drinking, we became the first food manufacturer in North America to install cutting-edge far-UVC downlights and sanitizing air filtration systems, which eliminate viruses like COVID-19 from the air. My son first heard about the technology from a friend, and we didn't hesitate to order and install them. The same technology is now being used by major airlines, long-term care facilities, and schools.

We moved as fast as possible, making these changes before health authorities even made their recommendations. But still, all of these measures took time to implement. Looking back, I think about the first two of weeks of COVID. I recall the panic taking hold, the incredible uncertainty. None of us knew what was going to happen.

And during the first weeks of COVID, the time we all remember, when the situation was changing by the minute, team members at our Sussex plant walked off the job. Two people working the same shift tested positive, and our employees said it wasn't safe. They said they didn't know what was happening. They said they would not work. And who could blame them? We all felt like that the first few weeks. We were all scared.

The team in Sussex walked out mid-shift. I will never forget the day. They left machinery running, cereal coming down the line. The floor manager couldn't stop them. They didn't turn anything off, they just walked out. There was complete panic on the floor. The manager was running around, desperately trying to shut things down. We lost thousands of pounds of product that day, at a time when we were already significantly behind on production. Thousands of dollars of equipment was also damaged.

I don't blame our team. I understand the panic of those first few days and weeks—I was feeling it too. We all were. I just wish they'd had faith that their health and safety was the most important thing to us—that as owners, it was what was keeping us awake at night. I have always prided myself on valuing our team members and showing our appreciation. They are our heroes; they are the people who cannot shift to working from home. They physically need to be in the plants, working the front lines making our food. The day our team members walked off the job in Sussex taught me we had to go even further in making them feel valued and secure.

It was at this point that we made masks mandatory. We had already introduced the physical distancing, and temperature checks, and other measures, but it was clear masks were a necessity. And since then, no one has ever come back to us saying they didn't feel safe. Also, right at the start of the pandemic, we introduced a "hero pay" premium of $2 an hour for each and every frontline team member. And to this day, we have kept this premium. Many other businesses rolled it back, but we felt it was extremely important to keep it. For us as a business, it was the right thing to do. As I said, they are our heroes.

By late March, the intense pantry loading had begun. Remember the shelves empty of toilet paper and other essential items? People fighting over what little was left in grocery stores? The irrational behaviour and panic-buying? Questions around global supply chain? It was a terrifying time. Governments had no choice but to declare food production an essential service, which meant we were operational and that demand for our products was still increasing. We had an obligation, we had to make sure we could still produce.

First, we had to ensure people were safe doing their jobs. I felt secure in that we had done everything possible. Then I asked myself, as a leader, "What else can I do?" The answer was to simplify production. I suggested to operations we start focusing on our bigger stock-keeping units, or SKUs, the products that had the widest distribution and sales. We had to simplify production and deprioritize the smaller SKUs. During this time, the first months of COVID, we also put the brakes on any new innovations—we had to put a stop to them. We had extensive plans to increase our EnviroKidz line, which we had to delay. We also had planned to introduce a low-sugar granola, which we ended up postponing by a year. There were several other products in the planning stages that all had to be shelved. We pride ourselves on our innovations, but we had to concentrate on the basic products our consumers were used to buying.

We also responded to specific demand where we could. For example, we made Love Crunch granola for one entire week, devoted an entire manufacturing facility to it—because there was such increased demand. Before the pandemic, we would sell about thirty-five thousand cases of Love Crunch granola in a month, but as soon as the pandemic started, that shot up to fifty thousand cases. One month we sold one hundred thousand! And it wasn't just Love Crunch; we also could not keep up with the demand for some of our other big sellers, like Heritage Flakes and Pumpkin Flax Granola. Our sales team makes a forecast on what they expect to sell, but we had no idea what to plan for. We were flying blind!

So the next phase was to increase operations to 24/7, something we had never done before. In the first quarter after COVID began, we produced three million pounds more product at our Blaine plant and one million more pounds in Sussex—a total of four million more pounds of food. I was shocked. This was unprecedented. We had never achieved anywhere close to these production levels before in our thirty-five-year history.

And that is how we continued: putting the health and safety of our people first, focusing on our production second. We spent millions of dollars on implementing the additional safety measures at our plants and have spent additional millions in "hero pay." But I believe that is a very small price to pay to ensure the safety of our people, and to ensure they feel appreciated.

Through the entirety of the pandemic, we have been extremely fortunate in that we have had just one very small COVID outbreak at our facility in Wisconsin, and none at our other plants. At the time, we immediately shut the Sussex plant down for three days, conducted an extensive cleaning and sanitizing process, and were able to contain the outbreak and reopen after seventy-two hours. We have had no other outbreaks. Team members have tested positive for COVID-19, but they contracted the virus outside work, and they did not transmit the virus to colleagues. We added free COVID testing for all our U.S. team members. Here in

Canada we take for granted that the cost of testing is covered by our healthcare system, but in America it wasn't. Some may have been discouraged from being tested because of the cost, so we eliminated that worry.

As I look back at the early months of COVID and reflect on what I learned, I think the main lesson is the importance of resiliency. Whether in business life or life in general, sometimes you will be thrown off the edge. It happens. And the question then becomes, what do you do? Slowly but surely you have to progress. These things are going to happen, and you have to keep on going. And you have to remember that this too shall pass.

I enjoy reading auto/biographies, and I often turn to those written by or about the people I admire, to seek inspiration. I read Joe Biden's autobiography during COVID. He has had a lengthy career that has taken him to the height of power in the Oval Office. But he has also had a life scarred by deep personal loss. When he was still young, he lost both his wife and baby daughter in a car accident. But he believed giving up was unforgiveable. I also turn to classic literature for inspiration during challenging times. I studied literature in university, and it remains one of my greatest passions.

Life has its way of presenting challenges. And I believe no challenge is insurmountable. You simply carry on. The COVID pandemic has represented one such challenge. And at the same time my family has had its own additional challenges. In the past year and a half, both my mother and sister have had strokes. My son-in-law has undergone cancer treatment and my daughter has had brain surgery. I am blessed to say they are all recovering. And I am well aware that despite the challenges I have faced, I know many, many people have gone through much more than I have.

During these hard times, in business and in life, there are also so many positives to hold on to. Everyone I know banded together. My family— and we are a family-run business—is closer than ever. We have so many wonderful people in our organization, I consider them to be my family too, and they care so much. They go out of their way to help and suggest solutions. To solve problems. I am so grateful for their caring attitude, grateful for all the wonderful people I have the privilege of working with.

Our frontline team members continued to manufacture our products. Our head of sales didn't miss a beat—he made sure sales were coming in. Shipping didn't miss a beat—they made sure product was going out. We did not sit in a corner, afraid. This is all evidence of the resiliency of our people, and of the organization. But it has only reinforced what I learned a long time ago: We are not in the cereal business. We are in the people business.

Robert Greenleaf is someone I admire greatly. He pioneered the concept of servant leadership. He wrote words that greatly resonate with me: "Leadership must first and foremost meet the needs of others." This was true for us during the pandemic. Our most important lesson learned: whether fulfilling the needs of customers or looking after the health and safety of your team members, always put your people first.

RECIPE UNLIMITED

Through the darkest days of the COVID-19 pandemic, CEO Frank Hennessey always took comfort from knowing Canada's largest full-service restaurant chain had the recipe for survival.

The 137-year-old company weathered the last global health crisis— the 1918 Spanish flu pandemic—and went on to create the spaces where Canadians gather for good food and good times. Now known as Recipe Unlimited, the company runs twenty-four iconic restaurant brands, including Swiss Chalet, The Keg, St-Hubert, and Harvey's.

Hennessey, named chief executive at Recipe in 2018, went into the pandemic confident his business was a resilient part of Canada's cultural fabric. His challenge was guiding more than sixty thousand teammates through unprecedented times, to ensure Recipe was still cooking when the country emerged from COVID.

Hennessey backed into a career in the hospitality industry after first considering law enforcement. Hennessey's first foray in restaurants was an eleven-year stint with General Mills Restaurants (now known as Darden Restaurants) working in operations before eventually being transferred to their buying division in Orlando, Florida. Recipe's predecessor, Cara Operations, recruited Hennessey to return to Canada to lead their buying group, where he also took the time to earn an MBA from the Rotman School of Management at the University of Toronto. He left Cara during a restructuring in 2009 and went on to become CEO of Bento Sushi, after which he took the helm at Imvescor Restaurant Group, which owned the Pizza Delight and Baton Rouge chains. Hennessey turned around Imvescor and oversaw the sale of the company in 2017 for $248 million.

At Recipe, Hennessey runs a company that traces its roots to the 1850s, when founder Thomas Phelan began selling apples and newspapers on Niagara steamboats. Phelan incorporated the company in 1883 as the Canada Railway News Co., which was subsequently shortened to Cara. At one point, the company was a leading supplier of airline meals, a line of businesses tested in 2001 when the 9/11 attacks curtailed air travel. Recipe sold its airline catering business in 2010.

In 2013, insurer and asset manager Fairfax Financial Holdings took a significant stake in Recipe. In the years that followed, the company acquired a string of familiar restaurant chains, including New York Fries, Pickle Barrel, The Keg, St-Hubert, and The Burger's Priest. As the COVID crisis hit, Hennessey oversaw a business that stocked store shelves with food and ran more than 1,300 restaurants in 300 communities across 11 countries.

Frank Hennessey

JULY 2021

"It feels rushed." The comment came across the table from a senior member of my team as the rest of the leadership group huddled in our boardroom to begin the most impactful conference call of my thirty-plus-year career in the restaurant industry. On the phone were over 1,000 franchisees and corporate restaurant managers, representing over 1,300 restaurants and more than 60,000 employees. It was March 16, 2020, the day before St. Patrick's Day, one of the busiest days in our restaurant calendar year—and I was about to shut it all down. Voluntarily.

The comment came as that team member watched my hesitation before initiating the call—a call that was already late getting started and one for which we had the line for only thirty minutes. We reserved 2 p.m., enough time to organize my comments after listening to the scheduled briefings from the premier of Ontario, Doug Ford, followed by Prime Minister Justin Trudeau, who was to speak at 1 p.m. I had assumed they would announce a complete shutdown of all retail business and non-essential travel. But we all know the dangers of assumptions.

Instead, the premier, looking like the boy whose dog ate his homework, essentially said nothing and the PM was late. I remember thinking that Ford must be letting Trudeau make the tough announcement (at this point in time, I did not have a good understanding of federal versus provincial jurisdictional rules for a pandemic). As my franchisees were beginning to queue for the call, we continued to wait. Finally, at 1:40 Trudeau emerged. And it quickly became apparent that he was not going to shut the economy down. I remember being stunned that neither of them had made the hard but obvious call.

Now I was left with a full boardroom and maxed-out conference call line. Everyone was waiting for me to speak. Was shutting down the right thing to do? It was no small matter and the decision would impact thousands of lives and livelihoods. Was it rushed?

Recipe (formerly Cara Operations) is Canada's largest full-service restaurant company. We are publicly traded, with twenty-four brands and three manufacturing plants, and are partnered with over eight hundred small business franchisee owners across hundreds of communities coast to coast. Our sales in 2019 were $3.5 billion.

I rejoined Recipe in May 2018 as CEO after having been with the company nine years previously in various leadership roles. I had gone through crises with the company before: the Great Recession in 2008, SARS in 2003, and the September 11, 2001, attacks, when the primary business of the company at the time was directly linked to the airline industry. Further, the company is 137 years old and had already survived one global pandemic, albeit a hundred years earlier. I knew the business was resilient, as long as we did not panic.

I'd had a dry run on crisis management only a few short months after taking over at Recipe. It was the fall of 2018 and the company was hit with a vicious malware attack that targeted most of our point of sales systems at the restaurant level. The attack prevented us from taking any type of payment except cash. While we never paid any ransom and personal data was not breached, it still took us the better part of a week to get all our systems back up and running.

In hindsight, during that crisis, I was too slow getting everyone together—information flowing in and out was out of sync, the right people were not in the room hearing information first-hand. People were working on their own priorities versus moving as one, and as a result, our response was sluggish. The fault was mine as I only assembled my war room on the second day after the attack—too slow when events are moving quickly. I was not going to repeat that mistake with COVID.

Restaurants are leading indicators of consumer confidence. Our first senior leadership group call on COVID occurred on January 29, 2020—two days after the first Canadian was confirmed to have contracted COVID-19. The call was in response to inquiries we were beginning to get around the wearing of masks. I had been watching the news and tracking what was happening in Asia, but now it was starting to get closer to home. We immediately activated our crisis management team and they began to work on preparing a COVID website to answer questions that might start coming in from our managers, teammates, guests, and franchisees. We closely monitored our social channels for any change to guest sentiment. Yet by the end of February, we had not seen any negative results show up on our daily sales reports. In fact, January and February restaurant sales were positive versus the previous year. But the storm clouds were building all around us.

Our first tangible sign of a shift in consumer behaviour due to COVID was surprisingly positive for Recipe. It happened in our sizeable retail sales division. These are the restaurant-branded products that we sell to grocery stores across the country. Products like St-Hubert sauces, Swiss Chalet pot pies, or Montana's ribs. In February, that business was up 36% versus the previous year—propelled in part by the federal minister of health suggesting on February 26 that Canadians stockpile food and medication. While it was nice to see that lift in retail, it was also not lost on us what that might portend. The weekend of March 7–8 was full of negative virus news. The talking heads on Sunday shows predicted the worst, quarantined cruise ship passengers were getting 24/7 coverage, and sporting events like regional tennis tournaments were being postponed. Still, by the week ending March 8, sales were down only 2%.

It was Monday, March 9 that our world began to change dramatically. Sales were down 14%, and on Tuesday they were down 16%. The storm walls really broke on Wednesday, March 11. That day, the World Health Organization declared a global pandemic, Ontario closed its schools for a few weeks, and within a two-hour time span U.S. president Donald Trump gave an unsettling address from the Oval Office, the NBA cancelled their season, and Tom Hanks declared he had COVID. It was that night when it first hit me that we were going to get shut down. It was no longer a matter of if, but when. By Sunday, March 15, our sales were down 44%.

The intensity was building—we all knew the world was about to change. While the politicians were saying "fourteen days to bend the curve," I felt that was just to mitigate panic. For me, the entire weekend of March 14–15 was a flurry of calls and scenario planning. Fortunately, I have a very supportive board and I had counsel from Paul Rivett, chair of Recipe. Paul and I would end up talking almost every weekend throughout the crisis. There was never much daylight between us and I always appreciated his guidance and his ear. I knew whatever decision I would need to make, I could count on his and the board's support.

Amid the chaos of that weekend, the doorbell rang at my house. At the door was a nurse. She had arrived so that she could take the normal samples needed for someone applying for a new life insurance policy. I had forgotten she was coming. One of the tests is for blood pressure. Now, even though I felt calm with all that was going on (I have never had high blood pressure), her little gauge suggested I was lying to myself. So, after some deep breathing exercises led by my wife and four more attempts by the nurse, we finally got a decent reading to record.

With the weekend over and my blood pressure normal, it was back to the boardroom thinking about our primary concern, the safety of our teammates and guests. One of our values as a company is "do the right thing"—if there was ever a time to live our values, this was it. So on that fateful Monday, the decision on what to do was clear to me. We needed to close.

As I announced our decision to the team on the conference call line, I made it clear that this was a survivable event if we all worked together and did not panic. To everyone's credit, not one franchisee complained about the decision. And while I worked on the press release to announce to markets our decision to close, the team at Recipe sprang into action to implement the crisis plan we had prepared across the last several weeks.

Crucial to our plan was the establishment of priorities. This was vital to creating clarity for all stakeholders and to keeping people on task. Our five key priorities were these:

1. The health and safety of our guests and teammates
2. The financial health of Recipe
3. Franchisee liquidity
4. Leveraging our off-premise brands and retail
5. Supporting our industry

Later that afternoon, a few hours after I had made the decision to close, the governments across Canada made moot any hand wringing I might have had when they began to order closures of dining rooms. What they would allow were takeout and delivery. Fortunately, some of our largest brands already did significant volume in both of those channels, which created a financial safety net as well as valuable intelligence that we could impart to brands with no experience in anything but in-house dining. The impact of closures varied across our network. New York Fries, led by the very able Craig Burt, was shut down almost completely due to their misfortune of being located within malls.

The key now was to ensure that our guests and our teammates were safe. The early planning started to pay off. Peter Vale, our SVP of Strategic Sourcing, and his team were unsung heroes throughout this whole ordeal, managing multiple disruptions to supply chains and shifting regulations. His team had secured masks and hand sanitizer—even though the latter was becoming increasingly difficult to find.

Innovative ideas were coming in from all across the system. Brian Robbie, one of our area managers at Harvey's, came up with the idea to put our payment device on the end of a hockey stick for guests coming through the drive-thru. That got some media attention, especially after the Great One, Wayne Gretzky, tweeted about it.

The restaurant transformations happened quickly, thanks to our franchisee and operations teams. Decals on the floor established the six feet rule, and masks, sanitizers, and new floor plans were all laid out to ensure that our guests and staff were safe. Our IT teams worked tirelessly to reconfigure our apps for brands getting into more off-premise business, while also translating all of our menus to have QR codes.

One of the things that I love about the people in the restaurant business is that when one of the most devastating events happens to their livelihood, their first instinct is to ask, "How can I help?" You can imagine that shutting down all restaurants overnight would create a lot of excess food inventory, but instead of throwing it away, groups such as Mark Sozanski's team at Montana's gathered to organize donations of perishable food to local food banks.

Many of our brands started up campaigns for frontline workers—including Ron Simard and the team at Swiss Chalet, who donated eighty thousand meals to first responders and healthcare workers. Dave Colebrook, president of Harvey's and Chelsea Kellock, VP of Marketing, continually came up with innovative ways for their brand to give back. Harvey's sent an RV across Canada to feed grocery store workers. They continued this program into the summer of 2021, giving away free burgers at vaccination clinics. Our Catering Division, led by Peter Higley, converted their operations from weddings to making healthy and nutritious meals for senior living facilities.

The collective team at Recipe ultimately donated more than $2.3 million, including 158,000 meals and 100,000 burgers.

While we were working to ensure our guests and teammates could be served safely and efficiently, we were also ensuring the financial health of Recipe. Our chief financial officer, Ken Grondin, is as competent a CFO as you will find in any business. He had built trusted relationships with our bankers and private noteholders, and they knew him to know his stuff. Recipe had a strong balance sheet coming into the crisis, but none of us knew how deep or how long the pain was going to be. On March 13, we drew on our revolving line of credit for $300 million—not that we needed the cash, but we just felt better with it sitting in our pockets.

Until we could properly assess the situation, we needed to preserve cash, not just ours but our franchisees, as well. In short, the taps needed to be turned off. That included cash inflow from franchisees to Recipe and outflows from Recipe to everyone else. We did not pull any rent or royalty payments from franchisees. We stopped all other collections from them as well, including payments for our IT programs. At Recipe, our senior executives voluntarily cut their pay and we slightly reduced salaries for all of our head office employees. Paul, the rest of the board, and I took no pay. We stopped dividend payments and stock buybacks. We cancelled or paused any capital expenditures projects. We put all of the hammers down.

We ran our burn models—something I had not been involved in since my days running some turn-around businesses. Recipe's business model typically generates significant free cash, so running out of cash is not something that keeps me up at night. But in this situation, we also needed to see what we could afford to do for our franchisees. However, as they say in those pre-flight safety videos before you can help anyone else, you need to secure your oxygen mask first.

Calculations were made for the typical three scenarios: good, bad, and worst. I recall Ken saying, "All the numbers will be wrong." While we had no precedent, we did observe where our sales had declined after the first two weeks of shutdown. We felt that our models would be close enough. Ken and I were confident enough to know that while Recipe would get hurt, the wound would be far from fatal. Further, we could still help our franchisees, but only if we in turn got support—especially from landlords.

Restaurant margins are notoriously thin. The industry quotes that pre-tax profit margins are less than 5%. Rents play a much more significant role in the unit economic model of a restaurant than they do in other industries. It can range from 6% to 12% of sales in full-service restaurants and can be as high as 20% in places like food courts. Many of those rents are fixed dollars, not a percentage of income—so you can imagine that unless relief was given, most restaurant owners would burn through their cash quickly once their revenue inflows were completely shut off and if their landlords still demanded that they be paid in full.

In the spring, Mark Eaton, our very skilled chief development officer, had the pleasure of dealing with me and Ken pushing him hard to be tough on landlords while also trying to preserve those same relationships in order to ensure we still had a business to operate in the future. To his credit, he managed to do both.

Across the country, the battle between restaurant owners and landlords was shaping up to be ugly. Lawsuits were threatened and some landlords actually locked the doors on their tenants. In fairness, many of the smaller landlords were also in a cash squeeze themselves. The landlord issue was causing major anxiety for our partners.

I felt strongly that we needed to remove the panic from our franchise partners and had to do it quickly. We wanted them to be focused on making the investments in personal protective equipment and pivoting their business and servicing their guests, not worried about whether they could pay rent and keep their homes. To do that we had to get ahead of this rent issue.

Once we had assessed our situation, Ken teamed up with VP of Finance Bob Ellis to brief our bankers and get us the needed covenant relief we required, including help for our franchisees. The solution was innovative, and it had to be since there was no playbook to follow. With Ken and his team being so early with the creditors, their solution became one of the models others would follow, and that solution included rent support.

The concept was simple: we would charge the franchisees a certain percentage of sales for their rent. Whatever was owed to the landlords above that amount, Recipe would pay. If they were completely closed by the governing authorities, there was no percentage rent to collect and we would pay what was owed to the landlord, or whatever Mark and his team could negotiate. We would keep this in place for the entirety of 2020, and the program was extended through the first three months of 2021.

We also lowered franchisee royalties. Combined with the rent relief, we estimated this cost to be about $40 million. While, as a result of our franchisee support, we took a major hit to the net income in our 2020 second-quarter results, we preferred to look at our action as an investment in our franchise partners and Recipe's future.

When we communicated our rent solution on yet another conference call with the franchisees, many of them did not believe it. There had to be a catch. But as soon as it sank in that this was real, their relief was palpable. One franchisee told me, "It's as if there was this massive weight on my chest that was crushing me and Recipe came along and simply lifted it off." That felt good.

Simultaneously, we had to organize our corporate team. Recipe is in the people business and our chief people officer, Julie Denton, could best be described as smart, calm, strategic, and able to carry a tremendous load. She genuinely cares about people. She does more things at Recipe than her business card would suggest, but I have not been creative enough to come up with a different title.

Julie was the main catalyst for us preparing ourselves, prior to COVID, to move to a flex work model. Recipe's main office is a hundred thousand square feet and is a completely open concept, I mean completely open. No one has an office. Thanks to our chief technology officer, Gary Black, whose team's efforts throughout the crisis were critical for our ability to pivot, the company's systems were prepared for flex work. Julie had the protocols all worked out; I just had not yet signed off on the policy. Call me old school but I wasn't completely on board with flex work before COVID. How would we measure productivity? What about team collaboration?

While I made the call to close all of the restaurant's dining rooms, I felt that our office should stay open as long as we had restaurants operating takeout and delivery. However, after returning home on March 18, I began to feel ill. It only lasted the evening, and maybe it was stress, but it was enough for me to make the call that perhaps having our office open was not the wisest decision. The next day we closed it completely.

My feeling ill that night, combined with the blood pressure incident from a few days prior, reminded me to focus on my own health. While I always considered myself fit, I greatly increased my workout routine and ensured I was eating properly. After all, I would not be very useful to my team if I myself was not healthy.

Fortunately, due to our preplanning, first started by the crisis committee at the end of January, we were able to make the shift to remote work seamlessly. At least to me, it seemed seamless. Gary had already secured three hundred laptops. We let our teams take the computer monitors and anything else they required, and we got back to work—this time in a completely remote workplace.

Remote working is interesting. Many books, I am sure, will be written on the subject. From my chair, the video call is a good medium to communicate information, but it falls short on connectedness. However, in a world of "stay at home" orders, it was a critical tool. Video allowed me to see the faces of my team. When were they looking tired or anxious? When did I feel we might be too relaxed (too many T-shirts or hoodies)? When was it necessary to be more of a coach than a taskmaster? That was the power of the video call over the phone call. Even if it meant that sometimes you had young or furry intruders.

I am in awe of how some parents managed through this with little ones literally climbing all over them. I will never forget one video call in which a very talented member of Ken's finance team was walking Ken and me through a report. Her kids were all around her and very, very much wanting her attention. Her ability to calmly stay focused on her presentation and not get rattled will go down as one of the most impressive feats of presentation poise that I have ever witnessed. Fortunately, my kids are older and out of the house.

Ensuring the team was staying engaged was vital. I did not want people "guessing" at our situation; instead, I wanted them to have the facts. Our communications cascaded from our senior leadership daily calls down to the brand and shared service teams. We regularly had our Top 100 calls (top managers in the company) and we increased our quarterly town halls to monthly. COVID was only part of the agenda, and over time it became an increasingly smaller part of the agenda. Julie's People Team created a long list of employee engagement initiatives and teams were encouraged to regularly check in with colleagues who lived on their own. We paid special attention to being mindful of people's mental and physical health.

In short order, we had taken care of the majority of our key priorities. We had ensured safety protocols for our teammates and our guests. We had ensured Recipe's financial health and the financial health of our franchisees. We had positioned our teams remotely and ensured that no one had to speculate about our situation. Brand operations teams had ramped up to do more takeout and to operate safely with new constraints. Most importantly—no one was panicking.

While working on the other priorities, we were also determining how we could further support our industry—in particular, independent restaurants. The $100 billion restaurant industry in Canada is vibrant and diverse. The sector employs 1.6 million people directly or indirectly—this is 8% of the Canadian workforce. The industry is the fourth-largest employer in Canada. Many of my favourite restaurants are small mom-and-pop places. Keeping the industry alive was not just the moral thing to do, it was also critical to the overall economy. Small independent restaurants did not have the resources or voice of a company the size of Recipe. How could we help them?

At the start of April 2020, I asked our internal Creative Team to establish a website that we called "One Table." The site included a mirror of our COVID website where people could access information and tools. It also contained interviews that our teams had conducted with independent restaurateurs across the country to help tell their stories. We pushed those videos out through our social media platforms. Their stories were incredibly moving and, together, told the tale of how vital restaurants are to the fabric of our local communities. It was very clear that unless financial help came quickly, many restaurants would not survive.

Political lobbying is something I never enjoyed doing and that I tend to avoid if possible, but this situation required me to reach out to mayors, MPPs, MPs, and premiers. Todd Barclay, who had the unenviable task of taking over the industry trade association, Restaurants Canada, halfway through the crisis, was a good guide and reminded me, continually, that losing my patience was not going to be helpful. Thankfully, financial relief was coming.

COVID generated a slew of new acronyms (I even added a few specific to Recipe). The first meaningful financial supports to come out of the federal government were CERB (Canada Emergency Response Benefit) and CEWS (Canada Emergency Wage Subsidy). Individuals impacted by

COVID were now given $500 a week and it was really designed for those with minimum-wage jobs. Unfortunately, this program had an unintentional consequence. All of a sudden we could not find staff. Many people were simply staying home and collecting CERB. Remember, our business was not completely shut; at this point, we were down 60% in sales, but we still needed people. It was a well-intentioned program, but one that simply did not work as planned.

CEWS was another story. I would credit this program with being one of the key lifelines given to Canadian businesses impacted the most by COVID. The program was generous, and once it was implemented, payment was immediate. Its intention was to keep people off the unemployment lines and to help businesses keep their teams employed and bridge them to the other side of the pandemic. That was exactly how we used the program. If we had not had it, we would have had to make different choices that would have negatively impacted many more people.

There were several other government programs—all were well-intentioned and some worked better than others. Navigating them took a team effort. Luis Rego, VP of Restaurant Central Operations; Courtney Hindorff, VP of franchising; David Blumberger, general counsel and VP of legal; and Rachel Wong, who heads up our Total Rewards, worked countless hours, along with their teams, to ensure that all of this was properly coordinated and sequenced, and, most importantly, they explained all of it to our franchisees.

However, we did not want subsidies, we wanted to open again. But when was that going to happen? How were we going to reopen? It's one thing to close 1,300-plus restaurants overnight, it is quite another to reopen them. We now needed a new playbook.

One advantage of our daily leadership calls was that we have executives across the country who provided first-hand accounts of what was going on. We were aware early on that the Government of British Columbia seemed to be taking the most business-friendly, common-sense approach to reopening. At least they appeared willing to work with the industry and they wanted the industry to give our views on how to safely reopen. To my knowledge, this was the only province that consulted the industry.

The assignment to work out a plan for how we would safely reopen at Recipe was given to Franco Tascione, COO of our Social Division, the division most impacted by dining room closures. I was confident that Franco's experience and his attention to detail would ensure all measures were accounted for.

Franco filled his team with leaders from a cross-section of departments and brands, including Andrea Winter, director of Occupational Health and Safety; Stephanie Roche, senior director of Central Training; and Christine Mulcahy, senior director of Food Safety and Quality Assurance. They came up with a very impressive, comprehensive approach to reopening. Unfortunately, over the next sixteen months, we would have to reference that plan several more times given so many fits and starts and waves of closures with no consistency across provinces.

Franco and his task force did such a great job at putting together the playbook, it prompted me to think about what else this cross-functional collaboration could produce. It led to our Way of Working (WOW) task forces (told you I added my own acronyms). In thinking about what I wanted WOW to do, I very much had the mantra of Paul Romer (Stanford economist) in my head: "A crisis is a terrible thing to waste." What lessons could we learn through this that could not just help us through COVID but actually make us a stronger business moving forward?

The results the teams produced were incredible. Not only was the output from these task forces meaningful, but it also brought back the feeling that we are in control of our own destiny and we can make our business better.

One creation of the WOW teams was our "Social Safely" program, which, through the leadership of one of our bright young stars, Yianni Fountas, we branded throughout our businesses. We understood that people coming back to restaurants would have two questions: is it safe? and is the experience worth it? The simple idea of the Social Safely program was to address the first of these concerns by providing transparency into all of the steps we were taking to keep our guests and teammates safe.

However, there was an additional step I wanted for our Social Safely program—I wanted rapid testing for our teams. A significant shareholder of Recipe called me in early October to talk about testing. They felt strongly, and I agreed, that testing was one way to get a handle on what was going on and could I get engaged on the matter.

I knew about initiatives such as the CDL program through the University of Toronto and I had been in touch with Abbott, makers of the rapid antigen tests. These are the tests that are the gentle nasal swab for home use, where you get the results in a few minutes—not the more invasive "brain tickler" tests. The first hurdle was Health Canada. They had not yet approved the use for Canada, and when they finally did authorize it, Ontario had a condition that only a trained clinician could administer the test. I was quite certain there was not an abundance of nurses readily available to give tests to servers and bartenders. All the provinces had their rules, but Ontario was critical to us as that is where most of our restaurants are.

The rule actually made no sense to me as the tests were designed to be used by people at home, just like a home pregnancy test. Several calls and more discussions ensued, now with Health Canada actually acting as an advocate for us, but there was still no movement from Ontario. Weeks went by, and just when I thought it was a dead cause, we got a call saying that if we could demonstrate how we would use the program and track results, we could be authorized to use these tests in our restaurants. Apparently, the Province of Ontario had thousands of these tests just sitting in storage. Julie became the point person on this project and took over the back-and-forth calls. We had a well-thought-through plan. Bob Belleau, a talented member of Gary's digital team, had his developers build yet another app that could help us track the number of people tested as well as results (without names, to maintain privacy). We just needed the administration of the test to be clarified.

Finally, they relented and allowed us to self-administer, but now a new hurdle. We would have to dispose of the tests in a special bio-hazard pail and arrange for a special bio-hazard pickup. Not only was that cost-prohibitive, but I was also imagining how those bio-hazard pails would look on Instagram. According to the manufacturer, the tests were being used all over the world and discarded in the garbage just like a tissue. Not one country or jurisdiction had that mandate other than Ontario and it was a non-starter for us, so Julie kept at it. Her persistence paid off when, finally, the last impediment was lifted. So, eight months after that shareholder's first call to me, we administered our first test to our employees, becoming the first restaurant company and the first retailer to do so in Canada.

By the spring of 2021, the opening and closing of restaurants was becoming very frustrating—particularly in Ontario. We were monitoring our restaurants very closely. We simply were not seeing the case rates that the province was more widely reporting. I was not surprised by this or by how fast restaurants were able to pivot towards social distancing protocols. Restaurants are one of the most regulated industries you will find. The food we make sustains human bodies. It needs to be safe. We continually take temperatures of our food, we use gloves, we constantly wash our hands, we sanitize tables. All of this has been going on for decades in the restaurant industry. We are inspected by local health officials, and at Recipe we conduct surprise random third-party audits, administered by an outside firm, to ensure we are complying with all food and sanitation safety protocols. So taking temperatures of our teams before starting a shift, moving tables apart, and wearing masks was not really a big stretch from our normal, everyday practices.

I was especially frustrated by how restaurants were being portrayed in the media. Every time reckless behaviour was on display, restaurants were being associated with it. Politicians, who absolutely refused to share any data with us, continually conflated restaurants, bars, and casinos together. They seemed to suggest that after some magical hour at night, restaurants turned into giant raves. I am not sure I have ever seen people dancing on the tabletops of a Swiss Chalet.

It was increasingly nonsensical. One thing became clear: political and health authorities simply did not want Canadians to leave their homes, regardless of the fact that at home was where most people appeared to be catching COVID. The stops and starts continued, and each time the new rules cost more and more money, wasted food, and strained the mental health of our teammates. Keeping abreast of all of the changing rules and regulations in Canada's healthcare system was itself a full-time job. In Ontario alone, there are thirty-four public healthcare units. Each unit seemed to be coming up with its own rules or interpreting provincial rules in its own way.

My thoughts around how the various provinces handled COVID would take up more space than this chapter could afford. And while the situation was frustrating, COVID could not consume us.

Due to the size of our business, I was surrounded by very talented leaders at all levels inside of Recipe. Derek Doke, president of Franworks, covered the west and was always a voice of calm and reason. His experience and insights were invaluable, especially as those provinces opened earlier and showed the rest of our network how to bring back customers. Richard Scofield, president of St-Hubert, was an especially busy guy. Richard runs not only the restaurants at St-Hubert but also our retail division for all of Recipe. In addition, he was the person representing our interests to Quebec. St-Hubert simply outperformed throughout COVID. Their performance is a testament to a culture that has been built and nourished for almost seventy years and also to Richard's leadership.

Not everything worked as designed and our foresight was not always perfect. The Social Safely commercial we produced only got limited airtime due to another shutdown, and we did not anticipate the massive third wave that hit Canada in the fall and winter of 2020/2021 (despite an early warning from one of our board members). It caused us once again to brush off our models and for Ken and the team to return to our lenders. Later, the Omicron variant presented a new group of challenges. But the good news was that we avoided major unforced errors. We knew that having a propensity for action was preferable to navel-gazing. In a situation such as a global pandemic, information is not perfect. We felt that if we had it 70% right, it was okay to proceed and we would course-correct along the way. Waiting for perfect information would have been disastrous—because there never was perfect information.

Despite the financial impact COVID had on our business, it did not alter our strategic plans. In fact, it accelerated them. That was because there was never anything systematically wrong with our business or our business plan. We were simply in a crisis event and we knew the crisis would pass and the business would continue. When that happened we wanted to come out on our front foot.

There is nothing good about a global pandemic, but the fact that it is global allowed us to learn. Various countries around the world were moving in and out of it at different stages. One of our values as a company is "be curious," and I was definitely curious to study what was going on. I did not want to rely on the local news sources—I wanted my own information from people on the ground. Even though Recipe does not have any significant international business, our supplier partners do.

We tapped into these resources to specifically understand how consumers were acting—what could we learn? I worked my network. One close friend of mine is a senior leader at a global luxury hotel chain. Her insight was invaluable. Another friend gave me first-hand accounts of how various parts of the U.S. were coming out swinging. His message came with a warning though: reopening would highlight a significant challenge—lack of staff.

Fortunately all along we had our frontline staff at the forefront of our thinking. In the beginning, we gave them premium pay. When Ontario went into its third shutdown, we set them up with a relief fund. It was the right thing to do as we felt strongly that they should not have to worry about how to pay their rent or feed their families. Our dishwashers, food prep, cooks, servers, bartenders, hosts and hostesses, and our managers and franchisees were the people who put themselves out into the community each and every day to serve their fellow Canadians. So we decided to keep paying our corporate hourly teammates and we encouraged our franchisees to do the same. The cost ended up being triple what we'd originally thought but it was worth it. When we emerged from lockdown, we had kept most of our experienced teammates engaged to help reopen and manage the surge in business. Everyone was grateful to be back to work.

Despite COVID, the business cadence continued. Earnings calls took place on time, brands developed new products, marketing campaigns were created and aired. Our construction team, headed by Paulo Ferreira, actually built and opened thirty-two restaurants—during COVID!

Other events got our attention as well. The social unrest that arose from the George Floyd tragedy certainly highlighted that we had our own work to do related to diversity, equity, and inclusion at Recipe. New task force teams were created.

We continued to hire and train new teammates and shape our portfolio. We opened four Ultimate Kitchens, a new concept designed for off-premise sales. We actually opened our first location at the end of March 2020. Many people applauded our speed in reaction to the pandemic with this new concept, but the reality was that it had been planned since the previous summer. It had nothing to do with COVID.

Our response to the pandemic demonstrated that a company as large and as complex as Recipe could still be agile. Being ahead of events, over-communicating to all of our stakeholders, and clearly establishing our priorities at the beginning allowed us and our partners to navigate the crisis and emerge ready to compete.

Recipe is now into its second century of serving Canadians. When future generations look back and reflect on this time in our company's history, I hope they recognize that it was our frontline teammates, supported by leadership at all levels within the brand and shared service teams, who successfully stewarded the company through troubled times.

I am extremely proud of the entire team.

RESTAURANT BRANDS INTERNATIONAL

Canada has its spring rituals. Snow melts, parkas get put away, and coffee drinkers across the country Roll Up The Rim of their Tim Hortons' cups to win prizes from the iconic restaurant chain.

As spring approached in 2020, José Cil faced a key decision on the signature contest at the country's largest restaurant brand. Cil, chief executive officer of Restaurant Brands International—parent to Tim Hortons, Burger King, and Popeyes—knew COVID-19 was beginning to pop up across Canada. However, in February and early March, there were relatively few cases and health authorities were still figuring out how the coronavirus spread.

Still, Cil and the Tim Hortons team decided to revamp the contest, which was set to give away $30 million in prizes. A full week before the World Health Organization declared COVID-19 a pandemic and the NBA and NHL shutdown, Tim Hortons withdrew the more than 80 million Roll Up The Rim paper cups that had been delivered to its restaurants and turned the contest fully digital across all Tim Hortons outlets in Canada and the U.S. The company said: "Tim Hortons does not believe it's the right time for team members in our restaurants to collect rolled up tabs that have been in people's mouths."

Scrapping the cup portion of the touchstone campaign was the first of many challenges Cil and the team faced in the pandemic. A lawyer by training, the Miami native joined the legal department at Burger King in

2000. He moved into the chain's operations in 2003, initially responsible for a region in North America, then running Burger King's operations in Africa, the Middle East, and several European regions. Cil left the chain briefly for an executive role at Walmart, running the retailer's operations in Florida, and rejoined Burger King in 2010 as president of the Europe, Middle East, and Africa region.

In 2014, shortly after Burger King merged with Tim Hortons and Restaurant Brands International, or RBI as it is colloquially known, was created, Cil was tapped as global president of Burger King. In 2017, Restaurant Brands International acquired Popeyes Louisiana Kitchen. And in 2019, parent Restaurant Brands International promoted Cil to CEO. The company is one of the world's largest restaurant companies, with more than 27,000 restaurants in more than 100 countries, and it generates approximately $33 billion in annual system-wide sales.

On Cil's watch, Restaurant Brands International shook up the quick-service industry by introducing its famous chicken sandwich at Popeyes in the U.S. in 2019. The combination of crispy southern fried chicken, pickles, and spicy mayo on a soft brioche bun—coupled with a timely and clever tweet—proved a huge hit, selling out across the U.S. and later in Canada. The chain was even forced to pull the sandwich off menus for several weeks to build inventory. And in 2020, when COVID headwinds were relentless, Popeyes recorded among the strongest same-store sales growth ever seen in quick-serve restaurants and held on to market share gains even as rivals introduced their own version of the meal.

At the start of the pandemic, when what we thought would just be a two-week March Break started to have no end in sight, Cil saw something different emerging from operations in China—weeks later he'd find himself at the White House in Washington, along with other restaurant leaders, to discuss the issues facing the restaurant industry during crisis.

José Cil

AUGUST 2021

Like many people, I'm a different person than I was prior to March 2020. In the pages that follow, I've done my best to bring you into rooms and conversations that stand out as pivotal moments for me during the pandemic. In recounting the constant shifts and turns, I'm reminded of how critical it was for us to act quickly and decisively, and how more often than not, our actions were based on the best available information at the time . . . until the time passed and new information shaped our thinking. We were charting new territory every day and the stakes could not have been higher. I have never felt more grateful.

It's incredible to consider all the people who enabled Restaurant Brands International (RBI) to follow our North Star—to do the right thing—at a time when no one really knew what that meant for certain. We came together as a village to share an awesome responsibility and support one another. RBI employees, restaurant owners, and supply chain partners worked tirelessly to help us continue serving guests safely and keep franchisee businesses afloat. Board members were engaged and responded swiftly to address the big decisions necessary to get us and our restaurant owners through to the other side. And while protecting their health and safety was always the foremost priority in our restaurants, hundreds of thousands of team members across the globe showed up every day to their jobs against the backdrop of so much uncertainty.

To those people, and especially those who suffered loss, I dedicate this chapter.

As a global company operating in more than one hundred countries, we regularly encounter a wide range of social, political, and regulatory issues that are unique to a particular country or region of the world, and we are well equipped with our teams to manage those issues when they arise. It might be the changing costs of food commodities, social unrest, new consumer privacy obligations, or updated food and packaging regulations.

In January 2020, our team based in Singapore flagged that a cluster of cases of pneumonia-like virus in China was beginning to result in heightened health restrictions in the region, and we were seeing traffic to our restaurants decline as our guests were increasingly staying home in an effort to curb the spread of this flu. China is an important growth market for us, where we have more than 1,300 Burger King restaurants and where our plan to open more than 1,500 Tim Hortons restaurants had been announced just one year earlier. The update on this regional outbreak was a pretty typical example of one of dozens of global updates that we review every week, and during that meeting we discussed the appropriate protocols our restaurants should be taking and then moved on to the next issue of the day.

Throughout that January, Sami Siddiqui, then regional president for our fast-growing Asia Pacific region, shared a series of updates that were concerning and seemingly isolated, but that in retrospect were our first glimpses of what was to come. Sami sent me an image from a Burger King China board meeting in Shanghai, where everyone in the room was wearing a mask. Even though it was common to see masks worn when walking outside in China, it was unusual to see an entire indoor board meeting taking place with them on. Another one of our colleagues, Jeff Galletly, had just become general manager of Tim Hortons for Asia Pacific. Jeff was in China for meetings and received a box of face masks from our Tim Hortons China team as a corporate welcome gift. In that moment, he didn't really know what to do with them, but he—and all of us—soon came to appreciate how important those masks would become.

By the start of February, we began to see the severity of the health crisis in China. Our team worked with our franchise partners to introduce new safety protocols for the restaurants in China and other markets in Asia that were affected at that early stage. Restaurant team members were asked to wear masks and gloves as they worked their shifts, and we initiated a deep cleaning protocol at frequent intervals in all restaurants. Our teams and franchise partners implemented what we thought were the most rigorous health and safety protocols that we had ever seen in our careers, which included mandatory temperature checks for all restaurant team members and guests entering the restaurants. We even established temperature checks for delivery drivers and added stickers to our takeout packaging indicating we had checked the delivery driver carrying that guests' food. But during all of this, North American media hardly covered what was quickly expanding as a crisis in Asia. Our corporate meetings at our global headquarters in Toronto and our U.S. headquarters in Miami continued as normal. Dealing with all our regular business issues, we were only occasionally reminded of the situation by the "intriguing" protocols that were underway on the other side of the world.

Unrelated to what was unfolding in Asia, I had just completed my first year as CEO of RBI. Even though I had been with Burger King for nearly twenty years, nothing really prepares you for the overwhelming responsibility of becoming CEO of a global company with (at the time) more than $30 billion in restaurant sales and over 25,000 restaurants around the world. On the day I was named CEO in January 2019, we had a town hall with the entire company, live-streamed in Toronto to Miami, Baar (Switzerland), and Singapore—our four major offices around the world. At that town hall, I unveiled our new vision—our Big Dream—to build the most loved restaurant brands in the world. This would mark the start of an exciting new chapter for the company, in which we would be brand-led and digitally focused and the guest would be at the centre of everything we do.

Throughout 2019, I had visited all our major regions and partners in the world. In addition to aligning the company behind our new Big Dream, I had been working with our senior leaders to develop a clearer sense of the values that we wanted to base our future growth on—the leadership traits we wanted in all our colleagues—and a compelling employee value proposition that would help us attract and retain the top talent in the world.

In late February 2020, we unveiled our new RBI values to the company, six inherent principles that would inform all our ways of working. This was not a bureaucratic exercise, where you send out an email and put your values up on the wall. We had done the work as a senior leadership team and with the help of dozens of colleagues throughout our company to understand how each value would contribute to our growth aspirations as "hard-working, good people." And one of the most important values we unveiled was on diversity—specifically "A wide range of voices and perspectives makes us stronger." This was especially important given our global footprint and acknowledgement that we would make better decisions if we had leaders around the table who had diversity in gender; diversity in race; diversity in sexual orientation; diversity in heritage and personal upbringing; and diversity of thinking, skill sets, and past experiences. Little did we know how critical this core value would soon be in our approach to responding to COVID.

By early March, North American media had discovered that this "regional outbreak" in Asia was on the verge of being declared a global pandemic by the World Health Organization (WHO). Everyone was mesmerized by the cruise ship *Diamond Princess* that was stranded off the coast of Japan due to an outbreak and the largest number of cases outside of mainland China. The situation was also evolving in Europe, especially Italy.

In the first week of March, Tim Hortons was launching our annual Roll Up The Rim campaign. As all Canadians know, this involves unrolling the top of a Tims coffee cup, often by using your teeth, to see if it has a winning prize printed on the inside of the rim. In the context of a public health emergency and heightened awareness of hygiene, a program that required people to hand over a chewed coffee rim to claim a prize quickly became out of the question. We made the difficult but correct decision to adjust the contest, and over seventy-two sleepless hours in a windowless Toronto boardroom, our team redesigned the contest to be almost entirely digital. We had already shipped eighty-four million cups to our four thousand restaurants nationally and we started the process of collecting and destroying or recycling them at one of our distribution facilities. This decision was ultimately about doing the right thing for guests and restaurant team members, regardless of the cost.

We were already on the path to digitizing this iconic contest through our app in the coming years, and the pandemic accelerated all those plans. Digital services are now foundational to providing almost contactless services with guests. Now, nearly 40% of every transaction we do in Canada is done through our digital loyalty program, Tims Rewards. And as for Roll Up The Rim, those chewed-up tabs are no more, and this contest has shifted to be 100% digital. I know a few of my colleagues pulled aside a sleeve of those Roll Up cups with the winning tabs to keep in their desk drawer—a memory for a future generation of what became the last paper Roll Up cups in Tim Hortons history because of COVID.

At the same time, our chief operating officer for Tim Hortons, Mike Hancock, had the critical job of determining what operations procedures should go into place immediately to protect team members, guests, and franchisees. Mike contacted our team in Asia, who were already a couple of months ahead of us in dealing with these new requirements, and we benefitted greatly from the playbook already established in our China and Asia restaurants. We had also adopted protocols at our restaurants in Europe, the Middle East, and Africa.

One of Mike's first decisions was whether to mandate masks in our restaurants—even though the rest of the industry and governments had not taken that step in Canada. Mike met with our supply chain team, who informed him that they could secure millions of masks within eight weeks at a very reasonable price—or millions of masks in two weeks at an astronomical "emergency" price. Mike made the difficult call to spend significantly more money to secure masks immediately and to then mandate them in all restaurants for team members as one of the first restaurants in Canada to do so—and before any government mandate.

We have about 1,500 passionate, entrepreneurial Tim Hortons restaurant owners in Canada. And with any group that large, there will always be those who agree and those who disagree with your decisions. We had a group of several restaurant owners who, in the moment, strongly disagreed with Mike's decision to pay more and be the first to mandate masks for all team members. But Tim Hortons is by far Canada's restaurant leader and we need to always act like it. Within a few weeks—when all of retail, restaurant, and hospitality moved to masks—we were in the enviable position of having a deep stock of masks in our warehouses when others were struggling to find them; the price we had paid ultimately seemed like a deal as demand for masks surged throughout North America.

The WHO declared a global pandemic on Wednesday, March 11, 2020. By that point, there were a growing number of COVID cases in the U.S., concentrated around New York City. My wife and I had been in Manhattan days earlier to help our daughter move back to Miami for a new job. As the numbers mounted, so too did a sense of wariness. Meanwhile, Canada had announced its first case of local transmission not directly linked to international travel in early March. Governments and health providers were struggling to understand what was happening and to formulate their responses. Workers were soon being urged to do their jobs from home if possible. School systems shut down shortly thereafter and border crossings were restricted.

In Toronto, local media was covering the story of an office worker who had come down with COVID-type symptoms, and TV images of medical workers in full hazmat suits were live on all the news channels, with the patient being moved out of a downtown office tower to an ambulance. That office was in the tower beside our global headquarters in Toronto— our colleagues were watching out of their windows as it played out live on the news.

Axel Schwan, president of Tim Hortons, and Duncan Fulton, RBI's chief corporate officer, knew that we were at a tipping point and needed to consider our options. They met with our technology team to evaluate whether we had the IT systems or online meeting software to support what was then the unthinkable decision to allow our entire office to work from home for a short while. They discussed details like whether our innovation kitchen team members could continue product development work on our Dream Donuts and what would become our Craveables lunch sandwiches. And whether tech support needed physical access to our servers on site or could access them remotely if they had to.

On Thursday, March 12, productivity in the office was dwindling and stories of more office workers in Toronto with COVID symptoms were dominating the news. Axel, Duncan, and the rest of the Tims leadership team met with more than three hundred employees to reassure them that we were evaluating all our options to keep everyone safe. Axel and Duncan still shake their heads today, recalling that we had hundreds of people crammed into a space—something that was so normal back then but that no longer makes sense in our current world. By the next afternoon, on Friday, March 13, we announced that we would work from home for a short while until things got under control. Employees were reminded to take their laptop cables and shoes from under their desk because we might be out of the office for up to a couple of weeks—a time frame that we all now know would be far, far longer.

As governments began to consider closing workplaces, retail stores, and restaurants, there was extensive discussion and debate in Canada about what constituted essential services that must remain open. It had never—ever—been a consideration for us that a government order could shut down our entire business for months or more. In addition to ensuring the safety and well-being of team members, guests, and restaurant owners, making sure we were included as an essential service became job number one. Everyone understood that hospitals, public transportation, banking, and grocery stores were essential, but we needed government officials to understand the case for why restaurants like ours were also essential services. We focused our attention on advocating for takeout, drive-thru, delivery, and outdoor patios as essential to our communities and as needed services for frontline workers who still had to travel every day to fight the pandemic. Canadians eat nearly half of their meals away from home—i.e., in restaurants—and the grocery and "at home" supply chain would not be able to meet the rise in demand that would occur if restaurants were shuttered.

We were fortunate at Tim Hortons to have more than 2,700 drive-thrus in our 4,000 restaurants; however, many other indoor-only restaurants suffered considerably throughout the pandemic. In fact, we argued along-side Restaurants Canada—the trade organization representing more than 30,000 companies throughout Canada—that restaurants have among the most stringent procedures in place to ensure the health and safety of food and beverage preparation. With added measures like mandating screening for team members and installing plexiglass barriers, Canadian quick-service restaurants were among the safest public locations anywhere. However, we were up against both politics and the "image" of indoor dining, so we ultimately had to rely on our drive-thru business and on quickly scaling up our home delivery service and other options like curbside pickup.

Drive-thru has been a feature of the quick-service industry for decades, but no one could have foreseen how important drive-thru networks would become in the economic survival of our and our competitors' restaurants. We had already been focused on expanding our delivery and takeout options before the pandemic, and as on-site dining closed, these alternative methods of getting food to people became an important part of our role as an essential service. This was a moment when it still wasn't clear how the virus behaved and whether and for how long it lived on surfaces. The precautions many people were taking included wiping down all their groceries with disinfectant and leaving purchased goods outside for a period of time before bringing them into their homes. With so many people sheltering at home and all the uncertainty of how the virus was transmitted, we had to remind our guests that we had safe and contactless methods of getting food and coffee to them—including implementing new trays on the end of a six-foot pole to hand over coffee, sandwiches, and baked goods without hand-to-hand contact.

I remember talking to our teams in both Canada and the U.S. and realizing that we needed to drop everything else we were doing from a communications standpoint to focus on explaining the functional benefits of our drive-thrus to guests. Marketing calendars and campaigns were shelved to focus our guest-facing messaging on health and safety.

Effective communications are critical in a crisis. We established a daily video call with more than forty of our RBI leaders from around the world. We had every subject matter expert we needed on these calls, representing all of our teams—food safety, quality assurance, health and safety, HR, operations, marketing, digital, communications, government relations, legal, and franchisee relations. This became the most important meeting of the day, and the group quickly grew to more than sixty as we realized we needed more advice from more areas of the business. It didn't dawn on me until about a week into those calls that we were fully living—and benefitting from—the value of diversity that we had launched to the whole company just a month earlier: "A wide range of voices and perspectives makes us stronger." We were the strongest we had ever been during those days when so many diverse points of view came together to help us make the best decisions for the company, our team members, our guests, and our franchisees.

We manage our priorities as a company and reward our team through bonuses based on achievement of goals in a bespoke program called Management by Objectives or MBOs. MBOs are aimed at connecting individual performance to company goals. At that point, we had about 600 MBOs shared by more than 1,200 corporate employees around the world. Each employee had five to seven MBOs aligned with the company goals and focused specifically on their individual priorities for the year, with clear, measurable outcomes that they needed to deliver to move our business forward. Less than a week into our new morning meetings, it became clear that nothing else in the company mattered more than charting a path through this wholly unknown period of disruption. I met with our chief operations officer, Josh Kobza, and our chief people officer, Jeff Housman, and we did something we had never considered in our company's history. We wiped out every employee's MBOs and instead listed five priorities with fourteen outcomes that were all that mattered, across all three brands, in every region around the world. We assigned the same five priorities and fourteen outcomes to every employee, regardless of their

level, and in 2020, our entire company pulled together with the singular
focus of doing the right thing for guests, our restaurant owners, and their
team members—and making sure that our business emerged as a strong,
stable industry leader.

Also during the spring of 2020, we quickly developed strong relationships
with government decision makers to help them understand our industry,
the actions we were taking to be responsible business operators, and how
we could partner with governments to communicate health messages to
Canadians and Americans—whether through signage in our drive-thrus
or card drops in our takeout bags. We have about 4,300 Tim Hortons,
Burger King, and Popeyes restaurants in Canada and about 10,000 in the
U.S. As an industry leader in both countries, we were privileged to be
invited by both governments to participate in a number of industry consultations and advise senior decision makers on policy options they were
considering.

One morning in May 2020, our general legal counsel, Jill Granat, called
me to say that the White House was seeking our opinion on several policies they were considering. I was anticipating a brief phone call with a
policy advisor, but then quickly learned that I was being invited to meet
with President Trump and a half-dozen other restaurant leaders at the
White House a few days later to discuss policy options on how to balance
the protection of U.S. citizens while continuing to stimulate the U.S.
economy. The meeting would include discussion of the Paycheck
Protection Program, a loan program for small businesses (many of our
franchisees would participate) backed by the U.S. federal government's
Small Business Administration, so I knew that it was important for RBI
to have a voice at the table.

My parents both emigrated from Cuba to Miami as children, and
although my father has passed away, I felt their pride in my being able to
represent our industry in this way in Washington. At the same time, this
was during the early days of the pandemic, when we still knew very little
about how the virus was transmitted. The world was in lockdown, and

although I have spent most of my career on planes, I had not taken a flight for several months. The idea of walking through an airport and getting into the enclosed air of a plane was daunting, but I needed to be at that meeting.

The journey to Washington, D.C., through deserted airports and on an almost empty airplane, was a surreal experience. I was told that when I arrived at the White House, we would be tested for COVID, and that unless they tapped us on the shoulder during the meeting, all was fine. I remember lying awake in my Washington hotel the night before the meeting, having gone through the airports and the plane ride, thinking: *Is my throat sore? Am I congested? Did I somehow get infected on the journey to our nation's capital for a meeting with the president?* It's funny what your mind can do when you know that the last place in the world where you want to find out you have COVID is while you're sitting down in front of the national media with the president of the United States.

The White House meeting was in the State Dining Room, an impressive if not imposing space used to host receptions and banquets for visiting heads of state with a large portrait of Abraham Lincoln above the central mantel. After going through all of the testing and being briefed by senior staffers, we were told to go ahead and find our seats so that we would be able to settle in quickly once President Trump arrived. The room was set up with tables arranged in a rectangular formation around an open central area.

As I walked around the room, looking for my seat, I saw Secretary of Labor Eugene Scalia, Secretary of the Treasury Steven Mnuchin, and Larry Kudlow, director of the National Economic Council. I was also looking out for fellow restaurateurs like Thomas Keller of the French Laundry, Niren Chaudhary of Panera, and Will Guidara of Eleven Madison in New York City, but I wanted to first find my seat.

When I located my name, I observed that I would be sitting next to Secretary Mnuchin, who was placed a socially distant six feet to my left, and as I looked to see who would be seated on my right, I couldn't see a nameplate in front of the chair. As I looked more closely, I noticed that the unmarked chair was in the centre of the table, directly in front of the mantel and the Lincoln portrait and flanked by two flags. Dozens of cameras were set up directly opposite. I realized I would be sitting next to President Trump, and the seriousness of the moment dawned.

I played football in high school and college, and some of the lessons I learned from competing in sports have been useful to apply in business. Mental preparation is essential, and coaches often have players study game videos of themselves and their opponents to learn how they react in different circumstances. In preparation for the White House meeting, I had watched online clips of a couple of similar meetings President Trump had hosted, one with a cross-section of business leaders and another with representatives from the oil and gas industry. In both cases, after delivering his opening remarks, the president had turned to the person on his left with his first question. In sports, players always have a tendency to repeat certain actions, and President Trump's tendency was clearly to go to his left (ironic, I know). Once I realized that I was seated to his left, there was no doubt in my mind that I would be called upon to start the discussion.

As soon as I realized that I would be up first to speak, I took some time to focus my thoughts. I knew it would be an important moment, with an opportunity to help frame the discussion of small business and worker protections, and I wanted to make sure I said what I needed to say on behalf of not just RBI but the entire restaurant industry.

President Trump and Vice-President Pence soon came in together, and not long after that we all sat down. President Trump spoke briefly in introduction and then turned to the topic at hand, saying "We're here with the leaders of the restaurant industry" and noting that we had been tremendously impacted by COVID. Then, sure enough, he turned to his left, looked at me, and said, "We'll start with you."

One of the things I made a point of emphasizing in my comments at the White House was the need to expand the Paycheck Protection Program past the eight-week deadline that had originally been envisioned. "When it was implemented, eight weeks probably seemed like an eternity," I said at the time. "But today we're in the tenth week of the pandemic and I think it's going to take some time for our restaurants and our owners to get back to the capacity levels and the traffic levels that we were seeing pre-COVID." I took the opportunity to suggest extending the program to twenty-four weeks, to allow restaurant owners to be able to manage through and rehire their employees over a longer period. In fact, the program ended up being extended for an additional year, through the end of May 2021.

That White House meeting was just weeks into the pandemic, when everyone still thought that the tide would start to turn within weeks. Looking back at that moment from the vantage point of more than a year later, as we continue to weather the effects of the pandemic and its repercussions, it's striking how much has changed economically, politically, and medically.

We were also working actively with Canadian provincial and federal officials to explain the impact that the lockdowns were having on small businesses, like those of our restaurant owners. We took part in dozens of meetings and small conferences that helped to make sure the narrative the federal government was hearing was balanced and accurate and helpful. All this behind-the-scenes work played a big part in how the Canadian government made important decisions to help businesses that were struggling. The Canada Emergency Wage Subsidy and the Canada Emergency Rent Subsidy programs were hugely instrumental in helping our franchisees and other businesses stave off disaster and remain operational.

Various provincial governments in turn reached out to us for assistance, given that Tim Hortons is such an iconic Canadian institution and that our footprint is in every community in the country. The Alberta government called requesting our help to deliver millions of masks to residents in that province through our drive-thrus. The Ontario government called asking us to reopen our washrooms in our highway locations so that truck drivers could continue to do their jobs. In fact, Premier Doug Ford in Ontario personally called Duncan on issues affecting our industry (and even once emphasized, in his morning news conference, how much he loved our new fresh-cracked egg breakfast sandwich!).

———

It's tempting to look back, with vaccination now widespread throughout Canada and a largely recovered global economy, and to lose sight of how much was at stake and how frightening the situation was in the spring of 2020. For so many people, including many of our restaurant team members, the simple action of showing up at work was an act of bravery.

We understood that restaurant team members were going above and beyond by continuing to do their jobs, helping to feed and fuel other frontline and essential workers. There were restaurant team members who contracted the virus in those early days or who had family members who got sick. We wanted to recognize their efforts and do what we could to help support them in such difficult circumstances. In mid-March, Tim Hortons and its restaurant owners set up a team member relief fund of up to $40 million that restaurant owners could tap into to support restaurant team members who had to stay home and miss their shifts if they got sick or if they needed to quarantine because one of their co-workers had contracted COVID. We implemented a similar sick leave approach for company-owned Burger King and Popeyes restaurants in the U.S., moves that were unprecedented for a restaurant company.

Our restaurant owners were invaluable partners. They were on the front lines and their livelihoods were at stake, and they could have responded in any number of ways. They were certainly feeling the pressure of the circumstances, but they came forward with a mindset of finding solutions to the problems that we were all facing.

We promised our Tim Hortons restaurant owners that we would not allow anyone to be left behind in this crisis. Through the spring of 2020, we led the restaurant industry in the level of support we made available to our restaurant owners. To support immediate liquidity challenges, we deferred rental payments (and in many cases absorbed rents outright, including for closed restaurants), negotiated custom-tailored bridge loan programs with Canadian banks, deferred many capital investment programs to the following years, and pulled forward various credits by almost a year, helping owners to put cash into their bank accounts to pay team members and keep their restaurants open.

In return, our restaurant owners knew that we had their back and they could focus on doing what they do best—serving their guests and their community. Tim Hortons has always been about community—from sponsorship of kids' programs like Timbit Sports and our Tim Hortons Foundation Camps to the millions given out annually to charities across Canada through the Smile Cookie program. So it was no surprise that the brand stood up and stood out during the pandemic. With our restaurant owners, and through our Tims coffee trucks across Canada, we donated coffee and baked goods to more than two million people at hospitals, long-term care homes, fire halls, and transit depots and donated 366,000 pounds of food to shelters.

In the early days of the pandemic, Mike Di Stasi, a Tim Hortons owner in Regina, Saskatchewan, started noticing paper hearts in windows across the city, put up as an expression of support and solidarity with frontline workers. Sure enough, he and his team members took up the effort and the windows at his locations were soon covered in hearts. And the brand's support for those on the front didn't stop there. At one of their daily emergency press conferences, Manitoba health officials recognized local Tim Hortons owners for their generous donations to feed and caffeinate lab workers who were working around the clock at testing sites. The initiative was spearheaded by restaurant owner Jamie Pope and others like her. That kind of informal and spontaneous effort was also reflected at the corporate level. Our Hero Cups campaign allowed Canadians to nominate hard-working frontline workers to be featured on limited-edition cups. The program allowed us as a company to express our deep appreciation by singling out hundreds of individuals who, like so many others, did so much to keep the country functioning at such a tough time.

Before the pandemic we had already started the transition to being a more purpose-led company. We had begun refocusing our corporate priorities, including our Big Dream and the values that now underpin our actions and decision making. And we went further. Inspired by our response to the biggest public health emergency and economic lockdown in the past century, and recognizing our responsibility and potential to do more to improve sustainable outcomes related to our food, the planet, and the people and communities we serve, we established Restaurant Brands for Good. Through this framework, we are integrating sustainability into our business strategy and holding ourselves accountable by establishing goals and measuring our progress to deliver more than great-tasting, convenient, and affordable meals that people love.

There's been much speculation about what a post-COVID world will look like. What will we leave behind and what will be altered forever? I prefer to look at it differently—what must we bring forward from this experience to continue making our company and the world around us better? My two biggest takeaways are rather simple: just do what's right, no matter how hard it is, and include a wide range of voices and perspectives—it only makes you stronger.

REVERA

Early in his career, Tom Wellner went back to school at Harvard University to polish his executive skills. But nothing they teach at Harvard, or any other business school, prepared the chief executive at Revera, a Canadian-owned global investor, developer, and operator in the senior living sector, for COVID-19. The virus poses a grave threat to the elderly and immuno-compromised and to those charged with their care. There is no business case study that dictates how to best protect Revera's fifty-five thousand retirement residence and long-term care home residents in three countries—clients who include Wellner's own parents—and the company's fifty thousand employees.

Mississauga-based Revera is one of Canada's largest operators of senior living centres, with more than five hundred properties across Canada, the U.S., and the U.K. One of the country's largest pension plans acquired the chain in 2007 for $780 million. Since then, Revera has grown into an international leader in the senior congregate living sector, acquiring own-ership of U.S.- and U.K.-based operators.

As CEO, Wellner's mandate at Revera was to reposition and expand the business, growing it through the acquisition and development of privately paid retirement residences across Canada, the U.S., and the U.K., while always ensuring residents enjoyed the best possible resident experience and care. Revera recruited the Prince Edward Island–born Wellner in 2014 from medical diagnostics company LifeLabs, where he was co-CEO following the take-private of the publicly traded CML Healthcare, where he was CEO. Prior to that, the graduate of Queen's University's life sciences, ICD-Rotman's Director's Education Program, and Harvard's executive education program was a global sales and marketing executive with Eli Lilly, and ultimately the president and general manager of Lilly Germany.

Pre-pandemic, in addition to keeping a strong focus on quality across all operations, a significant portion of the CEO's time was devoted to corporate strategy. Wellner is the architect of Revera's Strategy 2020, which transformed the company from a predominantly Canadian-operating real estate holding company into a collection of quality-focused operating platforms, all with strong development capabilities and a global footprint. Once COVID arrived in Canada in the winter of 2020, the Revera CEO and his team found themselves at the epicentre of the worst pandemic in living memory, where the company's priorities to ensure the safety and well-being of their residents and frontline staff became all-consuming.

Long-term care homes were on the front lines, and front pages, of the COVID crisis. During successive waves of the pandemic, Revera faced outbreaks in homes across the country, with staff and seniors falling ill and, tragically, dying. Residents' families were forced to keep their distance, causing understandable anguish. As case numbers rose, health authorities became involved in operations at a few Revera homes, responding to large outbreaks in Alberta, Manitoba, and Ontario.

Coming out of the pandemic's first wave, Wellner and Revera's chief medical officer, Dr. Rhonda Collins, formed an independent expert panel, led by Dr. Bob Bell, a former cancer surgeon and Ontario deputy minister of health, to help Revera understand how the virus had behaved in its operations. Also instrumental in this work was Dr. Calvin Stiller, chair of Revera's Quality Committee, a retired physician, entrepreneur, and Officer of the Order of Canada. This group of external expert advisors had full access to Revera's internal files and data and published a ninety-two-page report on the company, complete with recommendations, in December 2020. In a letter that opened the study, Wellner said he asked for the expert panel's audit "so that the solutions they prescribed could be applied immediately to counter the ongoing threat of COVID-19 so subsequent waves could be managed at the Revera sites."

Revera's report concluded that in preparing for the first wave of COVID, healthcare authorities neglected the issues facing seniors' homes in the push to ensure that hospitals were not overwhelmed. The controversial finding came out shortly after Wellner's grandmother passed away on Prince Edward Island, without the CEO being able to personally say goodbye and provide comfort.

To cope with the pressures that came with leading Revera during the pandemic, Wellner put a priority on staying fit, with a regime that included a daily run. In the coldest, darkest days of the first COVID lockdown, even a simple decision to go for a morning run became a test of the CEO's fortitude.

Tom Wellner

JULY 2021

On the morning of February 12, 2021, on the eve of the pandemic's third wave, I woke before sunrise to sub-zero temperatures. A light snow had fallen overnight and I pulled on my running tights, a toque, a headlamp, and shoes and left the house prepared for a dark, frosty run. Regardless of the season or where I've lived—growing up in Prince Edward Island, working in Hong Kong, Berlin, or London—I always run. I find it a therapeutic way to collect my thoughts. The cadence, the breathing, my mind and body in synchronized motion, it's almost meditative, and it is, for me, an invaluable stress release.

It's difficult to imagine there had ever been a more stressful juncture in my life than steering a multinational corporation through the extraordinary challenges of the COVID crisis, particularly a corporation responsible for the care and housing of more than sixty-five thousand seniors, twenty thousand of them in Canada. No other age group is more vulnerable to the novel coronavirus, and no other segment of the population around the world has suffered more death because of it. That heartbreaking reality has shaken the very foundation of the long-term care sector.

The streetlights were still on as I started up the road that morning. I jogged past Glendon College and its athletic centre, through a parking lot and up the hill near Sunnybrook Hospital. Recent jags of freezing and thawing had left the ground slick, and I slowed my pace at the small stretch of woods behind Sunnybrook Stables. The hill I usually run down to access the road home looked especially rough. Uneven skiffs of snow and cobblestone covered the slope and I stopped running. Carefully, gingerly, I tiptoed my way down and sighed with relief when I reached the bottom. Yet in the very moment I felt my body relax, my legs suddenly flew out from under me. A patch of invisible ice launched my feet up as high as my ears, tossing me backward into the air, hat and headlamp flying off as I landed hard on my back, my head cracking on the ice. I lay there dazed for several minutes before rolling from my back to my knees to collect the yard sale of running paraphernalia strewn around me, and then somehow I managed to half jog, half shuffle my way back home. A few days later, an x-ray revealed a neck and shoulder injury and two cracked ribs. Vertigo dogged me for weeks afterward.

As it happened, my fall that February marked the one-year anniversary of COVID-19 beginning to dominate my daily life as chief executive officer of Revera. Looking back, that bone-breaking mishap is an apt metaphor for the way the year had unfolded. No matter how prepared I thought I was, or thought Revera was—having built a mission-driven culture, assembled a strong team, practised pandemic-focused emergency drills—the new virus was a lot like that invisible patch of black ice: just when I thought catastrophe had been averted, COVID-19 slithered under-foot and jettisoned all assumptions. Within a matter of days in the winter of 2020, we went from cautious optimism to multiple outbreaks. Thankfully, most were small and containable, but in other homes the number of cases and deaths added up to unforgettable grief and trauma for our residents, their families, and our staff.

Of course, in the beginning everyone was running in the dark. Global experts and health authorities were offering conflicting direction on the importance of masking. They were not talking about asymptomatic spread-ers. The list of known COVID-19 symptoms they shared in the first wave of the pandemic proved to be incomplete. The national tragedy that we saw unfold in long-term care homes was used by critics to fuel a relentless stream of negative publicity around nursing homes. Heading up one of the largest long-term care operations in Canada suddenly had all the public relations charm of working for Big Tobacco.

As the first born in my family, I have a natural orientation toward responsibility, sometimes to a fault, and one of the unbearable aspects of leading through the devastation was feeling as helpless as I did at the base of that icy hill. Nothing in my career quite prepared me for the unique leadership challenges COVID-19 presented, forcing me to parcel my time and attention over an ever-growing span of urgent issues. Ultimately, the resilience and sacrifices of my team and staff helped to pull us up and out of the crisis, enabling me to lead us toward the safest ways to operate in these dangerous times.

This Is Not a Drill

Like most people, I first heard about the novel coronavirus in the news in early January 2020. Before the end of the month, it had spread from China to other parts of Asia, Europe, and then North America. Canada confirmed its first case on January 25. By then the new contagion had already established itself as a mortal threat to the elderly and I struck an executive leadership team to review and update our emergency measures.

Back then, most confirmed cases had been linked to recent air travel, and that February I was travelling myself, visiting our teams and sites in the U.K. Before I'd left, our executive team had gone through our annual risk management drill, assessing our readiness in the face of hypothetical scenarios that might compromise our business operations—including a pandemic. It's an excruciating exercise in which we evaluate anything that might impact us in the context of clinical, financial, and economic risk if disaster occurs. The goal is to make sure we have in place a business continuity plan to operate under any unfortunate circumstance. When I returned from London, the looming pandemic had punted the hypothetical into live action.

By the third week of February, Tricia Wade, our VP of risk management and Frank Cerrone, our general counsel, were convening our business continuity team meetings three times a week. We were still able to meet in person then, anywhere from eight to twenty of us, operations leaders from our different divisions, clinical and communications heads, and legal advisors. We identified issues that had to be tackled—and with the need for personal protective equipment (PPE) now much higher than pre-pandemic times, acquiring additional PPE was the most urgent.

All our residences stock masks, gloves, and gowns to handle the fifteen to twenty flu or gastrointestinal outbreaks our sites experience in a normal year. But with COVID-19 growing in momentum, we foresaw that supply wouldn't be enough for 2020. We started to hear that there was a global shortage and that Canadian cupboards were bare. So then came the questions: "What stock do we have? With COVID bearing down, what should we have, and where are we going to get it? And if we get it, how do we quickly ship enough additional PPE to the sites that will need it if they go into outbreak?"

Wendy Gilmour, our senior VP of long-term care, and Mary Brazier, our VP of clinical care, had both worked in hospitals during the 2003 SARS epidemic and had a strong sense of the supplies we might need. Still, when they recommended that we also pre-order extra body bags for the pandemic, I thought it was a morbid suggestion, but I gave it the go-ahead. After all, the main aim of the business continuity meetings was to provide team members an opportunity to share their thoughts, observations, and perspectives—even if they were different than my own.

But as we rushed to protect our staff and residents, most Canadian health system officials assumed it would be hospitals that COVID patients would overrun, as they had in China and Europe. The long-term care sector was cast as the understudy, there to help hospitals preserve their capacity as they cancelled surgeries, emptied beds, and took "off-loading" steps. As our data would later show, patient transfers from hospitals into Revera homes jumped more than 50% between February and April 2020. Given this increase and COVID's asymptomatic spread, some of the hospital patients transferred to us likely had COVID-19, while we were being advised that infected residents were not to be sent to hospitals.

Yet hospitals sat largely empty in wave one, and as the limited PPE stock was sequestered for them, the long-term care sector was basically left out in the cold. Various provincial health ministries had directed our usual national supplier to withhold PPE from long-term care sites unless— ironically—a home was already experiencing an outbreak. It was clear to me early on that we could not rely on third-party sources to give us what we needed, which sparked the creation of a collective across the sector to procure PPE for ourselves and for small operators and non-profits that would otherwise fall short. Eventually, we set up our own warehousing system to store an additional six months' worth of PPE beyond what we normally order from our national supplier.

From the moment our business continuity calls began, I vowed to myself that any decision I made would not only be made quickly but that it would be the right thing to do—morally and ethically—regardless of cost. When it came to operations, financial concerns would be thrown out. If we had to order ten million bucks' worth of PPE, we ordered ten million bucks' worth of PPE. If we had to spend on extra staffing or rides home for staff, we spent it.

I also vowed that taking the safest course of action, clinically speaking, would drive all my decisions. To that end, one of the first and most impactful moves I made was to have Dr. Rhonda Collins, our chief medical officer, be the primary source of clinical guidance for me and for all our staff. Having joined Revera in 2016 with a deep passion for the care of the elderly, Dr. Collins became the single source of pandemic-related communications to all sites. The last thing I wanted was any confusion around our policies or practices. With Dr. Collins's guidance, we set up early screening upon entry to our residences and instituted universal masking at our homes while health officials were still debating the efficacy of masks. Through daily emails, she kept our entire network updated and it worked well. People tend to trust their doctors more than their CEO (go figure), which is why I also made Dr. Collins our media spokesperson. I had no inkling then just how busy she would become.

The First Wave Hits

On March 12, one day after the World Health Organization declared COVID-19 to be a global pandemic, I received an urgent message to join a conference call about one of our retirement homes in British Columbia. The novel coronavirus was known to be spreading along the Pacific Coast, and a ninety-nine-year-old resident at our Hollyburn House in West Vancouver had tested positive for the virus. It appeared he had likely contracted it from a staff member who had also tested positive. The elderly resident had initially been presumed to have a cold or flu. But after our new screening measures detected the staff member's infection, we realized COVID had broken out. Both the staff member and the century-old gentleman were isolated, and remarkably, they both recovered.

The key lesson from that first brief outbreak at Hollyburn came after the discovery that the infected staff member had been working at multiple sites, as many of our employees do. We quickly realized that to reduce the risk of staff inadvertently transmitting the virus between sites, employees would have to commit to working at just one Revera home. It was a hard call to make, knowing the move could leave us short-handed. But the alternative was unacceptable to me, and on March 23, before any government directive, we restricted our employees to working at one site only.

At that moment, I thought we were in pretty good shape. But on March 24, I learned that COVID-19 had broken out at the McKenzie Towne Continuing Care Centre in southeast Calgary. It became our first big outbreak. I kept thinking we'd get a handle on it, but each day the situation was worse than the day before. The slow processing of test results by health authorities struggling to keep pace with growing demand did not help. Staff isolated residents suspected of having COVID and those whose test results were positive. I remember calling Wendy in desperation and saying, "My God—this is crazy! What do we need to do? Let's do whatever we need to do!" We shipped the site more infection control help, supplied more PPE, and provided more staff to support the local team.

It was in the grip of the McKenzie outbreak, which would ultimately claim twenty-one lives, that I realized this virus was going to be a historic contagion on par with the flu of 1918. Images streaming out of China, Europe, and the U.S. were showing us all what might lie ahead, and from our Sunrise operations in New York and New Jersey and our sites in the U.K., I had a chilling preview of just how bad it might get.

Crisis Management

My fears materialized by the end of March as COVID-19 broke out at nine sites. Through April, we were averaging an outbreak a day, with five major flareups all burning at the same time. While any site with a single case was considered an outbreak, and most homes remained virus-free, at the sites hit hard, staff, residents, and their families suffered intensely.

Our team calls jumped from three times a week to once a day, seven days a week. We heard progress reports, updates on case counts, and descriptions as to how the local executive directors were faring. If the on-site operations team was able cope on its own, great, but if help was needed—by way of executive support, extra staff, more infection control expertise, or resources—I agreed to deploy whatever and whoever they needed.

With some outbreaks, I wanted all the details; in other cases, details were speed bumps on the road to decision making and I had to say, "Okay guys, we have to go left, or we have to go right, or we'll be hit by a truck and end up like a flat squirrel." (The road of life is paved with indecisive flat squirrels.) In a crisis, people are looking for clear direction and I was fortunate that I could count on so many capable people ready to execute. When you can trust the crew on your boat in a storm, you delegate and get out of the way so they can get on with things.

From my standpoint, I was trying to make sure I spread my energy over the right spots. It was impossible to deal with everything that was happening at once. In between the virtual team meetings, I was having multiple calls to reassure various provincial health ministers that we were taking appropriate action. I was conferring with Peter Tsoporis, our VP of labour relations, as he tried to find common ground with nurses' unions who wanted their members to have N95 masks when there were no N95 masks to be found. Then I'd be on the phone with an Ottawa health official who wanted me to send in more executive support, and responding to emails from a man copying the premier as he slagged our staff while demanding hourly updates on his father, and fielding nasty emails in my inbox from strangers likening me to a merchant of death.

You absolutely have to compartmentalize.

To be an effective CEO you must be able to deliberately disengage to conserve enough mental capacity to tackle the priorities and focus on areas where you can make a meaningful difference. The breadth of stuff I usually deal with in a day is significant, but the pandemic expanded that range exponentially. In fact, Revera's long-term care division represents only 10% of our business, yet it was consuming 90% of my time. With outbreaks raging at our Canadian sites, and the virus laying siege to our international properties, I had to decide which fires I would battle personally.

Perhaps the most challenging aspect of leading during this time was my inability to physically be where I felt I was needed. In normal times, I often visited our homes and residences, but the lockdowns made site visits impossible—and it drove me nuts. On the one hand, I wanted to show that I was respecting the rules and keeping everyone safe by staying away. On the other hand, when there were homes facing outbreaks, and staff in those homes risking their lives, I wanted us all to get off our asses and out of our nice homes and be there. Not being present made me feel even more powerless against the virus, and I really had to adjust my mindset.

Like most of us confined to our homes, I found various ways to cope. Along with running and cooking dinners, I dosed myself with music. I've collected vinyl since I was eight years old, making my first purchase at Sam the Record Man in Charlottetown with money I saved from my lawn mowing business. During that first pandemic wave, my eclectic record collection became my respite as I reorganized our basement to a heavy mix of jazz, taking in Pat Metheny's "Wide and Far" from the album *From This Place*, and Chick Corea's "Now He Sings, Now He Sobs" from the album of the same name, trying to sort through the business issues I could impact and not to beat myself up over the things I couldn't change. Most days it worked well. But there were others when the frustration bubbled over.

One Friday morning after I'd been out for a run but had yet to eat break-fast, I sat down with my coffee and joined our daily team video conference call only to hear about yet another outbreak in one of our homes—and I snapped. I tore a strip off Wendy and John Beaney, our senior VP of retire-ment. I railed about being fed up with testing delays by health authorities and their inconsistent directions. Quite simply, I lost my temper and took it out on two people who were as stressed and fed up as I was.

As soon as I hung up, I was embarrassed by my outburst. I don't lose my cool very often, and I called Wendy and John back directly and apologized. It's crucial to me that my team feels respected and valued. Enabling people to feel proud of their contributions is one of the most rewarding aspects of leading. But it was hard to feel anything like that in wave one, when our people were falling ill and our residents were dying and, in the media, critics were blaming us for it. I also knew my team members were managing their own personal issues, with parents or other family members in need or a health condition that put them at high risk for the virus. Despite this, they were available at any hour determined to solve our most challenging issues.

By far, staffing was the most intractable problem we faced. Staff shortages have always plagued the sector, but in wave one we lost between 15 and 25% of our full-time employees to COVID infections, quarantines, and fear of the virus. We also lost many part-time employees to the one-site rule. Meanwhile, the workload had never been greater as a thin front line was left to don and doff PPE between residents' rooms, perform enhanced cleaning and infection control, organize cohorts, care for sick residents, and keep anxious families updated on loved ones they couldn't visit.

Restricting all visitors, including essential family caregivers, was the earliest pandemic measure undertaken and likely the most painful, as it kept husbands from wives, children from parents. I understood that personally. My own mom and dad live in a Revera retirement residence, and they have since moving from their beloved home in PEI in 2017. I was unable to see them for six months as they happened to be in a hot zone. I missed birthdays, holidays, and the regular precious visits that keep us closely connected. I felt the anguish of families who were locked out and sympathized with how distraught and fearful they were if the answers they wanted and deserved were slow to come. It is incumbent upon us to keep families informed. I pitched in from time to time to provide families with answers myself. The delay partly reflected the haphazard return of testing results, but it was also a side effect of having too few staff to provide timely information about one resident while trying to keep two hundred others safe at the same time.

Cathie Brow, our senior VP of human resources, led a drive to recruit extra staff and many of our executives jumped in to help. They launched a digital campaign and reached out to nurses' associations, public health bodies, colleges, universities, and even churches. They tapped agencies and hired temporary employees, regretful of the extra training burden it would place on existing staff. But none of this was enough to offset the number of employees we were losing to the virus in one way or another, specifically at sites where major outbreaks dragged on for weeks.

An Unwinnable War

I had visited Forest Heights, a 40-year-old, 240-bed brick building in Kitchener well known in the community, only once prior to 2020. The home confirmed its first COVID case on April 1 and infections among staff and residents continued to rise sharply over the following days. I sent Dr. Collins and her team to be my eyes and ears, and their report identified several factors that would combine to make Forest Heights one of our worst and longest outbreaks.

One of the most significant contributors was the building itself. Constructed in the 1970s, Forest Heights has small multi-bed rooms and shared bathrooms, and we had tagged it for redevelopment long before the pandemic came along. It was never designed to accommodate the wheelchairs and walkers of today's elderly, nor the social distancing space required to keep people apart during an outbreak. Neither did it help to have three different hospitals and two different public health units giving us conflicting advice on how to cohort our residents.

We certainly weren't the only ones contending with mixed messages. There's an unusual collegiality among competitors in long-term care, and three times a week I'd have conference calls with my counterparts at Chartwell, Extendicare, Sienna, and Responsive Group. We all found it constructive—and comforting—to try to interpret together the conflicting directives we received. Even now, the number of residents permitted to share a dining table varies—in one province, it's four people, in another it's two, though we're all dealing with the same virus.

In the end, the Forest Heights outbreak lasted 90 days. The virus infected 175 residents and 69 staff members, and 51 residents died. With so many dying in so short a time, the morgues were unable to collect the bodies quickly enough, forcing our staff to use the extra body bags I'd once thought would be unnecessary.

Death is no stranger in long-term care, but normally it's a rite marked by respect and compassion and grief shared with families. But COVID changed that. Death suddenly demanded a swift, cold, physical response. When our staff lost a resident to COVID-19, they could not pause to mourn. They had to follow new health authority protocols, immediately placing the deceased into a body bag to limit the spread of infection. They could not invite the family to collect the deceased's belongings, but instead had to place these in boxes for the family to retrieve later, and then had to disinfect the room. All while suppressing the sadness of losing a resident who, in many cases, had become a friend. Those images have never left me. I doubt they ever will.

At one point, in dire need of extra hands and help, we considered asking the province to step in and take over management. But on June 2, Ontario's Ministry of Long-Term Care issued a mandatory management order (MMO) that put Kitchener's St. Mary's General Hospital in charge, making Forest Heights one of eleven long-term care homes the province took over in wave one. I firmly believe that it was the right thing to have happened to help stabilize the site, and the St. Mary's team was wonderful in helping us achieve the right outcome. But as a leader, it was disappointing for me that it came to that. As CEO, I was not very excited to tell my board that the MMO had been issued. The Revera board had been nothing but supportive, but they also had to make sure they were covered in terms of exercising their fiduciary oversight and doing everything that they could do. (In May, families of the residents and unions representing Forest Heights had joined a class action lawsuit against Revera, alleging a series of missteps had contributed to the crisis.)

So the MMO was not something that I relished discussing with my board, but you have to get over your personal reluctance in these cases—you have to compartmentalize, get on with it, and carry on.

I could manage the challenges of the operational leadership side during the crisis—that's what I do. But it was impossible to separate myself from the stress and strain of contending with the unrelenting media coverage that came with it. The daily press reports of cases and deaths in long-term care accompanied a barrage of commentary that repeatedly vilified our sector—and that was too sprawling and unwieldy to mentally box away.

Thick Skin Required

Fuelled by the press, pundits, and opportunistic politicians, the public discourse revolved around the idea that for-profit long-term care homes were warehouses of neglect, designed to line shareholders' pockets at the expense of the elderly in our care. It made for a sensational storyline—but it was nonsense. Revera uses the same funding model as non-profit home operators, and in fact we subsidize our long-term care division, paying, for example, for clinical expertise and outside consultants to ensure we have the best practices in place.

We may be a private operator, but we are as close to a Crown corporation as a company can be, given that we are wholly owned by the Public Sector Pension Investment Board. What's more, some of the major factors that contributed to the COVID tragedy in long-term care had nothing to do with ownership; they were the result of decisions of health authorities and governments that barred us from timely access to PPE, testing, and even hospital care for our sick residents. If the needs of any other segment of the population had been so wholly overlooked or disregarded—if school children and teachers had been left without masks or tests—there would have been a collective outcry. Instead, the "for-profits are evil" argument detracted from the real issues. Interest groups hijacked the false narrative and used it for their own purposes. Without research-based evidence of any kind, they clung to non-empirical evidence to assert that for-profit homes had simply allowed COVID to run amok. But when data contradicted the assertions, they dismissed it.

A July 2020 study in the *Canadian Medical Association Journal* concluded that COVID was no more likely to break out in the homes of private operators than it was in non-profit or municipal homes, yet it was downplayed. The report found it was the age of a building—not who owned it—that was most predictive of larger, deadlier outbreaks. This was no surprise to me. Most of the nine Revera sites with the worst outbreaks had cramped, outdated designs. For years, I'd been working, and cursing, trying to redevelop Revera's thirty-two old stock sites in Ontario, which is the only province that even has an economic redevelopment plan and it's mired in red tape.

Yet these nuances were lost in the swarm of negative coverage, and what stung most of all was that staff who should have been celebrated for their service were instead condemned. Too rarely did our staff receive any acknowledgement of their efforts by way of kind words or the coffees delivered to other frontline healthcare workers. Too often it was a hostile media scrum and a volley of insults that greeted them on their way into work. From my perspective, the media had recklessly misinformed public opinion, and at some point I stopped paying attention to the coverage.

But the negative press was non-stop, and in time, the pandemic became political. On the national level, federal NDP leader Jagmeet Singh suggested that Revera was owned by Justin Trudeau's Liberal government and that the loss of life in our homes was due to the ownership structure. In fact, our company is owned by a pension fund that manages assets on behalf of federal civil servants—it is not under the control of either the bureaucratic or the political arm of the federal government. And ownership structure is not a predictor of outbreak outcomes. But these facts were lost in the political theatre. The media reported on the NDP attacks and perpetuated misinformation. This made for a truly sad and difficult dynamic in which to run a business, especially one with such a long, strong track record of providing excellent care for seniors across our network.

Paving the High Road

As wave one subsided in the summer of 2020, I had a chance to catch my breath. Pandemics historically have more than one wave, and I realized we had a short window to learn from the first wave before the second one hit. I wanted to know what worked, what didn't, and how we could do better in the waves to follow.

I kept coming back to the observation that when COVID breaks out, an overwhelming sense of panic can break out with it. Yet the need for clear, quick thinking in that moment is essential to contain the spread and communicate with families as we should. In my experience, if you have a suite of tools that you can easily turn to in a high-pressure situation and make automatic some of the things you must do, it gives you greater capacity to deal with things that are more bespoke.

My thinking was influenced by *The Checklist Manifesto: How to Get Things Right*. It was a 2011 *New York Times* bestseller by the American surgeon and writer Atul Gawande, who makes the case that having a thorough checklist at hand in an emergency can save lives in medicine but also in other realms. That's the essence of what I felt we needed—something that could be pulled out of a drawer and could enable any executive director to rise above the panic an outbreak can trigger by furnishing them with an itemized list of what must be done first, second, third, and so on.

The Revera board backed my idea completely. Previous leadership roles had taught me that you can earn your governing board's support by being upfront and transparent, and I met with my board twice a month throughout the pandemic. Board chair Mike Mueller was a constant source of confidence and support. I also had weekly calls with Dr. Calvin Stiller, the chair of the board's quality assurance committee. Everyone saw the checklist resource the same way I did—as a critical tool to control outbreaks and keep our residents and staff safe.

Having worked previously with David Burnie's management consulting firm, we engaged the Burnie Group to help us assemble the critical to-do lists as quickly as we could. We created templates related to communications, human resources, and clinical core processes and had the final product in hand in September 2020.

I take pride in what we came to call our "pandemic playbook." It is a pivotal contribution to protect the company and its mission, which matters to me deeply. I believe not only that we provide a service as essential as any form of social housing, but that we create environments that enable older adults to simplify their lives and focus on the things that bring them joy. Congregate living allows people to interact socially, to be spiritual and physical, and to remain mobile and engaged. But all of that is pointless if residents and their families feel that congregate living is unsafe.

To do better in wave two, or in any future pandemic, the board and I agreed that we had to explore the forces that helped or hindered our operations in wave one, an investigation we felt had to be conducted by an outside panel of experts. Talking with Dr. Stiller, I suggested we ask Dr. Bob Bell to assemble and lead the panel. I'd known Bob as the former deputy minister of health of Ontario during earlier efforts to redevelop Revera's older sites. I also knew him personally since his parents had lived at one of our retirement residences. Bob agreed to do it with a few conditions—he wouldn't take a penny for the work, and he and the panel he assembled would have to have unfettered access to our internal data, full editorial control of the report, and freedom to publish their findings and recommendations. It crossed my mind that the endeavour might leave us feeling naked and frost-bitten in the town square—but I got over it. We had to walk the talk. If we wanted to do better for ourselves, we had to live up to the highest standards of corporate responsibility. If we wanted the sector to benefit in the interests of the greater good, we had to share what we learned.

Among the panel's most compelling findings was that the outbreaks in our homes were predicted by the prevalence of community spread. If cases spiked in the area, COVID broke out in our sites about two weeks later. The finding shed light on the origin of our major outbreaks in wave one, just as the second wave was quietly building.

Wave Two and the West

By September 2020, we had reason to hope that the pandemic's second wave would not blindside us. We had our playbook as well as data that showed the masking, screening, and social distancing measures we had implemented in wave one had worked to significantly reduce the number of outbreaks we faced after the measures were introduced. But like that insidious patch of black ice, COVID-19 tripped us up again.

Manitoba had been relatively unharmed by the pandemic in wave one. But in early autumn, cases of COVID-19 spiked and Winnipeg became a hot spot where, tragically, two of our sites were hit with major outbreaks. One of them occurred at Maples Personal Care Home, a 200-bed site where the virus infected 157 residents and 74 staff and killed 56 people between October and January. Having had few cases in the spring, local health authorities were not prepared for the deluge and hospitals began transferring COVID patients into long-term care. At Maples, the staffing levels dropped to critically low levels. By early November, when many staff were too scared to come to work, our vice-president of operations in Manitoba inadvertently gave an incorrect tally of our staffing numbers at a media conference, stating that they were higher than they actually were. The VP had used staff planning sheets for his calculation, which I later learned was not an accurate account of how many employees turned up for their shift. He had otherwise done a great job, but the mistake became a lightning rod. After someone posted the true staffing levels on social media, the Winnipeg Regional Health Authority criticized us publicly for the inaccuracy. Manitoba's health minister called me at home, and after assuring him we were doing all we could to support the site, I jumped on a call with Wendy, Susan Schutta, our VP of corporate affairs and communications, and director of communications Larry Roberts, to issue an immediate apology for the mistake. But it was too late. The accidental misstep cemented the idea that we were villains, and the media ran with it. Manitoba's NDP leader, Wab Kinew, was quoted as saying Manitobans needed to gather their pitchforks and torches and run Revera out of town. Some people took him seriously.

Our VP of operations started receiving death threats, as did one of our executive directors in Winnipeg. We had to engage security staff for them and their families. I also began to receive death threats by email that made me feel personally vulnerable and concerned for my family, though less so since the senders were based in Manitoba. In this business, you get accustomed to a certain degree of nastiness. When family members who haven't seen their elderly parents for a long time pay a visit to them in long-term care and find that Mom or Dad has physically deteriorated, as the aged can do, we are sometimes on the receiving end of misplaced guilt and blame, and it has taken me time to grow a tough skin in response to that. But the death threats were something entirely different. I never considered that being the chief executive of a long-term care operation could be a dangerous job that could make me fearful of a physical attack. It's true the pandemic brought out examples of the best of humanity, but it also exposed the worst.

That November, COVID-19 also broke out at our Capilano Care Centre, a sixty-year-old West Vancouver site well past its functional life that we had slated for closure months before the pandemic. For several years, we tried to engage the Vancouver Health Authority to work with us to find a way to keep it open. But there was little interest until we informed them of our intent to close in September 2020. Unlike Ontario, B.C. has no economic redevelopment plan for outdated care homes and it is not financially feasible for us to renovate the site on our own. But the second wave hit just as we prepared to issue the closure notice and begin the year-long transition of relocating residents. Then the notice was delayed again after Capilano confirmed COVID-19 had moved in. True to the heartbreaking pattern of this virus hitting older sites hard, the outbreak lasted until January 2021 and took the lives of twenty-six residents.

Closure may be the fate of many older stock long-term care homes, particularly in high-density urban settings where there are few large available and affordable tracts of land. But even more important than the bricks and mortar needed to house the frail elderly is the need to ensure there will be enough trained nurses and personal support workers (PSWs) to provide the human-to-human care they require. Demand for caregivers already outstrips supply, and our aging population is about to dramatically exacerbate this lopsided equation. The negative media portrayals of our industry during the pandemic have hardly helped: who wants to work in the long-term care sector these days? We've even found it difficult to attract applicants for a business analytics role at Revera because the job description mentions that the position supports a long-term care business.

Carrots and Sticks

After the vaccine rollout began, COVID-19 deaths in our long-term care homes between January and June of 2021 dwindled to fewer than five. The media moved on to a different story as the third wave exacted a tragic toll in vulnerable, low-income communities. Long-term care deaths no longer accounted for the vast majority of Canada's COVID mortalities, but contentious issues remained as we worked to make sure our staff were fully vaccinated.

More than 95% of our residents had received both shots by July, and I couldn't have been prouder of our progress to help safeguard them against future waves of the pandemic. But efforts to vaccinate staff were more complicated. Despite providing rides to vaccine clinics and two hours off work to receive the shot, a worrisome percentage of our employees remained unvaccinated in the summer of 2021. I sympathized when vaccine supplies were limited early on, and I understood the initial hesitancy over a new vaccine technology. But after that, with supplies plentiful and tens of millions of people safely vaccinated, I had zero empathy for anyone working in health care who was choosing not to get the shot.

My parents had to spend yet another Easter quarantined in their room this year, after an unvaccinated staff member who had been chatting with my father—and my ninety-four-year-old father is a fabulous chatter—had tested positive for COVID. The staff member recovered, and my parents tested negative after seven days, but the experience only added to my determination to seize what I see as the moral high ground on this front. To my mind, the vaccination issue is muddled by our sense of individual rights. Yet anyone working in health care, where there are vulnerable people, should be required to have all the protection they can have, both for themselves and for the people they are serving. You don't want to be a spreader of any form of illness, and if you choose not to be vaccinated for religious or ethical beliefs, then perhaps you have not chosen the correct profession.

In July 2021, Revera became the first Canadian long-term care operator to make vaccination "an expectation of employment." We informed staff that those unvaccinated by July 7 would have to undergo daily testing and wear full PPE if interacting with residents. It was meant as both a carrot and a stick in the context of Canada's Charter of Rights and Freedoms.

The Road Ahead

There was a time in 2019 when I contemplated stepping back from Revera to pursue other opportunities. I'd made great progress growing the business, sharpening and refining its strategy. By then I'd been the chief executive for almost six years, about the length of time I'd spent in positions in the past, but I opted to stay. We were financially healthy and flourishing, breaking ground on new developments, acquiring businesses, and innovating. The pandemic upended all of this. As a CEO, it's been awful. We're having to recalibrate just to get to a sustainable economic model because our retirement business has shrunk considerably and the perception around the safety of congregate living has absorbed a profound blow.

Even so, for all the days the pandemic made me second-guess my decision to remain at the helm, I don't believe I'd make a different choice today. I still believe in Revera's mission to positively impact the aging years, and my parents bolster that belief. Since my mom and dad have been residents, my father has grown fond of his exercise class, has picked up new computer skills, and has been able to continue to live with my mother, who suffers from the early stages of dementia but feels safe and cared for.

From my perspective, the pandemic should stand as a once-in-a-century opportunity to accelerate improvements to our long-term care and retirement homes and the systems in which they operate. This crisis should be a rallying call to ensure we have enough capacity to house seniors in need, and enough nurses and PSWs to help care for them. I'd like to think we all share the desire to make sure the highest quality of life is considered paramount at any age.

Yet as I've led Revera through this scourge, I have had to accept that no matter how excellent your infrastructure or your operations, this virus can still find its way in. Outbreaks do not necessarily begin because of something you've done wrong—you may be doing everything right, but it can still find its way inside through the barriers we put up. As I told my board, despite all the lessons learned, initiatives undertaken, and protective measures put in place, there is no guarantee COVID-19 won't slither through again. I can't stop it anymore than I can prevent the formation of black ice.

This spring, after healing from my ill-fated February run, I swapped my running routine for a Peloton workout on a stationary bike. I managed to combine this with runs over the summer, though I haven't ruled out the possibility of hitting the pre-dawn pavement again this winter. Even if I may once again end up on a treacherous slope—I have to keep running.

RITCHIE BROS.

Picture a typical auction.

People crowded together in a confined space for hours, excited, talking constantly, and shouting occasionally. It is the definition of a COVID-19 superspreader event. As the pandemic swept through North America in the first few months of 2020, the challenge facing newly named Ritchie Bros. chief executive Ann Fandozzi was running a business that, at first blush, needed to be shut down.

Now picture the solution. Move the auctions online by accelerating the digital transformation of a B.C. company that's among the world leaders in sales of used heavy equipment.

Three Ritchie brothers—Ken, Dave, and John—backed into the auction business in 1958 when they decided to raise money to pay down a $2,000 bank loan at their father's Kelowna, B.C., furniture store by selling off surplus items. There were no reserve bids, and everything had to go. The event was a huge success.

By the 1960s, the brothers were selling industrial equipment at auctions across western Canada, with Dave Ritchie serving as CEO. Again, with no reserve bids, which meant there was always the potential to pick up a tractor, truck, crane, or road grader for a bargain price. In 1970, the company ventured into the U.S., holding an auction in Oregon. Over the next three decades, Ritchie Bros. expanded into Australia, Europe, Asia, and the Middle East. Dave Ritchie retired in 2004.

In 2019, prior to the pandemic, $5.1 billion of industrial gear changed hands at 40 Ritchie auction sites run by 2,400 employees in 12 countries. Fandozzi arrived in December 2019 to replace predecessor Ravi Saligram, who left the Vancouver-based company after five years to return with his family to the U.S.

In the winter of 2020, Fandozzi cut short a tour of Ritchie Bros.' far-flung operations, hunkered down at her home in Pennsylvania, and built a strategy for doing business during COVID. Technology was at the forefront of her plans. Fandozzi is a graduate of the computer engineering program at the Stevens Institute of Technology and holds a master's in systems engineering from the University of Pennsylvania and an MBA from Penn's Wharton School.

Ritchie Bros. recruited Fandozzi from the CEO role at car repair chain Abra Auto Body & Glass. She also led online carpooling platform vRide for four years, and held executive roles at industrial players Whirlpool, DaimlerChrysler, Ford, and Lockheed Martin, along with a stint at consulting firm McKinsey & Co.

The Canadian auction house found that their new CEO's skill at tying technology to the consumer experience was the cure for a pandemic problem. She also had the human touch needed to get deals done, flying to Reykjavik, Iceland, in the spring of 2021 to negotiate the company's largest takeover to date, a US$1.1 billion acquisition of rival Euro Auctions. Fandozzi and her teams settled the terms of the deal over two days of face-to-face sessions—the two teams chose the mid-Atlantic island because it didn't require quarantines.

Ann Fandozzi

AUGUST 2021

I was in Las Vegas for one of the world's largest construction equipment trade shows when North America started to shut down due to COVID-19 in mid-March 2020. I was surrounded by hundreds of thousands of maskless attendees from around the world, and miles from my home and family in Pennsylvania. Just three months earlier, I had joined Ritchie Bros., a Canadian-founded global equipment auction company, and now I had to lead us through the biggest obstacle we have faced in our sixty-plus year history—a pandemic that would impact nearly every aspect of work and life around the world.

We had been monitoring COVID overseas for weeks, but we had not fully understood the risk of a global pandemic. A few trade show exhibitors dropped out days before the March 10–14, 2020, CONEXPO event, but we spoke to our customers and they were all set to travel, so we would too. We had a customer event scheduled and paid for, so on March 11 in Las Vegas we hosted hundreds of people from around the world in one room . . . and we served food! The next day, the CONEXPO organizers told all exhibitors and attendees the show would be closing a day early due to new international travel restrictions in the United States. The following Monday, the Canada–U.S. border closed.

I was originally supposed to fly home from Las Vegas, change bags, and then fly to meet employees and customers in South Africa and Australia as I continued my tour around the Ritchie Bros. world to learn the ins and outs of the business. Instead, I flew directly home to Pennsylvania, and more than a year later I am still leading virtually from here, from a desk in the corner of my living room. Leading remotely during COVID has not been easy, but thanks to our amazing executive team and all our employees, Ritchie Bros. has experienced a lot of success over the past year, attracting record demand and achieving strong returns for consignors. Here's how we did it.

Before I joined Ritchie Bros., I certainly saw great potential in the company—that is what attracted me. Ritchie Bros. is one of the biggest players in a highly fragmented equipment sales market. Estimates put the global used equipment industry around $300 billion annually. And Ritchie Bros. only did $5 billion in sales when I joined. I could see a long runway ahead. What I did not know before joining was the strength of the team Ritchie Bros. had built.

Co-founder and chair emeritus Dave Ritchie set the standard decades earlier. Dave and his brothers Ken and John had built the company one customer relationship at a time—growing from a local furniture auction house in Kelowna, B.C., to a global company helping thousands of contractors each year. Dave's famous saying was "Treat a customer like a friend and they will be a customer for life."

That customer focus was evident from my first meetings with Ritchie Bros. employees in Cancun, Mexico, for our sales meeting in January 2020. I did not know anyone, so I circled the room to talk to everyone I could— the passion from our sales team for our customers was palpable. But in that first meeting, I was struck by how much time our presenters spent talking about process over people. We seemed in the weeds at times, and our administrative and field employee priorities appeared disconnected.

In Cancun and the weeks following, I met with as many people as possible to learn, but it was not until our massive Orlando auction in February 2020 that the business became full colour for me. Two hundred acres filled with equipment and trucks welcoming thousands of people from around the world—this was the Olympics of auctions, and in six days we sold more than 13,500 items for US$237 million. I had never seen anything like it. And yet the work behind the scenes was even more remarkable.

I was highly impressed with the work ethic of our employees. Our staff had been preparing for months for this event. They would arrive at the auction site before the sun rose and leave well after sunset. Many of our yard employees were covered in oil or dirt from head to toe as they lined up the next item for sale. It was a masterful performance. I knew I had a team that was willing to do whatever it took for our customers. But I did not know what was to come with COVID and how much we would be tested.

Establishing a COVID Response Team

I first started hearing about COVID-19 during our massive Orlando auction. We quickly held a board meeting where we discussed the relatively new disease and its possible impacts on our business, but I don't think any of us seriously thought we would see major impacts in North America. Still, we established a COVID response team immediately to closely monitor the situation.

To lead our response team, I chose our general counsel, Darren Watt, who surrounded himself with key stakeholders throughout the company to monitor different impacts. Choosing Darren turned out to be one of my best decisions. His legal expertise helped him handle the flurry of provincial and state stay-at-home orders, and his long history with the company made him someone everyone would trust, which ended up being extremely important given the amount of conflicting information in the news.

We issued our first email to staff about COVID-19 on March 3, 2020, informing employees that we were monitoring the situation and would be doing additional cleaning and sanitizing at our sites. We also restricted all non-essential travel to key affected areas outlined by the World Health Organization at the time and asked employees attending the big CONEXPO trade show in Las Vegas the following week to "refrain from shaking hands."

The next day we postponed our auction in Italy from March to April because the outbreak there had begun. Thankfully, none of our employees had been infected yet. In our email announcing the postponement, we ended with "There is no need for anyone to worry at this time. We just want to make sure we are fully prepared."

A week later, on March 12, we restricted all non-essential business travel until further notice and started to consider closing some of our administrative offices. Meanwhile, I was in Las Vegas at CONEXPO and was heading to our nearby site for our auction where we sold 2,700 items for US$44 million. The two-day Las Vegas auction—our last with on-site bidding—attracted more than 6,800 bidders from 57 countries.

The next few weeks would change our business forever.

Communication Is Key

Over the weekend of March 14–15, 2020, the world was turned upside down. North America was now seeing cases, and governments were planning shutdowns behind closed doors. The executive team and I were also busy that weekend: planning for 100% online auctions with no on-site bidding, prepping work-from-home plans for employees, and conducting serious risk assessments for our business. All the while our executives were busy travelling home from Las Vegas, with Canadian executives and employees getting home just as the border was shut—and then having to quarantine for two weeks.

Information about COVID-19 was unfolding in real time, and provincial and state shutdowns were coming fast and furious—each one different from the last. Our COVID response team, led by Darren Watt, worked closely with our operations executives in the U.S., Canada, and our international regions to decipher the shutdown orders: Were we an "essential business"? How many people could we have on site, if any? What signage was required on site? Each decision seemed to trigger another question.

We had to reinvent the way we did business. Ritchie Bros. has conducted in-person auctions for over sixty years. Suddenly, the approach that defined our company was no longer safe. Could our auctions still be successful with no one on site to raise their hand and bid? We were about to find out.

To stay focused at a time of great uncertainty, it was important to set a "True North," a single guiding principle that we would rally around. For us, the True North became the safety of our employees and customers. This focus ended up making all decisions that followed much easier: 100%

online auctions would help keep our field employees and customers safe, and work-from-home capabilities could help protect our administrative employees.

We also instituted daily emails to employees, keeping them abreast of the latest decisions and stay-at-home orders. These were a way to communicate key information and to keep our teams connected during a time of isolation. The daily emails, combined with monthly all-employee video town halls, were my biggest tools to communicate with staff around the globe. My original plan was to do a whole world tour to meet our employees—but that was no longer an option. It was virtual or nothing.

Going 100% Online

On March 17–18, 2020, we held our first site auctions with 100% online bidding in Columbus, Ohio, and Sacramento, California. There was enormous internal stress in the days leading up to the events. Our team members had to call hundreds of consignors to let them know we would not be allowing on-site bidding for their auctions; we had to adjust our online bidding technology to allow for more registrants; and we had to make sure all our regular on-site bidders were set up and confident with online bidding practices.

We were not sure what to expect on auction day. We went into the event confident we had done everything we could to make the move online easy to navigate. However, we didn't know how our customers would react. Jumping forward, we were thrilled to find the online auctions attracted far more clients than in-person events. Columbus registered 45% more bidders year over year, while attendance in Sacramento increased by 25%. This unprecedented demand helped drive strong prices for consignors.

Unfortunately, what worked for auctions in Columbus and Sacramento was not going to work for our international operations. By mid-March, much of Europe was locked down, meaning customers could not visit the site to inspect equipment in most cases, something they could still do in the U.S. and Canada. So, instead of a one-size-fits all solution, we decided to try conducting our international auctions with our timed auction system, which we traditionally used only for small consumer items and attachments.

With timed auction, buyers place bids in an automated online system, using set bid increments. People can set a maximum bid they are willing to pay and then walk away and let the system bid for them. It is an extremely popular tool, but we had never used timed auction to sell big excavators and cranes. Our first timed auction test was held in France, at our auction site in St. Aubin sur Gaillon. It was a huge success, achieving strong prices for consignors, with approximately 60% of the assets sold to buyers from outside the country, from as far away as Australia, Vietnam, and the U.S.

We were innovating, testing, and improving—just as Dave Ritchie had done. Dave introduced one of the first equipment websites in the mid-1990s and launched online bidding at Ritchie Bros. in 2002—leading the industry. When he first introduced digital bidding, Dave hoped we could eventually reach 10% participation from online customers. We were now at 100%, and demand was trending upward.

At this point, I started to fully understand the critical function we play in our customers' lives. I had worried our business could not work without on-site bidding, but we were thriving. Our customers rely on us to deliver results in good times or bad. If we were not able to deliver in a pandemic, they were going to find someone else who could.

Delivering Data into the Hands of Customers

Spring is always busy for auctions, especially farm auctions. Traditionally our agriculture team moves around the country, like a travelling roadshow, going from farm to farm across Western Canada, conducting dozens of auctions in a single month. But with COVID-19, we could not put our employees or customers at risk, so in late March 2020 we decided to test timed auction again, this time for our agriculture auctions. It worked immediately, with record-breaking registrations and skyrocketing farm equipment prices. Through sixty agricultural auctions in the spring of 2020, registrations were up 127%, with increased international participation.

We were having initial success, but in this new digital world, customers wanted more information than ever. There was a lot of uncertainty due to ongoing lockdowns. To help our customers be more confident when bidding, we began issuing a free monthly pricing report in April 2020. This would allow customers to see pricing trends for all major equipment categories. That information helped guide their bidding strategies.

Every year Ritchie Bros. sells hundreds of thousands of equipment items and trucks, and we track data on every single transaction. As a result, over the years, we've built massive files of pricing data. Internally, we use this material to help us better understand how pricing changes over time and how different factors, such as commodity prices and economic conditions, impact pricing.

Earlier in 2020, we launched a subscription-based market trends application to help customers better understand pricing through in-depth analysis of our data, asset valuation curves, and mix-adjusted price indexes. In April, we took it a step further by offering a free monthly report available to all customers.

A Big Test in Edmonton

The Ritchie brothers held their first auction outside of B.C. in Alberta, back in the 1960s and then went on to establish the company's first permanent auction site in Edmonton in 1976. Today our Edmonton site is one of the crown jewels of our operation—selling hundreds of millions of dollars of equipment each year.

Traditionally our spring Edmonton sale is one of our biggest events of the year. We usually bring in operations staff from across Canada and around the world to help us process the massive amount of equipment rolling in. But in 2020, the auction would be 100% online, and the Edmonton team was on their own for setup. All our field staff were separated into working cohorts and masked up. It was a monumental task, but the Edmonton team consigned and processed more than 10,000 items and registered over 23,500 bidders (up 33% year over year) in their spring sale. At the end of the five-day auction, we had sold more than $184 million of equipment.

The online-only event allowed us to maintain the safety of our employees and customers while still providing consignors the liquidity they needed during extremely uncertain times. Bidders registered from fifty-eight countries, with international buyers purchasing approximately 13% of the equipment, including two Caterpillar PL83 pipelayers, used in the oil and gas industry, that sold to a buyer from the U.K. for a combined $1.28 million!

The Edmonton test was a resounding success. Our auctioneers sold to an empty auction theatre while online bidders listened in. Yet the bids came fast and furious. Our new approach was working and our employees were safe.

The Front-Line Impact

By mid-March 2020, all our administrative employees were set up to work from home. However, most of our operations staff in the field were required to be on site to handle equipment, manage systems, and help facilitate in-person inspections. This team is an extremely dedicated group and works long hours for our customers.

With COVID, while our auction theatres were closed to bidders, our sites were otherwise open for customers if that was permitted by local regulations. Keeping our field operations staff safe was of the utmost importance—I could not live with myself if we did not do everything possible to protect them. While we quickly were able to establish cohort groupings, install "sneeze guards," and provide personal protective equipment to employees, I realized we needed a chief operating officer to help us coordinate and develop best practices and leverage our scale.

We had outstanding operational leaders, but we were entering a new way of doing business and I knew we would benefit from outside ideas. I brought in Jim Kessler, who had worked with me previously at Abra Auto Body & Glass—one of North America's largest car repair companies—to look at the entire auction network and establish new procedures and services. What else can we do to keep our employees safe? How can we get customers more information so they can still bid without visiting the site?

Are there other services and tools we can launch to help our customers in this new digital world?

Around the same time, our chief human resources officer was set to retire, so I brought in Carmen Thiede, someone else I had previously worked with at Abra and knew would be perfect for Ritchie Bros. Unfortunately, onboarding Jim and Carmen was not going to be easy as it was going to be all virtual. In fact, more than a year later, Jim and Carmen still have not met most of their direct reports in person. Regardless, they both dove headfirst into the deep end and got to work.

Carmen and I almost immediately began developing a plan to reward our frontline workers for their dedication. Companies like Walmart and Target were starting to add hazard pay of an extra dollar or two per hour for frontline employees, but we decided to create a virtual piggybank and surprised frontline employees with a four-figure cheque in the summer. Instead of an extra few bucks per paycheque, they got a big lump sum, and the employee response was amazing.

Simultaneously, Jim got straight to work with his team to develop new digital services to help safely facilitate in-person equipment inspection and give customers confidence in equipment while being remote. Previously, a customer could just show up on site and inspect any item they might be interested in, but we were now required to limit the number of people on site. We developed an online booking system to allow customers to book inspection times. We also offered bookings for equipment dropoff and pickup, which has proved very popular for the transportation companies we work with.

Black Lives Matter and the Power of Employee Resource Groups

I am a big believer in the power of communication and transparent leadership. Early on, when I first arrived at Ritchie Bros., I wanted to set up a regular cadence of town halls so I could speak directly to our people, honestly and openly. My grand plan was to travel the world of Ritchie Bros. and report from a different location each month, but I have been reporting from my less-grand living room for more than a year now.

We also set up an AskAnn inbox so employees could ask me questions, but it became so much more during the pandemic. Our employees working from home missed their colleagues, and our field employees missed the excitement of in-person auctions. I started receiving photos of employees working alongside their home-schooling kids, as well as baby photos. We also held a walk and photo competition, and so much more. Our company was finding new ways to connect and work.

This connection increased as we faced social and racial injustice issues throughout 2020. After the killing of George Floyd and the resulting Black Lives Matter protests, we had lots of outreach from our employees to my AskAnn inbox. Many members of our team wanted to do something tangible for social justice causes. We decided to establish a Black Lives Matter employee resource group (BLM ERG) to help support our employees. We now have more than a hundred BLM ERG members tackling a number of important issues, including training and education, community involvement, talent practices, and communications. The team has put on seminars on diversity in leadership, we've connected with diversity job boards to help with talent acquisition, and we've made charitable donations.

I'll let one of our leaders on the BLM ERG campaign talk about what it means in our workplace: *"The difference between performative support and genuine support is in the 'doing,' and Ritchie Bros. is doing more than just making statements," said Ritchie Bros. employee and BLM ERG chair Andrew Copeland. "The company is putting money into turning promises into action, and genuinely wants to understand what Black people in the workforce go through every day. There is an almost surprising willingness to shift ideals, and I think that's what separates this company from most of the others who declared their support for Black Lives Matter."*

Pushing for Innovation

On July 30 and 31, 2020, at one of our biggest auction sites in Fort Worth, we attracted more than 10,800 online bidders—a 108% increase year over year—to compete for 4,400 items. Typically, this auction would attract approximately 5,000 bidders on site and online combined, but our push to online only was increasing demand exponentially. A month later, our Houston auction attracted more than 11,100 bidders. It was becoming clear our online-only model was not just working, it was thriving. Unlike many other businesses that were having to constantly deal with closures due to COVID-19, we had chosen a safe, consistent, and effective way to do business. We were clearly essential—helping customers quickly turn their surplus equipment into cash so they could reinvest in their businesses.

At the same time, we were seeing strong returns from our timed auction system used for auctions overseas and farm retirement sales. We were also experimenting with combining smaller site events into larger regional auctions—pooling bidders together to drive stronger demand. In September 2020, we combined equipment from 16 different physical locations into four online regional events. Through the four events we attracted more than 1.5 million page views, with customers adding approximately 175,000 items to their watchlists and making 15,000 PriorityBids.

At the same time, we were heavily digitizing our marketing efforts, which was also paying off. For decades, we have been all about the print brochure, with each auction getting its own specially designed, printed brochure, mailed to tens of thousands of customers. By going all digital we could hyperlink items and maps for engagement and increase our target audience with no additional mailing cost.

Orlando and Edmonton 2021

As good as everything was going with our online-only auctions in 2020, we still were not sure how to handle our massive Orlando auction in February 2021. Florida had been a hotbed for COVID-19 cases and anti-mask sentiment. Meanwhile, our competitors in the region were planning in-person auctions and pitching that traditional approach as superior to our newly launched online experience. We knew we could conduct a successful online event—we had months of proof. However, we wanted to include feedback from our customers in the process. We had been working for months on new service ideas and data solutions and held a call campaign to outline our approach to our largest customers.

As we talked to customers in the weeks leading up to the Orlando event, we pitched a new, deeper auction experience, drawn from a significant acquisition we made in December 2020. Nine months into the pandemic, we bought Rouse Services, an industry-leading provider of data intelligence and performance benchmarking solutions. Rouse offers a toolkit that complements ours, specializing in rental and dealer data solutions. For years they have also been providing pricing reports on our auctions, so for Orlando in February 2021 we included day-by-day pricing breakdowns for key equipment categories.

With Orlando being a big destination auction, we also decided we would film videos of equipment operating to help those who could not inspect in person. We uploaded thousands of videos to YouTube—so many per day, in fact, that YouTube had to cut us off at one point. We ended up making a dedicated YouTube channel just for Orlando 2021. We also provided a concierge inspection service, allowing customers to FaceTime a certified inspector to inspect items they were interested in. Similarly, customers could pre-book equipment pickup and dropoff times.

Our February 2021 Orlando auction was a resounding success, attracting 22,700 online bidders from more than 80 countries, setting a new record for the site. More than 12,000 items were sold over six days for US$191 million, making it the largest online auction in our history!

Three months later, we were back for our giant spring auction in Edmonton and attracting 28,700 online bidders—up 22% from the massive registration numbers in May 2020. The site sold a record 13,600 items—the most for a single auction in our 60-year history—for CA$197 million.

What I Learned

The past year has taught me a lot about our company and what it takes to be a successful leader. Here are five of my biggest learnings:

1. I have always believed that business is all about people. If you put talented, well-intentioned people together, magical things will happen. The Ritchie Bros. team has proved this a thousand times over.

2. Communication is key. Everyone wants to come to work to contribute and feel valued. Communications play a very important role in connecting individual work to the company vision and performance. This is even more crucial in a remote work environment.

3. Safety, mental health, and work–life balance are essential. Our employees work so hard for our customers and we need to provide them the systems and processes to keep them safe, happy, and healthy, both physically and mentally. This is a critical management challenge we are working on every day at Ritchie Bros.

4. Be supportive and understanding of one another. This past year has been very difficult, and we must believe in the positive intent of each of our team members. I know with certainty that our team is doing the very best they can every day to support our customers. Unfortunately, this past year has loaded a lot of stress onto our people, some of whom have lost a family member or friend to COVID. Ask questions of your employees, don't jump to conclusions, and always believe in positive intent.

5. Finally, it's all about having a "True North" or rallying cry for team members to follow—to help guide them through difficult decisions. In good times, this can take the form of business objectives, like growth. In pandemic times, it's all about safety. Safety guided so many of our decisions over the past year and we benefited in so many ways. Whatever your "True North" is, communicate it clearly and live it daily to unite your team for success.

SIENNA SENIOR LIVING

In the summer of 2021, Sienna decided to give a sincere thank you to the thirteen thousand employees who carried Sienna Senior Living's retirement and long-term care homes through a gruelling pandemic.

Toronto Stock Exchange–listed Sienna awarded more than $3 million in shares to its team members, most of whom are hourly staff who have never previously owned stock in a company. Full-time employees who had been with the company for more than a year got $500 in shares, and part-time workers received $300. It is the only such program in the sector. The goal was to recognize the employees' dedication and to foster a sense of ownership in the company. In handing out the award, Nitin Jain said in an internal note, "As professionals in seniors living, you bring your whole selves to work every day—your compassion, skills and dedication to providing residents with a positive and caring experience. This has always been true, but never more obvious than throughout the COVID-19 global pandemic."

Sienna, with more than eleven thousand residents at eighty-three facilities in British Columbia and Ontario, was hard hit by the COVID-19 storm. Seniors proved the most vulnerable to the coronavirus, and outbreaks came fast and furious. Jain took the helm at Sienna in the midst of the gale. He was named chief executive in June 2020, following the departure of his predecessor. Jain joined Sienna in 2014 as chief financial officer and chief investment officer after serving as an executive with Canadian Tire and General Electric. A native of India, Jain spent the early stages of his career working in the hotel industry in Dubai and the U.S., then earned an MBA at University of Notre Dame.

Growing up in India, the future CEO learned the importance of wisdom and a love of seniors from his family there, where he saw his father take care of his sick grandfather for more than a decade. This experience was part of what drove Jain to rally the company and focus its actions and decisions around the purpose that it is a privilege to care for and serve Canada's seniors, ensuring they live with the utmost comfort, dignity, and respect.

Nitin Jain

JULY 2021

Being appointed CEO is an honour and a significant challenge. Being appointed CEO of any company three months into the first pandemic in a hundred years would mean the challenges were daunting. But being appointed CEO of Sienna Senior Living, a publicly traded company that operates long-term care communities and retirement residences, was all of these on steroids. This is my story and the story of Sienna's ten thousand team members and their incredible ability to stand up to COVID-19, never backing down until we were safe again.

The Beginning

It is safe to say this CEO role found me and not the other way around. With twelve hours' notice, on June 11, 2020, I became the president and chief executive officer of Sienna Senior Living upon the departure of the previous CEO. At the time, I was the chief financial officer and chief investment officer and had been with the company for six years. From the beginning, I was drawn to this complex industry. Seniors' living involves elements of hospitality, which is where my career began, and it is forecasted to experience significant growth based on current demographics. However, it is the service we provide to the residents that has always meant the most to me. I've met seniors from all walks of life, each with an incredible story to tell and a passion for doing the things they love. Take, for example, Monetta, a 94-year-old resident living near Ottawa who dreams of going sky diving when the COVID-19 restrictions are lifted; or Lucia, a B.C. resident who published her first children's book at the age of 82 and during the pandemic; or Eric, an 89-year-old retired professional baseball player who continues to share his love of the game with everyone at his retirement home in Sarnia. It is also significant how many Canadian centenarians are part of our communities—they represent some of our most treasured and vulnerable residents.

Sienna is a fifty-year-old company, and with more than thirteen thousand team members it is one of the largest Canadian operators in the seniors' living sector. We are a publicly traded company with assets of over $2.5 billion that owns, operates, and manages eighty-three long-term care communities and retirement residences in Ontario and British Columbia. Every home is a unique, tight-knit family unto itself, and like any family, we rallied around each other to get through an incredibly difficult and challenging time during the pandemic. We had homes that were virtually untouched by COVID-19 and others under constant siege. My early days as CEO were incredibly difficult. I wish my story had had a different beginning, but we found our way forward and have worked together to meet every challenge—and the challenges at times felt unrelenting and never ending. I am proud of where we are today, and although this difficult journey is not over, we can breathe again and look forward to better times.

When I took over as CEO, Sienna, similar to many other operators, was in crisis. The press release announcing my appointment as the new president and CEO went out at 8:45 a.m. on Friday, June 12, 2020. The familiar ding signalling a new email message began to sound in rapid succession on my phone. People across my network reached out with congratulatory messages, some of which I would characterize as "qualified congratulations," bearing some resemblance to letters of condolence. It didn't matter. I didn't have the luxury of time or a typical transition ahead of me. Looking back, one might expect this time would be a blur in my mind, but it's not. I remember acutely the moments of fear, anxiety, and sadness that came over me in waves, and they will forever be a part of me. I expect I will always carry them in some form. In my mind, these emotions honour the residents and team members who passed away, fell ill, or otherwise suffered at the hands of this cruel disease.

In the Eye of the Storm

The long-term care sector was hit hard in the early days of the pandemic. The virus swept through homes with relentless speed, attacking seniors and staff with precision. At the onset of the pandemic in Canada, it felt as though I was at a window, looking out as this novel virus caused the entire country to unravel. As Sienna's CFO and CIO, I was not part of the operations team, but I was close enough to understand everything unfolding. Things were happening both at deafening speed and in slow motion as governments and healthcare experts struggled to determine the right course of action to fight COVID-19. Was it airborne? Could it spread asymptomatically? This virus was moving faster than the answers were coming.

When I started as CEO, the Canadian Armed Forces were winding down their deployments in two of our Ontario long-term care communities, and we were partnering with a number of hospitals through management agreements for support in specific care communities. However, there was a fair amount of chaos created by the pandemic still circulating around us. I want to be clear: Sienna followed the guidelines and directives that the provincial governments and health units put in place. We acted as quickly as possible to procure personal protective equipment (PPE) and other critical supplies from any potential source anywhere in the world. We asked for help and accepted it. When we received advice, we took it. When we had to wait for answers, we implemented our own solutions to protect the health and safety of our residents and team members. In hindsight, the trajectory of the virus was largely set before it even arrived in Canada.

Few of us have faced a crisis of this magnitude in the workplace. The lessons we've all learned will fill books and case studies for years to come.

Calm the Chaos

It was mid-June 2020, and I needed to get Sienna's senior leaders to take a giant breath. They were under tremendous pressure, and anyone in the company who wasn't sick was likely working flat out without taking much

of a break. They were exhausted. We were continuously reacting to a barrage of external forces.

The ability to stay calm under pressure is a strength that I've worked
hard to develop over time. As a leader, remaining calm is a big part of the
job, and you have to resist the urge—and help others fight the urge—to
rush around in response to a crisis, while also making thoughtful and
decisive decisions. Make no mistake, I was scared and worried. We care for
more than ten thousand seniors. We needed to ensure that we understood
every action we were taking and the processes we were implementing,
and that they would contribute to protecting our people's health, safety,
and well-being. To regain our footing, we needed to have the right people
making the right decisions. Redesigning the executive team was my first
major undertaking as CEO. This was necessary to right our ship and get
us to calmer waters.

It is here that I want to stress that leadership is a team sport. One
person can't lead an organization the size of Sienna through a pandemic.
There were so many team members tasked with making critical decisions
that saved lives and prevented people from getting sick—staff like Denise
Bulmer, the executive director at Rockcliffe Care Community in
Scarborough, a "C building," meaning it was built over fifty years ago,
which makes infection control practices and processes even harder to
implement. A former emergency room nurse, Denise managed through
one of our most challenging outbreaks. Over 150 residents and more than
80 team members tested positive for COVID-19 at Rockcliffe. Throughout
the entire outbreak, Denise worked eighteen hours a day, stepping up to
provide direct resident care whenever necessary and leading a remarkable
response in partnership with the Scarborough Health Network. At every
virtual town hall meeting with families, someone would thank her for
her caring, passionate leadership. In the aftermath, Denise realized she
was so focused on getting through each day that the emotional toll of the
situation hadn't caught up with her yet. She shared that it wasn't until
being reunited with one of her residents who was in the hospital that it
hit her. When they saw each other for the first time after being apart they

cried and cried. They were both so happy and desperately wanted to put their arms around each other.

At the core of our pandemic response was the courage and determination of our leaders to keep pushing forwards.

Within the first two weeks of becoming CEO, I made several major appointments. I could see that we had seasoned people whose skill sets were not being maximized. It would have been easy to hold the line and make these changes when things stabilized, but I knew we couldn't wait. By identifying individuals best suited for their roles and elevating those people into more senior positions, our senior team gained strength in its diversity of skills and thinking. I am also proud to say that one third of the senior executive team identifies as a visible minority and 50% are women. The one thing *not* present is groupthink, which prevents us from getting trapped in the status quo. By the end of the first wave, Sienna had one of the strongest executive teams in the company's history and was fully supported by our equally solid and committed board of directors.

Surrounding yourself with great leaders, even those better than yourself, is one of the greatest challenges of any CEO. My mindset in rebuilding our executive team was that each person needed to have a skill set and a level of collaboration that meant I was able to trust any one of them with my life and the lives of others. This is the importance I had to place on the leaders I surrounded myself with at this critical time. It is also the type of quality individuals whom our residents deserve to oversee their well-being today and in the future.

Getting out From Behind a Desk

I am a big believer that you can't be an armchair CEO. You've got to leave your office and experience what your staff sees daily. I knew that getting out to our care communities, seeing the staff and residents in person, and showing them my appreciation and admiration for what they were going through was essential. I insisted that a robust schedule of tours be put together, while ensuring all safety protocols would be in place. Given the nature of how rapidly things were unfolding during the pandemic, there was no traditional hundred-day CEO plan to unveil, as my outlook was days and weeks, but I was determined to plan a comprehensive tour and to stick to that plan, no matter what. I needed to see for myself what other changes were required to emerge from the pandemic as a stronger, more resident-focused company and to prepare for Sienna's long-term success.

I prepared a big speech for my first visit to a long-term care community as CEO during the pandemic. I was nervous, and I didn't know if I would come up against a list of grievances as the new face of the company. I arrived early and started speaking to staff one on one as they trickled in for our meeting. By the time the whole team arrived, I had had the opportunity to meet everyone individually, and that's when I realized my visits would not be centred on speeches. Team members wanted the opportunity to share their experiences with me, to hear my thoughts and how we were going to move forward. This initial visit helped me understand what team members needed most from me.

Visiting with the residents and their caregivers was also eye-opening. They weren't shy about telling me how they felt, and I appreciated that as you can't fix problems you don't know about. Often, conversations found their way to food. One resident told me they loved pasta Bolognese and how much they missed it, while another shared their love of salad. Thanks to my background in hospitality, I know my way around a kitchen, and a small but heartfelt thing I could do came to mind. I promised them I would come back and cook for them, which I did. Finding my way around our kitchens, rolling up my sleeves to chop onions, dice tomatoes, and wash dishes was and is a sure way to get to know a home. Working in the kitchen and serving meals gave me a new appreciation of what it takes to feed our residents high-quality, nutritious food. Experiencing how rewarding it is to work side by side with our culinary teams and frontline staff, I continue to do this every opportunity that I have.

In January 2021, I visited one of our hardest-hit long-term care communities, located in a COVID-19 hot zone in downtown Toronto, a home that for many weeks had media cameras pointed at its entrance. I remember meeting a team member who had just returned to work after completing the required fourteen-day quarantine as a result of a positive test. Ontario was deep into the second wave and I will admit I was apprehensive about going into a home where more than a hundred residents had COVID-19. But this team member was so upbeat and happy to be back, insisting that there was no other place she would rather be. Her concern for the well-being of residents was completely transparent. To this day, that is one of the moments I lean into when I feel scared, tired, or frustrated.

Rather than being grand in my visits, I understood they needed to be about connecting with people and hearing the hard things they had to say. Whether it was about wages, or improvements they wanted to see in the home, people wanted to hear the truth from me and they appreciated getting it, even if it wasn't the exact answer they wanted. These experiences lifted me up. Seeing the bond between team members and their residents is the ultimate motivation for Sienna to set our standards higher than others.

Caring for an Aging Population

As CEO, I feel an immense responsibility for each resident, and our team feels the same way. It is why they chose this work, which has always been challenging. They understand what this work requires of them. Compared to ten years ago, seniors coming into long-term care today are older and have more complex health challenges. The medical needs of some of our residents were high before the pandemic, but during it, long-term care homes essentially turned into acute care units, the kind usually found in hospitals. To address this gap in our expertise, we hired Sienna's first chief medical officer whose career has been focused on care of the elderly. Having strong medical expertise as part of our leadership team provided us with the guidance we needed to take steps to significantly reduce the COVID-19 mortality rate experienced during the pandemic. We focused on strengthening the engagement and role of the medical directors in each of our care communities and brought a new level of rigour to quality improvement processes across the organization.

Strengthening our in-house infection prevention and control (IPAC) expertise was also a priority. We had relied on outside experts, who did their best to guide us, but this was not efficient. And to better understand infectious diseases, we hired a world-renowned chief infection prevention and control consultant who worked with team members, residents, and families to help them understand the virus, changes in practices, and the vaccines.

The next step in charting our new course was to focus on operational excellence. The pandemic prompted us to implement more robust quality improvement processes to fulfill our promise of providing excellent care for our residents. We formed a new quality committee of the board, similar to those found in hospitals and other healthcare institutions, to ensure we meet or exceed standards of resident care. In addition, we took steps to become a member of a North American–wide quality consortium to benchmark our outcomes against our peers and learn best practices. This is one of the ways we are committed to building back the trust our residents and families have put in us.

These changes crystalized what I believe is our purpose at Sienna, which is to ensure that our seniors age with dignity and respect. It is a privilege and honour to care for a generation of Canadians who have given so much. I believe that if we embrace this purpose, making the right decisions will always be easy. Growing up in India, where multigenerational households are the norm, my dad's father—my grandfather—lived with us. My dad was devoted to caring for my grandfather (Babaji) until he passed away at the age of eighty-four. Regardless of any challenges going on in my dad's life, my grandfather was always well taken care of. Babaji's daily presence in our home was one of the biggest influences on my life and on my understanding of the wisdom seniors possess. I have the utmost respect for our residents and I believe we must ensure they live their lives to their fullest.

Compassionate Leadership

Compassion isn't something we should have for just our residents. It must run through our entire organization, and it starts with the way we care for our team members in sickness and health. The physical, mental, and emotional well-being of our team members was tested every day of the pandemic. What was being asked of them was extraordinary, and for that, we needed to make sure they felt supported every step of the way. When a member of my family tested positive for COVID-19 and underwent fourteen days of isolation, I saw first-hand how lonely that experience could be. I realized some team members must have also felt very alone and that we should do more to let them know we had their back. We started sending care packages to any team member who had to quarantine. This was coupled with regular phone calls to check in and let them know we were thinking about them and hoping for their speedy recovery. Implementing our enhanced pandemic pay of time and a half for team members working in homes with significant outbreaks was another important way of showing our appreciation. Calling frontline healthcare workers heroes and saying thank you is important, but treating them with the respect they deserve is far more impactful. There were many unanticipated and unconventional costs, such as transportation, hotels, meals, additional frontline compensation, and the care packages, but the board of directors, senior executive team, and I were pleased whenever we were able to identify and offer something that might provide relief or comfort to the front line.

As for many people, balancing my physical and mental health was an ongoing struggle. I'm a husband and dad first, but this situation called for a great amount of my energy to be put toward my work. Fortunately, caring for seniors is a value my entire family shares, and their support for my work translated directly into me being able to push through some of the extremely important and difficult changes we needed to make.

When I had challenging days, I let my team know and I urged them to do the same. The pandemic put a wide range of never-ending pressure and stressors on everyone's plates. Nothing about this time was normal. People needed to feel safe in talking about how they were feeling. They were going through so much. Yet no one around me said, "I can't do this anymore." I wouldn't have blamed them if they had. I made sure people were taking time off to recharge and look after themselves. I encouraged them to ensure they had the right people on their team and could lean on them. It is easy to let highly motivated people keep going and to take their word for it when they say they are "doing fine." You have to make a conscious effort to actively support people's mental health. When team members embrace this level of duty and responsibility toward their job, those in leadership have a responsibility to take care of them.

I hope an important lesson we all take away from this time is that it's not weakness to ask for help or talk about how you are really feeling.

When You Stop Answering the Phone

One thing I feel we should have been better at during the onset of the pandemic is communicating with the families of our residents. Our frontline staff were overwhelmed trying to care for residents, and the first thing to go was answering the phone. Just imagine you are the loved one of a resident whom you can't see or talk to, and there is an outbreak of COVID-19 in the home—this must have been a very frightening position for family members of our residents to be in. In a number of ways, the pandemic pushed us to be more nimble than we were used to being, and our resolution of this issue offers a good example. In response to high call volumes to our homes, we implemented a centralized call centre, now staffed by five team members, so that family members trying to get information about their loved ones would be able to speak with a live person to get answers to their questions. We put a standard in place for all communication that every residence had to meet, and a separate team was dedicated to regular electronic communications. Virtual town hall meetings were implemented to ensure everyone was connected and kept up to date about the situation in each home.

These new investments significantly strengthened Sienna's Family Caregiver Engagement Program, which has resulted in better care for residents and a better experience for their families. In the fall of 2020 alone, we answered more than two thousand email inquiries related to COVID-19, hosted hundreds of virtual town hall meetings, and issued close to nine hundred e-newsletters. The feedback from families on our increased level of communication has been very positive. In the same spirit of providing information in a more timely and accessible way, we launched a new mobile app for our team members, which has been invaluable in connecting us with thousands of team members quickly and effectively. We did all this while in crisis, and I believe we have emerged more connected than ever with team members and families.

The pandemic has crystallized for the Sienna team how important family members are to the care of our residents. We have always viewed them as partners, and COVID-19 served to strengthen that. So many family members rallied around our residents and team members with kindness and generosity. Whether it was with homemade signs of support, meals, or words of encouragement on the phone, their shared understanding of this experience meant so much.

Strategy vs. Crisis

As the curve of the first wave flattened and life outside of the long-term care sector started resembling something closer to normal, Sienna developed a robust plan in anticipation of a second wave. Recruitment and retention of staff was crucial as the healthcare sector became even more competitive than usual. In addition to successfully increasing our workforce during the pandemic, the number of full-time positions at Sienna increased by 16% to two thirds of all jobs. As part of our plan for the second wave, each long-term care community and residence had its own dedicated four-month supply of PPE, as well as infection prevention and control education and training. Mandatory masking and routine testing were firmly in place, and we had the right medical expertise to help manage residents who contracted the virus and developed symptoms.

It felt like the worst was behind us. It was time to pull ourselves out of operating in crisis mode, to take a step back, and to divide our focus to include both the pandemic and a strategy for the company's long-term success. In making this decision, I was operating on sheer optimism fuelled by an invigorated senior leadership team, a new level of operational excellence, and a culture of accountability. As a leader, especially as a CEO, you have to bet on your people and give them hope. In truth, I had no idea how things would pan out, given the uncertainty of COVID-19. I did know that we could not control what was happening externally, but internally, I believed we would succeed if we stayed on track.

We also took this time to connect with our stakeholders and business partners. There is nothing like a crisis to find out who will be there to support you. I wish I could tell you that everyone we counted on came through, but that did not happen. There were also opportunistic parties who were trying to take advantage of our challenges, but we persevered. Coming out of the pandemic, we have developed a number of important and meaningful partnerships across many different sectors. They are helping us fulfill Sienna's mission, vision, and purpose.

Giving Back

The first wave of the pandemic was a humbling experience for most operators in the seniors' living sector. While we received a tremendous amount of support from many different partners, we still were on the receiving end of harsh criticism around some of our newly enacted protocols for IPAC and resident cohorting from others. This was a difficult pill to swallow, especially knowing how hard we were working. It was an unfortunate circumstance of conflicting opinions on the novel virus. But team members kept resident needs front and centre, working side by side with everyone who stepped forward to assist us. We accepted what was said about us because we wanted to learn everything we could about this virus and to keep it off our doorsteps. As it turned out, there were also many opportunities to share our knowledge of seniors' care and to extend a helping hand where it was needed.

Even in the midst of a pandemic, I am proud that we could collaborate with sector partners to create programs that provided much-needed PPE for smaller homes and millions of dollars of financial support for frontline workers across the Canadian seniors' living sector. We had the ability to step up and help when others needed us, and we did this because not doing so would impact people's ability to care for our country's seniors. We also took steps to create a new charitable arm, the Sienna for Seniors Foundation, to strengthen our ability to support organizations that seniors rely on. Giving back is part of our culture and is something our residents and team members do actively on a regular basis. For our inaugural gift, we chose to donate funds to the Scarborough Health Network to expand their new mental health hub, which serves many seniors in the east end of Toronto.

Second Wave

We genuinely thought we were ready for the second wave, but COVID-19 has an unrelenting cruelty about it. In many ways, we managed the virus more effectively the second time around. Better strategies helped reduce the mortality rate of the virus in our homes. But unfortunately, this time community spread was the dominant factor in determining where we would see the worst outbreaks. The term "COVID-19 hot spot" was coined to describe neighbourhoods that were experiencing high levels of community transmission. Sadly, our homes in these areas were impacted terribly by the virus. Studies on the long-term care sector have shown that the COVID-19 hot spots and older homes with four beds in a room and a single washroom were among the root causes of the pandemics' intense impact on long-term care homes.

During the second wave, COVID-19 hit schools, hospitals, and work-places. Long-term care continued to be impacted as well, but with our experience from the first wave, we at Sienna never reached the point where we felt totally out of control. November through January were long and dark, both literally and figuratively. Our emotional limits were being tested. Remarkably, people persevered. Lois Kirby, for example, a house-keeper and high-touchpoint cleaner at Traditions of Durham Retirement Residence, continued to view herself as a key member of the team who was crucial to keeping people safe. Lois told us that singing and talking to her residents while completing her daily tasks kept their spirits up. Everyone at

Sienna, regardless of the role, can tell you how their job supports the well-being of our residents. Making this connection is one of the ways we regularly refill our bank of resiliency.

In our homes, teams found innovative ways to celebrate the holidays, modify resident programs to meet IPAC protocols, and support a variety of technologies to facilitate virtual visits between residents and their loved ones. It was a sight to see: decorations were bigger and more festive than ever before, and huge light displays were erected outside many of our homes, not only for the residents but to brighten the spirits of the local community as well. With restrictions on the size of gatherings among residents, team members spent hours carefully designing individual activities and packaging special holiday treats and gifts to ensure everyone felt cared for during this special time of the year. There was still a lot of joy in our retirement residences and care communities. Although it was not the same, residents were still in many ways with their "family," and that counted for a lot, especially during the pandemic. At this point, the hope for a vaccine lay in the distance, out of reach but not out of sight.

Vaccines—Our Shot at a Normal Life
When the federal government announced the approval of the first COVID-19 vaccine for Canadians, we wanted to be prepared to assist with the rollout. We quickly pulled together a vaccine taskforce to ensure we would be ready to handle the logistics of an unprecedented mass vaccination rollout. This is my hope for how Sienna's culture of accountability and operational excellence will always manifest itself: prepared and ready to lead.

We will forever be grateful that provincial governments gave vaccine priority to seniors and seniors' living workers. This decision saved many lives and ended the outbreaks that besieged so many long-term care homes. Team members and residents bravely rolled up their sleeves to get the shot as soon as it was available. They showed the country how important it would be to get the vaccine, influenced their family and friends, and inspired other frontline workers. Sadly, the pace of the vaccine's initial rollout was no match for the virus, which continued to spread like wildfire. There was some palpable fear that we might never get out of this pandemic, and I had to fight against feelings of hopelessness and helplessness. Again, I dug deep to work on my psyche and be the type of executive who could talk openly about my mental health. I was surprised and buoyed to see prominent business leaders coming forward to share their mental health challenges on social media, especially on platforms such as LinkedIn. I think encouraging progress was made on this front, and I hope it continues.

In time, the vaccines caught up with the virus and began to work their magic. The number of outbreaks across our residences began plummeting. By February/March 2021, we knew the vaccines were working and that for us, mercifully, the second wave was coming to an end. Although we saw a dramatic change, it took many weeks for us to believe things would be okay. Even when we felt more reassured, we were determined not to let our guard down. Vigilance toward infection prevention and control remained firmly in place. So would our campaigns to increase vaccination rates among residents, team members, and essential caregivers.

This Is Our Time

As CEO, it was my job to help shift the company's mentality once we were finally out from under the siege of COVID-19. I wanted our teams to be proud of how they fought and how far we had come in turning things around. We were in a much different place than we were a year earlier, and for the first time, we had no fear of going back.

I was excited to share our vision for the future, a new focus on redeveloping older "C homes," and increasing our portfolio of retirement residences. This is our time to help lead the modernization of the seniors' living sector and help meet the growing demand of seniors across Canada. Now we are constantly looking out for the next infectious disease that could come our way. We are also working on bigger projects, accelerating timelines to build our culture of accountability and operational excellence. My new mantra to our team became "If your palms aren't sweaty and you're not feeling a little nauseous from the speed at which we are moving, you are not going fast enough!"

And there will be no trade-offs. For-profit companies can operate in this space as long as they know how special this work is and as long as they use their unique strengths to do what others cannot to meet the needs of seniors and support the teams who care for residents. I believe that shareholders will value our decisions even if it means at times forgoing more income or earnings per share. Ultimately, we want to create a sustainable business with a strong commitment to corporate and social responsibility.

There is still a lot of work to be done, and the spotlight the pandemic has put on long-term care will inevitably bring changes. We welcome the opportunity to improve the sector. Some of the advocacy work that we've been supporting for years will finally receive the attention it deserves. What we have collectively experienced is no small event. It is a time that will be imprinted on us all, forever.

When I think about why I am CEO of Sienna, the answer is clear to me—I believe in our ability to make a difference in the lives of Canadian seniors. When I think about how I attained this role and the mark I want to leave behind, I am reminded of the people who helped me reach where I am today. Success in the workplace isn't just about working hard. There is a path that twists and turns, and there are people along the way who help you make that journey. For me, I owe so much to my mom, who set me up for success long before I set out to work. She only finished high school but she taught me about life, setting the foundation that has made me the person I am today. My wife is my biggest supporter and is such a positive force in my life. After my two unsuccessful attempts at getting into business school she would not let me give up, encouraging me to be relentless in the pursuit of my dream of earning an MBA from a top American school. Without her belief in me, I would not have had the courage to try again, but thankfully I did because I was accepted on my third try. Her intelligence and love inspires and pushes me to be the best in all aspects of my life. I strive to be a better husband, father, person, and CEO because of her.

In my career, there are two key moments in my life when people saw my potential and took a chance on me. The first was when I met my aunt and uncle from Canada who were visiting the United Arab Emirates, where I was working eighty hours a week, making $200 a month, and struggling to get ahead. They saw that I was working hard yet not reaching my potential and offered me an interest-free loan to come to North America to pursue better opportunities. Then, when I could not afford to pay for business school, the University of Notre Dame awarded me a fellowship for my MBA. This critical assistance allowed me to achieve my goals and helped determine how I want to lead. Humility and gratitude are critical elements of my leadership style because of these experiences. I know they have served me well during this crisis because they have allowed me to see what is truly important.

SOBEYS

Grocers became an "essential service" overnight through the COVID pandemic, and Atlantic Canada–born retail group Empire (Sobeys), like many of their competitors, had to turn their operations inside out on a dime. Millions of food industry and retail workers continued to show up to support their local communities while many worked from home. Persisting through panic buying, sanitizing, and the continually changing COVID protocols, the frontline workers have been the true heroes of the food industry throughout the pandemic.

And of course, there was another boom—buying food online. In June 2020, with strict pandemic lockdowns keeping many Canadians confined to their homes, panel vans began appearing in Toronto neighbourhoods with the word "Voilà" written on their side in bright blue letters. The trucks were a sign that Michael Medline wasn't going to let a crisis go to waste.

Medline, president and chief executive of Empire Co. and grocery store subsidiary Sobeys, aggressively rolled out the Voilà home delivery service during COVID-19. Built with U.K. online retailer Ocado Group's technology, Voilà would fulfill orders straight from automated warehouses rather than tapping existing grocery stores. If it worked, Sobeys would be able to fill an online shopper's grocery list with fresher food. The challenge was launching a whole new platform in the midst of a global health crisis, but a year later, Sobeys reported that their online sales tripled during the pandemic. Voilà delivery trucks are now popping up across southern

Ontario and the company is launching the service in Quebec and Calgary in the coming years.

During a crisis that saw many CEOs hit a pause button on major projects, Medline went to fast forward. Sobeys launched a new e-commerce platform. Empire acquired a 51% stake in family-owned competitor Longo's for $357 million, after buying Farm Boy for $800 million in 2018. At the same time, Medline ensured his 134,000 teammates stayed safe and shelves stayed stocked in 1,500 grocery stories across Canada.

Nova Scotia's Sobey clan founded the grocery chain in 1907 as a meat delivery business, then opened their first grocery store in 1924. The family still controls Empire—parent to the Safeway, IGA, and FreshCo brands along with Sobeys—and hired Medline as chief executive in 2017.

A lawyer by training, with an MBA from William & Mary university in Virginia, Medline worked at the Ontario Securities Commission and law firm McCarthy Tétrault. He moved into executive roles by joining PepsiCo Canada, then moving to paper maker Abitibi Consolidated. Medline entered the retail industry in 2001 by joining Canadian Tire, acquiring and running its Sport Chek division before being named CEO in 2014.

Leading Empire and Sobeys through the pandemic prompted Medline to rethink the relationship between business and society. As Canada emerges from COVID-19, this CEO is making a case for kinder capitalism.

Michael Medline

Plexiglass.

As a hockey fan, I thought plexiglass was created to shield me from pucks. Now, I will never react to that word the same way again. The COVID-19 pandemic left me with an unexpected passion for plexiglass.

If you'd told me years ago that the defining moment of my career—one that will live on in my memory forever—was about plexiglass, I might have laughed. I don't manage hockey arenas—I run a company that helps feed millions of people across Canada. So if you'd predicted that, as CEO of one of Canada's largest grocery chains, I'd decide on a moment's notice to spend millions of dollars on an idea, unaware of the total cost, without consulting and without looking at data, I would have done more than just laugh. I would have told you that is just not how we do things at Empire Company. Yet that's exactly what happened. For me, it was the defining moment of the crisis.

It's human nature in moments of crisis to distill memories like these into a snapshot—a conversation, a decision-point, or an event where the magnitude of the emergency really hits you. Sometimes we even torture ourselves (repeatedly) by overthinking what we could have done, or should have done, or said, in those critical defining moments. *Looking back, I really wish I had . . .* is a common thought. Did our instincts serve us? Did we fall short? Did we make a terrible error? Was our judgment clouded? Did we treat our people well? What did our choices reveal about us as leaders? Those are the issues that are top of mind at Empire as I look back on our experience at our banner stores—Sobeys, Safeway, IGA, FreshCo, Foodland, Farm Boy, Thrifty Foods, Longo's, and Voilà— during the COVID-19 pandemic.

But I must admit, the task is triggering: if you've ever had the tendency to second-guess your decisions, writing an entire book chapter might get you there. Now that you're reading this book, you are placing yourself among a well-informed collection of people whose thoughts and ideas will reflect your view of how we did. History will judge us. And that is as it should be.

In retrospect, some things that happened over the past eighteen months are just not as important to me as I thought they would be. What's not important to me is whether we made mistakes. We did. Or whether we argued when the stress levels skyrocketed and split-second decisions were demanded of us. We did. Or whether working feverishly in a high-stress environment every waking hour on a 24/7 basis caused some short-term burnouts. It did. We are all human. Like everyone in Canada, we had our good days and our bad days. However, I'm proud to say that Empire had many more good days than bad.

Plexiglass came out of a very good day. It's a memory that stands out vividly.

Early one winter morning in March 2020, I was on an international conference call with grocers from around the world, including Asia, Australia, and Europe. They were already in the thick of the pandemic, weeks ahead of Canada. I was soaking up everything they had learned up to that point. On that call a grocer in Italy talked about the idea of using plexiglass as a shield to protect grocery employees and customers from airborne illness. Normally, a decision like that requires some due process. Our team is extremely agile when it comes to executing quickly, but in normal times we'd never embark on a major physical redesign of the front end of our stores based on a snap decision. But that is exactly what happened.

Our global grocery store leaders' conference call that morning was ninety minutes. My brain was racing. Right away, I thought plexiglass shields would be an amazing way to protect our people and customers. I didn't know how much it might cost to retrofit our stores from coast to coast, or even if it was possible. I worried that remaining on the call could be dangerous if it meant even a slight delay to a decision that could save lives in our stores. I felt that I needed to act—immediately. Even before that conference call ended.

My instincts told me that, even if it ended up costing us millions of dollars (it did), I knew it would be worth it if we saved even one life. I muted the call and texted our incredible head of real estate, Mark Holly: "Put in the order. Do it now!" I was all in on plexiglass. There was no time for consultation or due diligence. It was a pure gut decision. Then our Empire team took over and did what they continued to do throughout the pandemic—receiving impossible demands, they turned them into reality, often overnight. Plexiglass was just one example. We said essentially, "Okay team, we are putting up plexiglass shields at every checkout counter at every store. We don't know exactly how it will work. But we'll figure it out."

Our amazing team had a prototype plexiglass shield installed and operational in two Toronto stores within twenty-four hours. That's not a typo. At our Laird St. store in Toronto's East York neighbourhood, one of our long-time cashiers saw the prototype up for the first time and burst into tears of relief. That was all the feedback we needed. Fast-forward—and I mean fast—and within three weeks our operations team had installed plexiglass shields in all of our stores across Canada. That's more than ten thousand plexiglass shields, in over two thousand retail outlets in less than three weeks.

Our move on plexiglass was as close to a business miracle as anything I have ever seen in my career, and it led the way for customer-facing businesses across Canada. I'm eternally grateful to every teammate at Empire who made it happen. It helped me conclude that when it mattered, we would do the right thing for our people and our customers—the humane thing; that our board of directors and executive team would support an idea fully because it was an example of living our values and doing the right thing; and that I would do it again in a heartbeat—even faster if I could. I am certain it saved lives. No amount of leadership or crisis training prepares you for moments like that. But when your business has a strong set of values, it helps put you on the right course. As a leader, you're trained to always reset your team around your core corporate purpose to stay focused in the darkest or most challenging moments.

At the beginning, I quickly assembled a key executive leadership crisis task force and rallied people at every level of the organization around our newfound purpose as an essential service. We had never considered ourselves "essential" prior to the pandemic. This was a whole new world. We set three clear priorities:

1. Keep our teammates and our customers safe.
2. Keep our shelves stocked.
3. Never, ever, stop supporting our charitable and philanthropic causes. That was non-negotiable.

Every day, our team at Empire united around these three priorities. Every day we fought to do the right thing. Every day we stayed open. Every day our shelves were stocked (except for a few early adventures in paper product panic-buying). Every day we did everything we could to keep our customers and teammates safe, while ensuring we helped keep Canadian families fed. And every day we continued to relentlessly support and promote our charitable causes. We were determined to ensure our commitments to these worthy organizations did not become COVID-19 casualties.

What matters to me most now is what we take away from this. That's what I find most motivating about the opportunity to tell Empire's pandemic story. I can lay out what we did and why, while it's still top of mind, as other Canadian business leaders do here in this book. It then becomes about the lessons of COVID. We need to look forward. We were caught unaware by this pandemic. We cannot allow that to happen again. We cannot put people through that again.

Now is not the time to simply lapse back into business as usual. Our teams were emotionally and physically exhausted, but at Empire we are making time for deep reflection. As Canadians, I submit that it's time to ask ourselves big picture questions. As a country, what is our guiding light? In the business community, do we emerge from COVID with a "same old, same old" philosophy? Or does this pandemic change us, fundamentally, as corporate leaders and citizens? We know we will face more crises as businesses. Should post-COVID capitalism be the same as pre-COVID capitalism? Just saddle up and ride? I don't think so. We've made too many incredible strides during this pandemic to let that happen.

I believe the time has come for a more humane form of capitalism. Some have called it "kinder." The notion is not new. It has been discussed by business leaders and academics for decades. And I believe it's now vital that we talk about this openly in the context of Canada and the COVID-19 pandemic. The notion of kinder capitalism has been debated by academics since the eighteenth century, when Scottish political scientist and philosopher Adam Smith, in his book *The Wealth of Nations*, invented the concept of capitalism. Microsoft founder Bill Gates made a bold speech in 2008 calling for kinder capitalism, just months before he retired from Microsoft to focus on his foundation. Then, in 2019, a powerful group of American and multinational chief executives signed a joint statement declaring that maximizing shareholder profits should no longer be the primary goal of corporations.

Now is the time to have this kind of discussion in corporate Canada. Do we want to pursue a form of capitalism that acts on a range of factors beyond "what does this mean to the bottom line?" The pandemic laid bare the reality that our decisions as corporate leaders—the majority of them— need to be focused on human beings. When this awful time is behind us, I can't imagine looking at capitalism the same way again. Every single Canadian CEO I spoke to during the pandemic told me their first priority was not profitability but the health and safety of their teammates.

And when the chips were down for us at Empire and we feared a lack of PPE and cleaning supplies could potentially shut down some of our stores, it was other corporations—not governments—that came to our rescue. Our teams worked closely with others in the corporate world such as Scotiabank, RBC, RioCan, OMERS, Maple Leaf Foods, Cineplex, and Maple Leaf Sports & Entertainment. Those who were closed for business sent us PPE and sanitizer. They selflessly lent us their contacts and suppliers—despite facing some of the darkest days of their own. The people who run corporations stepped up and banded together to get our country through those toughest early days of COVID. That's the reality. And that's how it should be. COVID-19 didn't expose the evils of capitalism. It exposed the best side of capitalism. Now we need a concerted effort to build on that principle in Canada.

Let's be clear—without profit, there is no way for corporations to support humane causes. Kinder capitalism doesn't work without strength, growth, and funding. Profit is, in fact, critical: the pandemic made it clear that strong corporations play a vital role in building a better society. When our companies are healthy—when they run well and thrive—they can help do the same for our communities, our people, and our planet. Today's governments cannot do everything all at once. Did Empire wait for governments to pass legislation requiring plexiglass shields at all points of sale? No. We did it ourselves. We acted on what we believed, as corporate leaders, was in the best interests of Canadians. And we did it faster—much, much faster—than any government could.

COVID-19 has claimed so many with illness and death. This horrific disease has also broken down many of the social relationships and institutions we rely on to live a healthy and full life. Socializing with friends and family, going to school, nurturing a talent or a skill—when all of that was stripped away during government-imposed lockdowns, it exposed our raw need for social interaction, cultural engagement, and personal growth.

When COVID struck, Empire needed to focus on being essential in a world that was shutting down. We needed to be able to cope with what felt like a rollercoaster ride at breakneck speed and a series of violent corkscrew turns. Getting off was not an option. Decision making through the early months of this crisis was like participating in the lightning round of a game show all day, every day and every night. Initially, you may recall, there was even a difference of opinion about whether face masks were effective. I remember feeling incredibly guilty when I wasn't working, or if I took a short break.

During one of our daily Empire crisis calls over Zoom, we needed to make a decision about spending millions of dollars on personal protective equipment—masks and gloves for our frontline in-store teammates. One of our executives asked what impact the costs might have on our quarterly results. I was impressed by what happened next. You couldn't hear clearly over all the shouts of opposition. While our teammate had raised a responsible, traditional question, everyone else on the call vehemently disagreed. Every comment was a version of "We have to protect our people and our customers." I've never been prouder of our executive team than I was at that moment.

We faced dozens and dozens of such lightning-round decisions. Our Empire values—humane values, not spreadsheet values—gave us a framework for our quick decisions. For example, several other essential retailers were not publicly reporting outbreaks of COVID within their stores. We knew that, in the early days of COVID, sales at stores with outbreaks would fall significantly (and temporarily), for obvious reasons. Maybe old-school capitalism would have made the decision easier: Don't report publicly because it's not good for shareholders. But our priority at Empire was to do everything in our power to keep our customers and teammates safe. So we publicly reported our store outbreaks right from the beginning, and that practice soon became standard across the sector.

How could we keep making these fast decisions? How could we get them right, with so little time and input, and amid such uncertainty? For many corporate leaders, this is the most daunting question. It's also where a lot of organizations sometimes spin their tires and lose traction. That can happen when you don't have a clear set of values to keep you moving in the right direction. Fortunately, our values—and our teammates, who live them every day—are our greatest business advantage.

Our company was born in 1907 in Stellarton, Nova Scotia, where it was imbued with a strong sense of Sobey family and Stellarton community values. Members of the Sobey family serve on Empire's board of directors and work in our business to this day. They help us maintain that strong sense of values and compassion. The Sobey family values are the blueprint for the values our company lives by today, and they helped guide our decisions through the pandemic. We set aside any matters that didn't fall under one of these categories:

1. Be customer-driven and always place our customers first.
2. Be people-powered, understanding our people make the difference.
3. Be community-engaged, never relenting on our charitable and community commitments even at a time of crisis.
4. Be results-oriented, but do it with passion and integrity.

I tell you all this for a practical reason. One of my biggest "aha" moments during this pandemic took place not very long ago, as I prepared to write this chapter and share my thoughts. The truth is, in a fast-moving, roller-coaster-ride crisis environment, it's easy to fail. But it's even easier to be paralyzed. We saw that in the initial days of the crisis, when even governments seemed to have been overwhelmed (and understandably so). How did we avoid operational paralysis after being swept underwater by this tidal wave of disease?

I realized we avoided losing time and focus in those early days because we were operating from a solid bedrock foundation of values. No matter what breakneck speed we were travelling at, no matter how little sleep we'd had and how exhausted we were, we never lost sight of our values. They were so ingrained in our teammates that they knew what they had to do almost by instinct. Clear, basic priorities and steady values make it simpler to manage a crisis, even a crazy and unpredictable one such as COVID-19.

I think about the Great One, Wayne Gretzky, who is a hero of mine. It was said that his awareness of what he wanted to do on the ice was so clear that it "slowed things down" for him. It allowed him to see openings others couldn't see. That's when the magic would happen. I believe our clear priorities and values helped us slow things down a little bit for our teammates during this pandemic and allowed them to see the possibilities. To get creative and make firm decisions. In hockey, there is only one

Gretzky. At Empire, the pandemic demonstrated that we have a team stacked with superstar players.

Another lightning-round COVID decision had to do with how we paid our teammates. Now, before I say anything about this subject, I just want to make one thing crystal clear. No matter how many good decisions the executive team made, none of what our company did could have been accomplished without the incredible bravery and commitment of our 134,000 teammates from coast to coast. Without our people, I cannot even imagine the chaos that could have ensued. That goes for the dedicated frontline workers at our competitors across Canada as well. When it came to a discussion about the bravery and commitment of our people—not to mention how quickly they absorbed new sanitization policies and the intensified pace at one of the few places open for business—we knew we had to do something reflective of Empire's values when it came to pay. I started calling it "hero pay," and I was heartened to see the term enter the vernacular.

Our stores-first culture was one of our biggest assets prior to COVID-19, and our ability to act quickly when the pandemic hit drove that home. We empower our store leaders and franchise partners to make smart, creative decisions rather than using a top-down approach. It's led to some of our best programs. Our national Sensory-Friendly Shopping Hours program was initiated at a single store in Atlantic Canada, for example, before it rolled out nationally in 2019.

We could not have weathered this crisis without our incredible store leaders and great franchisee partners. They worked tirelessly through these challenging months, not just to tick off all the safety boxes but to do even more with new ideas and initiatives. Their incredible leadership shone through. I'm so proud to be on their team. They were the glue that held our company together. These leaders, who work in communities from coast to coast to coast, delivered a strong foundation of trust and stability that communities across the country needed so badly at a time of such deep uncertainty. Still, the pandemic took a toll on our people. They felt isolated. They were tired and stressed. I decided we needed to communicate like hell. We needed to over-communicate, then com-municate some more.

Communication was also a critical way to support our customers and maintain their trust. I began writing a series of online letters to our customers to make them aware of safety protocols in our stores. In one letter, I wrote: "Yesterday, I was reminded yet again that we have such a great team. One of our teammates put a poster together for her store filled with wonderful comments from customers and co-workers, to lift their spirits and cheer them on. At the centre of the poster she wrote 'Tough times don't last, tough teams do!'" That maxim became our ral-lying cry at Empire.

All told, I ended up writing and sending out sixteen letters read by millions of Empire customers. The dialogue was incredible. The feedback and engagement was rejuvenating and inspiring. Customers replied on social media channels, giving thanks to our frontline heroes (some even put up lawn signs!) and even suggesting other potential safety protocols. Some told us how baking and cooking together was becoming an essen-tial family activity during the extended lockdown.

Despite everything else going on, we launched our Family of Support child and youth mental health initiative in 2020. It supports Canada's thirteen children's hospitals by funding child and youth mental health services. That initiative is more relevant now than ever. Is that an example of kinder capitalism? Absolutely. Is it possible that by being a sustainably profitable corporation we can serve the community in greater ways than we could if we were not profitable? Most definitely.

Another important example of how we stepped up our service in the communities where we live and work is what we accomplished across Canada on diversity, equity, and inclusion (DE&I). I believe diverse com-panies make a greater impact in the communities they serve. At Empire, we are on a journey to rectify long-term institutional bias and racism. We're taking concrete actions to advance a culture of inclusion. We're proud that newer store-level programs have resulted in more women taking up historically male-dominated roles.

Our DE&I efforts could easily have been sidelined by the COVID crisis, but we were determined that would not happen. In fact, we took a giant leap forward as a corporation in terms of our efforts. During the pandemic, we implemented a new national DE&I strategy and we held workshops that helped our people gain knowledge and confidence about how they could be more effective with regard to DE&I.

As stressful as this time was from a pandemic perspective, our leadership on DE&I was a point of pride for our teammates. Nurturing a culture of inclusion, safety, and support for our people helped us deal with many of the COVID-related anxieties our team members were feeling. We also held mental health and awareness sessions to remind our people that it was okay not to be feeling okay, and we launched SobeysMentalWellbeing. com, a resource that provided our teammates with easy access to mental well-being resources and support.

The truth is that the DE&I work we did provided our people an outlet to think of something other than just the pandemic on a 24/7 basis. It brought our teams closer together. We are sharing more with each other about the customers and communities we serve and the diverse teammates we work with every day. That, in turn, is helping us attract and retain more diverse talent.

The pandemic also revealed a new spirit of collaboration and goodwill between grocers and our supplier partners. It's an understatement to say that, historically, these two groups have had a strained relationship. But during the early days of the COVID-19 pandemic, we came together as true partners, with the end goal of feeding Canadians. It was a welcome contrast that dissolved, for a time, some of the distrust and longstanding archaic industry practices in place prior to the pandemic—practices that worked against a healthy food-supply system and that weren't great for consumers.

Prior to the pandemic, my team and I sat down with a great supplier advocacy association, the Food, Health and Consumer Products of Canada (FHCP). We talked about improving the current model in a way that would benefit all ends of the supply chain, from retailers and manufacturers to farmers, local businesses, and consumers. FHCP had been calling for an industry-wide code of conduct for decades, one grounded in fair principles, transparent negotiations, and mutual understanding. Those talks went into overdrive as the pandemic progressed. We were working together, co-operatively, as never before. In light of all these positive changes, I felt Empire was duty-bound to take a firm stand on supplier relations. That's why we developed a Grocery Code of Practice in partnership with FHCP and sent it to federal government officials for review. It would be a shame to undo what several months of progress in the industry did to correct several decades of dysfunction in the sector.

I could give you a shopping list of initiatives we fast-tracked during COVID, such as home delivery and eliminating the use of plastic bags in our stores. Our pharmacies across the country have been proud to play a significant role in Canada's vaccination campaign. At the same time, we continued to support charities across the country through our community action fund. And we gave much-needed support to our Team Canada Olympic and Paralympic athletes on the road to the Summer Games in Tokyo (even sending athletes gift cards to help them stock up on groceries).

In Nova Scotia, our concern for the food security of senior citizens during the pandemic led us to provide a $100,000 donation of groceries to the Nova Scotia chapter of VON, the homecare agency that runs Meals on Wheels locally. It was the largest single corporate gift ever received by VON Nova Scotia, whom we worked with to select nutritious food items, based on client preferences, such as soup, crackers, and fruit. And one of our franchisees in Edmonton, Jerry MacLaughlan of our Belmont store, came up with the idea of hosting a "golden hour" of shopping for seniors only, to further protect them from this virus. Sobeys Belmont began implementing seniors hours on a Tuesday. The very next day, Empire rolled the program out at stores across Canada, another idea that quickly spread around the world among essential retailers.

There are many of these standout stories. In Markdale, a town in Southern Georgian Bay, Ontario, our Foodland store teammates decided they needed to help local businesses shuttered by COVID-19. They reached out to local suppliers, including closed restaurants and bakeries in the community, to put together a plan to sell as many of their products as we possibly could. It softened the blow of the initial shutdown. The feeling of so many Empire teammates across the country was essentially "We are not in competition with the other businesses in our communities; we are here to support them. Local producers support us, and we should support them."

For us, not everything in the pandemic has been about Gretzky-like moments, sunshine and rainbows. "Is it true you're charging $50 per banana?" we were asked in response to a Twitter rumour. No. "Have you hiked the price of toilet paper?" No. "Is it true you colluded with other grocery chains to end hero pay?" No. Never happened. And our hero pay program was restored when lockdowns were restored, as we promised it would be.

Inevitably, as the pandemic wore on, issues became increasingly politicized and government leaders didn't always appear to be willing or able to help. In fact, at times they fanned the flames. What will always stand out for me was a late summer federal committee hearing into alleged multi-company collusion over hero pay. It was spearheaded by a handful of MPs who chose to demonize the grocery industry, despite zero evidence of such "collusion." This was a huge insult for our team at a time when they were being pushed to the brink of exhaustion to keep Canadians fed and safe. It was demoralizing for our people who were leaving their homes every day to go to work, knowing the risks they faced. We spent a great deal of time preparing materials for a purely theatrical political hearing that I participated in, along with other Canadian grocery company CEOs. Oddly, two massive U.S.-based competitors with sizable market shares were, for some reason, exempt from this charade.

Bottom line? Collusion on hero pay never happened. The politicians knew that, but they didn't care because there were political points to be scored. Looking back now, I will never forget the anger and frustration my team felt about this event. It served no purpose whatsoever.

When we look back at this time in history, I wonder how corporations will be perceived. You hear a lot about corporations being greedy and lacking empathy. In my experience, the reality has been just the opposite. Businesses cannot go back and change any rushed, crisis-based decisions they made in the heat of the pandemic that didn't work out. But we can learn how to make better decisions in the future. We can create a set of Canadian corporate values that help frame those decisions. The "We are all in this together" mantra does happen to be true. We need to be less top-down and less siloed. The key to kinder capitalism won't be found in corporations talking to other corporations. It will be found by listening. Listening to our customers, our people, and our stakeholders.

Even after COVID is under control, we know there could be more infectious disease outbreaks. We also know there will be more frequent catastrophic weather events caused by climate change. In short: there will be more times when the way of life we enjoy as Canadians is under siege—this much we know—and as an essential service we will need to be there for our people and our customers again—and again, and again, and again.

If this pandemic taught me anything, it is that Canadian kindness is a special sort of kindness. We are a unique people. Our team will be eternally grateful for every single kind word at a cash register. We will never forget the gestures of thanks sent our way by Canadians. So, together, let's aim for a kinder and distinctly Canadian capitalism that serves all stakeholders and builds a better society.

TELUS

In his younger years, Darren Entwistle, Telus's chief executive officer, followed in his dad's footsteps as a Bell Canada lineman. While a student at Concordia University, Entwistle paid tuition by installing and repairing phone lines each summer. Looking back, Entwistle often reflects on that period in the early 1980s as a formative experience, an introduction to the importance of customer service excellence, personal accountability, and network superiority.

Fast-forward to the pandemic. By then, Entwistle had been running Telus for twenty years. He is a rare leader who started his career working on the front lines of his business. On his watch, Telus is Canada's top-performing telecom stock, with an enterprise value that increased five-fold to over $50 billion this year. Telus has also built one of the country's most recognizable brands, humanizing technology by leveraging the diversity of nature through the use of butterflies, lions, lizards, and other Telus critters in their creative.

Entwistle is also a CEO with ambitious, strategic growth plans for the organization. As 2021 began, Telus lifted the curtain on the global arm of its business by selling a portion of subsidiary Telus International in an initial public offering that has now become the largest technology IPO in Canadian history. Simultaneously, the Vancouver-based company continues to build out its Telus Health and Telus Agriculture units as leading players in their respective sectors.

Telus, along with major telecom companies around the world, entered the pandemic in the midst of a multi-billion-dollar, multi-year deployment of the 5G and fibre networks that will power the economy of the future. As one of the major telecoms in Canada, Telus played a critical role in keeping Canadians connected during the pandemic, on what has been consistently independently rated as the world's fastest wireless and wireline networks.

For a former lineman, and son of a lineman, Entwistle's priorities during the early stages of the COVID-19 crisis were clear. Job one was keeping Telus's eighty thousand employees safe while ensuring the company's customers were happy and connected in a manner that supported their safety and productivity. At the same time, Telus continued to be a world leader in community giving, contributing over $85 million and 5% of pre-tax profits in 2020 to their local communities.

As the following pages attest, throughout one of the most unprecedented periods in recent history, Entwistle demonstrates that he can lead a response that takes care of all the stakeholders Telus serves, a response that is similarly unprecedented in every sense of the word.

Darren Entwistle

AUGUST 2021

In early 2020, I was listening to a number of Telus team members who expressed deep concern about the worsening situation in China, with more people becoming infected with an unknown virus that we now know as COVID-19. At that time, I thought that the situation would be similar to the H1N1 epidemic, with only a small number of people being affected and the virus kept under control.

Following China's alert to the World Health Organization on December 31, 2019, regarding atypical pneumonia clusters in Wuhan, like these team members I had been following the emerging situation carefully. Given my personal interest in health, combined with the fact that Telus is a healthcare technology company, I reviewed medical articles and watched media interviews with healthcare experts. Most importantly, with eighty thousand team members serving clients in more than twenty-five countries around the world, I was worried for the welfare of our team and our customers.

Then, on February 7, 2020, I received a call from the CEO of our Telus International operations: a public health mandate issued by the Chinese government had closed our Telus International office in Chengdu, China. This is just one of the hundreds of client experience, digital, and IT delivery centres; administrative offices; and retail locations operated by Telus around the globe. Although our office in Chengdu was reopened six days later and no team members tested positive for the virus, it was among the first indications of the severity of the illness and the global implications of what was to come.

At that moment, I realized that the situation was worsening at a disconcerting rate. It was clear that our entire Telus and Telus International leadership teams would have to be creative and flexible in responding to the coronavirus, knowing that governmental response and the impact on team members and communities would differ greatly among the regions where we operate around the globe.

As I reflect on this eighteen months later, it brings to mind the many important plans Telus had underway at the time for 2020. Our team was embracing the new decade with our typical desire to make the world a better place, filled with optimism for the friendly future we were committed to building for the many stakeholders we serve. Indeed, 2020 was to be a milestone year for Telus: we were amplifying our network investments to support the arrival of 5G; we were preparing to turn our human and technological innovation toward connecting the agricultural value chain through Telus Agriculture; we were planning to extend our support for purpose-driven companies and entrepreneurs by providing early-stage financing through our Pollinator Fund for Good; and, after a decade of tremendous growth, we were anticipating a successful initial public offering for our Telus International business. These are just a sampling of the highlights of what 2020 promised for Telus. Similarly, on a personal level, 2020 would mark my twentieth year as a proud member of the Telus team and I was looking ahead, optimistically, to another year of connecting Canadians from coast to coast.

Just a few months into 2020, however, the world suddenly changed. While the optimism for the year ahead became uncertain, I could not be more proud of the way the dedicated Telus team responded to the many challenges associated with the pandemic. In short, our team passionately demonstrated that when things are at their worst, our customers, communities, and fellow citizens can always count on Telus to be at our very best.

Dedication to Our Telus Team

This chapter pays tribute to the Telus team's impressive and ongoing efforts to keep our families, colleagues, and fellow citizens safe, connected, healthy, and productive. I would also like to dedicate this chapter, in memoriam, to the Telus team members, globally, we so tragically and heartbreakingly lost to COVID-19:

Ana
Benjie
Dianne
Gabriel
Katherine
Leonel
Michael
Miriam
Richard
Richard
Sagabala
Sandy
Saurov

Our hearts are with the families of these team members and the many others who lost loved ones as a direct or indirect result of the virus.

Taking Care of All of Our Stakeholders

With the declaration of the pandemic, Telus quickly mobilized our human and financial resources, and in the intervening months we have worked tirelessly to keep Canadians connected to the social, educational, and economic resources that matter most, while also protecting the well-being of our team members, customers, and communities. This has been possible thanks to the incredible culture at Telus, one that inspires team members to thoughtfully take whatever steps are necessary to do the right thing.

Keeping Our Team Members Safe

In early 2020, when the coronavirus and its tragic impact were first beginning to make headlines, there were many priorities that immediately came to my mind, including how Telus would achieve our key goals:

- Safeguard the health of our customers while continuing to serve them in our essential stores and through customer installations, typically completed inside customer homes.
- Ensure uninterrupted service for our customers, given global supply chain issues.
- Enhance our digital storefront to serve the hundreds of thousands of customers choosing a digital purchase, upgrade, and customer support experience.
- Support small businesses in our local communities that had to close their doors as a result of pandemic-related lockdowns.
- Bolster the speed and consistency of our world-leading networks with so many people working, learning, and accessing health care from home.
- Leverage our considerable healthcare technology to ensure access to medical care and eventually to vaccines, knowing that government support around the globe would be inconsistent.
- Arm ourselves with data-driven, medically proven information to guide our response.
- Ensure no team members would lose their jobs.
- Enable our Telus International team members to work from home.
- Assist team members who were parents working from home and also helping their children to learn from home.
- Ensure the health and mental wellness of our team members, and also sustain team engagement despite the uncertainty and fear related to the pandemic, and the evolving working environments.
- Support low-income families and students who lacked the ability to stay connected with educational and healthcare resources, information, and loved ones.
- Provide assistance to healthcare workers on the front lines during this challenging time.
- Offer philanthropic donations to support pandemic healthcare research and operations.

- Continue generating strong results despite retail closures across the country.

As an initial response, our entire executive leadership team turned our attention toward how we could keep our team members and customers safe while ensuring the continuity of our business (and the employment of our team), connectivity for our customers, and support for our communities.

Telus Emergency Management Operations Centre

Our first move was to activate our Emergency Management Operations Centre (EMOC) teams across both Telus and Telus International to provide coordinated, centralized leadership of the emerging situation. Given the nature of the emergency, we concurrently established the Telus Medical Advisory Council, comprising specialists in pandemic leadership, primary care, infectious diseases, and health economics as well as public, occupational, mental, and digital health, to help guide our response to the developing health emergency.

As the magnitude of the crisis became clear and governments began implementing public health–related restrictions, ensuring the safety of our team members and those in our community became paramount. We effected an immediate vacation embargo for all Telus senior leaders to make sure our collective focus was entirely on the emergency at hand. Beginning in March, I held daily calls with the executive leadership team to ensure company-wide alignment in our response efforts as the situation continued to rapidly evolve. While we have since reduced the cadence of these calls, they continue to this day, enabling a concerted effort in our response to the emergency and to safeguarding the health and well-being of our team and customers.

Leveraging our pandemic planning framework and our longstanding Work Styles program—through which team members have access to the technology and resources to work where and when it is most convenient and productive—we responded quickly to the pandemic stay-at-home orders. These resources were critical in our ability to swiftly enable up to 95% of our team members, globally, with the tools, resources, and support to work from home—including our entire executive leadership team. This allowed our team to serve our customers safely and productively, while helping to reduce crowding in public places for those people unable to work remotely.

In this regard, it was also a priority to protect our team members who were required to work outside of their homes. Notably, our pandemic planning framework was customized for all of our unique work environments, including our administrative buildings. Each approach was reviewed by our Medical Advisory Council, and in addition to strict and comprehensive cleaning procedures, team members within our administrative buildings experienced a number of protocols focused on putting their safety first.

While we encouraged all Canadians to shop online whenever possible, in the early days of the pandemic, 136 essential Telus stores continued to operate across the country. We created a touchless in-store service experience, implementing strict health and safety measures that included plexiglass at the cash, triaging at the entrance, social distancing throughout the store, the mandatory use of masks, and cashless transactions. These protocols came into play again later in the summer of 2020, as the country reopened and retail locations began operating with numerous safety measures in place. Additionally, during lockdowns and periods of reduced traffic in our stores, some team members were redeployed to support busier areas of our organization. This proactive reassignment strategy resulted in full employment for our retail team throughout the COVID-19 crisis.

Equally important was our ability to provide virtual installations and repairs for customers in their homes, which led to Telus being the first Canadian telco to offer virtual installations as part of our response to the health crisis. Through this process, our team members left sanitized equipment on a customer's doorstep and provided support via a video call on their smartphone from the safety of their Telus vehicle. This touchless fulfillment process was also supported by a series of online demo videos, providing additional assistance to customers choosing self-installations.

It is with tremendous relief, and with great pride in the actions of our team, that I am able to share that, to date, Telus has not experienced any known cases of workplace transmission of COVID-19. This is a testament to the rigorous safety protocols we put in place and to our team members' commitment to serving our customers responsibly and safely. In addition, we acted swiftly to encourage quarantine and contact tracing for team members reporting close contact with anyone receiving a COVID diagnosis. As a result of the strong safety protocols and education we have provided to our team at work, the infection rate in the Canadian population as a whole is 70% higher than that experienced among our Telus team members.

Providing Meaningful Mental Health Support

Over the course of many years, Telus has developed a comprehensive health and well-being strategy that allowed us to effectively support the emotional well-being of our team members during a time fraught with anxiety and uncertainty. Building on this solid foundation, we introduced several new initiatives to enhance the mental health support for our team. By way of example, we augmented our mental health benefits to include $5,000 worth of support, and we gifted all Telus team members a subscription to the leading mental fitness app, Calm, which we also made available to customers on Optik TV. Through Calm, team members and customers have access to unique audio content dedicated to helping people manage stress, anxiety, insomnia, and depression—challenges that have, regrettably, become more prevalent as a result of the pandemic.

We also created voluntary, customized training to equip our people leaders with the practical skills to identify and provide support to those on their teams with mental health issues due to COVID and offered tailored mental health training for all team members. In addition, we have encouraged team members to utilize our extensive portfolio of mental health support programs and benefits, hosted company-wide well-being and mental health "Ask the Expert" sessions, and continued to expand our comprehensive mental health first aid network. The health and well-being of our team members remains an ongoing priority for us today, as we begin to navigate the post-pandemic world.

Recognizing the Exceptional Efforts of Our Team

Witnessing the incredible efforts of the Telus team to manage through their own anxiety and challenges associated with the pandemic while continuing to put our customers and communities first has been one of the most humbling experiences of my career. In this regard, our entire leadership team amplified our commitment to celebrating the exceptional accomplishments and perseverance of our team during an unprecedented and challenging year. We quickly developed new, customized recognition programs to highlight the grit, passion, and unwavering dedication of our team members in Canada and around the globe.

On a personal note, it was my responsibility to share a regular communication series, known colloquially as the "virtual hug," which provided an opportunity for me to connect with team members and reassure them they were not alone, despite the necessary transformation in our working environment. Importantly, through these communications, I was given the opportunity to acknowledge the incredible, selfless efforts of team members in caring for our communities. These communications were a weekly mainstay of my connection with team members throughout the initial challenging months of the pandemic. This excerpt from the inaugural bulletin to the team exemplifies my initial feelings of pride, mixed with a deep concern for the welfare of the Telus team, that continues to characterize my days:

> I am truly inspired by how our entire team has risen to the challenge and supported one another as we all adjust to a very new reality. I wanted to check in with everyone to make sure that you are all taking care of yourselves and your families, with a special emphasis on those with vulnerable loved ones. . . . Please stay safe and look after your loved ones and each other. We are all in this together and we are here to support you in any way we can.

As the country reopened, the vaccine rollout gained momentum and most of us began to feel more optimistic about the friendly future on the horizon, we revised the cadence of the communications to monthly. The team remains in my thoughts each and every day and it has been incredibly rewarding for me to stay connected with members of my Telus family in this way.

I am exceedingly grateful to the entire Telus leadership community for taking such good care of their teams during a challenging time in our history. Indeed, their exceptional efforts to support and motivate their team members contributed to a sense of connectedness as expressed through our annual Pulsecheck employee engagement survey. In fall 2020, our team's engagement score increased 3%, year over year. Indeed, this result, which would be considered impressive during a "normal" year, was extraordinary during a year like 2020. Certainly, camaraderie among the team increased as a result of regular touchpoints from leaders in addition to the proliferation of face-to-face, virtual interactions, including virtual recognition events, virtual "happy hours," and physical fitness challenges. When combined with our mental and physical health initiatives, the team has weathered the emergency with a feeling of our culture of caring taking on a new importance for the many stakeholders we serve.

Exemplifying Our Customers First Culture: Supporting Our Customers and Fellow Canadians Safely and Effectively

As a technology company—and an essential service—we are acutely aware of our responsibility for keeping Canadians connected, a responsibility that has been amplified exponentially since the onset of the pandemic.

Connecting Canadians Through Innovation and Investment

For more than twenty years, Telus has been demonstrating our courage to innovate by investing in network technology and infrastructure. These ongoing investments were accelerated in response to the pandemic, and, in concert with the ingenuity of our talented team, they allowed us to effectively manage a 50% daily increase in voice traffic and a near doubling of our multi-messaging service. To put it in perspective, our team's efforts to sustain our networks throughout COVID-19 have amounted to supporting Super Bowl–level traffic . . . every day.

Indeed, at a time when the human connection is more important than ever, our world-leading networks have been supporting Canadians in working and learning remotely, applying for critical government resources, receiving vital medical care, and staying connected to family and friends. I am extremely proud of our team's incredible efforts— enabled by our amazing engineers, technologists, and network innovators—to ensure that Canadians have had access to the tools and resources needed to stay connected.

Providing Important Connections to Our Communities and Each Other
Since the start of the pandemic, Telus has collaborated with regional health authorities and provincial governments to provide and expand broadband connectivity to hospitals and pop-up clinics nationally. These efforts enabled the connectivity to support healthcare workers in performing their critical, life-saving work, while also helping citizens stay connected to medical support and to loved ones affected by COVID-19. We also proactively monitored coverage and capacity for the hospitals, temporary hospitals, and screening centres in our service footprint to ensure a reliable connection was available for everyone who needed it.

Faith-based services and community programming have played a critical role in the lives of many citizens during this time of physical distancing. Understanding the importance of sustaining this critical connection, our team pre-emptively collaborated with community institutions to enable religious ceremonies to be broadcast virtually through our Optik TV service. Additionally, to enable seniors to stay connected, we facilitated the deployment of live video feeds from on-site chapels to residents of long-term care facilities. Moreover, throughout the pandemic, Telus has donated thousands of mobile devices and tablets to more than one hundred not-for-profit organizations and senior and long-term care homes across Canada, helping hundreds of patients and isolated seniors—many of whom were extremely or terminally ill—connect with their healthcare providers and family in a safe manner. These much-needed devices also enabled healthcare workers and other patients to stay safe and stay connected with family and friends, particularly in the earlier days of the pandemic.

Standing in Solidarity with Our Business Customers

For our business customers, we entered this brave new world of "business as unusual" together. Understanding the challenges they were facing amid pandemic-related restrictions across the country, we immediately offered our support and expertise. Accordingly, we shared our pandemic planning framework and resources, such as our workplace contract tracing guide, with more than half a million business customers, enabling them to leverage the processes and research completed by our team of business and medical experts to protect their own employees. We also helped to ensure the continuity of businesses across the country, empowering thousands of businesses with virtual work solutions.

To assuage some of the financial challenges resulting from the pandemic, we introduced our #StandWithOwners campaign, a $500,000 commitment to support, promote, and help business owners. In 2021, we renewed our commitment to stand with owners by dedicating $1 million to champion small business owners. As well, to support the mental well-being of small business owners, including the 48% who say they have experienced challenges with their mental health, Telus Business hosted a virtual discussion with business owners on mental health and wellness, which included valuable resources from expert panelists to help owners manage their health and support their employees' wellness. Telus's support through our #StandWithOwners program has been critical to small business owners, like Heidi and Scarlett of El Segundo restaurant, one of my favourite eateries on the Sunshine Coast. It was truly amazing to see Telus at work in my local community—a microcosm of the good the team is doing to help small businesses across the country.

Providing Help and Care When Natural Disasters Strike

As we directed our resources toward supporting our team, our customers, and our communities through the pandemic, citizens across the country continued to face other challenges, including flooding and wildfires. Exemplifying our commitment to our customers in communities impacted by natural disasters, the team expeditiously offered our support. By way of example, we mobilized our emergency flood response efforts in the communities of Fort McMurray and Fort Vermilion in the spring of 2020. Our network remained strong and consistent, keeping citizens connected to their loved ones and to critical information about evacuation plans. Furthermore, even as we continued our pandemic-relief efforts, our team supported community cleanup as customers returned home.

Similarly, in the summer of 2021, our team stepped up to assist British Columbians who were experiencing an early start to the wildfire season following days of record-breaking heat, including the families evacuated from their communities as well as the firefighters and first responders working tirelessly to keep our communities and fellow citizens safe. Indeed, our Telus team worked around the clock to support evacuees and emergency personnel across the impacted regions, providing hundreds of satellite and cellphones to keep everyone connected. Moreover, we provided care kits and waived fees for those tragically displaced from their homes as a result of the wildfires. This is yet another demonstration of our team's dedication to putting our communities first, particularly amid the most challenging of circumstances.

Providing Virtual Access to Health Care

Consistent with our collective desire to embrace change, Telus Health has been driving the digital transformation of health care in Canada since its inception in 2008. For me, this commitment to leveraging technology to improve the health outcomes of my fellow citizens stems from personal experience: I lost my dad as a result of an avoidable error, when he was accidentally—and heartbreakingly—given penicillin to treat an infection, despite wearing a MedicAlert bracelet clearly warning of his severe allergy to the drug. Tragically, similar stories and experiences are shared by hundreds of Canadians: when arcane scribblings on an antiquated paper chart caused grave harm to a loved one; or an incorrect prescription led to a negative reaction; or the inability to send timely information—often due to the use of archaic technology like fax machines—resulted in serious delays in care. Following my own experience with the challenges inherent in our healthcare system, I felt compelled to take this negative dissonance and recycle it into positive energy, which evolved into Telus Health.

As one of Canada's leading healthcare technology companies, we knew we had an important responsibility to keep Canadians safe and healthy. As the world took important precautions to practise physical distancing, virtual health care became critical in helping Canadians to securely monitor their health and that of their families, while also supporting vulnerable Canadians unable or unwilling to leave their homes. We quickly scaled, augmented, and deployed our suite of virtual care offerings, enabling Canadians to receive one-on-one, personalized, quality physical and mental health care in the safety of their homes, thereby helping to alleviate the pressure on frontline care workers and health centres and preserving precious capacity for those with urgent healthcare needs.

Similarly, we have been able to provide healthcare solutions to address the unique needs of our most vulnerable citizens. Through our Home Health Monitoring, we are enabling healthcare providers to virtually observe and support patients living with, or at risk of, COVID-19, and our LivingWell Companion service is providing personal emergency support for elderly citizens living independently. Likewise, we launched our Virtual Visit functionality, which enables doctors using Telus electronic medical records to visit their patients virtually, allowing both the patient and the physician to benefit from the safety of remote consultations.

Leveraging Our Technology to Bridge Digital Divides

Throughout the health emergency, the synergy between doing well in business and doing good in our communities has never been more evident. Indeed, over the course of a challenging year, Telus dedicated

$150 million in support of COVID-19 relief efforts, including helping build public healthcare capacity by purchasing new medical technology and equipment, and supporting the procurement of personal protective equipment. I was privileged to provide further support by donating three months of my 2020 salary to hospitals, community health centres, and critical COVID-19 research. This salary donation was matched by my family through the Entwistle Family Foundation to help maximize the Telus team's commitment to supporting health care and helping those most impacted by the pandemic. These donations were divided among the BC Women's Health Foundation to support virtual care technology; McGill University Health Centre Foundation in Quebec to enable ICU patients to connect virtually with loved ones; Covenant Health Foundation in Alberta to support vulnerable and isolated seniors; and Sunnybrook Hospital Foundation in Ontario to address the alarming increase in suicides during the pandemic.

Connecting for Good in a Multitude of Ways

At Telus, we understand that technology plays a critical role of the great equalizer, but only if we all have access to it equally. Since 2016, Telus's Connecting for Good initiatives have been helping some of our most vulnerable populations succeed in our digital society through Telus-subsidized access to the powerful technologies that support the success of Canadians at risk of being left behind. The health emergency highlighted the need to ensure all citizens had the tools to remain connected. It was my strong belief that as a technology company, Telus had a responsibility to leverage our technology to improve outcomes, which led to the expansion of our Connecting for Good programs.

Keeping in touch with family and friends made it easier for so many of us to navigate the pandemic. This basic necessity also motivated our Telus team to accelerate the expansion of our Mobility for Good program, providing low-cost wireless connectivity to more vulnerable, young Canadians transitioning out of foster care; to frontline healthcare workers; and to seniors, who have been disproportionately and heartbreakingly impacted by the pandemic—keeping them connected to loved ones and vital information while reducing feelings of isolation. More recently, we extended our Telus Mobility for Good program to provide mobile phones and connectivity for Indigenous women at risk of or experiencing violence.

Since the start of the pandemic, we have donated tens of thousands of phones, tablets, and plans to hundreds of not-for-profit organizations supporting vulnerable Canadians. By way of example, when Mount Sinai Hospital in Ontario notified our team that hundreds of their critically ill patients had no way of connecting with family in a safe manner, our team responded quickly, securing one hundred phones and having them delivered to the hospital within two days.

Similarly, we expanded our Internet for Good program, which provides low-cost access to high-speed Internet, to include people living with disabilities in B.C., Alberta, and Quebec. Moreover, to help ensure children could continue to learn from home and stay connected with their friends during school closures, we offered access to the program for students in need from kindergarten to grade twelve across B.C. and Alberta.

And as COVID-19 began to take a tragic toll on people living on the streets, we continued to provide primary and mental health care to people facing homelessness and others in need through our Telus Health for Good mobile clinics. Many of our clinics nationwide provide COVID-19 testing and assessments, as well as vaccinations for at-risk populations.

Staying Informed Throughout the Health Crisis
In the early days of the pandemic, our team felt a significant responsibility to share our healthcare, technology, and community knowledge and resources to help Canadians manage through this extraordinary time. This sense of accountability and our commitment to promoting fact-based resources led to the establishment of our Telus Talks podcasts, with veteran journalist Tamara Taggart. Tamara invited prominent Canadians, like B.C. chief medical officer Dr. Bonnie Henry, four-time Olympic gold medallist-turned physician Hayley Wickenheiser, *Dragon's Den* alum Arlene

Dickinson, and president of the Canadian Chamber of Commerce Perrin Beatty, as well as Telus's own vice-president of Telus Health, Juggy Sihota, and our chief neuroscience officer, Dr. Diane McIntosh. Over the course of more than eighty episodes, Tamara and her diverse selection of guests have focused on providing expert, insightful, and timely information, in an easily digestible and relatable format, to help address the many uncertainties surrounding COVID-19. This has driven significant listener engagement, often putting Telus Talks in the top 10% of all podcasts.

Providing the Tools and Resources to Give Back, Virtually

Our team's desire to give back has been amplified throughout the pandemic. One of the team's most selfless acts of giving involved the creation of our Telus-branded critter masks. These served the dual purpose of keeping those we love safe and protected while also raising over $600,000 for the Telus Friendly Future Foundation to support pandemic-related initiatives.

Impressively—although unsurprisingly—our team did not allow the public-health restrictions to negatively affect their commitment to giving where we live. In fact, with their characteristically spirited teamwork, they rose to the challenges the pandemic presented by creatively giving back more than ever. By way of example, to ensure we were still able to help those in need during the health crisis, we evolved our Telus Days of Giving into a year-long giving campaign comprising activities to be completed virtually or while adhering to social distancing guidelines. Starting in March 2020, our domestic team members and retirees sewed masks and gowns for frontline workers, delivered food and comfort kits to local food banks and families in need, conducted virtual phone check-ins with lonely seniors, and so much more. And beyond our borders, the Telus International team offered their support by distributing grocery baskets of supplies—purchased from small merchants—to families living in extreme poverty, and by purchasing personal hygiene products for seniors who usually made a living by selling crafts to tourists.

The resulting 1.2 million virtual and socially distanced acts of giving undertaken by our team in 2020 represented 1.25 million volunteer hours invested into helping build stronger, healthier, more connected communities. In total, in 2020, Telus contributed $85 million, representing 5% of 2020 pre-tax profits—more than any other Canadian company—to charitable and community organizations worldwide. I believe most people would agree that this is a remarkable feat by any measure, one that is made all the more inspiring against the backdrop of a worldwide health emergency.

Partnering with Government to Improve Outcomes for Our Citizens

In the early months of 2020, as we began to realize the true nature of the crisis, I reached out personally to our government partners at the federal, provincial, and municipal levels to assure them that the Telus team was ready to support their efforts in every way possible. I promised our partners that they could count on Telus to do whatever it takes, in collaboration with their administrations, to ensure that citizens across Canada remained connected and healthy, and that we would be there to answer any challenge for the welfare of our fellow Canadians. By way of example, we dispatched occupational health practitioners to remote locations, including mines in the Northwest Territories, and performed on-site COVID-19 testing to keep these employees safe.

This critical role we would play in supporting the economic, social, and educational health of our communities was reflected in our essential service designation and our immediate and sustained outreach. We responded with compassion and immediacy to requests for assistance in providing enhanced public sector connectivity—from government call centres to community spaces to healthcare facilities—and worked in tandem with our public sector partners to ensure they had the tools they needed to keep their administrations running and remain accessible to their constituents during the crisis.

Assisting Government Partners in the Vaccination Rollout

Among the many dates that resonate with me personally, December 9, 2020, has to be one of the most meaningful. On that day, the federal government approved the first vaccine for emergency use in Canada, and one could almost feel the collective sigh of relief. Help was on the way, and our Telus team was determined to be part of the effort. In anticipation of the arrival of the vaccines, our team had been proactively offering our support to our government partners for months. We offered our resources and technology, our buildings and other assets, and our logistics and health experts, including those on our Medical Advisory Council.

In my home province of British Columbia, we partnered with the government to build, staff, connect, and monitor call centres for the Immunize B.C. program in record time. This effort has not been without its challenges, and following a launch day that saw drastically higher than projected call volumes, as well as technical issues that prevented agents from logging in and being ready to take calls, our Telus team worked around the clock to scale capacity and respond to the unprecedented demand. Together, our team leveraged our technology innovation and human compassion to ensure that the inaugural group of citizens—our vulnerable seniors—received their vaccine appointments in a timely manner. The exceptional efforts of the 1,800 Telus team members, volunteering from all areas of our business to assist in the call centres and rallying together for the citizens of B.C., was nothing short of extraordinary. Importantly, their diligent efforts enabled our team to accelerate the province's vaccine rollout schedule and ensure that every British Columbian was able to receive a vaccine two months earlier than originally planned.

Continuing to Generate Strong Results for Our Stakeholders

Throughout an unprecedented year, we were able to do "good" in our communities because of the team's commitment to doing well by our customers and investors. Indeed, the Telus team's dedication to our social purpose culture earned us the loyalty of our customers and communities, while also driving industry-leading results. Notably, we were able to launch a new line of business, advance the strategy of an existing one, and reaffirm the synergies between success in business and success in our communities—a true testament to the dedication, agility, and grit of the Telus team.

Promoting Food Security Through Telus Agriculture

The health emergency identified vulnerabilities in our food supply that could be mitigated through transformative, connected technology. Notably, there was international concern that the pandemic's impact on the global economy would similarly disrupt the food supply chain, resulting in food insecurity for people in Canada and around the world. In this regard, it became more important than ever that we direct our human and technological innovation toward improving access to a nutritious food supply that is safe, sustainable, expansive, and connected. Telus Agriculture was introduced in October of 2020, with the mandate of creating a fully-connected agriculture value chain and improving outcomes for citizens by helping to safely and securely feed an increasingly hungry world.

Sharing Our Social Capitalism Thesis Through the Telus Pollinator Fund for Good

In 2020 we launched the $100 million Telus Pollinator Fund for Good, one of the largest corporate social impact funds in the world. The timing of this launch was critical, as we were providing early-stage financing to entrepreneurs, as well as new and established companies, enabling purpose-driven companies to scale and bringing socially innovative, sustainable businesses to life.

Evolving Telus International

Telus International (TI) is the global arm of our operations, with over 56,000 team members in more than 25 countries around the world designing, building, and delivering next-generation digital solutions to enhance the customer experience for some of the largest international brands. Taking TI public had been a long-time, strategic imperative for Telus and we were determined to demonstrate that we had the tools, resources, focus, and passion to advance TI's success, even in the middle of a global pandemic. Correspondingly, in early 2021, TI undertook an initial public offering (IPO), establishing a market capitalisation for TI of more than $10 billion and exceeding the $8 billion market cap of Telus in 2000, when we first embarked on our national growth strategy. With total aggregate proceeds of $1.4 billion, the TI IPO was the largest technology IPO in the history of the Toronto Stock Exchange.

Delivering Leading Operational and Financial Results

Our team's extraordinary efforts to keep Canadians connected, healthy, and safe also drove strong operational and financial results. Notably, in 2020, Telus delivered industry-leading results across numerous important growth metrics. In fact, it is a point of pride for all of us that Telus was the only national telco to report positive EBITDA growth in 2020, demonstrating our team's incredible dedication and resiliency during a truly unprecedented year.

Let's Make the Future Friendly, Together

In a year when the world needed a leader in social capitalism, it was more important than ever that our Telus family was able to deliver the solutions, resources, and care that made a meaningful difference in the lives of citizens, globally.

As the world looks optimistically ahead toward a period of recovery and reconnection, at Telus we will continue to bolster the robustness of our world-leading networks and to enable critical connections while supporting the most vulnerable among us. Over the course of the past eighteen months, we have seen the incredible accomplishments that are possible when we come together to amplify the good we can do in helping our fellow citizens in need. This is why we evolved our brand promise to invite others to join us in progressing toward a stronger, healthier, and more caring planet. Indeed, rather than declaring that the future is friendly, our refreshed brand promise—"Let's make the future friendly"—welcomes everyone to join us as we strive to make the world a better place.

There is hope on the horizon and I could not be more proud of the one hundred thousand Telus team members and retirees around the globe who have continued to provide unparalleled levels of connectivity, caring, and service excellence during a truly extraordinary time in our global history. Collectively, they have been my source of inspiration, pride, and motivation throughout the pandemic, as they will continue to be in the months and years to come.

WESTJET AIRLINES

Few industries were harder hit by the global pandemic than the aviation industry. As WestJet Airlines was taken private in December 2019 by Onex Corp. for $5 billion, the stage was set for an ambitious new era. Having grown from an upstart and irreverent airline in 1996, with three aircraft and 200 employees serving five destinations in Western Canada, to an international airline with 180 aircraft, 14,000 employees, and an aggressive play to entice business travellers, WestJet's future was not just bright, it was brilliant.

With the backing of Onex, the plan was to boldly expand into new markets and attract new customers. Ed Sims, president and CEO of WestJet, was relishing the fight to lead the carrier into this new world. No one imagined how hard and how fast the world's industries would be affected by COVID-19. Sims had lived through tough times in the airline industry. He was a senior executive at Air New Zealand when the carrier invested in Australia rival Ansett, which subsequently collapsed in 2001, resulting in sixteen thousand lost jobs. He was working for Air New Zealand in 2008 when they suffered a tragic hull loss that resulted in the death of seven colleagues.

A native of Wales, Sims started his career in the travel industry on the front lines, as a check-in agent at London's Gatwick Airport. He subsequently worked for travel companies Thomas Cook and Richard Branson's Virgin Group, and spent ten years at Air New Zealand, running the airline's international travel operations. He then served for six years as CEO of Airways, New Zealand's air navigation service, before joining WestJet as an executive vice-president of commercial in 2017. WestJet tapped Sims as CEO in 2018, and he both expanded the carrier and oversaw its sale to Onex.

While leading an airline through a crisis can be challenging, Sims recognized the need for empathy and humour to make it through.

Ed Sims

JULY 2021

It was the best of times, it was the worst of times, it was the age of wisdom, it was the age of foolishness, it was the epoch of belief, it was the epoch of incredulity, it was the season of Light, it was the season of Darkness, it was the spring of hope, it was the winter of despair, we had everything before us, we had nothing before us, we were all going direct to Heaven, we were all going direct the other way—in short, the period was so far like the present period, that some of its noisiest authorities insisted on its being received, for good or for evil, in the superlative degree of comparison only.

These famous opening lines from Charles Dickens's *A Tale of Two Cities* were written in a wholly different age, with a radically different set of circumstances, but they could scarcely describe the chaos and confusion of the coronavirus pandemic any more effectively.

While we all looked for silver linings that may yet emerge from this human tragedy on an epic scale, I found an oddly personal one. As an English literature graduate running an airline in an industry ravaged by loss of demand, I found myself taking solace from the awareness that all we have endured in the last eighteen months has happened before. To use Dickens's beautiful words, in every epoch, in every age, some form of existential or human-caused threat has tipped our world on its head. Suddenly, all those twilight hours too many years ago studying the wisdom of previous generations not only made sense but helped me stay calm.

From Shakespeare describing carnage in the Scottish monarchy with "So fair and foul a day I have not seen" to the Irish poet W.B. Yeats portraying the Easter Rising as a period when "The best lack all conviction, while the worst / Are full of passionate intensity," we have all been here before. Other nations, previous generations, saw what we saw, suffered as we have suffered, and had the resilience and spine to survive and thrive.

Don't be alarmed by this point of my story—this will not be an essay on literary history, and I have just about exhausted the few quotes I still remember. This will, however, be a reflection on how one person found composure and conviction to be able to cope through a situation unseen not only in the corporate world nor just in one country, but across all aspects of modern life across the globe.

I have often been asked if, in hindsight, we at the WestJet Group of Companies would have done anything differently in responding to the pandemic. I suppose there are always actions or decisions that could have gone another way, but in the moment I often thought of the adage "Measure twice, cut once." You analyze the situation, make the decision, and move forward. There were many tough calls that impacted thousands of people and led to many sleepless nights. Despite all this, as the CEO responsible for leading WestJet through, I never once had any doubt about our survival. Not once—and here's why.

The last year and a half all blurs together, and many of the challenges we faced were happening simultaneously. As I write this, it feels like I'm telling you a linear story in which one sequence of events took place only after the previous one had concluded. But all of this was happening concurrently, though many of the biggest and most complex issues lay ahead.

We entered 2020 on a roll. In December 2019, we had successfully closed our private equity purchase by Onex, the largest deal of its kind in aviation history. By February 17, 2020, we had presented the board-approved five-year plan at an annual event we call Summit, where every manager from across Canada meets in Calgary to plug in and find out what's in store for the coming year. The energy was palpable. Having successfully rolled out our Boeing 787 Dreamliner the previous summer, we were now serving London, Paris, and Dublin non-stop from Calgary and were slated to add Rome in three months' time.

Three days after Summit, the first reported COVID-19 case appeared in Canada, and six days later there were twelve confirmed cases. The excitement about our future prospects was still there, but we were desperately seeking a better understanding of what this all meant and what impact it would have on Canadians and on flying.

The aviation industry is focused on safety. Without that, we are nothing. Every single employee knows inherently that we are only ever one incident, one loss of attention, one missed communication away from unimaginable tragedy. It's why we train so hard, why we are rightly heavily regulated, why we build checks and balances into every single procedure to prevent incidents and learn from those that, sadly, occur.

And yet nothing in thirty-five years of experience prepared me for that Sunday afternoon of February 29—coincidentally WestJet's twenty-fourth anniversary. I will often review future bookings on a weekend as they come in, to get a sense of the week ahead and to determine if strategies we have put in place on the scheduling or pricing front are taking hold. Suddenly, like the old-style Wall Street numbers board in a bear market, our numbers turned from black to red.

Of course, we were aware of the situation in Wuhan. We were all concerned by travel patterns for Chinese New Year and the thought of viral spread. We had spent many of the previous days establishing inventory levels of face masks, gloves, and sanitizer to protect our people to understand what we had and to begin understanding where we were going to get more if required. But on that unforgettable afternoon, we had no way of knowing we were on day one of a trend that would see seventy-two consecutive days where cancelled flights outweighed new bookings. Pre-COVID, a single day with cancellations outstripping bookings would have been considered a disaster. A drop of 1% or 2% of demand, year over year, would have been cause for alarm and would have sparked many a strategy session to understand how to recover from single digit demand decreases. To go more than two months with negative bookings was more than alarming—words could not express our level of concern.

By March 13, 2020, the federal government was putting travel restrictions and quarantine measures in place as Prime Minister Trudeau said to Canadians, "If you're abroad, it's time to come home." Borders around the world began closing. Within days, WestJet stood up its Incident Command

Centre (ICC). Every airline has an Operations Command Centre (OCC) where flight plans are filed and flights are monitored twenty-four hours a day. It is the central nervous system of the airline. Airlines also have at the ready an ICC—designed to deal with any number of emergencies in the air or on the ground anywhere in our operating world. Twenty-four different functions and departments met daily—a thirty-minute stand-up meeting at which we reminded ourselves of unintended consequences and of the interdependency of every decision. Each leader communicated on their function as if their business lives depended on it, and we made crucial decisions at lightning speed.

We grizzled airline veterans tend to do crises well. We practise responding to all aspects of a crisis in hopes we'll never have to use the skills we continuously hone. As luck would have it, our OCC and ICC were in the middle of a renovation as the pandemic hit. We were building our OCC/ICC for a future that saw widebody aircraft in all parts of the world, and we had begun this work long before we had heard of the coronavirus. But our ICC sprang to life in a training classroom, and we began meeting three times a day in those early weeks. The ICC is set up much like a mission control you would see in the movies. The incident command director (ICD) runs the show, and each team reports back to the ICD with updates on their situation. Where are our aircraft at each point in time? If we are grounding the fleet, where are we parking these aircraft? Are our crews safe? Can we procure hazmat suits, gloves, sanitizer, etc., and get them distributed across our network? These were the early days of our response—focused on safely bringing down our network while ramping up our hygiene efforts to protect those continuing to fly.

We realized early in our response that bringing together all the key personnel needed to run our airline into the same room at the same time—in the middle of a pandemic not well understood at this point—was an infection risk we could not continue to take. Enter Microsoft Teams. Our IT team would tell you that our implementation of Teams to run our business virtually was an overnight success that was years in the making. Core personnel in the OCC would remain on site, but the remainder of those in these meetings would connect remotely. Over the next several months we met thrice daily, then daily, then three times a week. As our contingency plans began to take shape, the calls transitioned from ICC to Business Continuity Centre (BCC) meetings, focused now on what needed to be done to keep our airline alive. If that sounds dramatic, a look at a few key metrics will underscore how difficult this has been.

- Within 14 days, more than 90% of demand disappeared.
- Pre-pandemic, we would fly roughly 2.5 million guests per month. From March 2020 to September 2020, we flew 1 million people in total.
- With 180 aircraft in our fleet, ranging from 78-seat Q400 Turboprops to 320-seat Boeing 787 Dreamliners, 80% of our fleet was now grounded. No one to fly and nowhere to go. Each of these idle aircraft was a stark reminder that aircraft can't make money if they're not in the air. More importantly, our people aren't working and our guests aren't getting where they need to be.
- On one day in May we flew 700 guests. That's slightly less than 1% of our normal daily average. It's still hard to believe even after all this time.

Through these ICC calls, we determined quickly that we didn't have time for exhaustive analysis. As we scoured every news source and official statement to understand what might be coming next, I was struck by a statement by the World Health Organization's Health Emergencies Programme executive director, Dr. Mike Ryan, who said that being prepared was paramount, adding, "If you need to be right before you move, you will never win. Speed trumps perfection. And the problem we have with society at the moment is everyone is afraid of making a mistake. Everyone is afraid of the consequence of error. But the greatest error is not to move. The greatest error is to be paralyzed by the fear of error."

We took those words to heart. We tasked our procurement team to find masks, gloves, gowns, sanitizer, face shields, and protective eyewear. We knew we needed this personal protective equipment (PPE) fast, and we needed lots of it. As borders closed and anxious Canadians looked to come home from abroad, we were asked to operate over a hundred repatriation flights. We flew to destinations for which we weren't previously authorized—South America as one example. The approval process would ordinarily take upwards of six months, but we had approval in six days.

Our people deserve 100% of the credit for the way in which WestJet responded. They stood up, passed the baton, and solved problems like no team I have ever witnessed. They treated triumph and adversity as the impostors they are (apologies, Rudyard Kipling!), with serenity, diplomacy, and acuity while chaos reigned around them. It was jaw dropping.

By far the most challenging metric, and the toughest to write about, is the impact of the pandemic on our employees. We lost 70% of our people—some furloughed or temporarily laid off, some prematurely retired, and many permanently out of work. For many of our employees, we tried to offer some choice so that they could have some of the decision making in their hands. We asked if there were, among our people, those who would stand down so that our airline could stand up. Amazingly, more than ten thousand WestJetters were willing to sacrifice to help our airlines live to fight another day.

I vividly remember a particular day when I was filming a video update at our front reception and I watched employee after employee filing out with cardboard boxes, unsure of when, or if, they would be returning. Here I was, recording an update for our people and our guests while the gravity of decisions made were unfolding in front of me.

I had been through a total airline collapse back in 2001, post-9/11, with Ansett Australia. On a terrible Friday a matter of hours after the horror in the U.S., sixteen thousand airline workers lost their jobs in one hit. That experience was a critical reminder to our beleaguered HR colleagues at WestJet that their role was to focus on every job they could save, without becoming preoccupied by the jobs that were sadly to be lost. But this was much easier said than done when those lost jobs were held by friends, close colleagues, and confidantes.

We were not entirely without assistance in managing our workforce challenges. The federal government moved at pace to set up schemes to cope with the spiralling worldwide financial plight. The Canada Emergency Wage Subsidy (CEWS) was a lifeline for hundreds of thousands of workers nationwide and it proved invaluable in helping us keep our people connected and close at hand. But it was one of very few lifelines in a disorientating and turbulent storm.

On March 25, 2020, the Canadian Transportation Agency (CTA) issued a statement that refunds to travellers in the form of travel credits or vouchers were acceptable considering the situation in which Canadian airlines found themselves. On the one hand, passengers who have no prospect of completing their planned itineraries with an airline's assistance should not simply be out of pocket for the cost of cancelled flights. On the other hand, airlines facing huge drops in passenger volumes and revenues should not be expected to take steps that could threaten their economic viability.

Just about every other jurisdiction in the world provided sector relief through low-interest loans and grants. The U.S., almost immediately, introduced the CARES Act, injecting $57 billion in aid to the aviation sector. European airlines received just under 38 billion euros. Commensurate with this financial support was the requirement to provide refunds to original form of payment, which took place very quickly. Canada, on the other hand, took a slower approach. While aid was being provided to cash-strapped airlines in other countries, it wasn't until November 2020 that then-Minister of Transport Marc Garneau stated that negotiations with Canada's airlines would begin immediately. It took another four months before the first agreement was signed, by Air Canada. As I write this, the WestJet Group of Companies has yet to reach an agreement with government—sixteen months after the start of the pandemic and travel restrictions being put in place.

The airline industry is a force that drives economies. In Canada's case, we are the second largest country in the world by area, so airlines are crucial to move people and goods around the nation. We provide the lifeline, the heartbeat to this beautiful country that the railway network provided a hundred years ago. In 2019, the International Air Transport Association published *The Importance of Air Transport to Canada*, a report in which they noted that 630,000 jobs in Canada are supported by the air transport sector, which contributes more than $49 billion in GDP. It was, and remains, a tremendous source of disappointment and frustration that, during the pandemic, Canada's approach to air travel and the aviation industry did not support the valuable role we play.

Federal politicians were all but impossible to pin down on specifics, regarding either financial relief or the lifting of some of the world's most draconian restrictions and closures. At times, their elusiveness reminded me of T.S. Eliot's practical cat Macavity: "You may seek him in the basement, you may look up in the air—/ But I tell you once and once again, *Macavity's not there!*" What were clearly, and sadly, not in the air at this low ebb were WestJet aircraft.

With these aircraft not in the air, the work involved in putting them to rest, temporarily, was considerable. As demand cratered all around us, we began putting planes into what's called "active storage," which takes approximately 200 work-hours to complete for each aircraft. The key word here is "active," with the engines, auxiliary power unit, hydraulics, and pneumatics needing to be run every seven days. These "tails," as aircraft are often referred to, then need to be serviced at 14, 30, 60, 90, and 180 days, with each check requiring 60 work-hours over the course of a week. So, while it might be assumed that the maintenance costs fall to zero when we're not flying, those costs remained yet another financial challenge to overcome. But the ongoing servicing ensured that our aircraft were maintained to the same high standard we are used to at WestJet and that we could bring them back relatively quickly when demand returned.

At this point, we had no idea how long this crisis would last. As much as we were singularly focused on just the pandemic, other challenging hands were dealt to us at the same time. On June 13, 2020, a hailstorm hit Calgary, producing a tornado, torrential rain, and tennis-ball-sized hail. Members of our technical operations team, realizing that upwards of fifty of our aircraft were parked in Calgary and that hailstorms are not uncommon at this time of year, knew that these planes could be extensively damaged if their sensitive flight surface areas, like flaps and ailerons, were not protected. The damage to aircraft could easily approach $100 million if they were left unprotected.

Amazingly, there is a silver lining in this cloudy story that comes about from a very Canadian approach. Months earlier, the tech ops team had built a slingshot from available materials in the maintenance shop and used ball bearings to simulate hail. They now purchased different thicknesses of rink board—the plastic covering around every hockey rink—and a thinner plastic used for lawn signs. Standing six feet away from the plastic samples that were taped to the wall, they fired ball bearings at the various samples. The first ball bearing went through the plastic sign sample—and the drywall. The "ball bearing hail" dented the one-eighth-inch-thick rink board and dented the drywall behind it. Amazingly, the one-quarter-inch sample of rink board stopped the ball bearing—we had a solution! Six thousand dollars in plastic later, and some speedy work by our aircraft maintenance engineers on one summer evening, protected those aircraft on the ground and saved WestJet untold millions.

While this quick thinking and ingenuity saved the planes, our head office building was not so lucky. The storm flooded our main campus building in the basement, as well as three floors up as water poured in the HVAC system. Hail flooded the downspouts and froze solid, leaving the gushing water to pour in through the ceiling. More than $1 million in damage was caused to the building and its contents. Now we had the job of repairing this extensive damage in addition to responding to the pandemic.

To add further pressure, we had to deal with the issue of the Boeing 737 MAX. Prior to the pandemic, this aircraft was our biggest challenge, as it had been grounded around the world as a result of two tragic accidents in 2018 and 2019. With large-scale changes approved by aviation regulatory agencies, we now had to look at ways to convey how safe this aircraft was while also trying to navigate the pandemic. In January 2021, just shy of two years from its grounding, the MAX returned to service once again. I believe the concern around this aircraft was muted because of COVID, and with excellent work from many of our teams at WestJet it was introduced with less attention than we anticipated. It will be, ultimately, one of the safest aircraft ever to fly the skies. No aircraft has been more scrutinized than the MAX, and that will serve airlines and the travelling public well for years to come.

As the pandemic took hold, two critical criteria emerged above all others: cash and communication. The preservation of cash in the business, managing liquidity at an acceptable level, and minimizing outgoings took the place that generating revenue had previously occupied. We obsessed over every dollar where spending could be avoided, asked suppliers to share some of the pain our staff were going through, and cancelled orders and projects unless related to our safe operations. Looking back now, the simple reality that we removed 70% of variable costs from an already frugal business seems scarcely credible. But that's what we achieved, collectively and collaboratively, to ensure the survival of our beloved airline.

Communication with our people, with our guests, and with our shareholders was no less fundamental to surviving this first phase. We had concluded our change of ownership with Onex just seventy-seven days prior to the first wave of the pandemic striking Canada. The owners and management were understandably nervous, needing to assure ourselves about contingencies and continuity. In those early stages I talked to Onex hourly, where we agreed that the pain we would incur of our own volition would hurt infinitely less than pain imposed on us by circumstances. You cannot become a helpless victim in a crisis—you must establish control, especially when you sense you have none. "Keep calm and carry on" never seemed more apt.

Our guests were also craving that same sense of reassurance. We re-emphasized that safety would always feature above all else, not just in the provision of PPE on all flights but in the furnishing of travel insurance, the facilitation of refunds where we had cancelled flights, and the scheduling of repatriation flights to bring thousands of stranded Canadians back home.

As for communicating with our own people, we learned anew that dialogues are so much more important than monologues. From the time I started at WestJet, I had written a weekly blog on the business that was published at 8 a.m. on Fridays (we called it EdTalks; I thought it was very clever). But that was never going to be the right vehicle for communicating during a crisis. So we started regular webinars using Microsoft Teams, where over four thousand WestJetters weekly heard the latest developments from me, relevant executives, and subject matter experts. They could ask questions—and they asked hundreds of them. Often, they were seeking reassurance or good news we simply could not provide. They were looking for certainty we didn't have. In uncertain times, we found that our people looked for assurance on everything from European flight schedules to progress on government support for the sector—all areas with little clarity or certainty.

Obviously, I always wanted to ensure our webinars were serious—they needed to accurately reflect the position in which we found ourselves. The magnitude of layoffs and the grim demand outlook, combined with the very serious nature of the virus itself, needed to be respected. But as weeks turned into months of the pandemic, I realized we also needed to release tension for the presenters. Hence, finding a way we could enjoy some humour while still maintaining the gravity of the situation was important.

Early in the pandemic, on March 22, 2020, I stepped up to the small whiteboard in my office and wrote down what I believed would be the three phases of this crisis from WestJet's perspective: "Liquidity, Stability, Recovery." It's still there today (although someone did stop by to write a fourth category of "Retirement" once I had announced I would be retiring at year's end. COVID has apparently not put an end to people being smart alecks). The predicted sequence turned out to be remarkably accurate. Its forecast timespan was just tragically over-optimistic. Instead of the three phases neatly reflecting the sequential financial quarters of 2020, those first two phases dragged on. And on. And on. Indications of potential financial relief moved from days to weeks to months without end. Any joy at seeing out the end of 2020 with an increase in demand and WestJetters returning to work was quickly extinguished with the realization that a year could actually contain eighteen months, every day at times leaving us all feeling like the actor Bill Murray in the movie *Groundhog Day*.

As the Canadian winter started to bite, we saw some green shoots of hope. Rigorous arrival testing regimes for travellers at Toronto Pearson Airport and a well-executed and unique inbound testing regime in Calgary provided COVID positivity indicators below 50% of those in the broader community. Provinces began tentative reopening and social distancing, and masks and sanitization almost eliminated seasonal flu. Vaccines came into view with warp-speed regulatory approvals, and we all became armchair experts on the relative values of Pfizer, Moderna, and Astra Zeneca.

But this was a rollercoaster ride, where the dips were sharper, steeper, and longer lasting than those brief upward, pleasant interludes. Pre-departure tests became mandatory. Trips to relatively unaffected beach resorts were suspended, partly triggered by the fashion of "flight shaming" prominent public figures who had sought respite from the cold only to find more heat than they could ever have imagined upon their return. Lengthy quarantines and mandatory and expensive hotel stays upon return put a punitive stop to putative travel plans. Law-abiding Canadians took the advice that "now is not the time to travel" literally and stayed at home, despite so many efforts to re-emphasize that no one had actually contracted COVID mid-flight.

There were bright moments that I reflect upon fondly that demonstrated how our people showed up in the face of the pandemic. WestJet celebrated its twenty-fifth birthday in February 2021, and we took time to celebrate those twenty-five WestJetters who are still here a quarter century on. We re-enacted our very first flight from Calgary to Vancouver with "day-one" WestJetters operating the flight and the remainder of those day-ones along for the ride. It was an important reminder that the mission of enriching lives that we set out to accomplish twenty-five years ago continues today.

I received many letters and emails from guests who passed on their experiences of travelling during the pandemic. They were a wonderful shot in the arm (pre-vaccination) as each told a story of how well WestJetters were showing up in the face of adversity, how safe guests felt because of the safety and hygiene procedures we had put in place, and how impeccably our people were providing service. In fact, through most of the pandemic our Net Promoter Score (NPS), which is a customer service metric used to measure customer satisfaction, rose to the highest levels in WestJet's history. These NPS results demonstrated that people wanted to feel safe and that, across every flight, we were surpassing their expectations.

At the time of writing, many of the restrictions that have been in place for so long are being lifted. In each jurisdiction around the world where a restriction is removed, we are seeing an immediate increase in demand, reaffirming our confidence that once we are allowed to travel again, we will do so. We firmly believe that more than a year without seeing loved ones, without meeting in person, without people feeling sand between their toes has created huge pent-up demand. Our post-COVID world will need social, cultural, and personal bridges as we have never needed them before, and air travel has the unique ability to make our world feel smaller and our connection with each other easier.

In fact, I am no different from so many people in this situation. The primary reason and driving force behind my decision to retire at a relatively young age is rooted in the fact that it will have been two years since I have seen two of my three children by the time I am back in New Zealand. I lost my parents and sister young, and our time here on earth is simply too short not to embrace the time we have with loved ones. We all knew that inherently, and COVID has put it in the spotlight, under the microscope, or any other analogy you can think of to say that we should embrace the relationships we have. Many of the pundits who say air travel will not return to the way it was need only to speak with a handful of those who have been separated from loved ones. And they should step aside from the entrance to the airport—the people are coming.

So this former student of literature remains optimistic despite it all. More than optimistic: Inspired by the courage, vision, and resilience of those who have shared this wild ride with me over the past fifteen months. Fuelled by the knowledge that this too shall pass—that tough times seldom last while tough people always do. And driven by the spirit of those who have seen crises over the centuries and who survived before they thrived.

I keep searching in vain for pithy airline references in Chaucer's *Canterbury Tales* or Milton's *Paradise Lost*. No need. They and many others wrote simply about universal truths that endure no matter when they were written. Ultimately it is the strength and spirit of human nature that will prevail against this terrible pandemic. I saw that clear fact multiplied many times during the pandemic's course, in the actions of the WestJetters I was fortunate enough to share the foxhole with. Maybe the poet William Wordsworth captured it best in the eighteenth century when he wrote that the "best portion of a good man's life [is] / His little, nameless, unremembered, acts / Of kindness and of love." I was fortunate enough to have been surrounded by thousands of such acts during this crisis. There was no one I would have rather shared that foxhole with than resilient WestJetters.

While none of us can yet say with certainty how this will all end, I remain convinced that "the best of times" remain ahead for us all.